The Wooden Plane

ITS HISTORY, FORM, AND FUNCTION

The Wooden Plane

ITS HISTORY, FORM, AND FUNCTION

John M. Whelan

Illustrated by the Author

ASTRAGAL PRESS
Mendham, New Jersey

Library of Congress Catalog Card Number: 92-76137
International Standard Book Number: 1-879335-32-8

Published by
THE ASTRAGAL PRESS
5 Cold Hill Road, Suite 12
P.O. Box 239
Mendham, New Jersey 07945-0239

Manufactured in the United States of America

Table of Contents

Foreword

We live in an age in which almost every manufactured object has been made with a minimum of human intervention. The phrase "untouched by human hands" has been in use for so long that it is a cliche. Factories in which the human has not yet been replaced by a robot often expect most of their human workers to function as robots. They create interminable replicas that are indistinguishable one from the next, with no vestige of human workmanship beyond that of the original designer. The engineer, perhaps, may feel satisfaction in creating and maintaining these instruments of production. The designer leaves his print, but sees his design given shape by others who get little pleasure in mass producing it. The machine operator feels little connection with his product.

Increasing numbers of workers earn their livings by manipulating abstracts, symbols on paper or in a computer. In pursuing one's vocation, only an artist or one of the few remaining craftsmen can produce an object, see that it is good, and feel the satisfaction that comes from knowing that his or her own hands produced it.

Many feel the lack of this satisfaction, the partnership of the mind and the body in creating something. Some find substitutes in creating a better golf or tennis swing, some in producing fruits from the earth. Others turn to the crafts that were a part of an earlier, simpler life. The working of wood is one of these. Those who find pleasure in this form of accomplishment acquire an affection for tools.

Even those who do not turn to such personal creation enjoy a vicarious pleasure in objects bearing the stamp of their creator. "Hand made" or even the less demanding "hand crafted" labels commonly increase the appeal of an article offered for sale. And those pieces that combine the creative genius of an artist's mind with the sensitive craftsmanship of his hands are the most appealing.

While modern examples are found in the works of Sam Maloof or James Krenov, among others, this is a major appeal of the furniture of the past. There are some who will admire an object simply because it is old, but for most it is the admiration of the talent of the maker and the loving attention he gave to making it; not "good enough" — but as well as he could.

The current interest in restoration of old homes not only for public appreciation as at Williamsburg but for private residence again reflects the desire for surroundings that show the mark of caring craftsmanship —

i

craftsmanship that goes beyond the bare requirements of a smooth wall, a flat floor, and adds the careful attention to detail that converts adequacy to attractiveness.

The tradesmen of the past who made the masterpieces of furniture so greatly desired today, and those who sculpted the moldings, pilasters, staircases of the mansions, respected their tools as well as their work. Their tools hold interest for us, not only because they were instruments of creating the works we admire, but in their own right. They preserve for us the generations of experience and innovation that went into the design of these instruments, that they might do their task quickly and well. Some of the subtleties of design are still being rediscovered today, as old tools are being restored and put to use. But beyond function, the maker of the tool demonstrated his affection for it in the additional touches that mark it as his creation, not someone else's. Some of the early European tools appear at first to be wood carvings, and require a second look to identify them as functional objects. The later British and American tools were less elaborately decorated, but reward close examination with individual details that reflect the pride of the maker: a particular tiny gouge cut to terminate a chamfer, the curve chosen for eye appeal rather than need.

The era of the wooden plane as an instrument of commercial production is at an end, except for those craftsmen devoted to authentic restoration or recreation of the masterworks of the past. Nonetheless, its development presents a microcosm of the application of man's ingenuity to his natural resources for the enhancement of his comfort. The story of the plane brings to us a clearer picture of the life of past centuries, in which hard manual labor, in addition to craftsmanship, was required to win the bread of the working classes. Aside from the simple pleasures of collecting old artifacts, the plane rewards close examination with insight into the character of its maker and user. In use, it provides gratification through sharing a learning experience with the workers of more than a century ago.

The recent decades have seen a dramatic increase in the number of enthusiasts who admire and study these tools. It seems likely that this appreciation will continue to grow. Thanks to these students, the information available on the subject has increased enormously, to the point that summaries such as this one seem to be indicated.

Introduction

MATERIAL COVERED

The objective of this work is to collect and render accessible the information that has become available on the form and function of wooden woodworking planes. The principal interests are their physical form, the tasks they were designed to accomplish and how they were used. An attempt is made to trace development of the various functions over time and to contrast styles and implementations in different countries.

The book has been written to be accessible to those who have little familiarity with the subject as well as to the expert. The terminology is defined as it is encountered, and is available in a glossary. Even the most common planes receive attention, along with the rare and unusual. The discussions, I hope, will bring new information to the knowledgeable. The objective is to permit identification and naming of the vast majority of wooden planes, and to provide an understanding of the uses to which they were put. The book cannot hope to be complete. The collecting fraternity has learned much which has not yet been published, and new information continues to appear. And there are many planes found (so-called "oneoffs") which were made just once, for some forgotten purpose, and which will continue to provoke wild hypotheses for years to come. This work will serve a further useful purpose if the absence of a plane from these pages inspires the sharing of information, with the author or with a wider audience through publication.

I hope the audience for this book will be a broad one — that it will prove useful not only to collectors, but to curators in identifying unfamiliar planes and in creating accession records; and to those woodworkers, restorationists, and others reproducing classical furniture and architectural details, who have interest in the hundreds of molding profiles that are illustrated and described. I hope architects and craftsmen will gain inspiration from the study of earlier methods and ideas.

Not covered in this volume are the metallic and transitional planes (planes using metallic members for the fixing of the cutter). There is minimal coverage of biographical data on individual planemakers. These may be found in Goodman (1978) and in its forthcoming revision by Rees, and in the works of the Pollaks (1987, 1989); their dates are repeated here only where it helps to place the time frame. While some attention is given to how the tools are used, I cannot pretend to offer anything beyond elementary instruction in practical shop use.

Coverage of information available only in languages unfamiliar to me was not attempted. The omission of Scandinavian, Mediterranean, near East and other references does not imply their lack of importance, just lack of trade literature or English citations available to me. In particular, the Netherlands will undoubtedly reward further study. The Dutch tool association established two years ago (AMBACHT & GEREEDSCHAP) should bring forth particularly interesting material. Gerrit van der Sterre, one of its founders, recently informed me that he has evidence of a professional planemaker, Mijghijel Cornelisz, registered in Amsterdam in 1600.

ORGANIZATION

Because of the author's fond hope that the book will serve as a reference, each section has been written to stand on its own without reliance on material to be found elsewhere, making it unnecessary to look outside of any section for facts needed in using it. This has resulted in some repetition, for which the author asks your indulgence. Drawings are repeated wherever they may be of use, some several times. Illustration numbers are given as chapter number, colon, ordinal number, and a repeated figure has a new number, corresponding to the chapter in which it appears. Instructions in using the coding systems for plane types are given in detail in appendices, with simplified versions in the main text.

To avoid the use of footnotes, references to the literature are given simply by the author's name, followed by a year (in parentheses). This should suffice to find details of the source of the publication in the Bibliography.

The illustrations were drawn by the author in a simple style intended to convey information, not esthetic appreciation. Rather than using shading to represent rounded edges (as opposed to sharp edges which are solid lines), these are indicated by multiple dashed lines. Plane profiles all represent the tool as viewed from the rear by its user, and are the same as would be obtained by placing the front of the plane on paper and tracing around it. The cutting edge is represented by a heavier line.

Acknowledgements

The concept for this book was formulated by Emil Pollak, and it was at his instigation that the work was undertaken. He has been most supportive, and his editorial talents have greatly clarified the text. Martyl Pollak has been similarly helpful, and her patient talent has provided the format.

Sir Isaac Newton, and others before him, have felt that they stood on the shoulders of giants. There are many who have provided broad shoulders for me. The pioneers in acquisition of knowledge of the tools of the past include Henry Mercer, Josef M. Greber, W.L. Goodman, and Kenneth Roberts. Their works, and those of Seth Burchard, Charles Hummel, Paul Kebabian, R.A. Salaman, Alvin Sellens, Roger Smith, and Philip Walker, have provided a large part of the information presented here. The cahiers of M. J.F. Robert were most useful for information on French and Swiss planes, and the bulk of the material on Japanese tools came from the work by Toshio Odate. Kenneth Kilby was a major source for cooper's tools.

It is hardly necessary to mention the classics of the past such as the work by Joseph Moxon, which provide a motherlode for our information. They will appear frequently as references in the text.

The journals of the tool history societies have provided a wealth of information — Early American Industries Association (the Chronicle), Midwest Tool Collectors Association (the Gristmill), the now inactive British-American Rhykenological Society (Plane Talk), and the English Tool and Trades History Society (Tools and Trades), to name a few. To the many contributors to these, I express my gratitude.

Much of the information presented here was obtained through private communication with, or examination of the tools of, fellow tool enthusiasts. While I cannot hope to list all from whom I have learned in this fashion, special thanks are due Henry Allen, Roy Arnold, Alan Bates, A.M. Beitler, Jack Bittner, Benjamin Blumenberg, Carl Bopp, Lee Donnelly, Harold Fountain, Robert Fridlington, Charles Granick, William Gustafson, Joseph Hauck, William Hermanek, Kenneth Hopfel, Charles and Walter Jacob, Donald Kahn, Herbert Kean, Paul Kebabian, John Kesterson, Gene Kijowski, Thomas Lamond, Harry Ludwig, Dominic Micalizzi, J. Lee Murray, Robert Nelson, Harry O'Neill, Francis Pfrank, William Phillips, Emil Pollak, Roy Schaffer, Roger Smith, Raymond Townsend, Paul Weidenschilling, Robert Westley, Robert Whitacre and Steve Zluky.

Herbert P. Kean has shared freely his enormous knowledge in this field. He reviewed the work in great detail, and gave me two full days of discussion clarifying technical details. He revealed several errors on my part, and improved the clarity of many descriptions; for which he has my deepest gratitude. As I remained unconvinced by some of his suggestions, any remaining errors are my responsibility alone.

Philip Walker most kindly reviewed the bulk of the text, and made several valuable improvements. My thanks to him, and to his associates Roy Arnold and Mark Rees for their comments. Joseph Hauck's review produced helpful suggestions. Jay Gaynor was kind enough to examine an early draft of the numerical classification system of Appendix 3 and provided encouragement for its development.

I am especially grateful to four people who most kindly agreed to review glossaries in their native languages (with English definitions) submitted to them by a stranger. Jean Mario Fischlin examined the French, Günther Heine the German, Toshio Ōdate the Japanese, and Gerrit van der Sterre the Dutch.

Chapter 1

HISTORY OF THE PLANE

The axe, adz, chisel, drill, and a crude saw were all known in the Stone age, and served man in shaping wood for millennia. These tools remained the same, although much improved in function, during the Bronze age. The plane was a product of a later time, a date that can only be roughly estimated.

EGYPT The historical record of tools prior to the birth of Christ rests heavily on the relics of ancient Egypt, where they were preserved, along with furniture and decorative pieces, in the dry climate. The contents of the tomb of Tutankhamen, who died in ca.1350 B.C., are perhaps the best known of these. Many people have seen some of these magnificent artifacts at museum exhibits, and know at first hand the high level of skill of Tutankhamen's cabinetmakers. The joinery of the fourteenth century B.C. included most of the techniques still used by the masters of the seventeenth and eighteenth centuries. It may seem impossible to a modern woodworker that this work was accomplished without the use of a plane; but it was. Moreover, it was most likely done entirely with tools of copper or bronze. No iron tools have survived from this era.

The wood was shaped primarily with the adz, with the final surface achieved by rubbing with blocks of pumice or sandstone, using sand as an abrasive. Their adz, like our plane, took many shapes to fit it for different tasks. It had a blade of bronze (or earlier, of copper) not unlike a plane iron in shape. It was longer than wide, with an edge made with a single bevel on the side facing the handle, and was affixed to the handle with thongs.

The adz of our era has the blade fixed to the handle in such a way as to present the flat side of the cutting edge parallel to the line of the cut. It is swung from the shoulder with a long handle, from the elbow with a shorter one, and from the wrist in the sharply curved bowl adz. In each case the curvature of the blade matches the radius of the swing. The Egyptians had similar tools, some of which must have been used in a different fashion. A straight blade mounted at an acute angle to the handle, and one on an S-shaped handle, suggests that they were pulled rather than swung. Then, too, certain frescoes appear to indicate that the adz was also used as a scraper, with the blade nearly at right angles to the work.

The finish and the flatness attained on Egyptian wooden surfaces was equal to that obtainable by planing and called for similar techniques. The "lost arts" attributed to the Egyptians, such as the method of hardening bronze to allow better cutting edges, have not been documented. It may well be that they also had methods of using an adz which became "lost arts" because they were made obsolete by the invention of the plane.

Skill in working wood with bronze tools and without the use of the plane was not restricted to Egypt. A well-formed wooden folding stool survives from the Northern Europe of about 1500 B.C.

GREECE Homer, about 850 B.C. (half a millennium after Tutankhamen), sang of Odysseus smoothing his bed with the bronze—the adz. The Greeks probably had woodworkers of skill comparable to those of Egypt, but there is little in the way of documentation for this. The best evidence of their wood-working equipment comes from items preserved in the tombs of Egypt after it was brought under Greek rule by Alexander the Great in 332 B.C.

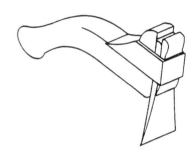

Fig.1:1—Early Greek adz

The smelting of iron was practiced in the Caucasus before 1700 B.C. and had spread to Syria and Palestine by Tutankamen's time. Although Odysseus used bronze, elsewhere Homer speaks of the hiss of iron being quenched by the smith. Iron did not immediately replace bronze, even when it was available. However, it had largely done so by the time of the Greek rule in Egypt. Greek adzes with an iron blade fastened to the handle by an iron band, as shown in Fig.1:1, are found from this period. (The same form still remains in use today in rural areas of Spain.) The blade was fixed within the band by a wooden wedge, in the style to be used later in planes. It appears that not only iron, but the plane and several other tools, were brought to Egypt by the Greeks. Plane shavings, which are unlikely to be confused with adz shavings, were found (under the mummy and as pillow stuffing under the head) in Egyptian sarcophagi from the period of Greek rule.

The earliest known name for the plane is the Greek "rhykane". A Roman lexicographer about 120 B.C. (Marcus Tarentius Varro) indicated that the Roman "runcina" was derived from the Greek. The plane was named in a poem of about 270 B.C. (by Leonidas of Tarento). It would appear that the plane was commonly known in Greece and Rome by the third century B.C., although no examples of early Greek planes, or even depictions of planes, have survived. Their absence in art is perhaps not surprising. Handwork was for slaves, not citizens, and the tools of handwork were not often considered as suitable subjects for artists. The fabled Daedalus is credited with a great many inventions and, although planes were not mentioned in early Greek accounts, they were among the tools shown in a depiction of him on a Pompeian wall (1st century A.D.).

The plane, then, existed in the fourth century B.C. in Egypt, brought there by the Greeks. It was not known to Homer in the ninth century B.C. This sets a probable time frame, and a reasonable estimate would place the invention in the Golden Age of Pericles, in the fifth century B.C.

How did it come about? We may speculate that a clever Greek, using his adz as a scraper, placed a block of wood between its handle and the work to maintain a constant angle, and liked the result. He made a new handle, with a projection to serve the same purpose as the block. From there, a sole to rest on the work and support the blade is a logical next step.

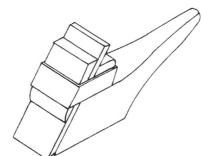

Fig.1:2—Greber reconstruction of transitional form between adze and plane

Greber, in his *History of the Plane*, has made a convincing reconstruction (Fig.1:2) of a tool of transitional form between a hand adz and a plane, in which the wooden handle of the adz is extended forward to provide a sole behind the blade. This would approach the action of a modern chisel or edge plane (as seen in Fig.1:3).

It is possible that a tool of this type was known well before the time frame postulated above, but was considered a form of adz not requiring a new name.

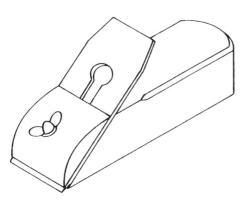

Fig. 1:3—Modern chisel or edge plane

Another important discovery remained to be made: that pressure on the wood in front of the blade produced a smoother cut. The true plane appeared when the blade was moved from the front to the interior of the plane's body. This was a major event in the history of woodworking, providing the key to further development. We may surmise that it was the Greeks who evolved the form found in the two planes surviving from

3

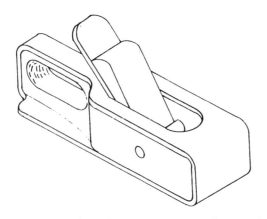

Fig.1:4—Author's free reconstruction of a smooth plane buried at Pompeii, A.D. 79

Pompeii (A.D. 79). A reconstruction of one of these is shown in Fig. 1:4.

W.L. Goodman, in his *History of Woodworking Tools,* prefers the theory, offered by G.A. Norman (1954), that the plane evolved from the scratch stock or a similar tool. The Vikings used molding tools on the edges of their ship planking, as shown by an example found in a ship buried in about 850 A.D. near Oseberg in the Oslo fiord. A Lapp molding plane (Sandvigske Samlinger, Norway) may well be derived from such molders. As shown in Fig.1:5, the blade was bedded at a steep angle at the rear of the body. A grip projected forward, suggesting that the tool was pulled in use. Vertical dovetail slots in either side of the tool could accept a fence for guiding the cut. Both Greber's and Norman's proposals are reasonable, but until further evidence provides a definite answer they must be regarded as no more than interesting hypotheses.

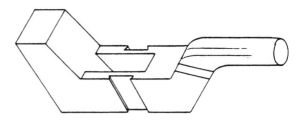

Fig.1:5—Early Lapp molding plane

ROME   By the beginning of the first century, the plane was well known. Pliny (A.D. 23-79) treats it as a common tool. The earliest surviving planes were recovered from the ruins of Pompeii (buried A.D. 79). Their appearance (Fig.1:4), although different in detail, is remarkably similar to the planes of our era. A wooden body was encased in a rectangular frame of iron 0.4 inch (about a centimeter) thick, forming sole, front, top and back. The top rear was narrowed and a horizontal slot through the wood formed a grip for the right hand. Dimensions were 8.3 inches (21 cm.) long by 2.4 inches (6 cm.) wide. The irons, 1.4 and 1.6 inches (3.5 and 4 cm.) wide, were bedded at about 45° and protruded through a narrow slit in the sole. They were fixed in position by a wedge bearing on a round iron rod across the throat.

A number of other planes from Roman times have been found throughout Roman-occupied Europe. The blades were narrow, less than 1.75 inches (45 mm.) in width, and were held by a wedge bearing on a bar across the throat.

4

The handles were usually horizontal slots through the stock for fingerholds, in front and back or just in back. Iron soles, or iron sheathing on a wooden stock, predominate. The jointer or long plane was known, as shown by its appearance in a Pompeian wall painting. The Romans used not only bench planes, but rabbets, grooving and other planes as well. Some of the surviving Roman irons appear to have had profiled cutting edges, for use in molding.

NORTHERN EUROPE   The scarcity of specimens from the Dark Ages (476 A.D. - 1000 A.D.) was formerly believed to mean that the art of planemaking was lost with the fall of the Roman empire and was only rediscovered during the Renaissance. Indeed, the few examples that have surfaced are more primitive than those of the Roman era, but enough have been found to suggest a continuous history. The oldest example known from the peoples of northern Europe was found in the Vimose bog on the Danish island of Fynen (Fig.1:6), and is dated at about 300 A.D. It is narrow, 10 inches (26 cm.) long, of hexagonal section tapering toward each end. The ends were upturned, recurved and carved. The iron was held by wedging it against a peg across the mouth, in the center of the plane. A hollow in the sole suggests that it was used to round spear shafts.

The present method of fixing the wedge in slots cut in the sides of the throat was first seen in a plane found in Bergen, Norway in the residue of a fire known to have occurred in 1248. This innovation was widespread by the

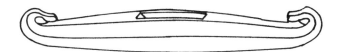

Fig.1:6—Danish plane ca.300 A.D.

beginning of the sixteenth century. (It is interesting to note that the older method, using a peg across the throat, has been revived and is used in some contemporary planes.)

The architecture and furniture of the later Middle Ages (1000 A.D. –1500 A.D.) made fewer demands on the workers of wood than were made by the styles of earlier times, and the plane received little attention. The tenth century monk Theophilus describes smoothing altar tables with a drawknife. Homes, even cathedrals, were built without the plane. The Coronation Chair, built for Edward I of England (1272-1307) and still used for British coronations, is illustrative of the work of that period. Massive, square, elaborately carved, it may well have never felt a plane.

The Gothic styles of the thirteenth century replaced some of the carving, which had predominated as surface treatment, with planed surfaces. Moldings assumed importance, in particular the linen-fold forms, and the planes (hollows and rounds) used to start this pattern became important. The planes acquired their present names: HOBEL in German before the fifteenth century, RABOT in French somewhat earlier.

The joiners began to disassociate themselves from the carpenters, forming their own guilds during the fourteenth and fifteenth centuries. They regarded the plane as their instrument, and attempted to prevent, by legal means, its

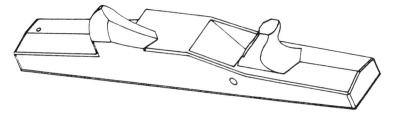

Fig.1:7—English plane of 1545

use by carpenters or other woodworkers. They were successful and the schism remains embodied in language as different names for joiner and carpenter, Tischler and Zimmermann, menuisier and charpentier. The ban held until the sixteenth century, and even later in some parts of Germany. By then the skills of the two trades had evolved along different lines, and the joiners had less reason to fear competition from the carpenters.

Our knowledge of the evolution of the plane in the ninth to the fifteenth century rests largely on the art of the period, as surviving specimens are rare. The sixteenth century has given us more examples. The recent trove recovered with the ship Mary Rose, which sank in 1545, provides the first concrete information on the tools of England of that era. A reconstruction of a wooden plane of about 20 inches (50 cm.) in length is shown in Fig.1:7, and others will be seen later. We can hope for more as the practice of underwater archaeology expands. A glimpse of the plane style of the Netherlands of 1596 was provided by the tool shown in Fig.1:8, recovered from an expedition of that year that was wrecked on the island of Novaya Zemlya bordering the Barents Sea. Their stores, including this smoother and several plane irons, were retrieved in the 1870's.

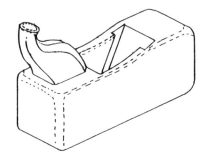

Fig.1:8—Dutch smooth plane of 1596

The collecting of tools as objects of interest rather than of use began in earnest at about this time. August I of Saxony, Elector of the Holy Roman Empire (1553 - 86) owned 8700 tools, most made especially for him, highly decorated and carved but with fine working qualities as well. The collection contained over three hundred planes of many types. Although these may be presumed to be rather more ornate than the working man's tools of the period, they speak to the range available. We will return to details of some of these planes in later sections.

RENAISSANCE With the Renaissance of the fourteenth through six-teenth century came a taste for less massive and more diverse furniture styles. The simple shaves used previously acquired new forms and importance in forming cabriole legs. New functions for the plane, too, proliferated during this period. Curved surfaces required planes with curved soles to shape them. Several types of grooving plane are present in the Elector's collection, interest in frame-and-panel construction having increased. With them, planes for shaping the panel edges appeared. Planes for cutting dovetails were men-tioned in a 1587 inventory of the Elector's Dresden collection. Moldings became more elaborate, and to the bevels, hollows and rounds of the earlier Gothic period were added ogees and complex molders. The "stuck" moldings (cut in the material of the structure) were supplemented by "planted" moldings cut on separate pieces of wood and then affixed.

The major changes in the bench planes over this period were in appearance, not in function. The evolution of the handle is shown in Fig.1:9. The Roman style (A) was retained in southern Europe, with the horizontal

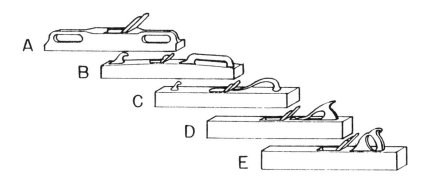

Fig.1:9—Evolution of bench plane handles

slot emerging from the stock as the flat-iron type handle shown in early Italian frescoes (B). The slot expanded upward, over time, through the shepherd's crook type (C) shown in Félibien (1676), intermediate forms (D) and culminating in the closed grip of the nineteenth century (E). Northern Europe took a different course. The rear grip was dispensed with (at least in the shorter planes) and was replaced by a front horn. This appeared first in rudimentary form as a buttress for the left thumb in long planes, and developed through various ornate forms to the standardized horn of modern Continental planes.

The Baroque and Rococo periods of the seventeenth and eighteenth centuries saw an explosion in the demands upon the joiner for more and more elaborate furniture. In turn, they demanded more of their planes, and created them in great variety. The new taste called for surfaces adorned with painting and figured wood to replace the Gothic carving and tracery. The older arts of mosaic with stone were applied to inlay and intarsia, and veneer became an important design factor.

Centuries of profligate use had depleted Mediterranean forests, and the Dutch East India company at the beginning of the seventeenth century imported exotic woods to fill the needs. Veneer, hand sawn and much thicker than the material we know today, became important. Gluing these thin pieces to secondary wood not only stretched the supply, but permitted use of highly figured grain too unstable to serve as solid boards. Veneer called for development and mastery of specialized tools, such as toothing and scraping planes. Holland, with access to the imported woods, led in development of these arts and provided training for the Royal cabinetmakers of the day.

As furniture design changed, a higher level of workmanship was required in joining the lighter elements of these new, more delicate styles. The mortise and tenon joints formerly cut with saws and chisels now had to fit more accurately, and fitting planes such as rabbet and shoulder planes were needed. Drawer runners were inserted in grooves in case sides. The cross-grain grooves called for a special tool, the dado plane. The drop-leaf table required concealment of the gap between leaf and table when the leaf was down, and a new profile (and the planes needed to form it) was devised.

Furniture styles followed each other in rapid succession once the break with Gothic was made. Rulers vied with each other to have the finest palaces and furnishings. The masters of furniture design and construction acquired new dignity and stature as the aristocracy competed with each other for the latest and the best. Veneering in ebony was a mark of fine work, and the French masters took the title "ébéniste" as befitting their rank above that of the menuisiers or joiners, and on a par with artists and sculptors.

Widely regarded as at the pinnacle of elaborate furniture creation was the workshop established at the Louvre by the "Sun King", Louis XIV, in 1668. Presided over by André Boulle, it produced work admired by royalty and imitated in the workshops they established. Standard moldings would not serve in such work, and the molding planes of the period were often designed and made for a specific job.

The Renaissance came more slowly to England. Gothic style and oak construction persisted until about 1660. Furniture making then became a specialty, and lighter styles appeared. The reign of William and Mary (1689-1702) saw the fashion shift to favor English walnut. This coincided with the rise of veneering techniques. Highly figured sections from crotch or burl permitted the creation of symmetrical patterns by book-matching or quartering. These grains were unstable and only practical as veneers. Walnut was particularly attractive if molded on the end grain, and thicker sections were used as borders. Molding planes were modified to handle these new requirements, and replaced carving tools as the principal means of adornment.

RISE OF THE PLANEMAKING TRADE   Prior to the eighteenth century, almost all planes were made by their users. This was part of the "arte and mysterie" that was imparted to the apprentice by the master, and his early training included the making of plane stocks for the blades the master provided. There was little standardization of form, and the maker was free to indulge his fancy in style and decoration.

There is little doubt that some tradesmen were better than others in making planes and could be persuaded, for a consideration, to make one for a mate. But there is no evidence for the establishment of plane-making as a separate trade until the seventeenth century.

There are a number of early planes from the Netherlands which show a distinct standardization of form, characterized by stylized carving and bearing carved dates. An example is shown in Fig.1:10. Burchard and Walker (1985) have presented evidence that these were made by a small group of professional plane-makers. Forty-two planes of this type were marked with the initials I A, found to be the mark of Jan Arendtz. (The letter J was usually rendered as I until the nineteenth century.) Examples of his planes are dated 1663-1664. A number of other initials have been found on more than one plane of this genre, and these are presumably maker's identifications. There

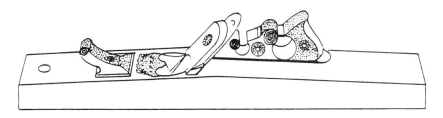

Fig.1:10—Dutch plane, 18th century

9

is mention of a group of planemakers within an Amsterdam joiner's guild in 1614, and evidence that planes of this type were exported. This area cries out for further investigation, and it appears that the Netherlands may claim the first plane-making industry.

Planemaking was a distinct trade in England before 1700. Thomas Granford, "plainmakr" has been documented in 1692. The custom of embossing the maker's name on the end grain of the upper front end of the plane was established probably by Thomas Granford ca.1700 and by Robert Wooding shortly thereafter, and has been used in England and America ever since. (Incuse rather than embossed names gained favor in the nineteenth century.) The colonies were not far behind in establishing planemaking as a trade. Francis Nicholson was producing and signing planes in Wrentham, Massachusetts, in about 1730. French workers continued to make their own planes until the late eighteenth century. Roubo (1769) assumed that woodworkers would buy their plane irons but make their own stocks. Germany appears to have resisted until the nineteenth century, with the tradesmen making their own plane bodies and having irons made to fit them. Eventually commercial manufacture was established in Europe, by Joh. Weiss in Vienna (1820), Lachappelle in Strasbourg in 1840, Lemainque in Paris in 1849, and others.

The growth and subsequent decline in America of the wooden plane, as it was supplanted by metal planes and then motorized tools, will be detailed in a later section. These changes were less precipitous in other countries. In recent years the resurgence of interest in handcraft has increased the demand for wooden planes, and plane types out of production for many years are reappearing in modern tool catalogs.

WRITTEN HISTORY OF THE PLANE   With the exception of a few fragmentary early works, the publication of descriptions of contemporary woodworking tools did not begin until the sixteenth century in Germany and Italy, and the end of the seventeenth in England and France. These facts were regarded as proprietary by the workmen, and not easily elicited by those few authors who did not regard them as beneath the concern of gentlemen. We are fortunate in having the works of Félibien, Moxon, Roubo, and especially Diderot and D'Alembert to record the tools used at that time.

Research on early tools is a recent development. For the historical information presented here, we are indebted to the studies published by Mercer (1929), Greber (1956), and Goodman (1964) among others.

The pioneering research of W.L. Goodman and his colleagues has provided biographical data for over a thousand British planemakers and dealers. His classic work *British Planemakers from 1700* is referred to so frequently that its second edition is commonly abbreviated BPII. The corresponding task for the United States was pursued by Kenneth Roberts in the decades after 1950; his summary, *Wooden Planes in Nineteenth Century America*, is familiarly known as WPINCA. The research of many others, including contributors to the *Chronicle* of the Early American Industries Association and to the quarterly *Plane Talk*, were added to these and published in 1983 and 1987 by the Pollaks in their *Guide to American Wooden Planes*.

CHINA   The history of the plane in the Far East is largely unknown in the literature of the West, though probably more will become known as translations from Far Eastern works on this subject become available. I have found no evidence indicating that the plane was known in China before early European contacts; yet their style is quite different, suggesting independent development. Early Chinese planes had blades beveled on both sides, but the Western single bevel was accepted in the latter part of the nineteenth century. They retained a long rounded bevel, however, in contrast to our straight one. Their blades were mounted at an angle of 31-32°, but the double bevel raised the effective slope of the cutting surface to 43-45°. With the change to single bevel, the bedding angle was increased, but many Eastern planes use lower than our "common" or 45° pitch.

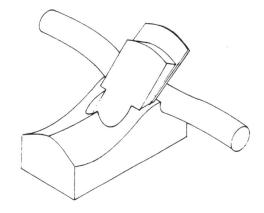

Fig.1:11—Chinese plane

The single cutter in early planes was held in place with an iron wedge, lodged against a steel pin across the throat. Later planes adapted the Western cap iron, and some also used the Western wooden wedge fitted into side abutments. For handgrip, the smooth planes and some molders have transverse rods dovetailed into, or piercing, the stock behind the blade. The top of the stock usually tapers downward toward toe and heel. An example is shown in Fig.1:11.

Authorities conflict on whether the early Chinese pushed or pulled their planes. Tools collected around 1870 usually had fences on the right. One authority concluded, on this evidence, that the Chinese were left-handed! When it became known that the Japanese pulled their planes, the more reasonable assumption was made that the Chinese did, as well. This ignored the fact that some early central European rabbeting planes (filletsters) had fences on the right, and worked quite well when used on boards edges and pushed. Chinese planes function equally well either way — so, for that matter, do Western planes. In modern Chinese planes, the shape of the body remains unchanged and they are pushed. As we shall see presently, the form which reached Japan from China was called a push plane. The bulk of evidence favors the view that the Chinese have always pushed their planes.

JAPAN   The earliest tool used in Japan for surfacing riven and adz-smoothed boards was a spear-shaped double edged knife, flat on one side (Fig.1:12). This was used with the worker in a sitting position, and was drawn toward him. While it would not qualify as a plane in the Western concept of the meaning, it was called YARI-KANNA (the form variously transliterated as

Fig.1:12—Japanese predecessor of the plane

kanna or ganna means plane). A considerable amount of Chinese technology made its way to Japan in the sixth century and later, and it is reasonable to assume that this included their tool styles. By the fifteenth century, riving logs had given way to ripsawing with the ŌGA, a large one-man saw much like the Chinese tool. Shortly thereafter a push plane, the TSUKI-KANNA appeared, in form much like the Chinese (tsuki means push). The iron was held by a wedge, and it had a transverse handle. The shape is better adapted to use in a standing position than in the sitting posture familiar in Japan. There was a period of ferment while standing-sitting, push or pull options with the new tool were evaluated. Ōdate (1984) cites a seventeenth century drawing in which carpenters are depicted using both push and pull styles. On the southern island of Kyushu the Chinese form is still in use, perhaps because of immigration of Korean woodworkers. Elsewhere in Japan, however, the plane lost its handles and it was used by pulling.

The body of the Japanese bench plane (Fig.1:13) is low, the iron short, thick, and thicker at top than bottom. A very hard steel face is laminated to a soft back. The steel face is hollowed out behind the cutting edge to make flat honing of this face easier. It fits tightly into wedge-shaped slots in the cheeks, acting as its own wedge. This remains the principle holding method even in their double-iron forms, although the loose cap iron is of a wedge

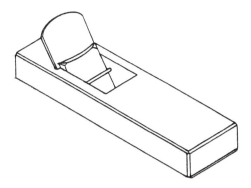

Fig.1:13—Japanese hand plane

section and also serves as a wedge against a steel pin across the throat. The mouth is narrow, and the front of the throat runs parallel to the iron or nearly so for a short distance to keep the mouth narrow as the sole wears or is dressed.

Nearly all of the Japanese planes are pulled, although they work equally well in either direction. In the classical posture (still used by some), the woodworker is seated on a floor mat before a low (1 foot, 30 cm.) bench. No vises or other holding devices are used, the workpiece being held by the worker's foot. In this situation, a push plane (or saw) would be most inconvenient. The Chinese, in contrast, work on a bench as we do.

The Chinese and Korean practice was to plane on a sloping beam. The posture is much like a Western cooper's, but with board and plane interchanged. This was accepted as an improvement for long boards by the Japanese; however, the worker stood near the low end of the beam and pulled the plane toward him.

While Japan may have acquired the idea of the plane from the West through China, it is evident from the above differences that they have followed a rather different path of development. Their planes are capable of the highest level of performance, but require much effort for their mastery.

DATING PLANES   Through reference to the works of Goodman or the Pollaks, it is possible to determine within narrow limits the age of most maker-marked planes, with a certainty unusual in other artifacts of their vintage. In the absence of a maker's mark, a few design features may be of use in approximate dating of English or U.S. planes. Wide flat chamfers (over 3/8 in. (10 mm.)) were predominant in the eighteenth century, but became narrower toward its end and later were replaced by rounded edges. Rear handles were frequently offset toward the right before 1800 (the French apparently never offset). Very early 18th century English molding planes usually range between 9¾" and 10" in length, but by the late 18th century, the shorter 9½" (24 cm.) was usual. Planes in the mid-Atlantic states followed the English style, and New England accepted the new standard ca.1800. At about the same time a style of tool chest became popular in which the molding planes were stored on end in the bottom, with a sliding compartment (till) above them for other tools. Unfortunately older planes too long to fit under the till were shortened, and many lost their maker's names along with their front ends.

The wedge finials of eighteenth century American and English molders and fitting planes (such as rabbets) were usually cut to circular arcs. Later, elliptical patterns predominated. (These are illustrated in Chapter 5.) Comparison of the wedge pattern with those of known makers may be of help. These may be found in Pollak (1987 and 1989). The particular pattern of stop chamfering of the toe and heel of the plane, the shape of the cove of the step, and other features provide characteristics helpful in identifying certain makers or geographical locations. The work of W.L. Goodman is a valuable source of this sort of information.

The criteria given here are not to be fully relied on, as many exceptions are found. With the experience gained by close examination of many planes it is possible to develop a sense of the age (at least for English and American planes) similar to that attainable in the study of furniture.

With planes from other countries, this is more difficult. Certain types of planes, such as bench planes, remained relatively unchanged over centuries. The English custom of signing planes with the full name of the maker was not adapted on the Continent, and the initials often seen on these stocks may have been carved by owner rather than maker. Stamped initials were common only on the products of some of the planemakers of Holland, and dates for a number of these have been reported by Burchard and Walker (1985). Continental planes were often dated in the course of embellishing them with chip carving, and if this appears to be contemporary with the making of the plane (and not a later addition by an owner) it provides good evidence. It is a mistake, however, to assume that all early planes were decorated. A carved plane is much less likely to be consigned to the scrap heap than a rude one, and the ones that were preserved by chance, such as in the sunken ship Mary Rose, are indeed rude. Conversely, the assumption that a carved and decorated plane is old is risky. There are twentieth century craftsman who adorn their tools.

THE WOODEN PLANE
IN THE HISTORY OF AMERICA

The early settlers in the new world recapitulated, in a few decades, the preceding millennia in wood use. They were perforce their own carpenters and joiners. Timber was abundant. A home could be built with axe and chalk-line, and furnished with little more. However, the plane was needed for even the simplest improvements. The Pilgrims had brought some wood-working tools with them: John Alden was recruited for the voyage because he was a cooper, and his tool chest sailed with him. Barrels were essential in storing food for the winter, so he was a valuable asset to the colony. His tools and skills were also called upon to make the first furniture, and some of his work survives.

Boatbuilding was one of the earliest industries. An American-built ship sailed up the Thames in 1638. Whaling followed, and the coopers were kept busy providing barrels for the oil. Within a few decades of the first harsh winter, the colonies prospered. New colonists arrived, and brought with them the skills of their European apprenticeships. While outlying settlements still fought Indians, joiners from London founded shops in Boston: Henry Messinger in 1641 and Ralph Mason about the same time. William Gibbons and William Russell started making furniture in New Haven around 1640.

In contrast to the earliest settlers, those who followed brought significant financial resources with them. New Amsterdam, though founded in 1623, showed little growth until the Dutch West India Company provided incentives which enticed burghers from the Netherlands. Pennsylvania was settled in 1683 by people of means, bringing fine furniture and the skills to make more. By the early eighteenth century many cities were prosperous enough to support makers of fine furniture and builders of ornate homes. A small industry of one-man shops arose to provide the planes they needed. The first dozen or so of these were located within a fifty mile radius of Francis Nicholson's shop in Wrentham, Massachusetts.

The wealth of the Connecticut River Valley provided patronage for the builders of fine furniture, and many of these pieces are to be seen in museums. Initially, the taste for heavy Gothic styles brought with the original settlers from England and Holland predominated. The use of heavy cornice moldings, which could overhang by 8 in. (20 cm.), is a characteristic of the kas, a heavy linen cupboard of early New York homes. Some Connecticut pieces appear to have been influenced by this, with cornices composed of eight or ten elements individually cut by standard molding planes. Lighter styles followed,

15

in accordance with English trends. High quality, sharp planes were important, as sandpaper was not generally available until after 1750. Final smoothing was by scrapers and scraper planes, or abrasive rushes or the skins of certain fish.

Stirrings of innovation arose in the colonies, prompted by the availability of mahogany from Cuba and the West Indies (a bonus of the sugar trade). This permitted sawing drawer fronts from thick slabs of fine wood, and inspired the block front style. New techniques in the use of planes with curved soles must have contributed to the finishing of these pieces. The form was brought to a pinnacle of perfection by the Goddards and Townsends of Newport, Rhode Island, in the latter half of the 18th century.

By the latter half of the 18th century America was producing furniture believed by many to be equal to the best that England could supply. The styles of Chippendale, Adam, Heppelwhite, Sheraton, making use of the new world's mahogany, were copied here (from their publications) a decade or so after they were adapted in England. They were modified, to the point of becoming a new style called Federal and associated with Duncan Phyfe (1768-1854). As in Europe, the new styles needed no basically new forms of plane for their creation. Modification of existing tools and new profiles sufficed.

The furniture built for the very rich naturally dominates the material seen in textbooks and museums. A refreshing look at the creations of the rural cabinetmakers and the tools they used to make them is to be had in the Dominy collection at Winterthur and in the volume by Charles Hummel (1968). The Dominys worked in East Hampton, New York, from about 1760 to 1840.

The demand for new types of molding planes arose primarily for architectural use. The colonists, once having attained the comfort of a tight house, began to seek to improve its appearance. The earliest houses were sturdily constructed by housewrights, many of whom learned their trade in England. A first major improvement was to sheath the fireplace walls with vertical boards, planed (on the room surface only) and half-lapped with rabbet planes. A house later to be occupied by Paul Revere was built in Boston in the third quarter of the seventeenth century with such sheathing, with the joints concealed by use of a shallow quirk ogee plane on either side. Its exposed ceiling beams had their corners softened with a quarter-round plane.

An alternate sheathing, which continued in use into the eighteenth century, used the same wide pine boards but grooved both sides of one and tapered both edges of the next to fit the grooves. A plow, either fixed or movable, served for the grooving and a simple jack or similar plane could have done the tapering. The joint was again softened with a chamfer or a simple molding. If this wainscot covered only the lower portion of the wall, it required a finishing touch at its top. This was initially a plain strip of wood, but soon acquired an elaborate molding as a chair rail.

By 1700, harbor towns on the New England coast were prospering from foreign trade and money was available for more decorative touches. Pine paneling, as opposed to sheathing, came into use about 1720. Inch-thick pine, again planed only on the exposed side, formed stiles and rails joined by pinned mortise and tenon joints. Thinner panels of pine, beveled on their edges, fitted into grooves in these. A little later, the edges of the panel framing were decorated with molding planes.

The pilaster (a flat vertical member suggesting a Greek column) appeared as a suitable enhancement on either side of the fireplace. These were usually vertically fluted, stopped at either end. The fluting plane cut the center, and a gouge finished the ends. At the top, horizontal moldings simulated the capital and entablature: a small one for the architrave, a flat section for the frieze, and a large molding for the cornice. These short moldings were relatively complex, but were quickly made using repeated application of simple hollows, rounds, and ogee planes.

The cornice of the pilaster was soon extended to ring the room at the junction of wall and ceiling. Cutting these in the longer lengths required called for a plane to finish the elaborate profile in one pass, and New England planemakers began making planes wide enough to cut the full cornice molding.

Trim was now required as framing around door and window casings. These were initially just flat boards with rounded edges, but soon were required to be elaborately molded. These architrave moldings were highly individual at first, and obviously made by using combinations of simpler molders, but later certain forms were produced by wide molders.

Elsewhere in the home, on baseboards, mantel shelves, staircase handrails and elsewhere, still other types of moldings required their own planes. With increasing prosperity, the homes of the rich were no longer decorated only with straight moldings, however complex. These soon became but the starting point for further elaboration with carving tools.

The nation in 1830 consisted of 24 states with a total population of almost 13 million. During the next two decades this was swelled by seven states and ten million people, four million of whom were immigrants. The building of a canal system provided work for the new Americans not only in its construction, but in the industry and the new markets it generated. The growing population was absorbed not only on the farms but increasingly in the cities. Water provided transportation and also power, and most factories were powered by waterwheels. With the canals opening broader markets, plane manufacturing expanded from the early centers in New England and the major Eastern cities to central and western New York, eastern Pennsylvania, the Connecticut River valley, and Ohio.

These two decades saw a surge in American technology. The demand for better ways of doing things covered all fields. Samuel Colt set up to make his revolver, Morse invented the telegraph, McCormick the reaper, Goodyear vulcanized rubber. In woodworking, the rotary sawmill replaced the up-and-down mill, the Woodworth rotary planer patents were incorporated in a thousand machines. Machines for making moldings proliferated, and factories were established to make woodworking machinery.

The availability of milled lumber, the need to house the growing population, and the cost of labor combined to change house construction techniques. Stud framing replaced post-and-beam. The making of furniture, too, began to be taken over by machine. Lambert Hitchcock had established a factory in 1818 to make furniture parts for sale to cabinetmakers, and soon it was mass producing finished furniture. The furniture industry of Grand Rapids, Michigan, was started in 1848 by William Haldane's factory. By 1908 Sears Roebuck would sell you a "massive side board, carved oak, serpentine front" for $14.65. There was little room for individual handwork in the mass market.

The manufacture of wooden planes, too, was included in the move to mass production. Housing the rapidly growing population of the United States and satisfying their demand for ornate moldings provided the incentive for an explosive growth in plane production. The early small shops were replaced by large factories. The history of the Union Factory (Roberts 1983) provides a fascinating illustration of the change. One of the small shops that made wooden planes by hand was operated by the brothers D. and M.Copeland in Hartford, Conn. in 1822. They took as apprentice Hermon Chapin, agreeing to teach and board him for four years while paying him a total of six hundred dollars. Chapin was 21 at the time, with a knowledge of the lumber business gained from his father. He apparently did very well as an apprentice, as after three years he formed a partnership with D. Copeland, built a water-powered factory, and hired and boarded hands. He bought out his partner in 1828. Making full use of power and innovations in plane-making machinery, he increased sales from $5000 in 1828 to over $32,000 in 1848 (a double-iron jack plane sold for $1.00 at that time). Another large manufacturer, Baldwin, outpaced Chapin by making 60,000 planes in 1860.

The economy of the North continued to expand, especially during the years of the Civil War, as the making of war goods scarcely diminished exports.

After the war, huge fortunes were made by some and a good living by many. Furniture styles appeared in rapid succession. The demand was for the newest style. The extravagant mansions of the Astors and Vanderbilts were filled with ever more elaborate creations, and the average family did its best to copy these.

The business of planemaking prospered. Patents on planemaking machinery began to appear, and the tedious hand operations were mechanized. But the Yankee ingenuity which increased the rate of wooden plane production also brought about the invention of metal planes and eventually the downfall of the wooden plane. The Bailey plane patents of 1855-1867 were acquired by the Stanley Rule and Level Co. in 1869 and these metal planes were vigorously marketed. From 6500 units by 1871 total sales grew to three million by 1898, and the demand for wooden planes plummeted. By 1925 there were only two surviving wooden plane factories (Sandusky and Chapin-Stephens). Four years later both had sold out.

Dissatisfaction with machine-made furniture and Victorian excess appeared. John Ruskin in the 1850's preached a return to handicrafts to escape the dehumanization of the machine. William Morris agreed, and his factory (built 1861) produced simpler forms, of which the Morris chair is perhaps the best remembered. The Arts and Crafts movement in England toward the end of the nineteenth century was followed by the Mission furniture of the beginning of the twentieth. Gustav Stickley's Craftsman styles and Elbert Hubbard's Roycraft returned to solid wood, straight lines, simple and honest construction. The Shakers had long before adopted functional design and absence of ornament in furniture for their own use. The planes they made and the appealing simplicity of the work they produced (1789-1920) are still admired at Hancock Shaker village and other locations.

Another indication of dissatisfaction with mass produced furniture was the growing demand for well-made reproductions of eighteenth century masterpieces. Wallace Nutting was one who responded to this. He established a shop in Saugus, Mass. in 1917 to reproduce fine furniture, and returned to handwork for critical areas. His success was not monetary, but his work commands respect today. Other fine cabinetmakers survived to produce superb work for a limited but wealthy clientele.

The simpler styles in furniture were within the capability of home workshops, and with increased leisure the average person could pursue woodworking as a hobby. Popular magazines arose to cater to this new interest. Most professional workers of wood were under severe economic constraints as to the amount of handwork they could use, but not so the amateur. He could afford the luxury of spending whatever time it took to do it as well as he could. Over the past fifty years, the home workshop has been a common feature of the home. In the recent past, the amateur has rediscovered the capabilities of hand tools as opposed to his first love, the power tools. In particular, he has learned the almost sensual delight of using a properly tuned plane on fine wood. Some, self- taught, have learned the techniques and now produce work comparable to that of the legendary masters. At the risk of offending lovers of antiques, it is probably true that there are many first-rate makers of fine furniture alive today that compare favorably with the makers of earlier times.

There is no better way to learn to appreciate fine furniture than to try to create it yourself. An appreciation for well-built furniture is reappearing outside of the enclaves of the very rich, and several fine schools are training young people in the skills of designing and creating it. There is new demand for authentic reproductions (as opposed to copies simplified for factory production); some of these require hand planing. The art of working wood has come full circle with James Krenov and his disciples, who emulate the old masters by making and using their own wooden planes.

Chapter 2

BENCH PLANES — AN OVERVIEW

The name "plane" derives from the tool's original purpose, which was to create a flat or plane surface. Over the years, the plane has acquired many other functions and shapes, but let us begin with the original - and still the most common - form. These are called BENCH planes, presumably because they were in such constant use that they were to be found on the bench rather than on a shelf. They are characterized by their flat bottom, a cutter not exposed on either side of the tool, and by the fact that the shavings escape through an opening at the top. Before considering the individual types of bench plane, let us cover the uses to which they are put, the names and variations of their several parts, and some general characteristics which serve to suggest the age or origin of the tool. Many tools of other function, to be covered later, developed from the bench plane. Those which retain the top shavings escapement will be termed bench type planes, and most of the details covered here apply to these as well.

BENCH PLANE FUNCTION

Today, when we seldom see a board that has not been machine planed, it is easy to forget that this luxury was not available in the eighteenth century. A planing mill was invented in England in 1791, but saw only limited use. The modern rotary planer dates to 1828 in the United States, and was not widespread until about 1850. In earlier times the woodworker was faced with a pitsawn flitch, a hewn balk, or a riven section of log rough-dressed by a hatchet or adz. It was up to him to reduce the rough surface to a smooth and level one. Further, in most cases, he had to shape two adjacent edges to planes at right angles to this surface and two ends mutually perpendicular to edge and surface. Finally, the workpiece had to be hand planed to the desired thickness, finishing with a second surface parallel to the first. This used to be a standard first exercise in the use of hand planes in woodworking courses, and is an exercise guaranteed to increase your respect for the tradesmen of that day.

The task may be divided into several stages, and the evidence of older planes tells us that this was usual. Superfluous wood was removed with a roughing plane, which had a wide mouth and took thick shavings, using a single iron with a distinctly curved edge. This was commonly used in diagonal strokes cutting across the grain at 45°.

After nearing the proper size and flatness, the gouge-like tracks of the roughing plane had to be removed and the surface made "tried and true". It was "tried" by checking for flatness in length and width, usually simply by comparing the surface with an edge of the plane sole. Warping was found by placing straight pieces of wood, one at either end of, and at right angles to, the board. Sighting the top edges of these "winking sticks" (boning strips, winding sticks) revealed any warp, which had to be corrected by planing wood from the high corners. The plane used for corrections during "trying" is still called a trying plane in England. It had to remove significant amounts of wood and had a mouth opening to allow this. Its cutter was slightly rounded as a compromise between the opposing objectives of cutting deeply and leaving only shallow depressions in the surface.

Having attained a "true" surface, final smoothing was accomplished by use of a smoothing plane with a narrow mouth and straight edged cutter to remove the tracks of the previous plane.

Where two trued boards are to be joined by gluing edge to edge, to make wider stock, the two edges must meet exactly over their full length if the joint is to be sound. Here the finishing plane must be long, usually over 20" (51 cm.). A short plane can dip into hollows and deepen them, while a long one rides over them and only cuts off the high spots. The boards would be clamped face to face in a vise, edge up, and a long "jointer" plane used to create a true edge. Cutting both at the same time not only gave a wider support for the plane sole, but ameliorated any deviation from a right angle caused by failure to keep the plane exactly horizontal (the error in one edge being exactly compensated by the opposite error in the other). When a paper-thin, continuous shaving could be taken the full length of the piece, it was ready for trying with its mate to make sure that no light could be seen between them.

With the ready availability of tried and true boards, the need for roughing planes decreased sharply. As we will see when we take up the individual plane types, the planes formerly used for this service markedly changed in design although they often retained their old names. Modern metal planes, from smooth through jack, fore, and jointer, are nearly identical as purchased except for their length, and the old names are now used only to specify their length. This change of meaning, which evolved during the 19th century, has caused some confusion in naming. An 18th century jack plane is rather a different tool than one called a jack plane in 1900 (as described in Chapter 3).

BENCH PLANE STRUCTURE

A typical bench plane of the nineteenth century started as a center plank of beech, steamed and seasoned for three years or more. The stock was oriented with growth rings horizontal, the bottom or sole toward the bark. It was pierced by a vertical passage, the throat. (Features named here are labelled in Fig.2:1.) The opening at the sole — the mouth — was narrow, as the pressure of the sole in front of the mouth on the work being planed helped to resist tear-out and rough cutting (see Appendix 1).

The rear wall of the throat slanted backward at an angle of 45-50° to provide a bed for the cutting iron. The bed was notched to provide clearance for the head of the screw joining the iron and cap iron, or chip breaker.

The front wall of the throat just above the mouth (called the wear) was also slanted backward, less steeply. As the sole of the plane wore or was dressed to restore planarity, the mouth widened unless the front wall was

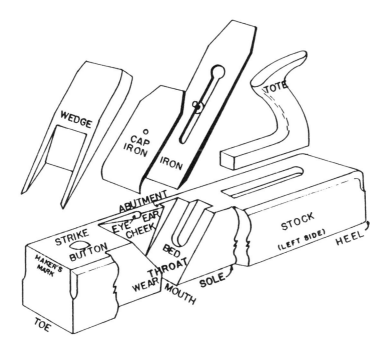

Fig.2:1—Bench plane nomenclature

sloped at the same angle as the bed. The slope chosen for the wear was a compromise between maintaining mouth size and providing clearance for the shavings. Above the wear the front wall broke to a forward slant, to provide increased room for the shavings to escape.

The side walls of the throat (the cheeks) thickened toward the bed and were there cut away to form the wedge grip (ears, abutments). The top inner front edge of each cheek was provided with a chamfer (called eye or turnout) to ease the task of the fingers seeking to clear the throat of a choke, when the shavings jammed.

The wedge angle was about 10°. The angle between the bed and the abutments of the wedge grip was less because the combined cap iron and iron were thicker at bottom than top. These angles were carefully matched, with the bulk of the pressure taken at the lower end of the cap iron if chatter was to be minimized. That portion of the lower end of the wedge that did not bear on the abutments was removed and a taper provided to prevent shavings hangup.

Wedges were not interchangeable. It is not uncommon to find a plane with a wedge that appears to be of the right size and shape, but which does not hold the blade firmly when in use. This may have resulted from an exchange of wedges or irons with another plane. An accurate fit required scraping the wedge and trying with the specific iron to be used.

Although the plane appears as a massive piece of wood, the front and rear portions are joined only by the thin cheeks outside the abutments. These take the full stress of the wedging. In final trueing of the sole by planing, it is important that the iron be wedged in place (although well retracted). Failing this, the sole behind the mouth (called the back wood) is pushed down by the force of wedging and plane performance suffers.

The weakest part of a bench plane is the short grain in front of the abutments, which take the full force of the wedging. It is not necessary to use a forceful blow of the mallet to seat the wedge. A major cause of splitting the plane at this point, however, is seating the wedge tight in winter and leaving it through a humid summer. The cross-grain of the wedge expands as it takes up moisture, while the long-grain of the wedge slot does not.

As the removal of the iron from the longer planes is normally accomplished by a mallet blow on the top of the stock above the toe, better quality planes are fitted with an end-grain hardwood or metal strike button at this point. In the case of the shorter, unhandled smooth plane, it is placed in the heel. Behind the throat the top of the stock is mortised to receive the handle (tote or toat) which is shown as an open jack handle in Fig.2:1. A longer plane usually has a closed tote.

The terms LEFT and RIGHT are ambiguous, in that they refer to different sides depending on which end of the plane you face. Common usage refers to left and right sides of the plane as they appear to the worker using it: that is, to one facing the heel of the plane. Similarly, the right side of the iron is that on the right side of the plane, even though it is on your left when you are looking at the maker's mark.

MAKING BENCH PLANES

While the wooden bench plane appears to be a simple tool, the making of it demands skill. A few critical points can make the difference between good or poor performance of the finished product. The mouth opening (the distance from the front of the mouth to the cutting edge of the iron) should be no larger than the thickest shaving to be passed. This minimizes splintering or tear-out of the surface being planed. The bed should be flat, supporting the iron over its entire back surface, if chattering is to be avoided. The sole must be flat if it is to cut a flat surface, and to assure pressure on the work immediately in front of the mouth.

The procedure for making a jack plane by hand was described by Armour (1898), and more detailed instructions are available (e.g., Perch, 1981) should you be tempted to try. The wood chosen should be from a plank cut through the center of the tree, and the body taken from this as close to the bark as possible without including sapwood. It is cut to length and planed square, and the side nearest the bark chosen as the sole. (It was generally believed that this was the harder part of the wood — in fact there is little difference, but the choice is correct for reasons of lower growth ring curvature and fewer defects.) If the grain is less then perfectly straight, the orientation is chosen which minimizes chipping: that is, with grain running down from toe to heel.

Construction lines are laid out. The mouth outline is scribed on the sole, the slopes of the bed, abutment, and throat front on both sides, the throat outline on top. (Scribed lines remain on the sides of many older tools.) The bulk of the wood within the throat is removed with gouge and mallet. A small hole is drilled from the center of the mouth opening through the stock at the bed angle, taking care not to cut below the bed line. A planemaker's saw (thick blade, little height) inserted in this hole cuts the mouth outline. A chisel removes wood to the wear (the slope at the front of the throat). With this opening, the abutments may now be sawn, and a narrow chisel used to clear the wood between sawcuts. The critical step is now the paring of the bed, finishing it perfectly flat without ridges from overcutting. The wedge slots are pared with a chisel and finished with a float (a tool like a file but with sharp cutting ridges across its width). The cheeks, wear, and throat front are pared with skew chisels. A trench is chiseled in the bed to provide clearance for the cap screw, if a double iron is to be used.

The wedge is made and its taper carefully fitted to the abutment and the iron to be used. The fit should be exact, but tighter at the bottom near the cutting edge to minimize chatter. The tote is shaped, inlet into the top of the stock and glued in. The strike button is installed, and the plane finished by cutting eyes and chamfers or round edges. Finally the iron is wedged tightly but above the level of the sole, and the sole planed exactly flat and square to the sides.

This hand procedure, with perhaps a few individual preferences as to order of operation and finishing style, probably describes that used for centuries - until the middle of the nineteenth century in America. Patents on planemaking machinery then began to appear in England and America. An example is Henry Dewey's device for cutting plane throats (31 Mar. 1857, U.S.16,954).

Mass production by the Sandusky Tool Company toward the end of the century (Wildung 1955) started by steaming beech (to drive out sap and loosen bark) and air drying for four years. Machine sawn into blocks of appropriate cross-section and 52 inches (132 cm.) long, it was returned to seasoning sheds until called for. Lots of four to eight hundred stocks were cut to length on a twin saw, machine planed on two sides at once, then again on the other two sides to a perfect square section. A machine called a "beater" roughed out the throat, another cut the cheeks and mouth. A mortiser cut the trenches for tote and cap screw clearance. A room closed to prying eyes contained a proprietary machine which pared the bed and throat front, another machine cut the eyes. The irons and wedges were fitted by hand, and another worker applied the finishing decorations — at a rate of two hundred planes per worker per day. The planes were inspected (piece work rates meant that the worker suffered if his work was not up to par), and finished by linseed oiling (or later by varnishing).

Hand cutting of a plane throat is a task to challenge the ability of a woodworker to use a chisel. A much easier method is to make the plane in two halves, left and right, which allows sawing the bed. An occasional user-made plane is seen with this construction. Krenov (1977) gives his procedure for making the tool in three parts — which is completely satisfactory now that we have modern adhesives.

WOODS

Although yellow birch was favored by the earliest New England plane-makers, American beech has been the mainstay of the planemaking industry in the United States. Other woods used on a commercial scale for premium planes were applewood, boxwood, rosewood and (rarely) ebony. Ship planes are found made from other tropical woods such as lignum vitae or cocobolo which were available in seaports. Craftsman-made planes are found in maple or live oak (which make excellent planes), cherry (less durable) or virtually any other wood at hand — even softwoods in a pinch. In Great Britain, English red beech predominates, along with the same premium woods. White beech is offered as an alternate. Recent planes from The Netherlands are of white beech, as were many of the 18th and 19th century examples (although walnut handles were common).

In Germany, hornbeam is preferred. For hard service and in premium planes, a sole of lignum vitae is applied. Switzerland and Austria use, in addition, pear, maple, apple, and cherry; whitebeam is seen in Alpine planes. In France, the quality scale ascends from beech to hornbeam, pear or apple, and cormier. This last, almost unique to France, is called service tree in English, but is practically unknown in the United States. Botanically Sorbus domestica, it is related to whitebeam and mountain laurel, and is superior to both, approaching boxwood in performance. On some planes it rates the proud imprint "cormier" or "Véritable cormier".

The Scandinavian countries favor birch, those along the Mediterranean, evergreen oaks. These, related to the holm oak of Europe and the live oak of the southern United States, are cross-grained woods difficult to work but very durable.

Modern Chinese and Japanese planes are usually of their local oak, occasionally with sole inserts of ebony or other hard wood. Older Chinese planes are often of rosewood or other dense tropical wood.

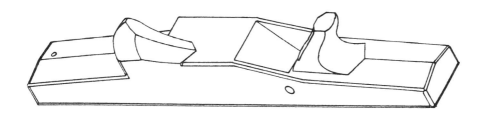

Fig.2:2—English plane of 1545 (wedge and iron are missing)

HANDLES OR GRIPS

In the days when large blocks of seasoned wood were easier to come by than good glue, it was usual to hew the entire plane, grips and all, from one piece of wood. Several of the planes recovered with the Mary Rose, an English warship which sank in 1545, were made in this fashion (Fig.2:2). Some large planes of 16th through 18th century middle Europe were made without handles, or with simple grooves along their sides — to be used by simply grasping the stock. There are hints that this was not completely satisfactory, as some have leather straps or wooden laths nailed to their upper surfaces; obviously after-thoughts. The very long jointers used by coopers and others are mounted upside-down on legs and need no handles.

ROMAN handles (Fig.2:3A) are those found in the oldest surviving planes, of Roman origin. The stock is penetrated horizontally by slots, fore and aft in long planes, or just one behind the blade for shorter ones (rarely, just one as a front grip). This style persisted as a rear grip in southern Europe into the eighteenth century. The top of the stock around the handhole was cut away to provide a more comfortable grip, and it was frequently decoratively carved. Long planes supplemented this rear grip with the provision of an additional improved grip for the left hand, either by carving the top of the stock or by providing pegs. Roman front grips were still used occasionally in Austria and Italy in the nineteenth century, but they were unknown in Germany and France.

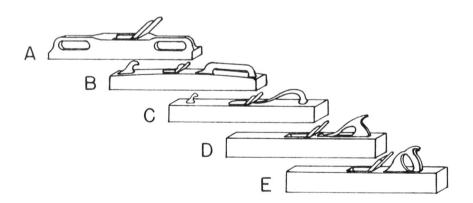

Fig.2:3—Evolution of the bench plane handle

FLATIRON grips (Fig.2:3B) are similar in shape to the Roman, but are elevated above the top of the stock. Usually integrally carved, they may also be applied. A fine example survives in a varlope (jointer) of the French joiner

Pierre Montpeyroux (1828-1910). Here the front grip is provided by a low protuberance from the top of the stock, carved to provide a comfortable abutment for the left hand gripping the stock.

SHEPHERD'S CROOK (Fig.2:3C) is a further modification in which the flatiron is raised slightly, the rear riser thicker than the front, which joins the stock after a reverse curve. It is shown in plates from Félibien (1676). Here again an abutment is provided for the left hand. Conversion of the Shepherd's crook to an early English grip as shown on the trade card of John Jennion (1732-57) requires relatively minor change. The addition of a shark's-fin shaped projection at the top is the major difference (Fig.2:3D).

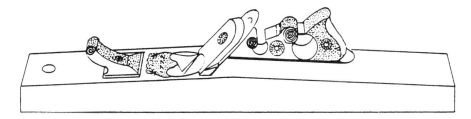

Fig.2:4—Dutch plane - 18th century

DUTCH grips (Fig.2:4) are seen in larger numbers than the rare types listed above, although still not common. These have the general outline of the Jennion type handle, but the central opening is smaller and the forward portion is carved into one or more scroll shapes. This rear grip is invariably accompanied by a front grip consisting of a square-based post leaning sharply forward, usually tipped by a volute. They were apparently standardized by a group of Dutch planemakers near the beginning of the 18th century, although earlier prototypes are known. These were accepted as a significant improvement, as they were popular for over a century. They are quite uncomfortable to hands used to the later saw-handle types, the opening in the rear grip being large enough for only one or two fingers.

There has been much discussion as to how this grip was used. The placement of the rear grip at the extreme right side of the stock suggests that the fingers of the right hand gripped the side of the stock, with the thumb behind the grip. An etching dated 1608 appears to support this theory (Sayward 1985). Further credence is lent to this interpretation by the existence of Norwegian long planes with rear bosses obviously designed to be used in this fashion. However, this leaves unexplained the function of other features. Was the larger hole intended as an alternate thumb placement for this method of holding? Why the triangular top extension?

The suggestion has been made that the grips adapt themselves well to using the plane backward, pulling it toward the user — as is sometimes convenient when awkward grain is encountered.

The shape of the back of the grip and its placement on the side (the left side if pulled) forms a comfortable grip for the left hand, while the front grip now serves for the right hand. Perhaps some as yet undiscovered description will end speculation and provide us with the facts.

CLOSED TOTE or FORE-PLANE grips (Fig.2:3E) are the latest development of this evolution. W.L. Goodman (1964) shows profiles of totes intermediate between the Jennion grip and the modern version, and points out that its development coincides in time with that of the modern saw-handle (this tote is sometimes called the saw-handle grip). The palm on the right side and three fingers through the opening, the thumb on the left and the forefinger

JACK HANDLES

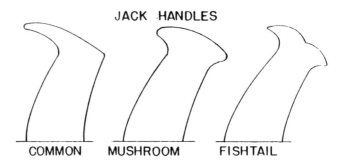

COMMON   MUSHROOM   FISHTAIL

Fig.2:5—Jack plane handle types

projecting forward provide a secure, comfortable grip. This removed the necessity for the front handle, which almost disappeared from the English plane.

JACK handles appeared later, perhaps because of lack of room on the shorter jack planes for the closed tote. They are essentially the closed tote with the front riser removed. Even the jack type can cause interference. Worker-made jacks are found in which the top of the cutter was bent forward to avoid hitting the grip. Although I have found no documentation of use of the terms by tradesmen, variants of the form are known as mushroom and fishtail by tool dealers and collectors, Fig.2:5.

Bench plane totes were usually offset to the right of center until about 1800 (although the Jennion trade card shows them centered), whether as a holdover from the Dutch style or for valid reasons is not clear.

PEG grips are usually front grips, less often found both front and rear, and were the first grips used on the long planes. They are vertically inserted in the top of the stock, and range from rudely cut posts through turned shapes

(Fig.2:7A) to elaborately carved features (Fig.2:7B). The famous Novaya Zemlya smoother of 1596 (Fig.2:6) is fitted with a peg whose shape clearly foreshadows the modern horn grip. Peg grips were not used by English or American makers.

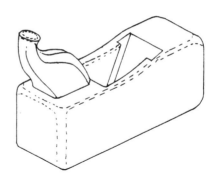

HORN grips are the predominant form on short Continental planes, though uncommon in the English-speaking world. A vertical carved post mortised into the top front of the stock of a smoother is depicted in the Durer 'Melancholia' of 1514 (Fig.2:7B), while another example was

Fig.2:6—Dutch smooth plane of 1596

recovered with the Vasa, a Swedish ship sunk in 1628. This mounting method apparently lacked strength, as it was replaced by the method in use today (Fig.2:7C). A step is made in the front of the stock so that the sole projects forward under the base of the horn, which is fitted into the stock by a vertical sliding dovetail. (The step predates this mounting method, and is seen in early smoothers with peg grips.) A horn was commonly used on French long planes until the 18th century.

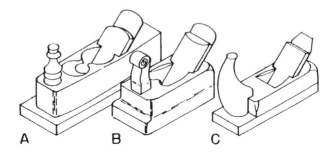

Fig.2:7—Peg and horn front grips

Swedish planes in the Wildung collection at Shelburne Museum (Vermont) have horns carved in a manner seen by Mr. Wildung as symbolic of Viking ship figureheads. Tool dealers sometimes use the term "ship's prow" to describe this type. A number of French and German short planes of the eighteenth century used horns of this type, sometimes elaborately carved (Fig.2:7B). The shape of the horn evolved into the modern form which resembles the butt section of a cow's horn: round, tapering, helically twisted to conform to the left hand (Fig.2:7C). It is commonly the sole grip on short Continental planes, the right hand gripping the rear of the stock (it is also occasionally seen on longer planes with rear totes). A recent modification is elevation of the rear of the stock to form a collar under the cutter, providing a more comfortable grasp for the right hand.

A small graceful plane shape originated in the Rhineland (Fig.2:8). It was most often made in The Netherlands but has been copied by the Scandinavian countries; a few were made in England. The body slopes downward toward the front, then sweeps upward to form an integral front grip. It has been called a whale plane or a scroll plane in English.

TRANSVERSE grips are staves mounted horizontally across or through the stock of the plane: there is no generally accepted name for these, but the descriptive one will serve. Examples may be seen in the front grip of Fig.2:9 or the Chinese plane of Fig.2:10. They may be permanently mounted, or the plane may be equipped with pull-holes — horizontal holes through the stock through which any handy dowel, or a rope, is inserted.

GALLEY or SIDE grips are not seen in English or American planes, but were fairly common in nineteenth century and earlier French and German carpenter's planes. The top of the stock is extended sideways and pierced vertically to form finger slots running front to back, as in Fig.2:9. Less frequently, the side handles are not pierced, but simply

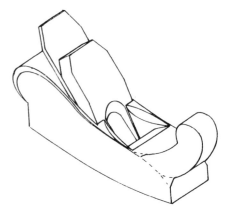

Fig.2:8—Integral front grip

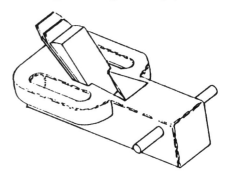

Fig.2:9—Plane with side
and transverse grips

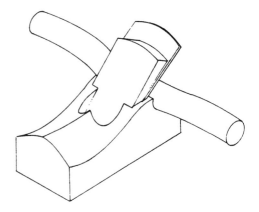

Fig.2:10—Chinese plane

grooved for finger holds. (Transverse handles are also sometimes called galley grips.)

CONTINENTAL CHARACTERISTICS

While early Continental planes varied widely in style, by the 19th century certain idioms had developed which may be useful indicators of the country of origin (indicators, not guarantees). The front horn strongly suggests Continental origin, although some were made in England and the U.S. A pronounced rounding of the heel is found on many short planes, but on both heel and toe of a long plane suggest Austrian or German origin. These may also have a longitudinal groove along the sides at the level of the stop in the chamfer.

English, American and Dutch wedges usually have front and back parallel at their top ends, and break to the wedge angle from the front. French and German wedges, however, commonly maintain the wedge angle for their full length. Bench plane wedges are not normally notched to form a finial. When they are, the shapes often conform with the styles usual in their molding planes, shown in Fig.2:11. A triangular notch is taken out of the front to mark a finial. French wedges may have a slight front-to-back rounding of the top; the German tend to be flat-topped.

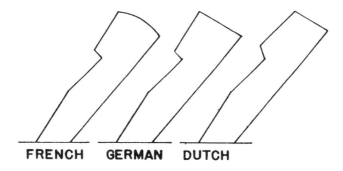

FRENCH   GERMAN   DUTCH

Fig.2:11—Continental wedge profiles

PLANE IRONS

The irons of the earliest planes were narrow, presumably because tool steel was an expensive commodity and needed a great deal of care in forging to preserve its virtue. Wrought iron (the only form available before development of the blast furnace in the fourteenth century) was carburized by long contact with carbonaceous material at high temperatures (but below the melting point). This produced "blister" steel, in which the carbon content and therefore the hardness varied sharply from point to point in the mass. Uniform material was obtained only by repeated forging, folding, and welding. The ultimate in this process is the renowned Damascus steel, or the blades of Japanese Samurai swords. Great care and expertise was required in forging, to avoid spoiling its quality. It is no surprise that the earliest plane irons were narrow.

The technique of welding a cutting edge of steel to an iron tool was known in the 12th century. It continued to be used for plane irons long after crucible steel — cast steel — became available in larger quantities in England after Huntsman's work in 1740.

The planes irons recovered from the 1596 trove on Novaya Zemlya were tongue-shaped, narrowing in width toward the top. This form persisted into the 18th century in The Netherlands (some can only be removed through the bottom of the plane). They were thin, about $3/32$ inch (2.4 mm.) at the cutting edge and $1/16$ inch (1.6 mm.) at top. By the late 18th century bench plane irons throughout the West were parallel-sided and tapered in thickness.

The thickness varies from 0.16 - 0.19 in. (4 - 5 mm.) at bottom to 0.06 - 0.1 in. (1.5 - 2.5 mm.) at top. The wedge shape may have originated as a natural result of welding the steel tip to the body and dressing the final product, but it does have the advantage of resisting the thrust of the work better. A patent by William Hovey (10 Mar.1830, restored U.S. 5867X) describes running steel and iron blanks through eccentric rolls to produce this taper. A disadvantage of the tapered iron is the widening of the mouth opening as the blade is ground down in use. English bench plane irons were usually round-topped (as were the wedges) in the mid-18th century, with squared off or octagonal tops appearing later. So-called parallel irons, without taper, (thickness: 0.16 - 0.18 in., 4 - 4.6 mm.) were offered in England in the late 19th century, but are not often seen in wooden planes.

The early English planemakers acquired the irons for their planes from the makers of edge tools. The planemaker's name (and sometimes his location) was stamped on the top front of his plane; in like manner the maker of the iron impressed his name on the top face of the iron. These stamps were often ornate, including a design of some sort as a logo. Perhaps this arose as a way of making their wares identifiable to those of their patrons not proficient at reading. Different designs were later used by some makers to identify discreetly their first, second, and third quality lines.

A number of these stamps for both English planemakers and plane iron makers are reported and illustrated by Goodman (1978) in *British Planemakers from 1700*, along with the then known working dates of the makers. These may sometimes provide a clue as to the age of the plane. However, the iron marks should not be considered conclusive unless there is reason to believe that the iron is the one originally supplied with the plane. Some of the early plane iron makers were William Crosby (mark William Crosbe, -1718-1742), John Hildick (1720-1760), Thomas Allen (1730-70), Edward Dingly (1735-75), Robert Moore (1750-70). The top of an iron marked by Moulson Brothers (1824-1912) is sketched in Fig.2:12.

Fig.2:12—Iron maker's mark

The invention of the CAP IRON (shown in Fig.2:1) as a way of improving the cut was made in the early part of the 18th century, presumably in England. (It is documented there in about 1730, and was advertised for

Fig.2:13—Continental capped rabbet iron

sale in Philadelphia in 1767). It was almost universally available by 1800. Its function is discussed in Appendix 1. Initially it was simply a second iron turned over and laid on top of, and unconnected to, the cutting iron. It compounded the problems of setting the iron and ways were soon found to join them. Cap irons unconnected to rabbet plane irons were sometimes used, particularly by the American planemaker J.R. Tolman, but they were not common. Continental capped rabbet irons are joined by a screw and peg, as in Fig.2:13. An early solution was simply to screw the two together, but this usually didn't survive more than one or two grindings. Then the cap iron was slotted and held to a tapped cutter by a screw. This required a slot in the wedge to clear the screwhead, and weakened it too much. Finally the present scheme of slotted cutter and threaded cap iron was adopted. Older cap irons may have a thickened section or a brazed nut to provide sturdier threads.

Another device used was the LONG SCREW (Fig.2:14). The cap iron was fitted with a pair of lugs projecting through a slot in the cutter, threaded to take a screw parallel to the irons. The head of the screw fitted a notch in the cutter, and prevented length-wise motion. This was popular in France and Austria, rarely seen elsewhere although it appeared in the Sheffield 1889 list and a version was patented in the

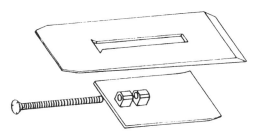

Fig.2:14—The long screw cap iron

U.S. in 1832 by Wm. B. Reynolds, (U.S.7158X). A design fixing the cap iron in the throat, with the wedge between it and the cutter, was short-lived.

A number of other designs have been patented and occasionally an example surfaces. For example, Horace Harris (18 Sept. 1855, U.S. 13,575) encased the cutter in a box-like cap iron with longitudinal screw adjustment. Benjamin Shelabarger (28 Mar. 1844, U.S. 5,486) devised a cap

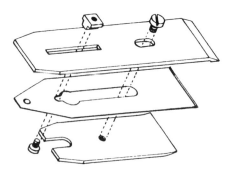

Fig.2:15—William Kellet patent

iron which permitted passage of the shaving between it and the cutter, exiting through an opening in the cap. This really acts as a fixed mouth opening rather than a cap iron. William Kellet (16 Sept. 1884, U.S. 305393) patented a three-piece assembly using a thin steel cutter clamped between cap iron and iron body. One found in a Reed and Auerbacher plane is shown in Fig.2:15.

Far Eastern   While the Chinese plane iron is similar to those of the West (except for the previously mentioned double bevel in older planes), those of Japan are quite different. They are made by forge welding a thin sheet of high carbon steel to a thicker piece of wrought iron in the finer blades, or of mild steel in the common. The blade is short, about 4½ in. (11 cm.) long, and about $\frac{5}{16}$ in. (8 mm.) thick at the top. As previously described, the blade is thicker at top than bottom, and serves as its own wedge in fixing its position in the side slots. The corners of the cutting edge are cut away at 45° to prevent the shaving from fouling in these slots.

For the sharpest edge on any plane blade, it is essential that the front of the blade (opposite the bevel) be perfectly flat. The steel face of the Japanese blade is slightly hollowed at the center, which means that less material has to be removed in honing the front flat. Best performance is reputed to come when sharpening has reduced the flat between edge and hollow to a minimum. Beyond this point, the blade must be peened on the soft side to regain the flat. This requires skill, as the steel is glass-hard. As supplied, the steel edge is much harder than a Western blade and brittle. The toughness improves with use, perhaps because the heat generated by the rapid Japanese stroke provides a small amount of tempering.

A recent innovation replaces this hollow with a shallow hollow horizontal cylindrical curve on the steel face. Flat grinding of this face (commonly done on a steel plate called a kanaban) then produces the desired narrow flat.

Japan adapted the chip breaker or cap iron toward the end of the nineteenth century. These are carefully sharpened and fitted to the main iron, and are not attached to it. Most often they are held in place by their wedge shape bearing on a steel pin across the throat, although planes are sometimes seen with the cap iron serving as a wedge holding both irons in the cheek abutments.

VARIANT BLADE MOUNTINGS

It has been mentioned that early planes use a wooden or metal pin across the throat in place of cheek abutments to secure the wedge. A variant of the top escapement seen (rarely) in French, Swiss and Italian planes completely encloses the bench plane iron and wedge in a slot in the top of the body and provides a separate channel through the stock, opening at the top, for the shavings. This was called the BRIDGE mounting by Greber (Fig.2:16).

Fig.2:16—Bridge mounting of the plane iron

A patent by E.W. Carpenter (27 Mar. 1849, U.S.6,226) describes the use of two wedges, one behind the iron and fixed to the bed, in addition to the usual one. By moving the rear wedge, the mouth opening can be varied. This device has been seen in a number of bench planes. It also shows up in molding planes, and it is suspected that in this case it was used to change the pitch of the iron by moving the rear wedge to the front of the cutter.

William Hopper (16 Jan. 1855, U.S.12,234) describes the placement of the wedge behind the blade in conjunction with a movable metal piece to adjust the mouth opening. H.L. Kendall (8 June 1858, U.S. 20,493) screws a wedge to the front of the throat. By moving it downward and trimming it, the mouth opening is narrowed, helping to offset the widening of the mouth that resulted from wear and the trueing of the sole. A variety of designs for adjusting the opening have been used, usually involving a sliding section inset into the sole fixed by a screw through the stock. Modern horn planes with this feature are called REFORM planes.

Chapter 3

BENCH PLANES - INDIVIDUAL TYPES

ROUGHING PLANES

English and American   The English roughing plane of 1700 and earlier was called the FORE plane, as Moxon (1703) tells us, because it was used before the others. The same plane was called a JACK plane by house carpenters. Unfortunately, Moxon took his illustration of a jack plane from Félibien (1676) (Fig.3:1A) so that it represents French practice of a quarter century earlier rather than the English jack of 1700. That plane probably looked more like the type shown on Jennion's shop sign (Fig.3:1B).

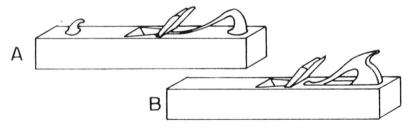

Fig.3:1—Early roughing planes

The jack plane of the late 18th-early 19th century was used in surface preparation prior to the availability of machine planers. It is shown in Fig.3:2A and, in contrast to the late nineteenth century style (Fig.3:2B), it had a single iron (narrower than that of the other bench planes) with a distinctly rounded cutting edge and a wide mouth to pass the thick shavings. These jack planes are sometimes found with the sole slightly rounded, as well, although not as sharply as the cutter. It is not clear whether this was done deliberately, as in some parts of the Continent, or a result of greater wear on the outer edges. The tote was open and usually offset to the right.

The uneven surface left by the roughing jack plane may often be seen on the hidden parts of early furniture (backs and under drawer bottoms). Roughing jack planes (sometimes called HACK planes) are not necessarily

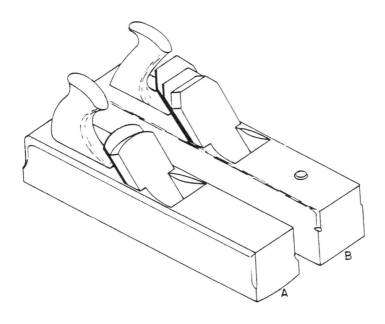

Fig.3:2—Jack planes of the late 18th and the 19th centuries

old. Standard jack planes of much later vintage are often found with their cap irons discarded, their cutting edges sharply rounded, mouth widened, and perhaps with their soles slightly rounded. The need for the roughing plane still existed, although the roughing jack was no longer commercially made.

The SCRUB plane is an English or American name for the German Schropphobel (Fig.3:3A). These were most often imported, but were also

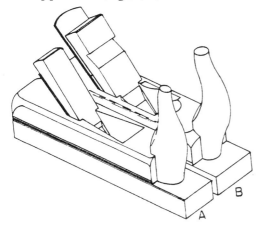

Fig.3:3—German scrub and smooth planes

made in the U.S. by at least two suppliers after the Civil War and sold as BULL or GERMAN planes. The Sandusky Tool Co. made both regular and a special short (6.25 in.; 16 cm.) size. The Hammacher, Schlemmer catalog of 1896 listed them as HORN SHRUP planes, an interesting intermediate anglicization of Schropphobel or Schrupphobel. They were also called BISMARCK planes in England. They were listed as HORNED SCRUB planes after World War I, and during that period were imported from Germany by the Columbia Tool Company.

Continental   The German SCHROPPHOBEL, also called Schrupphobel and many other variations (Fig.3:3A), is a narrow plane about 9.5 in. (24 cm.) in length fitted with a front horn and a thick single iron with a sharply curved cutting edge. The sole is flat, the mouth wide. The upper surface of the front step, characteristic of the horn grip, is usually carried backward as fluting, or at least a scribe mark, to visually separate the sole from the rest of the body. The upper body has rounded chamfers for a comfortable right-hand grip. Joh. Weiss & Sohn (Austria, 1909) listed blade widths of 1.1 - 1.5 in. (27 - 39 mm.), and offered plain, finger-jointed lignum vitae, or steel soles.

With the exception of the above Schropphobel and the Schrobber described below, the early Continental roughing planes evolved in the same fashion as the English jack. They retained their original names and basic forms, but replaced rounded edges on their irons with straight edges and had mouths narrowed. Just as with the English and American jack, planes originally intended for work on machine-planed lumber may be found which have been modified to serve as roughing planes. These planes are treated with the other bench planes in the following sections, but are included here to reflect their original purpose.

The 1915 catalog of D. Stolp (The Netherlands) pictures a plane essentially identical to the Schropphobel under the name BLOKSCHAAF MET HOORN, SCHROBBER. Prior to the 18th century the ROFFEL, often unhandled, and the VOORLOOPER, with Dutch grips, were roughing planes that corresponded to the English jack and fore planes of that era. As with their English counterparts, their sharply curved cutting edges were often accompanied by a slightly rounded sole.

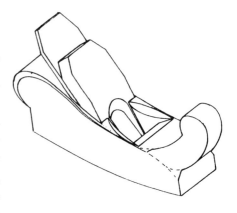

Fig.3:4—The Gerfschaaf
(whale or scroll plane)

The GERFSCHAAF (whale or scroll plane) (Fig.3:4) is frequently found with rounded cutter and other indications of use as a scrub plane, its normal application in later years, although it was originally a smooth plane.

The French VARLOPE derives its name from the voorlooper and has similarly changed its function. It is no longer a roughing plane, but a jointer or try plane. The DEMI-VARLOPE (24 - 26 in., 60 - 65 cm.) is a fore plane that is sometimes converted into a roughing plane. (It is described under Long Planes).

The name RIFLARD originally denoted a hand plane with or without a horn, a little narrower than a smooth plane, with a single iron 1.2 - 1.4 in. (30 - 35 mm.) wide and having a rounded cutting edge. The Féron catalog (France) of about 1940 uses the same name for a tool which would be called a fore plane in a contemporaneous American catalog. The bilingual Lachappelle catalog (France, 1945) equates RIFLARD avec corne (with horn) with the Schropphobel. Another French name given for a roughing plane is RABOT À DEGROSSIR.

La GALÈRE (galley) (see under smoothing planes, Fig. 3:13) is a name that has been applied to several variations of the roughing plane. One of these is a relatively wide plane with two transverse handles. The German equivalent is the KETSCHHOBEL; in Austria, the SCHROPPZWEIMANDL (two man scrub). These differ from their smooth plane equivalents only in the curvature of their cutting edges and their wide mouths.

Japanese   The Japanese HERASHI-KANNA (cutting-down plane) has a stock like the common Japanese smoothing form, hira-kanna (more fully described under smooth planes). It is distinguished from the smooth plane by a wider mouth and a curved cutting edge on the single iron, and by a rather higher body (1½ in.; 40 mm.). As with all roughing planes, it is often used to cut diagonally across the grain. An intermediate form between this and the smooth is the ARA-SHIKO roughing plane, used to remove rough saw marks.

TRYING PLANES

To recapitulate, the original function of the TRYING plane was to follow the roughing plane and bring the workpiece surface to planarity, ready for smoothing. The function may be served by a variety of plane types, depending on the size of the workpiece.

Moxon (1703) defines the jointer as a long—and the smooth as a short—finely set, straight-edge plane, a definition that still stands today. He makes no mention of a plane of a length between the fore or jack (his roughing plane) and the jointer. An English *Builder's Dictionary* of 1736 defines the fore-plane as does Moxon, adding the fact that it is 18 in. (46 cm.) long. It also includes a LONG plane of about 24 in. (61 cm.) in length, which, it states, prepares the way for the smoothing plane on surfaces or, if for the edge of a board, the jointer. By 1800, English tool lists named five bench planes of decreasing lengths: jointer, long or long trying, trying, jack or fore, and smooth. In the 1910 Sheffield list, although the size selection (8 to 30 inches;

20 to 76 cm.) was still available, the names had diminished to three — trying, jack, and smooth. In 19th century United States, the name fore plane had acquired a meaning as intermediate in length between the jack and jointer — the latter being available in several lengths.

As the need for roughing planes and sharply curved cutting edges decreased, bench planes were most often supplied with straight-edged irons, leaving it to the user to shape them to his needs. In practice, the cutter of the jack was usually sharpened with a slight curvature as it was generally the first to be used. If heavier cutting was called for, an old smooth or jack with a worn sole and open mouth was called into service and modified (unless a scrub plane was available). Trying would be done with a plane of length appropriate for the workpiece, either a jack with blade of little curvature or one of the longer planes.

JACK PLANES

English and American   The word jack was a general term frequently used to convey the feeling that something was common, everyday, usual. It is therefore not surprising that the most common plane came to be called the jack. If a household had but one plane, it was a jack: if a tool kit was purchased that had only one plane, it was a jack. The early jack has been described under roughing planes: Fig.3:2 compares an early roughing jack (3:2A) and the later standard version (3:2B). As made in England or America in the nineteenth century it is a plane commonly 14 to 16 in. (36 to 41 cm.) in length. The cross-section is about three in. (7.6 cm.) square, with a flat sole and a jack, or open, handle (although closed totes are found, rarely). The upper edges of the body are rounded, and round chamfers stop half-way down the side edges.

Most manufacturers offered a choice of cutter width, with 2¼ in. (57 mm.) most common. The irons were straight-edged as bought, but were rounded by grinding to suit the purpose and individual taste of the user. If rapid wood removal was to be the principal use, the blade edge was curved to allow about ¹⁄₁₆ in. (1 - 2 mm.) to show when the corners of the edge were flush with the sole. If this was to be the only plane used, the edge was left straight with only the corners rounded. Heavy cuts with a straight blade choke the plane, while light cuts with a rounded edge give only narrow shavings and many more strokes are required. Both single and double irons were offered by almost all suppliers, but double irons are the most commonly found. Until the middle of the 19th century in the United States (and later in England), a choice of German steel or cast steel blades was offered, the latter at a premium.

Front handles are rarely found on English or American wooden jack planes, although some types with a front knob or a horn were offered by the Ohio Tool Co. The front of the stock was held by the left hand with the thumb on the near side and the fingers crossing the top. This was used to apply downward pressure at the start of the stroke, with pressure released as the stroke continued. Downward pressure by the right hand prevented dubbing (rounding the edge of the work) as the stroke was finished.

To remove the blade, the stock is held in the left hand with the thumb on the wedge, to keep the iron from falling out. The front top of the stock is struck with a light mallet (on the strike button or start, if present). In setting the blade, a tap in the same spot or on the upper rear chamfer decreases the exposure of the edge. A tap on the top of the iron increases it, or "shows more iron" as a tradesman would say.

There are a number of variations of the jack, the most common being the RAZEE JACK, in which the rear portion of the top of the stock is cut away to permit a lower placement of the tote (Fig.3:5A). This directs the thrust of the plane more in line with the motion of the blade, and decreases the frictional drag. The name razee derives from a term used to describe a ship which had an upper deck removed, and indeed the style first appeared among ship

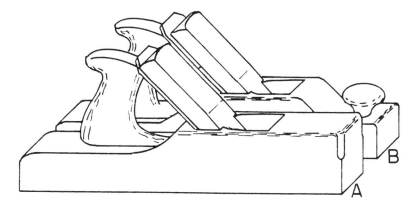

Fig.3:5—Single and double razee jack planes

carpenters. Some suppliers listed these as SHIP or RAZEE JACKS and did not differentiate, while others offered different planes under the two names; the SHIP JACK having a narrower iron, always double. Narrow razee jacks and longer razees are often found made of heavy tropical woods (which were more readily available in seaports). These are referred to as ship planes, and

longer razees are often found made of heavy tropical woods (which were more readily available in seaports). These are referred to as ship planes, and usually have closed totes. A razee jack somewhat shorter than the common jack is called a TECHNICAL JACK in England. A jack cut down both fore and aft was listed by Ohio Tool as an "improved" plane but is popularly called a DOUBLE RAZEE (Fig.3:5B).

Ship planking must fit snugly against the curved frames of the hull. To fit a convex curve, the planks had to be hollowed slightly. A jack with a slightly convex sole, called a BACKING OUT JACK (Blumenberg 1990), was used for this purpose. (A standard jack served for doing the convex rounding.) The backing out jack should have matching sole and blade curvature, differentiating it from a roughing jack.

The GERMAN JACK is an English plane of common jack dimensions without the rear tote and having a front horn or peg grip. The same name is sometimes used in the U.S. for the American copy of the German Schropphobel, or roughing plane. The STRIKE BLOCK (described in Chapter 4) still serves as a jack in Scotland.

A few unusual types, rarely seen, should be mentioned:

The BOXMAKER'S JACK is a razee jack with double iron mounted at extra pitch (about 40° from the horizontal versus the normal 45 - 50°); it was listed by Sandusky.

A patent was issued (Achenbach, 6 Jan. 1885, U.S.310163) on insertion of metal cross-pieces in the sole of the plane, in front of the mouth and well behind it. The inventor claimed superior performance on cross-grained wood. The plate before the mouth would, indeed, reduce wear at this point. Planes with this feature were sold under the Ogontz Tool Co. label (a Sandusky Tool Co. brand name).

A wooden jack, sawn in two horizontally and hinged, was described in Spons *Mechanics Own Book* of 1886. The blade was held in the upper part, and edge exposure was changed by screw adjust-

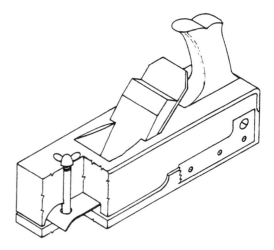

Fig.3:6—"Split" jack

ment of the position of the lower part, as shown in Fig.3:6. A similar method was used briefly by Bailey (U.S.) in early metal planes.

Ccntinental Continental planes are not often found in the jack size range. The ROFFEL in the Stolp catalog (The Netherlands, 1915) closely resembles the American jack, although the shape of the tote is somewhat different. The French galère or the German Ketschhobel, described under smooth planes, may be found in this length. Lachappelle (France, 1945) lists as a RABOT GALÈRE or KETSCHHOBEL, a carpenter's plane just under 14 in. (35 cm.) long with a 2.2 - 2.4 in. (57 - 60 mm.) wide double iron. It has a rear closed tote on a razee body and appears to borrow from the English styling. It was listed along with the more usual transverse or galley handled forms of the same name in the smooth plane size range 11.8 in. (30 cm.). The functions of our American jack are normally performed on the Continent by shorter planes or by their roughing planes.

Japanese The Japanese NAGA-DAI-KANNA is of a length that would be considered jack size in the West, with the body of hira-kanna shape (Fig.3:7) . It is used, however, primarily as a jointer. The sole is slightly hollowed across its width, as described under Japanese smooth planes, in order to maintain contact with the work at its mouth, toe and heel. The planing beam (Fig.3:8) mentioned earlier in Chapter 1 is a timber with a flat upper surface mounted at a slope, with the worker

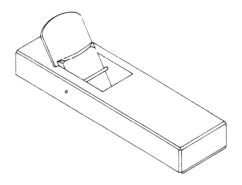

Fig.3:7—Japanese hand plane

standing at the lower end and pulling the plane toward him. This may be equipped with a ledge on one side to scrve the same function as the shoot board (covered in Chapter 4). The naga-dai-kanna may be used with its side resting on this ledge to shoot edges. A special plane made for this purpose has its throat located off center in the stock, to provide greater distance between the iron and the side resting on the ledge. This avoids having an unused section of blade edge, and also provides for frequent dressing of the plane side to maintain an exact right angle to the sole.

The jack function (dimensioning the work after roughing) is affected by the CHŪ-SHIKO, similar to the Japanese smooth planes but with a slightly rounded cutting edge.

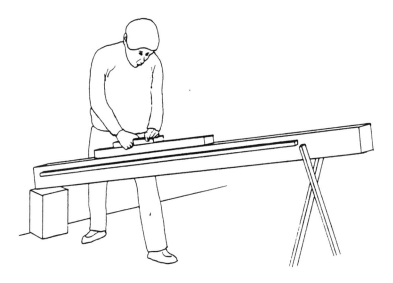

Fig.3:8—Japanese planing beam

LONG PLANES

English and American   Bench planes longer than the jack serve two purposes: trying, or making sure the surface planed is flat; and jointing, preparing edges for joining with glue. In general, the shapes of the bodies of the planes used for these two purposes are identical except for dimensions. Trying planes would have the edges of their irons slightly rounded, while jointer irons should be dead straight. However, it would be a mistake to read the original purpose of a plane from the iron presently installed. Irons are too readily exchanged. The two types of long planes will be treated together here with the understanding that the longer planes, and those with wider irons, were probably intended for jointing.

Comparison of planes across cultures on the basis of length is not useful, as the size ranges for different purposes in different countries are not uniform (as we have already seen with the jack size range).

In the United States during the 19th century, there was general agreement that planes in the length range 18 - 22 in. (46 - 56 cm.) were called FORE planes and those 22 - 30 in. (56 - 76 cm.) JOINTERS. Except for the fact that the fore plane and jointer usually had closed handles and the jack an open handle, the description given earlier for the American jack applies equally well to longer planes, including the variations that were offered.

The English names for these planes and their lengths, as given by Holtzapffel (1846), were TRYING (22 - 24 in.; 56 - 61 cm.), LONG (24 - 26 in.; 61 - 66 cm.) and JOINTER (28 - 30 in.; 71 - 76 cm.). Later, the name trying became generic and referred to the whole range.

Continental   In Germany the general name LANGHOBEL or long plane includes the RAUHBANK for the range 22 - 28 in. (57 - 70 cm.) and HALBLANGHOBEL (half-long) or HALBBANK for the shorter examples. Prior to the 18th century the Rauhbank had either no handle or simple pegs (Fig.3:9A), while an applied rear closed tote was usual thereafter (Fig.3:9B). As its name (rough bench) implies, it was originally used for roughing, but later the name continued in use for finishing planes used by joiners. The house carpenters used a longer plane, the FÜGBANK, which was 28 - 39 in. (70 - 100 cm.) long and had a single or double iron 2 - 2.5 in. (51 - 63 mm.) wide,

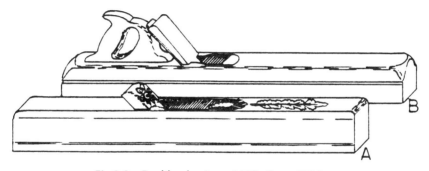

Fig.3:9—Rauhbank. A: ca.1600; B: ca.1900

with the same appearance as the Rauhbank. The two larger planes (Rauhbank and Fügbank) were still listed by Weiss (Austria) in its 1909 catalog. The German word "bank" means bench, reflecting the earlier custom of using the longer planes inverted and set on legs, as with the cooper's jointer (see Chapter 13—Cooper).

The French used the DEMI-VARLOPE which is about 24 in. (60 cm.) long with a 2 in. (50 mm.) wide iron; and the VARLOPE, 26 - 35 in. (65 - 90 cm.) long with a wider iron 2.5 - 3.5 in. (65 - 90 mm.). Lachappelle (Alsace, 1945) lists a 26 - 28 in. (65 - 70 cm.) long closed-tote plane as a Raubank or varlope. RIFLARD was the French equivalent of fore plane; the name was used over time even though the plane it referred to changed. As shown in the Féron catalog (France, ca.1940) it could easily pass for an American fore plane. Féron also lists a razee jointer under the name GALÈRE À POIGNÉE ENTAILÉE.

The long planes from The Netherlands of the late 18th and early 19th centuries are easily recognized by their grips (Fig.3:10) and the stylized carvings and dating. The VOORLOOPER is roughly in the fore plane range, the REISCHAAF, or RIJSCHAAF, longer. A work of 1700 (Witscn) depicts the planes of that era, unfortunately with rather poor definition. A "ry-schaef" is shown with a rear grip intermediate between a shepherd's crook and a Jennion tote (Fig.3:1 A,B), and a "voor-looper" with what appears to be a rear thumb

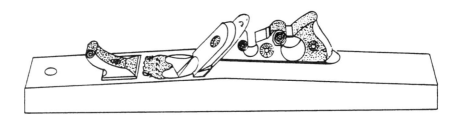

Fig.3:10—18th century Dutch reischaaf, or rijschaaf

abutment. Both have the forward-sloping peg front grip of later Dutch planes. Both Nooitgedagt (ca.1890) and Stolp (1915) of the Netherlands show the later version of both planes, looking much like the American fore plane and jointer with the exception of having handles of an earlier style.

French long planes have survived with carved and decorated rear shepherd's crook grips. Planes from the Tyrol may be seen in museums with Roman rear grips. It is difficult to date accurately or even to assign a locality to planes of this type in our present state of knowledge. They are apt to be described simply as Continental in auction listings and given names corresponding to the American or British size ranges.

SMOOTH PLANES

English and American   The most common smooth plane in England and the U.S. is the so-called "coffin" shape smoother (Fig.3:11A). The "square" type (Fig.3:11B) was no longer preferred after about 1800. Smooth planes range between 6.5 and 9 in. (17 - 23 cm.) in length, or about 1.5 in. (4 cm.) longer for the handled versions (Fig.3:11C). Their slightly rounded sides give

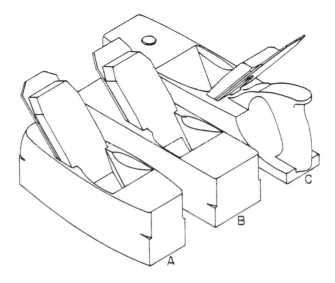

Fig.3:11—Smooth planes: "coffin", square, and toted

maximum strength at the cheek abutments while permitting easier handling. The oval shape was exaggerated by some makers into a near teardrop form. The upper edges, especially at the rear, were rounded to give a more comfortable grip. The iron is commonly about 2 in. (5 cm.) wide, most often double (although single-iron versions were offered by most suppliers), and originally came with a straight cutting edge. Many joiners kept several smooth planes, each with a different blade contour. Very slightly rounded edges were useful where heavier cuts might be needed; edges with just the corners rounded for ordinary smoothing, and a special plane with a narrow mouth and a dead straight, well-honed edge for the finest shavings of a final polish.

Variations on the coffin shape include a SHIP SMOOTH which was listed by several makers and differed only in having a somewhat narrower body and iron (always double). These would be difficult to recognize today without a maker's number, as their widths overlapped the common smooth plane range. Smooth planes in tropical woods, if narrow, are apt to be described as ship planes. A BOXMAKER'S SMOOTH, or FLOGGER, is an oval smooth with a pitch about 35° from horizontal. In England, an oval smooth squared at the front and fitted with a horn is called a TECHNICAL SMOOTH —the shape is quite different from the narrower Fausthobel (described below under Continental), which was also available. American manufacturers offered a variety of smooth planes with rear handles, with closed totes either integral with the stock or applied. Jack handles are rarely found. In some cases front knobs were provided. The closed totes were sometimes offered as either round or right-handed, the latter asymmetrically rounded to suit the right hand. In all cases the handled smooths were razeed at the back. The Ohio Tool Company catalog 23, ca.1910, even listed a double razee with a front knob. The handled planes, although perhaps cumbersome for small jobs, were significantly less tiring in prolonged use.

Continental   The German name FAUSTHOBEL (fist plane, like our term "hand plane") (Fig. 3:3) refers to a body type that was used for several purposes. It is about 9.5 in. (24 cm.) long and fitted with a front horn. If made with a wide mouth and having a rounded edge on its iron, it is the Schropphobel (Fig.3:3A) which was mentioned earlier with roughing planes. The SCHLICHTHOBEL is a slightly wider plane of the same shape, which has a single iron of straight edge with rounded corners. It was used to remove the grooves left by the roughing plane, serving the function of the American fore or trying planes. A still smoother finish calls for the DOPPELHOBEL (Fig.3:3B), using the same body as the Schlichthobel but fitted with a double iron and tighter mouth. A somewhat shorter version (7.5 - 8 in.; 19 - 20 cm.) is called the PUTZHOBEL (polishing plane) and it would be used in the final stage of finishing. Joh. Weiss (Austria, 1909) listed all four planes with plain, lignum vitae, or steel soles. It listed a skew version of the Doppelhobel and one with an adjustable mouth; and a version of the Putzhobel, with the cutting iron set at a high angle, for hardwood. The double irons were fitted with the long screw (Fig.3:12). Modern versions of these planes are still being made. An adjustable mouth horn plane is currently imported from Germany and sold in the U.S. under the trade name RE-FORM. As is evident from the above, Germans tended to use

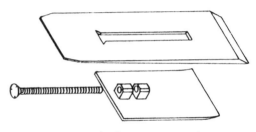

Fig.3:12—The long screw cap iron

50

the shorter body plane, which we would call a smooth plane, for all purposes from roughing through finishing.

The Fausthobel was made in the U.S. by Greenfield and Chapin-Stephens in the late 19th century and sold as the GERMAN SMOOTH. After World War I it was made by Sandusky in two lengths and sold as the HORNED SMOOTH and HORNED JACK. Shortly thereafter Sandusky discontinued production in the face of competition from similar planes imported from Germany and distributed under the name of Columbia Tool Company.

In The Netherlands, the same sequence of operations would be followed. After the roughing planes (BLOKSCHAAF MET HORN, ROFFEL, or VOOR-LOOPER), one would use an ENKELE BLOKSCHAAF (single iron) followed by a DUBBELE BLOKSCHAAF (double iron). The 1915 Stolp catalog shows the blokschaaf as quite similar to the English rectangular smooth plane. So does the ca.1890 Nooitgedagt catalog, but it also lists horned versions. The blokschaaf of the mid-18th century is wider and lower, with carved and dated adornment at the top. It looks the same as the bossing-schaaf (Fig.4:16) except that it does not have a rabbeted sole. However, the famous earlier example retrieved from the Novaya Zemlya expedition of 1596 (Fig.1:8) is of a shape surprisingly close to current European planes.

An old form of smooth plane is the GERFSCHAAF (Fig.3:4), called in English a whale or scroll plane. Mr. Henk van Dijk provides the information that the name derives from an obsolete verb "gherven" meaning to finish or put in order.

Carved and dated bench planes from The Netherlands have survived in significant numbers, undoubtedly because of their attractive appearance. 18th century English and American bench planes, which were generally un-adorned, are rare, most having been discarded when worn out.

The French word RABOT is translated simply as "plane"; unspecified, it means a smooth plane, but to be specific it may be called RABOT À RAPLANIR. Dated planes of the mid-18th century are usually fitted with a front horn of the ship's prow type. More recent ones resembling the Fausthobel (Fig. 3:3) may be called RABOT À CORNE, or horn plane.

Féron (ca.1940) shows rabots closely resembling rectangular English smoothers, and also offers a steel soled version. The catalog lists, under coachmaker's tools, two shorter smooth planes (6.7 in.; 17 cm.) made of cormier (servicewood), the RABOT PLAT À CARRÉ (rectangular) and the RABOT PLAT À NAVETTE (oval). Lachappelle lists the single iron German-style Schlichthobel as RABOT SIMPLE avec corne, the Doppelhobel as RABOT DOUBLE, and the Putzhobel as RABOT À PLANIR.

On the Continent, house carpenters frequently used different tools than did joiners for similar work. In Germany, their plane in the smooth size range was known as the KETSCHHOBEL (from a dialect word meaning lug or haul laboriously). It has two transverse handles for use by two men. In Austria it was called ZWIEMANDL or two-man: Weiss (Austria, 1909) lists a SCHLICHTZWIEMANDL 11.5 in (29 cm.) long with a 1.9 in. (48 mm.) wide iron; and a DOPPELZWIEMANDL, the same plane with a double iron. The French version of this plane is

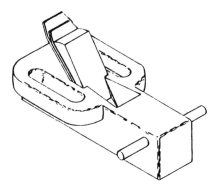

Fig.3:13—Galère with side and transverse grips

called la GALÈRE, or galley — presumably referring to the effort of using it. These were probably used in planing floors by two men facing each other — a return stroke is difficult working alone on your knees. More commonly, the GALÈRE had galley, or side, handles (described with other handle types in Chapter 2). It may have, in addition, a fixed front transverse handle (Fig.3:13) or simply a hole for one. Dated Dutch planes of this type are occasionally seen, and similar planes were known in 15th century Italy. (The name "galère" is also used by Féron to mean a long jointer.)

A smooth plane salvaged from the Swedish ship Vasa (sunk in 1628) is quite similar to French smoothers of the mid-18th century. Swedish planes of the early to middle 18th century, which may be seen at the Shelburne Museum (Shelburne, VT), had changed but little. One of these has a heart-shaped throat reminiscent of the planes from The Netherlands of that era. A more recent example (ca. 1840) has a spool-shaped peg handle.

Far Eastern   The Japanese common plane HIRA-KANNA (Fig.3:7) is quite different from Western styles. The stock is rectangular in length and cross-section, usually more than twice as wide as high. Made of Japanese oak, it may have ebony inlays in the sole. The blade is thick, squat, thicker at top than bottom. It fits tightly into slots cut in the cheeks of the stock. In single iron planes the blade thus serves as its own wedge. Double iron tools have a sharpened cap iron unconnected to the cutter. It is usually bedded against a metal pin which crosses the throat (although cheek abutment fixing is occasionally seen). Bed angles are usually about $38°$ for softwood, between this and $45°$ for hardwood (some modern tools are offered at $47\frac{1}{2}°$). The cutters are available in widths from 1.2 - 2.8 in. (30 - 70 mm.), with 2.4 - 2.6

in. (60 - 65 mm.) the most common. Plane length tends to vary with blade width, although wide short planes are also seen. Block planes may be as short as 5 in. (13 cm.) or even shorter for special purposes. Usual length is 11½ in. (29 cm.), with planes used for jointing up to 18 in. (46 cm.) or more. The blade is a lamination of a thin, very hard high-carbon steel front and a soft back, with corners of the cutting edge removed at 45°. The steel face is hollowed out above the cutting edge to facilitate honing of the flat face opposite the bevel. In use, the plane is pulled toward the user.

Proper adjustment of the blade exposure in the hira-kanna is an art requiring practice, and much more attention to detail than is needed for the Western styles. The dai, or plane body, must first be stabilized for the humidity level of the shop in which it is to be used (storage for years is not unusual). The blade, with inked sides, is inserted into the side slots and withdrawn. The side slots are then pared wherever marked with the ink. The process is repeated until blade and slots are in complete contact, at the position of proper blade exposure. After this, the sole is flattened and very slightly hollowed so that it contacts the planed surface only at the mouth and toe or mouth, toe and heel.

The difference in bed angle reflects a somewhat different planing style. Much emphasis is placed on using heavy pressure and a very rapid stroke. Although, as is obvious, the mastery of the Japanese plane is difficult, the results they obtain are striking. The plane is the finishing tool for much Japanese work, and neither sandpaper nor applied coatings are required.

After the roughing planes, an intermediate plane CHŪ-SHIKO is used, having a narrow mouth and slightly rounded iron, almost always with a chipbreaker. This dimensions the stock and prepares it for marking out. A fastidious shokunin (craftsman) will have two of these, the finer one used after proper thickness is reached. After shaping the stock, the JŌ-SHIKO (or SHIAGE-KANNA) finishes the surface. It cuts the finest of shavings and has a mouth no wider than needed to pass these. This plane may have either a double or a single iron: the mark of a master is to finish awkward grain with a single-iron plane. These blades are hand-forged by ironmasters using techniques developed by the sword-makers. The best, forged in traditional manner by the most experienced, command incredible prices as works of art as well as superb tools. Here again, a craftsman will own several finishing planes with the finest reserved for special purposes.

Modern Chinese smooth planes (Fig.3:14) are still largely user-made. The stock shape may be similar to the Japanese or higher, sloping downward toward toe and heel. A transverse handle is usually fitted on top of the stock behind the throat. The plane, in contrast to Japanese custom, is pushed.

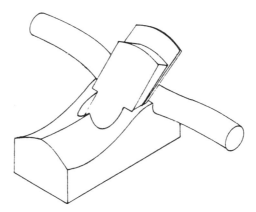

Fig.3:14—Chinese plane

Planes from Indonesia occasionally appear in this country. These imports are often elaborately carved in animal shapes and fitted with transverse handles behind the blade, in the style of Chinese planes.

Chapter 4

OTHER SURFACING PLANES

VERY LONG PLANES

Jointers longer than the bench jointer (over 32 in.; 81 cm.) were called FLOOR planes by American house carpenters. As the name implies, they were designed to level wooden floors, but also served for jointing long boards. They have been found as long as 40 in. (1 m.) with irons up to 3 in. (76 mm.) wide. The TANK JOINTER, offered by two American firms, and the BACK-MAKER'S JOINTER, in an English list of 1871, are presumed to be long planes used in planing staves for the large vats (sometimes called "backs" in England) used for cattle watering troughs or for various industrial purposes.

The COOPER'S JOINTER is a very long plane, mounted with sole uppermost on legs or clamped to the edge of a bench. The several forms used by coopers are discussed in Chapter 13—Cooper, which describes the cooper's work and tools. They are mentioned here because these planes were also used by other trades such as crate- and box-making and chairmaking.

SMALL PLANES

Planes shorter than the smooth plane (less than 6 in. or 15 cm.) have been produced in a number of shapes for specific purposes. The smallest of these, most common in brass but reasonably common in boxwood or other hardwood, are the VIOLIN or VIOLINMAKER'S planes used by luthiers in shaping the surfaces of musical instruments. The task of adjusting the thickness and contour to obtain the correct resonance is a delicate one. It requires the use of a variety of soles; flat, convex front to back (compassed), convex side to side (rounds), and convex in both directions (spoon). These planes are small, usually under 2 in. (5 cm.) in length. Normally made by their users, they vary widely in style, but most often have the shape of miniature bench planes. Occasionally these are seen with rear extensions in the shape of an awl handle or a rod and knob. These latter are called PALM planes.

THUMB or MODELING plane is a more general name that includes violin planes as well as any type of plane under 5 in. (13 cm.) in length. These names are applied to side escapement forms as well as the bench type.

Coachmakers used smooth, compass, and other bench type planes in this shorter size range. Marples and Preston, among other British catalogs, listed COACHMAKER SMOOTH and similar planes with curved soles. I know of no physical characteristics which distinguish small bench planes used by coachmakers from similar planes made by other tradesmen

Planes of these smaller sizes were apparently not standard items for most American manufacturers (except for the toy planes covered below). They are not found in American catalogs and are rarely found with American plane-maker imprints (though small signed British planes are seen more frequently). The Japanese versions, CHIBI-KANNA, in the shape of small hira-kanna, are still made in great variety.

The WHIP plane is a short smoother (little more than 3 in., 8 cm. long), usually steel soled. The name derives from their original use, which was in tapering cane sections that were then bound together to form whip handles. The abrasive cane made short work of a wooden sole, thus the steel reinforcement. Some had plated bodies as well.

TOY planes vary from crude items with sheet steel blades incapable of effective cutting (used to stuff children's toy tool boxes), to reduced scale versions of bench planes which could perform effectively in small hands. The Chapin 1874 catalog listed, as toy planes, smaller-sized tools at slightly below the price of standard planes, and, as "toy tool chest supplies," planes by the dozen at one-third the price.

In England, a slightly smaller or lighter version of any standard tool may be called a GENT'S or GENTLEMAN'S tool, implying it to be for amateur use. A LADY'S tool is even smaller and usually more ornate.

Short planes with the mouth close to the front of the sole are useful where smoothing must be done on a surface abutting a vertical obstruction. This body style is rarely seen in the United States as a wooden plane, although versions made of metal are.

While all-wood examples are found, wood is not a strong enough material to stand up under use if the distance from mouth to nose of the plane is made too short. For this reason, the front of the mouth is commonly formed by mounting a strip of brass across the stock just in front of the blade. This is illustrated in the CHARIOT plane (Fig.4:1). A popular type in England, it has a profile somewhat like the Gerfschaaf (rounded back, stock raised to form the front grip).

The BULLNOSE plane (Fig.4:2 B and C) permits an even closer approach to an obstruction. These resemble small Smooth planes that have had a portion of their front end truncated and have a brass plate fitted in its place. They are usually 3 - 6 in. (8 - 15 cm.)

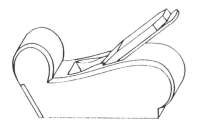

Fig.4:1—Chariot plane

long. Where working very close to a vertical obstruction is required, the metal nose plate must be mounted vertically or at a backward slant, as in Fig.4:2B. Both bullnose and chariot planes frequently mount blades with pitch less steep than normal. Both were pictured in the Sheffield 1876 list, and found use in cleaning rabbets and fitting tenons.

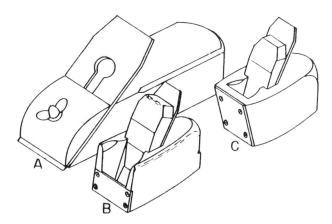

Fig.4:2—Edge plane (A) and two bullnose planes (B and C)

The removal of the sharp edge or arris where two surfaces meet, by cutting it away on a diagonal, is called chamfering. A chamfer is often more attractive if it does not continue to the ends of the arris, but fades in a gentle curve leaving the arris untouched at the ends of the member. This is called a stop chamfer, and is best accomplished by a short-nosed plane such as a bullnose. This gave rise to an alternate name for the bullnose, CHAMFERING SMOOTH plane. The illustrations labeled as bullnose planes in the Sheffield 1876 list were reproduced in several British catalogs. James Howarth (England 1884) called them both chamfer planes, while Mathieson (Scotland, 1899) gave us the name "champhering smooth" for Fig.4:2B. The name "chamfer plane" is a poor choice, as it has another commonly accepted meaning. This, and a variety of other planes designed for chamfering, will be described later in Chapter 8 "Planes Forming Angled Surfaces."

The EDGE plane, also called CHISEL plane or PIANOMAKER'S plane (Fig.4:2A), has no mouth. The blade projects forward beyond the sole, and thus can reach a vertical step. These are rarely found in the United States (except for the metal Stanley No.97 cabinetmaker's edge plane) and then are user-made. Without pressure on the work in front of the blade, only light cuts are safe if a rough surface is to be avoided. An alternate approach is used in a Japanese plane, the HIRA-BŌZU-KANNA (Fig.4:22), where the sole of the plane is cut away behind the mouth, permitting the stock to clear the obstruction.

PLANES WITH INTERCHANGEABLE SOLES

G. Gladwell (England, ca. 1824) devised a plane whose body was in two parts, the lower body separable from the top and held in place by a sliding dovetail joint. The lower sections were interchangeable, permitting various functions by changing sole and iron. Such planes were also made by J. Armour (England, -1826-28).

The concept survives in the PATTERNMAKER'S plane. The lower part of its stock is attached by screw fitments and is removable. It may be replaced with one of a set of soles of various curvatures, at the same time changing the blade to match. It is found in both smooth and jack size, with soles predominantly round across in different radii; but often with compassed or concave lengthwise types as well.

This concept was carried a step further by Thomas D. Worrall (29 Aug. 1854, US 11,635 and later patents; Fig.4:3). He made a variety of planes with interchangeable stocks marked as made by the Multiform Moulding Plane Co. (Boston) or Lowell Plane & Tool Co. (Lowell, Mass.). In the original form, these had molding plane (side escapement) stocks with the lower portion removeable. Interchangeable lower sections, with a variety of

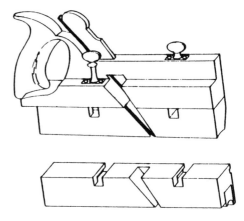

Fig.4:3—Worrall patent plane and interchangeable sole

sole profiles, had transverse T-slots in their upper surface which were engaged by brass thumbscrew fittings in the top member to hold them in place. Later, the stock was reduced to a handle to which a variety of essentially complete planes with T-slots could be fitted. The objective, to save space in tool chests, must have been well received since a considerable number of these have survived in spite of a short (1854-58) production period.

PLANES WITH IRONS BEDDED AT HIGH PITCH

English and American   The TOOTHING plane is a fairly common tool much like a short coffin smooth plane except for a nearly vertical bedding angle (Fig.4:4A). It is fitted with a toothed iron, a single iron with fine grooves ranging from 20 - 36 per inch (8 - 14 per cm.) in the steel (front) face of the blade (Fig.4:4B). In almost every case, these grooves are not symmetrical, but have vertical walls on the right side and slanted walls on the left. When ground to a bevel, the cutting edge resembles that of a very fine rip saw, facing the right side of the plane's user.

The plane has two uses. Holtzapffel (1875) and others give the purpose as roughing the backs of veneers and the surfaces to which they are to be glued, to make a tooth for better adhesion. James Smith (1816) and Peter Nicholson (1823) recommend its use to level cross or twisted grain. Evidence seen in 18th and early 19th century furniture (Albright, 1972) proves that the toothing plane was indeed used on end-grain, and on surfaces not intended to be glued. Experiment shows that the plane serves well for levelling awkward grain, and gives a surface ready for the scraper. The asymmetry of the grooves would seem to assist this use, as skewing the plane in the usual direction presents the rip-saw edge in the proper orientation. The finding of toothed blades more heavily worn in the center than at the edges also indicates this usage.

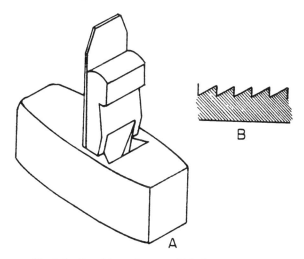

Fig.4:4—Toothing plane and blade cross section

Extensive testing in wood technology laboratories has shown that toothing is ineffective as a means of improving adhesion. A better bond is obtained with a cleanly planed surface than with a toothed one. However, since generations of tradesmen invariably used a toothing plane on surfaces to be veneered, and many of today's workers still do, I find it hard to believe that the practice would have survived unless it served a purpose. There may well be some adverse factor encountered in practical shop practice which is not taken into account in controlled laboratory experiments, and which is mitigated by toothing. As one example, restorers often encounter awkward surfaces difficult to render smooth by planing, and find that use of a toothing blade gives better glue adhesion in these cases.

As with square smooth planes (Fig.3:11B), SQUARE TOOTHING planes are rarely seen, although one of these fitted with a jack handle was made by the planemaker John Veit (Philadelphia, 1857-99). At least one SKEW TOOTH-ING plane with a skewed iron exists. Pitch in toothing planes varies from as low as 60° to a slight forward slant (100°). An English toothing plane of jack size is known.

The toothed blade has a long history. A Roman plane of the second century was found to contain one, and other early toothing blades have survived. It is not known whether it was first developed for levelling or for surface roughening. The former use requires following with a scraper to produce the final finish, so that it is not surprising that some vertically bedded planes are found fitted with straight-edged blades to act as scraper planes. In fact, some have blades that have been sharpened on either end; one straight, one toothed. A better form of SCRAPER plane has a short body with the iron mounted vertically or tilted slightly forward, and often with the blade edge turned with a burnisher as in a hand scraper (Fig.4:5; enlarged view in circle).

Several vertically bladed wooden planes used in other trades may be mistaken for wood-working tools. A jack with a nearly vertical iron is used by organ-builders to level cast sheets of tin-lead alloy to be formed into organ pipes (see Chapter 13—Organ Builder). A plasterer's tool is described below.

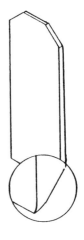

Fig.4:5—Scraper blade

Continental   The French RABOT À DENTS and the German ZAHN-HOBEL (both literal translations of tooth plane) are quite similar. The stocks used are like those of their common handplanes with front horn (Fausthobel, Fig.3:3), fitted with an erect toothed iron. Féron (France, ca. 1940) also shows an unhandled model with a square stock. In The Netherlands Stolp (1915) and Nooitgedagt (ca.1890) both show a square unhandled TANDSCHAAF quite similar to the French model shown in Féron.

A wooden stock with several vertical slots at random skew angles in the sole, each fitted with a steel blade (usually toothed) is used by plasterers and stone masons. The French call it a CHEMIN DE FER (railroad) or RABOTIN.

Japanese   The TACHI-BA-KANNA (standing blade plane) is of the usual hira-kanna shape (Fig.1:13) except for its pitch of 90 - 100°. A smaller version of this, the DAI-NAOSHI-KANNA (stock scraping plane), is reserved for maintaining the sole of other planes. Both may have either smooth or toothed blades.

THICKNESSING PLANES

English and American   Where wood strips must be planed to a precise thickness, a bench plane may be fitted with fences, one on either side of the sole. These straddle the workpiece, and touch bottom on the bench surface when the proper thickness is reached. These are commonly called REGLET planes, from their use in cutting the strips of wood (reglets) used as spacers in setting type. They are found with either fixed or vertically adjustable fences.

A similar tool, the SLAT plane, was used for making the slats of venetian blinds. These may have slightly concave across (hollowed) soles to leave the slat slightly rounded. The TAMBOUR plane is an exaggeration of this with deeply hollowed sole, which was used to cut the strips later bonded to canvas to make the roll-tops of desks. An elaborate thicknessing tool is treated later in Chapter 13—Organ Builder.

Japanese   Important features of Japanese homes are shoji, light frame-works of slats supporting a surface of rice paper and sliding in grooves. These serve in lieu of walls, providing movable partitions of living areas. A form of reglet plane, the KUMIKO-KEZURI-KANNA or grid shaving plane (Fig. 4:6) is made with sole wide enough to plane several slats at once. It is simply a wide hira-kanna with fences fixed to both sides of the sole. A variant provides a spring-loaded pressure plate (usually bamboo faced) in front of the blade, intended to prevent buckling of very thin grid strips.

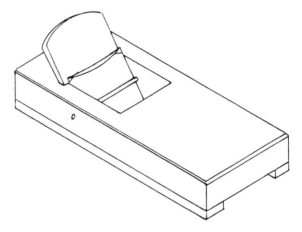

Fig.4:6—Japanese grid shaving plane

THE STRIKE BLOCK AND ITS DESCENDANTS

Moxon (1703) describes the STRIKE BLOCK as a plane shorter than the jointer with a straight, flat sole, used for shooting (planing) short joints and for fitting miter joints. Both the plane and the name seen to have been borrowed from The Netherlands, where the STRIJKBLOK was in use earlier. The pronunciation is very similar, but strijk refers to ironing or smoothing, not striking. One suspects that puzzlement over what the English name meant led to the variant STRAIGHT BLOCK.

For use in fitting miters, the strike block was held in the left hand, with the sole up, and the work pushed across it. Moxon states that for larger miters the work was held in a vise and a smooth plane was used. Planes of rectangular shape, square in section or somewhat wider than high, usually without jack handles, and with blades at 45° or less from the horizontal were sold as strike blocks in England into the 20th century. An example by W.J. Armour, who worked in London 1878-87, is 12 x 3 in. (305 x 76 mm.) in size and unhandled. It looks like a larger version of Fig.3:11B. (The name strike block was also used for the MITER plane, which is described in the next section.)

Mention of the STRIKE BLOCK or STRAIGHT BLOCK is made in 18th century lists, but descriptions are lacking. A plane in the Dominy collection at Winterthur Museum dated 1793, that is 11 in. (28 cm.) long and has a jack handle, strike button, and flat sole qualifies for the name (Fig.4:7). At first glance it might be mistaken for a short jack plane.

We may perhaps gain understanding of the continuous evolution of English planes by speculations inspired by Moxon's description. The two uses he gave for the strike block could have been served by the earlier smooth plane, but both were better served by a larger plane; and the strike block appeared.

One use for this new tool was in beveling the edges of wooden panels, to permit them to fit into grooves in the stiles and rails that support them. This was an improvement over the jack and smooth that were previously used for this purpose. It is tempting to speculate that this use gave rise to the alternate name "panel plane" for the strike block, since the name survives in the metal panel planes of Spiers and Norris.

A simple bevel is not as pleasing, in a panel, as a sunken bevel. This style could be cut by outlining the center of the panel with a grooving plane, followed by cutting away the outer sides of the grooves. It was undoubtedly

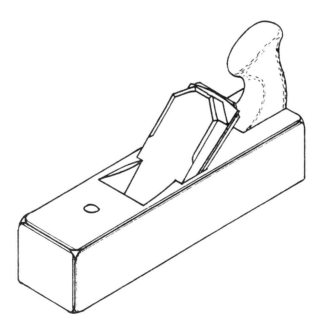

Fig.4:7—Dominy strike block

not long before it was discovered that the same result could be attained with one tool: all that was required was to cut away the right side of the strike block's sole to expose the side of the iron (as in Fig.4:12). The new version could sink the bevel without interference by the right cheek. Now we have a tool fully deserving the name "panel plane". These are not common tools, as continuing evolution produced the badger and panel raiser. These three are discussed in the next section.

The other use of the strike block was to trim miters and to plane end grain. The strike block was superior to the jointer for this, but performed better if the pitch of the iron was lowered. This variation of the strike block made it more suited to the specialized use and less suited to serve as a short jointer, so that a new name was needed. What better than "miter plane"? One gets a feeling of the ferment caused by change from the multiplicity of names appearing in early 19th century lists.

The Gabriel inventories of 1791 and 1793 listed single and double "pannel" planes, a "mitere" at twice the price of the single panel, and straight blocks at about the smooth plane price. The evolution of the panel raiser seems to be indicated by the listing of jacks rise and smooth rise, which I take to mean jack and smooth size panel planes.

By 1826 a Sheffield catalog (J. Wilks) showed a "strait block," a "pannel plane," and a "mitre plane" with stop and iron reversed (original spellings used). This last appears to be a description of a plane (the English mitre plane) which appears fairly often in English auctions, but is unknown in the U.S. except for a few imports.

The miter plane was known on the Continent well before 1700, so that it seems surprising that it did not find its way to England. Nicholson (1858) describes using the "straight block" for cutting miters, and does not describe the miter plane. It appears that the miter didn't become popular until somewhat after that date.

The English wooden MITRE PLANE is usually about 12 in. (30 cm.) long with a snecked iron bedded at very low angle, and with its bevel up. (Fig.4:8). (The above is the English spelling and will be used hereafter to refer to the English style of the plane, while the American spelling "miter" will mean the rather different American form.) It normally has a boxwood block fitted into a vertical mortise, forming the front edge of the mouth. Wear is faster than normal in end-grain service, and the end grain boxwood block resists this. Further, the block can be knocked downward as needed to restore the mouth. (The Japanese smooth plane is sometimes found with a similar device dovetailed to the front of the throat.) Occasionally a mitre plane is seen with a skew iron and without this mouth adjustment.

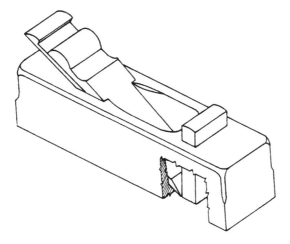

Fig.4:8—English mitre plane

It is not clear whether the metal mitre plane derived from the wooden one, or the wooden version succeeded the metal as a less expensive alternative. They were both listed in the 1826 catalog cited above. Both are capable of performing both functions of their progenitor, the strike-block. Both were still listed in English catalogs until about 1920. A significant advantage of the bevel-up mounting of the iron is that it can be supported on its bed right up to the cutting edge. With bevel down, support ends at the upper end of the bevel. The disadvantage is that the low blade mounting angle required by the mitre plane puts great strain on the feather edge of the stock at the lower end of the bed. The steel cased mitre plane therefore is much more durable than the wooden one.

The American version of the MITER plane (Fig. 4:9A) is quite different. It resembles an oval smoother, only longer and narrower, with its single iron bedded at 30 - 40°. Occasionally one is seen with a square, rather than an oval, stock (Fig.4:9B). Unlike the English mitre plane, the iron is most often bedded bevel

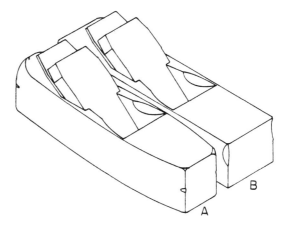

Fig.4:9—American miter planes, oval and square

65

down. This requires an unusually small sharpness angle (it must be smaller than the bedding angle). The bevel down placement meets the requirements for best performance in end-grain work, where a low pitch is called for, and where a small clearance angle is acceptable. Steel soled miter planes of very low pitch are occasionally seen with bevel-up mounting, the reinforced sole providing additional support.

Several American catalogs offered miter planes with double irons. A cap iron is not needed to break the shavings in end-grain work but helps to prevent chatter. The double iron miters may also have served as smooth planes: their low pitch would be useful on soft woods.

Another form used for cutting end grain or miters is the SHOOTBOARD, MITER SHOOTING or MITER BLOCK SHOOTING plane. This plane rests on its side (which must be exactly square to the sole) in a rabbet in the shoot board which controls its motion. The workpiece is secured to the board at the proper angle for the miter to be edge-planed accurately. Several versions are known. Mathieson (England, 1899) listed a pair of steel soled unhandled smooth planes with skew irons (right and left hand) as mitre or shuteing planes. Marples (England, 1909) offered "mitre shuteing" planes in lengths of 12 or 22 in. (30 or 56 cm.) with choice of straight or skew single irons and soles with or without steel plating. These had handles attached on the side, rather than the top, of the stock. Most American makers offered similar planes. One version had two skew irons in the same stock, and was listed as a PICTURE FRAME MITER plane (Fig.4:10). Hammacher, Schlemmer (New York City, 1896) offered the same tool under the name SHOOTING PLANE. It was sold with a shoot board that had a glass plate for the side of the plane to ride upon. A few examples are known of a 13 in. (33 cm.) long plane of square

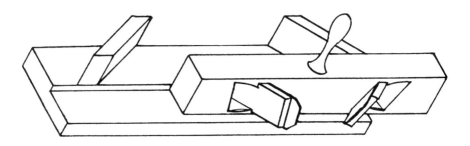

Fig.4:10—Shoot board and plane

section with side-mounted handle and metal fittings on toe and heel for attachment to a patented metal shootboard (Joseph Jones, 3 Jan.1871, U.S. 110,765).

Continental   The French use a plane that they call VARLOPE À ONGLET (miter jointer). Joiners commonly kept several, each with a different pitch. Roubo (1772) describes it as a plane 13 - 14 in. (33 - 36 cm.) long for such uses as mitering picture frames. The German miter is called the VERGATT-HOBEL or HIRNHOLZHOBEL. The Germans discovered the advantages of all-metal planes for low bed angles quite early. These are known dating as far back as 1644. Wooden ones are uncommon. The few known are about 5.3 in. (135 mm.) long and have their irons bedded at about 20°. The portion of the sole in front of the mouth was usually iron-plated.

The STRIJK-BLOK of The Netherlands, mentioned earlier as the archetype of the strike block, is 12 - 15 in. (30 - 38 cm.) long, with rectangular body and unhandled. Nooitgedagt (The Netherlands, ca.1891) listed it with either single or double iron.

Japanese   A modern Japanese plane, the KAESHI-BA-KANNA (reversed blade plane) uses the bevel-up blade mounted at the normal Japanese bed angle (37-38°) or slightly lower.

PANEL RAISING PLANES

English and American   Frame-and-panel construction is used where it is necessary to allow for the cross-grain expansion and contraction of wide wooden sections under changing conditions of humidity. A frame of vertical stiles and horizontal rails is made, with grooves on the inside edges into which the panel is fitted. The panel is not firmly attached, but is free to move within these grooves as its dimension changes. The edges of the panel (which was made of solid wood, thicker than today's plywood) had to be reduced in thickness to fit these grooves.

In early chests, and in early American wall paneling, the panels were often flat on the visible side, and the edges were reduced in thickness by bevelling the inside. Alternatively, a simple bevel was cut on both surfaces. Later, it was customary to make the edge thinning a decorative feature (Fig.4:11). A central area (the reservation) of the visible side of the panel was outlined by a shallow step or molding profile. The area outside of this (the

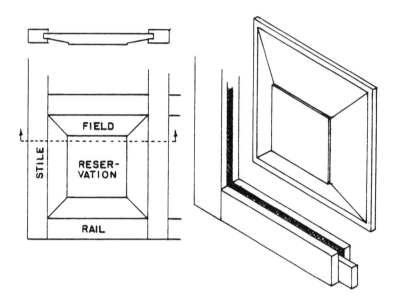

Fig.4:11—Frame and panel construction

field) was reduced in thickness until the edges fit the groove (perhaps with help from a bevel on the hidden side). A simple rabbet forms a flat fielded panel, and planes to cut this type are known. More often, the field slopes from reservation to edge; or slopes, then breaks to a section parallel to the reservation surface to enter the groove. The four slopes, one for each edge of the panel, meet in lines extending diagonally from the corners of the reservation. These provide increased visual interest, as does the reflection of light in different manner from the different slopes. Skill is required to cut these slopes as plane surfaces and to exactly the same depth, so that they meet in perfectly straight lines joining the corners of the reservation precisely.

A bench plane can work no closer to the step than the distance from the end of the iron to the side of the stock, and so cannot raise a panel without help. A large panel may be fielded by cutting grooves with a panel plow or similar tool to outline the step around the reservation, followed by use of a bench plane to sink the field. For smaller panels a faster method was found.

The PANEL plane may be described as a jack, strike block or similar plane which has been modified by cutting a rabbet in the lower right side of the plane just deep enough to expose the side of the cutter as shown in Fig.4:12. (The wooden panel plane is not to be confused with the quite different metal

68

plane of the same name.) In most cases the iron is skewed, as this helps both by keeping the plane against the step it is cutting, and also in cutting the cross-grain. In a variation called the SLIPPED PANEL plane (Fig.4:12), a strip of wood which filled the rabbet could be screwed to the stock to restore its original shape as a smooth plane or strike block.

One of the earliest surviving English panel planes (very similar to the one in Fig.4:12) is stamped Robert Wooding, dating it between 1710 and 1739. It measures 8.5 inches long and 2.5 in height and width (216 by 64 mm.), has a single skew iron and is unhandled. In common with many similar early panel planes, it has nail holes on the left side of its sole, testifying to the need for addition of wood strips to serve as fences. Another shortcoming of the early form is the fact that the cross-grain cutting at the top and bottom of the panel had to be preceded with a saw cut or some other way of preventing a ragged edge to the step.

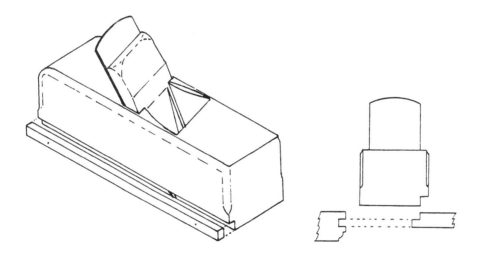

Fig.4:12—Slipped panel plane

An early American panel plane marked Tho. Grant (New York, late 18th century) illustrates one of the variations (Fig.4:13A). It has a cove (a hollow quarter circle) cut in the side of the stock in place of the rabbet, and cuts a quarter round step in place of the usual vertical one.

A panel plane with rabbets on both sides of the body, to expose the blade edge on both sides, is called a COACHMAKER'S DOOR CHECK plane in England. These were made in both smooth (COACH DOOR SMOOTH) and

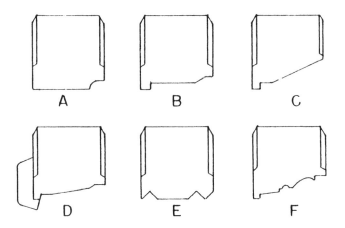

Fig.4:13—Profiles of panel raisers

jack size (COACH DOOR JACK). The oldest survivor of this style known to me is dated 1755, although the type was described much earlier. It was used to plane the rebates serving as door stops in door frames. Smooth and jack planes with this modification are found in the U.S., and are called COACH-MAKER'S RABBETS (unfortunately, as the same name is used for common rabbets with short soles). A long plane of this type was called a TENONING plane by D.R.Barton & Co. in its 1873 catalog. It was equipped with a nicker iron, and appears to be sized for cutting large tenons as in post-and-beam construction. This type of plane was used more extensively on the Continent, as we shall see below.

Although the panel plane in its original form had no fence, a variety of types with fixed fence are also called PANEL planes in the U.S. They may also be called PANEL RAISERS. Several types are seen in Figs.4:13 and 4:14. They may cut a short slope as the step (Fig.4:13B, made by R.C.Carter, New York, 1847-49), a long slope without the step (Fig.4:13C, C. Harwood, ca.1800), or both in one profile (Fig.4:13D, also made by R.C. Carter). D.R. Barton and Co.(New York) shows a simple version in its 1873 catalog (Fig.4:13E). In this example, a bench plane with skew iron and nicker is modified with two V-grooves in the sole, and the corners of the iron's cutting edge are removed to match. Holding the plane at an angle, one groove serves as the fence and the field is cut at the plane angle. An unusual form (Fig.4:13F) by Martin (Pennsylvania, 1773-1801) has a short slope with a quirk ovolo and astragal molding adorning the step.

Fences as provided by the maker (either integral with the body or as movable attachments) made the plane easier to use. The moveable, or filletster

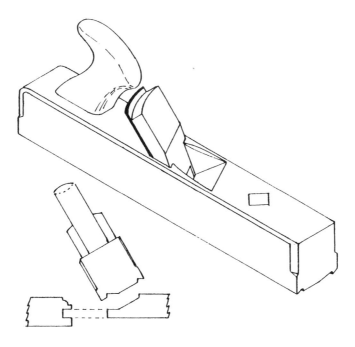

Fig.4:14—American panel raiser

type, fence is seen in Fig.4:15. Other improvements followed. To avoid splintering the step as the plane cuts were made on the two cross-grain sides of the panel, spur or nicker irons were used. These are knife edges that sever the grain of the wood ahead of the right side of the edge of the main cutter (Fig.4:15). As the panel plane evolved into different types, new names were

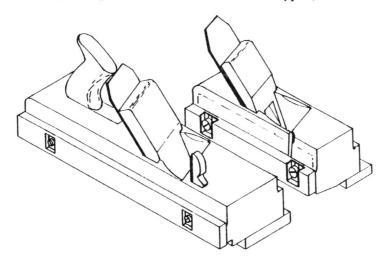

Fig.4:15—Panel raiser, left; panel fielding plane, right

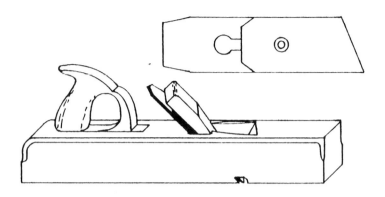

Fig.4:16—Badger plane and iron

introduced and another method of exposing the corner of the cutter was developed.

In the BADGER plane (Fig.4:16), the skew iron (usually double) is mounted in a throat canted toward the side of the stock. As a result the right corner of the cutter peeps out at the joint of sole and side. The badger plane was developed near the beginning of the nineteenth century; the first mention I have found is in the Marshes and Shepherd list (England, ca.1838-46). The badger comes in both jack and smooth sizes. It may be (infrequently) fitted with depth stop and fence, sometimes with a spur. The edge subject to wear against the step of the fielding is frequently boxed. The badger has the advantage of being able to cut a deep rabbet, unrestricted by a step (unlike a panel plane). However, this is of little value in panel raising and has the disadvantage of creating a weak feather edge to the plane's stock where the iron is exposed. (Brass reinforcements are often seen as repairs in old badgers). The cutting of the badger's throat is described by Armour (1898) as requiring special care. The badger was fairly popular in England, to judge by the number of survivors, and also in Japan. It was still being "made to order" in 1884 by James Howarth (England). It had little popularity in the United States; Chapin was one of the few makers to list it (in its 1874 and 1890 catalogs).

The various types of planes used in panel raising have given rise to more than the usual amount of confusion in their naming. This is illustrated by the Sheffield list of 1870. In addition to panel, slipped panel, badger, and badger with two fences, there was a smooth raising, smooth with badger mouth, jack raising, and jack with badger mouth. The last four were deleted in the 1876 list and presumably were variations that did not survive.

A distinction in naming sometimes used by English dealers is to call the panel plane fitted with filletster fence and full-length side stop a PANEL RAISING plane. If the sole and iron show a break, so that the edge of the panel is made horizontal for a short distance before beginning the bevel or curve (Fig.4:15 right), it is a PANEL FIELDING plane. The distinction is frequently ignored, and the panel produced by either is called a fielded panel. A panel raising plane with a pronounced curve to the bevel may be named to suit, as a COVE RAISING plane. All can vary from unhandled short planes to wide planes of jack length and handle.

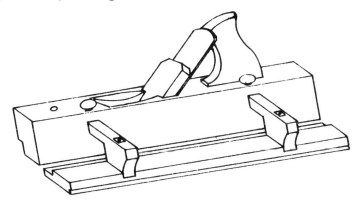

Fig.4:17—18th century American slide arm panel plane

In the United States the fenced planes are commonly called PANEL RAISERS (Fig. 4:15 left). They were listed in catalogs as RAISING planes in width sizes (priced per inch of width, 2¼ up to 4 inches) or as PANEL or RAISING JACK (the latter two names synonymous) in a single narrow size. It is amusing to note that Greenfield (Massachusetts, 1872) and Chapin (Connecticut, 1874) used the same drawing, one to illustrate the panel or raising jack, the other to depict the raising plane. The panel was offered with an optional "cut" (nicker) and moving fence; the raising plane was fitted with "stop and cut" — a wooden side stop and nicker. It was also offered by several makers with a fence mounted on slide or screw arms rather than screwed to the sole. An 18th century panel plane with slide arms is shown in Fig.4:17, this one unusual in that the iron was not skewed. The raising plane, whatever called, was a fairly common tool in the U.S. in the 18th and early 19th centuries. It was usually about 14 in. (36 cm.) long and had a jack handle.

Shorter planes — 8 to 9 in. (20 – 23 cm.) long — were often preferred in England (Fig.4:15 right). These are usually found with the typical bench plane throat and skewed double irons bedded at 50°, a depth stop and a filletster fence. The cutting edge is in the form of a very flat V, one leg horizontal to cut the edge and the other for the slope up to the reservation, as shown in the American plane of Fig.4:14 lower. A moveable fence permitted changing the size of the field by changing the extent of the horizontal section. The right side of the blade is sometimes sharpened to clean the vertical step.

Occasionally an older panel fielding plane is found with a side escapement in a molding plane shape. These have soles generally less than 2 in. (51 mm.) wide with a break to the horizontal, as above.

I have seen only right-handed panel planes by the older makers. These force cutting the field in a clockwise direction around the panel and must cope with grain reversal unless the stock is very straight of grain. One modern maker now offers both right- and left-handed forms.

Continental   The Dutch BOSSINGSCHAAF (Fig.4:18) is their panel raising plane. It has the same body shape as the Blokschaaf (see smooth planes) but normally has a skew blade. As in English practice, they are found both with badger mouths and (more frequently) with a rabbeted side. They were made with integral fences, although some have survived fitted with moving fences mounted on staves fixed in the stock. Here the setting is held by wedges through vertical mortises in the fence. Both Nooit-gedagt (The Netherlands, ca.1890) and Stolp (The Netherlands, 1915) catalogs list two: one unfenced (zonder geleider), the other (met geleider) with fence mounted on round staves and fixed by thumbscrews.

Fig.4:18—Dutch bossingschaaf or panel raising plane

The German version is the PLATTBANKHOBEL, a smooth size plane with integral fence and rabbeted sole as in a panel plane. Weiss (Austria, 1909) lists a horned type with straight or skew iron, and also fenced models with German screw-arm fences, straight or skew single irons or skew double irons, with nickers optional.

The French panel raiser is called GUILLAUME À PLATE-BANDE, or simply PLATE-BANDE; it is quite similar to the German Plattbankhobel. Later versions of jack size with closed razee totes were also made. They may have a second

74

iron to cut a molded step forming the border of the reservation. Early examples had a fixed fence, and changing the width of the field required tacking fillets of wood to the sole inside of the fence. Later a filletster fence was used. Lachappelle (France, ca.1890) listed these both unhandled with an adjustable metal fence, and handled with a filletster fence.

A slightly narrowed smooth size stock with rabbets to expose both sides of the cutter edge was called the ABPLATTHOBEL in Germany, the RABOT À ÉLÉGIR or thinning plane in France. Féron (France, ca.1940) lists a wide version with closed tote and two skewed throats — in effect, two panel planes in one body — as the VARLOPE À FEUILLURE, which is presumed to be of use in panel raising.

Japanese   A Japanese smooth plane with rabbets on the bottom of both sides is called an ŌSAKA-SHAKURI-KANNA, an Osaka grooving plane (Fig.4:19). It is quite similar to the western planes (coach door, etc.) except for its lower body and the placement of the throat near the heel of the stock. It is used as a plow to cut the grooves which accept the top rails of sliding partitions. As in almost all Japanese planes, it is pulled, and the rear blade placement provides a more comfortable grip. In some instances the usual Japanese cheek slots are used; in others the iron is wedged against a throat pin, using the chip breaker as the wedge. A somewhat larger version of this plane has been made to cut grooves for western-style window sash. The Japanese prefer to cut these, rather than form them with stops and parting strips. Another form seen only in Japan is the SEME-KANNA or attacking plane. The sides of the stock are sloped inward, instead of using rabbets, to expose the blade. It is used to plane (usually cross-grain) a surface up to a slanting projection.

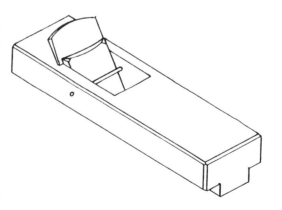

Fig.4:19—Japanese Osaka grooving plane

The badger type of blade mounting is well represented in Japan. The KIWA-KANNA or WAKI-KANNA (corner cutting plane) is a modification of their smooth plane and is found in both right-hand and left- hand versions, with or without chipbreaker. These may be equipped with nicker irons for cross-grain work, as in tenoning

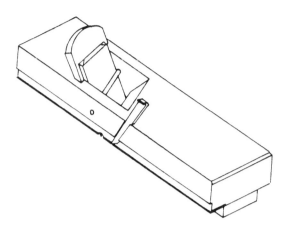

Fig.4:20—Japanese badger plane with filletster fence

(YOKO-ZURI-KIWA-KANNA) and also with a filletster fence (AI-JAKURI-KIWA-KANNA, Fig.4:20. The dark line shows a brass wear plate). Another uniquely Japanese plane is a badger plane with the side of the stock (the one having the blade exposed) sloped sharply inward, the SUMI-KIWA-KANNA. It is used to cut the male member of the sliding dovetail joint.

Paneling is uncommon in Japanese architecture, but raised elements similar to panel reservations are used, for example, in cabinet doors. These are cut with a special set of planes which do not rely on fences for guidance and are all in the general style of the hira-kanna or common plane. The SUMI-MARU-YOKO-ZURI-KANNA (corner rounding plane, Fig.4:21) serves to remove wood leaving a concave step at the raised portion. It may be of badger form with a rounded sole corner, or like a panel plane with the rabbet edge rounded. It has a thin single iron. It is followed by the HIRA-BŌZU-KANNA (rounded flattening plane), which is a common plane with the sole cut away behind the mouth. The rear of the plane can thus overhang the raised section of the work and the stroke is begun at the curve, working along the grain (Fig.4:22, next page).

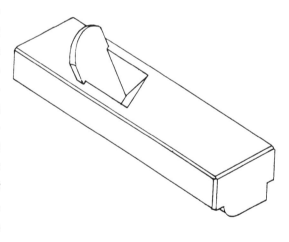

Fig.4:21—Japanese corner rounding plane

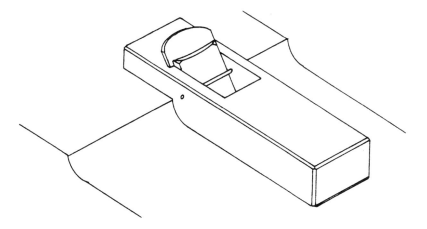

Fig.4:22—Japanese relieved sole plane

Chapter 5

THE TWO MAJOR TYPES OF PLANES

Planes are not the most effective means of removing large quantities of wood; they are best brought into action after other tools have done the preparatory work. Bench planes are used primarily to refine and finish a surface that has already been roughly defined by tools such as axe, hatchet, or saw. Curved surfaces as well may be roughly shaped by sawing, and planes then employed to bring them to final shape. These are simply bench planes whose soles have been configured to serve on curved surfaces. They are refining and finishing tools, if you will, rather than shaping tools.

Once the main outlines of a project have been realized, there remain details to be introduced. A table top, for example, may need a particular profile at the edge where a drop leaf is to be attached, and a rounding or decorative molding at its other edges. The amount of wood to be removed for such purposes is easily within the capability of a plane. Let us call those planes designed primarily to create a desired shape, rather than simply smooth it, FORMING planes.

As with most attempts to divide any subject into classes, there will be gray areas. In some medium-sized tasks one workman will start with the plane; another will first remove excess wood with a chisel. To say this another way, one will use the plane as a forming tool, the second will treat the same plane as a finishing tool. Another area of confusion might be varying use of the same tool. A simple bench plane with a piece of the sole edge cut away (the panel plane) is a finishing tool when used to smooth a surface, a forming tool when forming a panel.

Fortunately, there is a method of separating planes into classes that is unequivocal, yet which roughly parallels the split into finishing and forming tools. The latter are usually required to cut deeply, but over a narrower cut width. They are generally narrower than finishing planes. If the plane were to be made in the same body type as the bench planes, the shavings would have only a narrow passage for their exit, and the plane would "choke", or jam with shavings. The solution to the problem was to change the plane's shape. The side of the plane was opened to permit the shavings a direct exit.

In classifying planes, there are a number of cases where it might be difficult to decide whether the tool was for forming or for finishing. In contrast, it is easy to see whether the shavings escape from the top of the body or from the side. Let us call the latter SIDE ESCAPEMENT planes, and refer to the former as BENCH TYPE or BENCH THROAT. This will determine the order in which we take up the various plane types in future chapters. It is a key feature of the numerical classification system that is designed to help the reader identify a plane by providing an index based on the plane's shape. (See Appendix 3.)

This nomenclature is essentially a more closely defined form of one now in common use that differentiates among body types, lumping together as "molding planes" all narrow planes with side exits for shavings. This may be useful, but it is not strictly true. There are very wide molding planes with top shavings exits, and there are many types of side-exit planes which do not form moldings.

SIDE ESCAPEMENT PLANES

We may suppose that an early version of the side escapement style was invented when a throat was cut in the side of a body, the wedge and iron being held in an open groove.

A plane of this form was recovered from the ship *Mary Rose*, sunk in 1545. The stock sketched in Fig.5:1 is the oldest surviving open-throat example known to me, but it is probable that the form was in common use well before this date. Many of the planes illustrated by Félibien (1676), one of which is seen in Fig.5:2, were made in this way.

Early Continental furniture makers often made open-throat

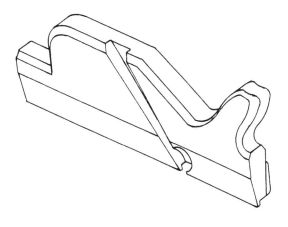

Fig.5:1—Early open throat stock, ca.1545.

molders, this being the quickest way to create a tool for the need at hand. They are rarely finished carefully or given the decorative touches characteristic of other tools. It seems apparent that they were not intended for long service and, in fact, the design would seem to invite stock warpage after short service. Some are seen with cap irons, dating them well after Félibien's time. Hastily made and crudely finished tools of this type are also found in America, but they were not made commercially.

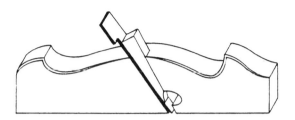

Fig.5:2—Rabbet after Félibien (1676)

The open-throat form is improved in two ways by planting a batten over the upper portion of the wedge slot. The body is strengthened against warping, and risk of the wedge slipping out is decreased. With improved adhesives, this construction is serviceable and was accepted by some French commercial makers, as seen in the Peugeot planes (France) of Fig.5:3. Earlier, however, a better body was made by cutting the throat through a solid piece of wood.

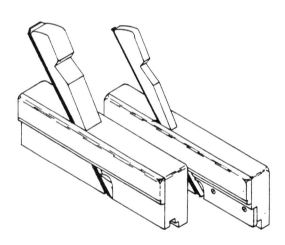

Fig.5:3—French tongue and groove planes showing batten construction

In both open-throat and batten construction, the iron is like a narrow bench iron, of uniform width over its length. The batten shape requires that the body of the plane be wider at top than at bottom, if the side of the iron is to reach slightly beyond the right side of the sole. This was not acceptable in most countries, and was soon changed by reducing the width of the upper portion of the iron. The cutting end, as in the open throat construction, reaches the right side of the stock, but the upper part is reduced to a shank ½ in (13 mm.) or less wide. The wedge, not constrained by the need to allow a passage for the shavings, could (together with the shank) completely fill a tapered mortise through the upper stock. The side of the plane body is sawn away to form the side escapement, and the lower end of the wedge is cut away on a slant to divert shavings toward this. (An alternate round escapement is used in rabbet and dado planes, seen in Chapter 6.)

WEDGES

In contrast to the bench type of wedge, the side escapement construction uses a thinner wedge, the distance from front to back being greater than it is from side to side. The use of a notch in the wedge to form the finial is almost universal, and invites its use as a striking surface in the removal of the wedge. This invitation should be declined. Even more so than in the case of the bench planes, the short grain will not take much pressure or impact. It is not advisable to use more than a gentle tap on this, as the sheared finials on many old planes testify. If a light rap with a mallet on the front top or the heel of the stock does not free the wedge, it is much safer to clamp the wedge in a

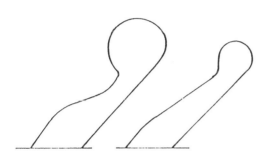

Fig.5:4—Two wedge variations by Robert Wooding

wooden bench vise (or a metal vise suitably protected with softwood padding) and apply pressure or shock to the stock along the line of the wedge. The top of the finial is often seen to have been mushroomed by repeated hammer blows used in tightening the iron. This would not have happened to the tools of a good workman. If the wedge is properly fitted and the blade not set for too deep a cut, a light tap with a mallet (not a hammer) is all that is required to seat it firmly.

The various forms used to shape the upper end of the wedge provide clues as to the age and geographical source of a plane. Wedge outlines have been thoroughly catalogued by the Pollaks (1987) and others, but perhaps a few comments are in order here.

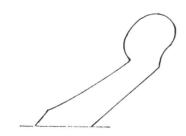

Fig.5:5—Relieved wedge of Jo. Fuller

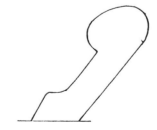

Fig.5:6—Later wedge form of Mutter

The earliest planemakers appear to have made their wedges one at a time, to judge by the variations found. Two by Robert Wooding (England, 1710-1739) are shown in Fig.5:4. He and most of his contemporaries usually cut the top of the wedge (the finial) in the shape of roughly three-quarters of a circle. This shape is a reasonably good diagnostic of an 18th century plane. A form with the back of the finial relieved was favored by some early New England makers; an extreme form made during the later years of Joseph Fuller (Rhode Island, ca.1800) is seen in Fig.5:5. Toward the end of the 18th century, a number of makers chose to replace the circular form with a tilted elliptical shape. George Mutter's (England, 1766-1812) later wedges were made in this form (Fig.5:6), although his earlier wedges had circular tops.

In making large numbers of planes, it was practical to cut a number of wedges at one time. Special planes were made to cut the wedge finial (as described in Chapter 13— The Planemaker) so that the planes of a given maker during one period all had wedges of the same finial shape.

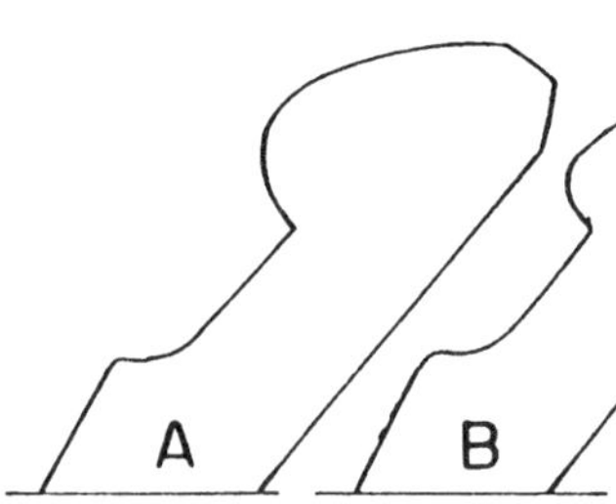

A variant of the elliptical wedge finial appeared in eastern Scotland in

Fig.5:7—A: wedge by D. Malloch; B: wedge by S.F. Willard

the mid-19th century. The top, or striking surface of the finial, was flattened. At first this was so slight as to escape all but the closest examination and could easily be mistaken for distortion from hammer impact. (Perhaps the original purpose was to minimize such damage.) The curve at the rear of the finial was also flattened to meet the top at an angle, as shown in the wedge of D. Malloch (Scotland, 1850-1870; Fig.5:7A). This variant was introduced to Canada by Scottish immigrants, and an emphasized version was adapted by a number of Canadian planemakers (Tool Group of Canada *Newsletter,* Vol. 4). An extreme version is shown in Fig.5:7B, a wedge by S.F. Willard (Canada, 1876-1884), in which a third flat is added at the front of the finial.

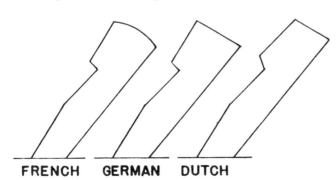

FRENCH   GERMAN   DUTCH

Fig.5:8—Continental wedge profiles

The wedges favored by Continental planemakers (Fig.5:8), as mentioned previously, use straight line segments for the most part (although finials like the English forms are not unknown). The finial is usually demarcated by two straight cuts. The taper continues unbroken to the top of the wedge in most French and German planes; the former may have a slight curvature of the finial top, while the German and Austrian are usually flat. The wedges of The Netherlands resemble the German except for the narrowing of the finial toward the top.

IRONS

Irons for planes with side escapements are commonly of iron faced with steel, as are bench plane irons. They are normally thinner than bench type irons, and are tapered in thickness in the same manner. The top is cut back, or "shouldered", to form a shank often less than ¼ in. (6 mm.) wide. Certain types of plane (e.g., rabbets) have shavings exit on both sides; their blades are double shouldered to center the shank. For most others, the shank is located on the left side (Recall that the left side is to the left of the person using the plane.)

Early irons were made individually by hand forging, but in commercial production they were made by forge welding a steel strip to an 8 x 6 in. (20 x 15 cm.) rolled iron rectangle. The appropriate shapes were then punched out of this.

Planes designed for cutting across the grain are usually equipped with NICKER irons, also called SPURS, in addition to the main cutter. These are fitted with knife edges that sever the wood fibers of the work immediately in front of the sides of the main cutter. Without them the cut would splinter the edges.

Details of the methods used in making side escapement planes are presented in Chapter 10 under Molding Planes. (Some of the terms used are best defined in that chapter). Material in the following chapters will be organized primarily by the task accomplished by the tool. While most tool types are predominantly of one body style, it is not uncommon to find the wider plane with a bench mouth and the narrower one with side escapement; or to have different styles favored in different countries. The same function may then be covered in two places, giving cross-references.

PARTS COMMON TO BENCH
AND SIDE ESCAPEMENT PLANES

There are several functional parts of planes that may be found in either bench or side escapement types and which may be common to planes of differing functions. It may be useful to name and outline these here for comparison and reference.

DEPTH STOPS

These serve to stop the cutting action of the plane when the desired depth is reached, and insure a uniform depth of cut.

An INTEGRAL STOP is one formed by the body of the stock, and is immoveable. An example is shown in the left plane of Fig.5:9. A FULL SIDE STOP is a wooden piece the full length of the stock, with vertical slits through which wood screws attach the

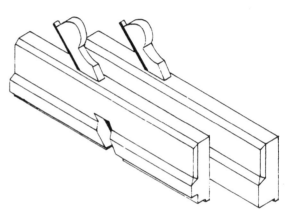

Fig.5:9—Left: integral fence and depth stop
Right: integral fence

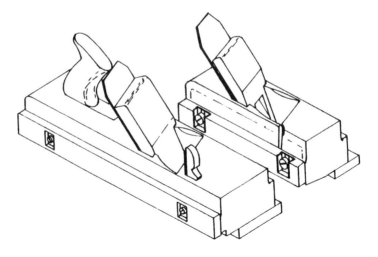

Fig.5:10—Panel raisers with full side stops and filletster fences

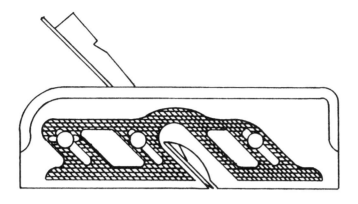

Fig.5:11—Continental plane with cut out full side stop

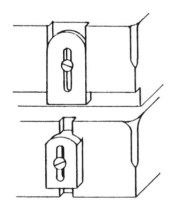

Fig.5:12—Two types of wooden side stop

stop to the right side of the stock. The slits are usually countersunk and lined with brass to provide a bearing surface for the head of the wood screw. This type is most often seen in panel raisers, as shown in Fig.5:10. It cannot be used with side escapement planes unless a part of the fence is cut away or the escapement is changed to the left side of the plane. Both methods are seen in some Continental planes. In the former the cutout is on a diagonal parallel to the bed, and the adjustment slots are cut at the same angle to keep the opening at the throat as its position is changed. The fence is usually attached by wingnuts rather than wood-screws. A brass version with similar shape is preferred in planes of later vintage (Fig.5:11).

A SIDE STOP is a shorter member, sliding vertically in a dado in the side of the plane body. The WOOD SIDE STOP, seen in older or lower grade planes, is a slotted wooden block, fixed to the stock with a common screw. Two versions are seen in Fig.5:12. The BRASS SIDE STOP is the brass version, using the same mounting. The variant whose foot sweeps outward in a curve

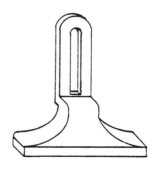

Fig.5:13—Filletster side stop

85

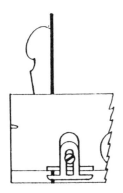

Fig.5:14—Dado brass
side stop

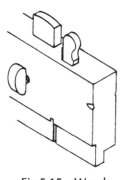

Fig.5:15—Wood
screw stop

from its vertical slide has been called a FILLETSTER SIDE STOP (Fig.5:13). The DADO BRASS SIDE STOP differs in that its foot turns under the stock and into the step of the dado plane, rather than outward (Fig.5:14).

The WOOD STOP slides in a vertical mortise through the plane. If fixed in place by a wooden screw threaded through the stock, it is called a WOOD SCREW STOP (Fig.5:15).

The BRASS SCREW STOP is adjusted by means of a cap screw or thumb screw extending through the top of the plane body. Its external member, in the FILLETSTER SCREW STOP form, appears similar to the filletster side stop, but the vertical slide has an extension behind it which slides in a slot in the plane. This extension is threaded to take the adjustment screw. Removed from the plane, it appears as in Fig.5:16. The same fixture with a thumb-screw in place of the cap screw is more usual; it has been called the "plow fashion" filletster screw stop. When used on sash fillet-sters, this stop frequently has the rear section of its foot elongated. The DADO SCREW STOP has the same method of adjustment, but the metal can be enclosed in the plane body with only the foot protruding at the bottom, in the dado's step (Fig.5:17) .

The PLOW SCREW STOP (Fig.5:18) is similar to the dado screw stop but has a longer foot, an appreciable fraction of the length of the stock. The foot reaches inward to the skate, or metal sole of the plow, at its ends, but is cut away in the middle to avoid interference with the blade or the shavings. In the premium plows, the thumbscrew is not relied

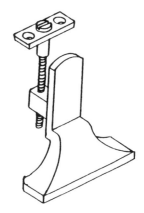

Fig.5:16—Filletster screw
stop

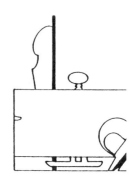

Fig.5:17—Dado screw stop

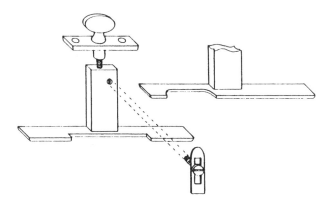

Fig.5:18—The plow screw stop (church window type) and sash filletster type

upon entirely but a secondary fixing is made after adjustment. A brass thumbscrew through the side of the stock and bearing on the vertical member of the stop is described as SCREW STOP WITH SIDE STOP. Another variant threads a thumbscrew or cheesehead (flat fillister head) screw through the vertical member of the stop, the head of which projects through a vertical slot in the side of the stock. This slot is usually framed with brass, and frequently the top of this is finished with a dormer or arch shape. The variation has acquired the designation CHURCH WINDOW from the fancied resemblance. In still another variation, one English maker has added a ratchet to the adjustment screw. Several of these forms will be seen in the chapter on plows.

The "IMPROVED" SASH FILLETSTER SCREW STOP is identical with the plow screw stop with the exception of the different shape of the cutaway portion of the foot, to match the different clearance requirements.

FENCES

A fence is a member attached to the plane; it rides the edge of the workpiece as a guide in keeping the blade cutting parallel to it. An INTEGRAL fence is a downward projection along one edge of the sole (Fig.5:9). The FILLETSTER fence (Fig.5:19) is a wooden member the size of the sole and about ½ in. (13 mm.) thick. It is held to the plane sole by wood screws passing through crosswise slots in the fence — the slots usually recessed and lined with brass to avoid wear by the screwheads. The slots permit adjustment of the fence from almost complete coverage of the plane sole to exposing a major portion of it.

The FILLETSTER ARM fence is a similarly shaped member suspended from wooden arms. The arms pass through holes in the stock and are cut with deeper sections (shoulders) at one end. They descend to meet the fence at its proper position with respect to the stock. They may be of the form shown in Fig.5:20 (wedge arm), or the arms may be threaded (screw arm).

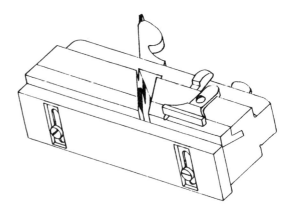

Fig.5:19—A filletster fence attached to the sole of a moving filletster

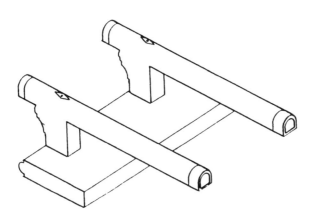

Fig.5:20—Filletster wedge arm fence

PLOW fences (Fig. 5:21) are hung from arms in similar fashion. The fence body, however, is quite different. It has a deeper face on the guiding edge, and is deeply molded into roughly triangular shape in cross-section, with molding repeated on the front. (The moldings are individualistic and often serve to identify the plane's geographic origin or even the planemaker.) The fence projects in front of the stock to avoid mishap at the near end of the cut. A variety of arm types have been used, and are described in Chapter 7 under plow planes. The SASH FILLETSTER fence is quite similar, and many of the arm types described under plows are found on these as well. In contrast to the filletster fence above, the sash filletster fence need not be mounted low enough to pass under the body of the plane.

The above descriptions apply to English and American planes. On the Continent, arm fences use an opposite suspension. The arms are fixed in the stock and slide through the fence. The advantage is that the protruding arms are to the left and less in the way; the disadvantage: the fence must be of the same height as the stock and is bulkier. Again, further details are given in Chapter 7 under Continental plows.

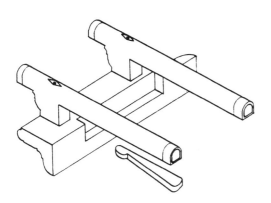

Fig.5:21—Plow fence

The COOPER'S fence rides on the stave ends of a headless barrel and serves to guide the cutting of grooves within it to hold the heads. It is commonly a separate piece, larger than the body carrying the cutting edge. To increase stability, it must contact a significant fraction of the rim, so it usually has a semi-circular outline. The ends of the fence may be extended to provide handholds, giving a shape like a "fore-and-aft" or "deerstalker" cap (see Chapter 13 under Coopers).

Chapter 6

RABBETING PLANES

A rabbet is a rectangular step cut in the edge of a board (Fig.6:1). Its uses are manifold. It is used for a common corner joint in casework (Fig.6:2 left), in the lap joint in wainscot or siding (Fig.6:2 right), and in many other places where a simple butt joint will not serve. The rabbet cannot be cut by a bench plane, as the blade cannot get into the corner. This was the reason for the conversion of the jack to the panel plane, you will recall (see Chapter 4). Besides the panel plane and other bench type tools capable of rabbeting, several other imple-

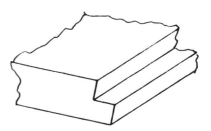

Fig.6:1—A rabbet cut in the edge of a board

ments were designed for the same purpose. Open-throat rabbeting planes are shown in Félibien (1676, Fig.6:3), and were probably in use much earlier.

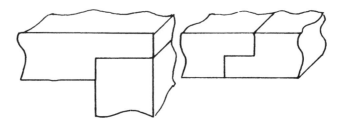

Fig.6:2—Rabbet used for a corner joint (left) and a lap joint (right)

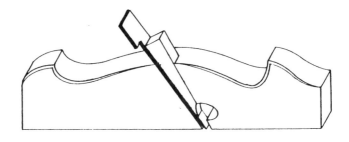

Fig.6:3—Open throated rabbet plane after Félibien

90

Blades which may have been used for rabbeting survive from Roman times. There are many planes used to cut rabbets, but the name RABBET plane has been appropriated by one type.

RABBETS

English and American

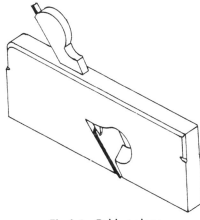

Fig.6:4—Rabbet plane

A RABBET plane (in England called the REBATE) is a plane of rectangular cross-section, higher than wide, with a blade whose cutting edge is slightly wider than the sole. Its characteristic feature is a snail-shaped shavings escapement which opens to both sides of the stock (Fig.6:4). In older planes, this was simply a large hole drilled through the stock and extended in a reverse curve to intersect the throat. Later, a tapered auger or ream was used. This produced a shape which not only gave better direction to the shaving but was more pleasing to the eye.

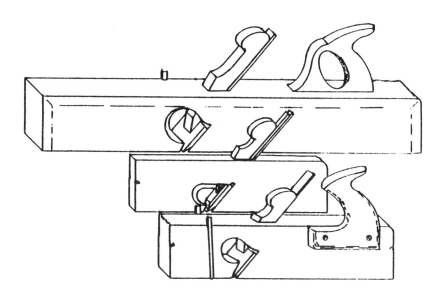

Fig.6:5—Bridgebuilder's rabbet with closed tote (top); shipbuilder's rabbet with separate cap iron (center); jack rabbet with offset tote (bottom)

The blade is slightly wider than the stock for about an inch or so (25 mm.) up from its cutting edge. Above this both sides are cut away to leave a central shank to be held by the wedge. Pitch (the angle of the blade with the horizontal) is most often about 50°, although higher and lower are found. The rabbet is not usually fitted with spurs or nickers, although one or two "cuts" were offered as options by most makers. These were simple affairs, a steel blade held by a force fit in a tapered sliding dovetail in the side of the stock ahead of the iron (two are shown in Fig.6:5 bottom). Other options available were shoulder boxing (the insertion of strips of boxwood in the sole to increase wear resistance), and full face boxing (see Fig.6:6). (Additional information on boxing will be found in Chapter 10.) The common rabbet, of standard length (about 9.5 in.; 24 cm.), is listed in most catalogs as available in width sizes from ½ to 2½ in. (13 - 63 mm.). Larger and smaller sizes are

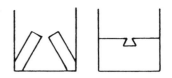

Fig.6:6—Shoulder boxing (left); full face boxing (right)

seen infrequently. The smaller sizes have the upper stock enlarged, and the iron shank moved to one side. An uncommon type has the stock enlargement placed low enough to serve as a depth stop. These are called SHOULDER RABBETS.

Today, of course, rabbets are cut by dado heads in bench saws, or by power routers or other power tools, and rabbet planes are used only for finishing or fitting. Earlier, the rabbet plane cut the rabbet from scratch. The simple rabbet needs a guide of some sort to get it started, perhaps a batten clamped to the workpiece. Another option was to nail a temporary fence to the sole of the plane, as the nailholes often seen in the soles of the wider rabbets tell us. There does not seem to be much point putting an integral fence on the simple rabbet described above, since the exposure of the blade on the left side of the stock is then of no use. There are many alternate solutions, to be taken up shortly.

Another limitation of the simple rabbet plane is that cutting the rabbet to a uniform depth over the full length of the cut requires care and frequent measurement. A means of stopping the cut when it has reached the desired depth helps. One such way is an integral depth stop, formed by the body of the plane, as in the shouldering rabbet described above. Other methods used are discussed later.

SQUARE RABBETS (Fig.6:7 left) have their cutting edge perpendicular to the sides of the body, and are less common than SKEW RABBETS (Fig.6:7 right) whose blades are mounted at a skew angle of up to 20°. The skew places the right side of the iron forward, and tends to hold the plane against the side of the rabbet it is cutting. It also directs the shaving away from the cut ("off the bench"). The escapement is cut to encourage this, being wider on the left of the stock. (Square rabbets may have symmetrically cut escapements.) The right side of a skew iron must be beveled for clearance, though only rarely is it also sharpened. Left-handed rabbets (with opposite skew and escapement larger on the right) are not unknown, although they do not appear in the catalogs.

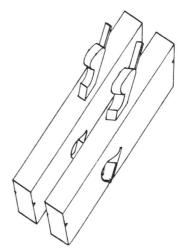

Fig.6:7—Square rabbet (left); skew rabbet (right)

Rabbets are found with closed totes cut integrally with the body, similar to those on bench planes (Fig.6:8). More often, the handled models were of jack size with open jack handles and inevitably called JACK RABBETS, although most catalogs (except for Sandusky and Barton) listed them as "handled rabbet". The handles are sometimes offset to the left side of the stock (Fig.6:5 bottom), or mounted slanting to the left, as a way of increasing the hand clearance. (See Raglet, in Chapter 7—Grooving Planes). Jack rabbets are most often found with two nickers (one on each side), although these were listed as options in most catalogs. This reflects the fact that rabbets were cut cross-grain, as well as along the grain.

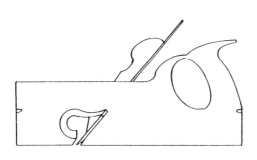

Fig.6:8—Rabbet with integral closed tote

The rabbet has been made in many variations. It may be as short as the COACHMAKER'S, which are often less than 7 in. (18 cm.) in length, or as long as the BRIDGEBUILDER'S (Fig.6:5 top). The latter have closed totes and are 20 - 30 in. (51 - 76 cm.) long, with wide irons. The Arrowmammett Tool Co.'s 1858 catalog listed the same tool as a SHIP CARPENTER'S RABBET 22 in. (56 cm.) long and 2 in. (51 mm.) wide. Rabbets may be compassed or rounded, or the lower side of the stock may be rounded in a horizontal plane to permit planing rabbets inside a curve (COACHMAKER'S DOOR RABBET, Fig.6:9). RADIUS RABBETS (Fig.6:10) have the stock curved in a horizontal plane longitudinally, and will work either inside or outside a curve. Rabbets longer than 10 in. (25 cm.) are commonly called SHIP or SHIPBUILDER'S RABBETS, especially if fitted with separate cap irons, as made by J.R. Tolman (Massachusetts, -1841-49-; Fig.6:5 middle).

While simple rabbets are not found with integral fences, they *are* seen with adjustable ones. Both wedge arms and screw arms were used. Arrowmammett (Connecticut, 1858) listed SCREW-ARM RABBETS in widths of 2 to 2½ in. (51 - 63 mm.), as did Alex. Mathieson and Sons (Scotland, 1899 catalog). Fences with arms could be purchased separately and installed into holes bored in the stock of a common rabbet so that screw-arm rabbets are often user modifications.

The coachmaker often had to trim both side and bottom of a rabbet in final fitting. He often had limited space in which to work. One of his tools was the T-RABBET (Fig.6:11 center) in which the sole is extended beyond the width of the stock (cross-section an inverted T). This offered a clearer view of the surface being worked, and provided

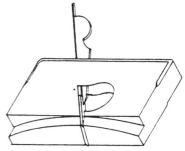

Fig.6:9—Coachmaker's door rabbet

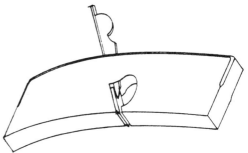

Fig.6:10—Radius rabbet

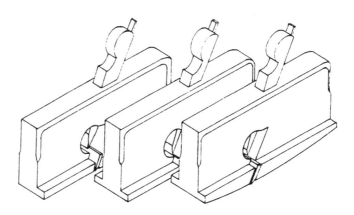

Fig.6:11—Coachmaker's rabbets: L-rabbet, left; T-rabbet, center; Compassed T-rabbet, right

a bit more room for finger clearance. It also permitted paring either side of a groove by applying the tool sidewise. Less frequently found is the L-RABBET, whose sole is extended on one side only. This is shown in Fig.6:11 left, together with the COMPASSED T-RABBET (Fig.6:11 right), which has a longitudinally curved sole. These planes

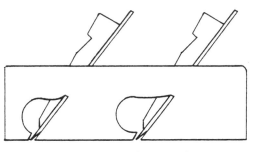

Fig.6:12—Bullnose rabbet combination

are also found with their sole extension made with an iron plate. A rabbet with a very short sole in front of the iron is called the BULLNOSE RABBET, although metal planes soon replaced wood here. At least one combination bullnose and regular rabbet is known (Fig.6:12).

Steel cased rabbet planes, called SHOULDER planes (Fig.6:13) were made by Spiers, Norris and others in Great Britain in the latter half of the 19th century and later. They were popular and widely imitated. The earlier models have thick metal soles dovetailed to metal sides; while later, thinner folded steel was used. The metal casing was stuffed with hardwood, often rosewood or ebony, and the wedge was made of the same wood or, for better holding power, of a somewhat softer wood. The iron was mounted at low angle (about 20°), bevel up.

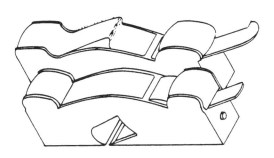

Fig.6:13—Shoulder planes

The steel sole supported the iron very close to the cutting edge, as in a steel miter plane, minimizing chattering in end-grain cuts. Skew mountings are sometimes seen. The wedge finial is usually cut in a form which provides a palm rest to improve the grip, and the upper edge of the stock is shaped in graceful curves. A form with an upward projection in front of the wedge, to buttress the grip, has been dubbed a RHINO-HORN (Fig.6:13 rear). The Shoulder Plane proved useful in trimming rabbets and in fitting tenons, and all-metal versions are still being made today.

A rabbet plane with an adjustable mouth (Fig.6:14) was patented by T.J. Tolman (13 Jan. 1857, U.S.16,412). The sole in front of the mouth was a separate block secured to the stock by a bolt and nut, and adjustable forward or back. The iron was double, Tolman being one of the few U.S. makers to use a cap iron in a rabbet plane.

The side wall of a rabbet or groove may need finish planing. The SIDE RABBET (Fig.6:15) serves this function, as does the T-rabbet. The former is a thin molding plane with the stock tapered nearly to a point at the bottom. The iron (one is shown lying on the stock in the figure) is mounted almost vertically, sharply skewed, sharpened on its side edge which projects from the vertical side of the stock. They were supplied in right- and left-handed pairs. Another form, the side snipe, is treated later.

An unusual variant is a plane of L-shaped cross-section with a cutting edge projecting horizontally from the lower leg of the L. A steel-sheathed example is in the Mystic Museum collection. Another uses an L-shaped cutter to cut on the side (Fig.6:16). The design would serve to trim the side of a wide groove.

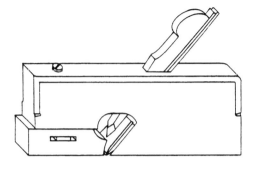

Fig.6:14—Patented adjustable mouth rabbet

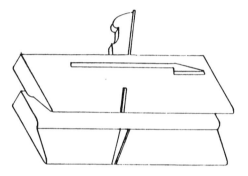

Fig.6:15—Pair of side rabbets and an iron

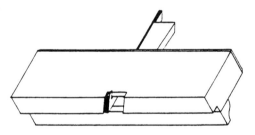

Fig.6:16—Side rabbet with L-shaped cutter

Continental Most of the above varieties of the rabbet are known on the Continent — in various national idioms of body style, but with the same business end — plus some variations of their own. The plane sometimes listed as FRENCH COACHMAKER'S RABBET in English or American auction catalogs is called the GUILLAUME À QUEUE, or tailed rabbet, in France (Fig.6:17). It has a particularly graceful stock, rising in front and rear for handgrip, the rear in a breaking wave shape. Guillaume (which also means William) is the French for rabbet plane, although they do not restrict the name to planes with the

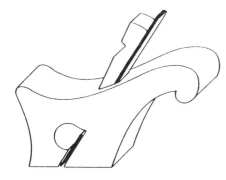

Fig.6:17—French coachmaker's rabbet

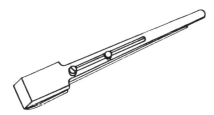

Fig.6:18—Cutter fitted with a cap iron

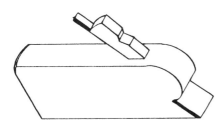

Fig.6:19—Stop rabbet or chisel plane

rabbet type throat as we do. The German is SIMSHOBEL, the Dutch BOOR-SCHAAF. A DOPPELSIMSHOBEL has its cutter fitted with a cap iron, attached with a screw and a peg (Fig.6:18).

Variants of the rabbets have received names in France and Germany which have no formal equivalents in English. They distinguish between planes used for roughing the rabbet (SCHÜRF-SIMSHOBEL, GUILLAUME À ÉBAUCHER) and for finishing it (SCHLICHT-SIMSHOBEL, GUILLAUME À RECULER). Roubo called a shorter rabbet with 60° pitch a "standing rabbet" — GUILLAUME DEBOUT. The Germans call this a "steep" rabbet — STEILSIMSHOBEL. An easily confused name is GUILLAUME DE BOUT (end rabbet) with no sole in front of the blade - this is imported from Germany and sold here as a STOP RABBET or CHISEL plane (Fig.6:19). Roubo describes still another type of rabbet used for final fitting — the GUILLAUME À ADOUCIR or easing rabbet. It has rounded sole edges and the iron, set square, is sharpened on both sides as well as the bottom. This gives a clean inner corner to the cut.

The French side rabbet (GUILLAUME DE CÔTÉ) is found in a shape like the English, and also in another version. The iron is mounted at a sharp angle to the side of the stock and with a slight backward slant (Fig.6:20). The lower side of the stock is slightly angled and plated with iron, and the cutting edge protrudes through a slot in this. A similar design was used by Stanley in its metal side rabbets (Nos. 79, 98, and 99). The GUILLAUME À DEUX FERS (rabbet with two irons) has two throats arrayed as come-and-go. It is steel-soled and was used by pianomakers for planing ivory. The DENTS DE BOUVET is a shoulder rabbet with sole narrowed to leave an integral depth stop on either side.

Japanese Far eastern rabbets may take shapes quite similar to modern western ones, or may be seen in shapes reminiscent of ancient Continental planes. The Chinese form resembling our rabbet is usually of rosewood or other dense wood, and often has a curved top to the stock, dropping at toe and heel. It is pushed. A similar form is seen in Japan (they call it a comb-shaped rabbet) but with the throat near the heel. It is grasped with one hand at mid-body and pulled. More often, the Japanese rabbet (SHAKURI-KANNA) has a flat top with a concave hollow at the top of the heel where the iron and wedge emerge. The iron is laminated, and is sometimes used with a chip breaker. The bed angle is lower than in a Western rabbet (42-45°) and the wedge is sometimes placed behind the iron. It is interesting to note that the name mizotsuki-kanna is still in use, a remnant of its use as a push plane when first introduced (mizo-kanna is the general name for a grooving plane, tsuki means push).

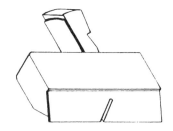

Fig.6:20—French side rabbet

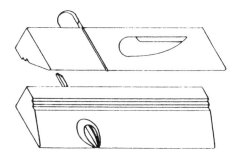

Fig.6:21—Japanese side rabbet

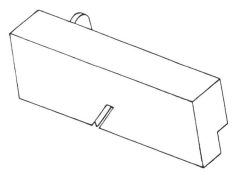

Fig.6:22—Japanese side rabbet

The Japanese side rabbet (WAKI-TORI-KANNA) in one form uses a Japanese marking knife as the iron (seen lying on the stock in Fig.6:21), wedged into a thin stock with edge exposed on its side. For use in trimming sliding dovetails, the bottom of the stock is shaped in an acute V (HIFUKURA-KANNA; Fig.6:21). Another form is like a badger plane of large skew, but with the top side of the stock cut away in a rabbet (Fig.6:22). It is used with this narrowed side inserted into the groove, to plane its side. A third type (NIMAI-WAKITORI-KANNA) functions like the French form described above.

FILLETSTERS

The characteristic round escapement of the rabbet and dado planes was not developed for decoration, but in answer to a need. In other side escapement planes, the shank of the iron is on one side, and the wedge lies against one cheek of the throat. The lower edge of the wedge is tapered on its free side and serves to direct the shavings toward the side vent. In the rabbet and dado, the centrally located shank and wedge are less effective at guiding the shavings, and a normal molding plane throat would tend to choke.

In rabbeting planes that are fitted with an integral fence, the iron no longer extends from side to side of the sole and no longer requires the central shank. As in other forming planes, the side mounting of shank and wedge means that a normal straight-edged throat will serve, and as the straight-edged throat is easier to make, the round rabbet escapement is usually dispensed with. Such planes are no longer called rabbet planes, although they still cut rabbets. They are FILLETSTERS or, in England, Fillisters. This has led to some confusion in naming. Some planes with integral fences used to make heavy cuts — as in half-lapping boards — are still subject to choking and are fitted with the round escapement. Chapin (1874) offered to cut a rabbet throat in his No. 151 moving filletster for an additional twenty-five cents.

There is a tendency to call any plane with a curved throat a rabbet, whether fenced or not. This is not incorrect, as it *is* used to cut rabbets. However here the name filletster will be used for any rabbeting plane with an integral fence, no matter what the throat shape. This seems to be consistent with the distinction made in France and Germany. They are listed in the following sections.

STANDING FILLETSTER

English and American   The STANDING FILLETSTER is a forming plane with a flat sole and an integral fence (Fig.6:23). The form is an old one; an example is pictured in a fifteenth century Italian intarsia. The simple form without integral depth stop (as opposed to the half-lap, below) is almost unknown in the U.S. One made in 1770 is in the Dominy collection, and inventories of that era often list filletsters (under various imaginative spellings) at values suggesting that the simple, not the moving, filletster was meant. They are not found in American catalogs — "filletster" invariably meant the moving type. They do appear in English listings from the Gabriel inventories (England,

1791-93) to the Marples catalog (England, 1909), but are not common even in England.

If fitted with an integral depth stop, the standing filletster is useful for cutting half-lap joints or simple sash bars (another English name is GREENHOUSE RABBET, from the latter use). If sized to cut a square rabbet (Fig.6:23 left) it is called a HALVING or HALF-LAP plane in the U.S., and as such is listed in many catalogs — with plating and handles as options. Nonetheless, it is not a common plane. One made by Cesar Chelor (Massachusetts, 1753-84) survives. Even rarer is a form which places the depth stop between the fence and the blade. This is used on the edge of the board, and the rabbet is cut on the far side (Fig.6:24). This type has been seen with the maker's mark Gardner & Murdoch (Massachusetts, 1825-42).

Simple standing filletsters are sometimes seen with nickers, fitting them for cross-grain rabbeting. Depth stops in the form of a brass fitting attached to the side of the stock by means of a screw (brass side stop) are occasionally seen, but may be later additions.

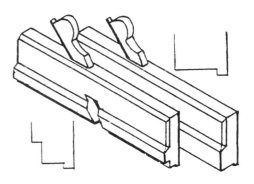

Fig.6:23—Standing filletsters

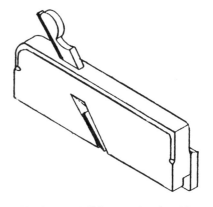

Fig.6:24—Half-lap, cutting far side

Continental   These planes were apparently more popular in France, where they are called FEUILLERETS. Both straight and round escapements were made, and nickers and full-length metal depth stops were listed as options. They were made in right- and left-handed pairs, as well as with left- and right-hand throats combined in one stock. The latter were listed by Féron as made with open throats, one of the few commercially made planes so made. The balanced thrust of the two wedges removed the threat of warping. Both of the above half-lap forms (parement and contre-parement in French) were made.

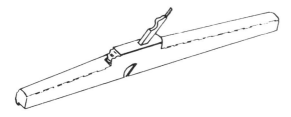

Fig.6:25—Continental long filletster

The German standing filletster (FALZHOBEL) was available commercially in sizes of cut from 6 to 27 mm. (¼ to 1 inch). Long filletsters (53 cm., 21 in.) were listed as house carpenter's tools.

Some Continental catalogs offered a choice of right- or left-side escapement, with those on the left cutting through the fence. As described below for the moving filletster, the shaving cut by a skew blade (right side leading) must change direction to leave through an escapement on the right. This apparently caused more problems with choking, and called for this modification.

The long, slender planes shown in Fig.6:25 were apparently quite common throughout the Continent, from the frequency with which they appear. Among other names, they were called JOIGNEUX in French or FLUCHTHOBEL in German. The shape has won them the nickname of "couleuvre", or grass snake, in the French Alps. These are of eighteenth century or earlier appearance, often with carved decorations and early flat- iron or Roman handles, and highly individualistic in style. The style is not necessarily a guarantee of age, as the tradition may have been honored by later user-makers, but they are attractive and sought after. With integral fence (frequently on the right), no depth stop, and circular escapement, they are usually called "CONTINENTAL RABBETS" in current English-language listings. Lengths to 43 in. (110 cm.) are found, and the wood is often evergreen oak or other prized species.

Both left-hand and right-hand models are seen, as well as both in one stock — in this case two throats facing each other on the same side of the fence, or facing in the same direction on opposite sides. Double filletsters are also found with two throats facing in opposite directions in the same stock, on opposite sides of the fence. As the sides are identical, the same tool is obtained by turning it end for end — presumably to have a roughing and a finish blade.

MOVING FILLETSTER

English and American   The MOVING FILLETSTER (Fig.6:26), or just filletster in the U.S., was developed in the eighteenth century. It is a wide side escapement plane with a skew blade usually 1¼ in. (32 mm.) wide or wider.

101

The stock has a step cut in both sides to form a handhold. The throat is cut through only about two-thirds of the stock, leaving room on the left side of the sole to attach a movable fence. The fence is a rectangular billet of wood about ½ in. (12 mm.) thick, screwed to the sole with two, or less often three, wood screws. The screws pass through slots in the fence, nor-mally recessed and lined with brass.

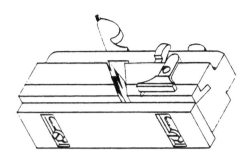

Fig.6:26—Moving filletster

These permit the fence to be fixed at any position, from covering nearly the full width of the blade to exposing almost all. The tool is also called a SIDE-FILLET or SIDE-FILLETSTER.

In the wedge-arm (Fig.6:27) or screw-arm filletster the fence is carried on arms instead of being screwed to the sole. As the widening of the sole to carry the fence is no longer needed, the left step is rarely used and the stock is narrower. The fence itself is of the same thickness as in the sole-mounted version, but is wider to enable it to carry the arm shoulders. These are rather rare — almost un-known in England.

Moving filletsters were popu-lar and are fairly common, usually found with nicker, boxing, and a depth stop — although these were all options in catalogs. An-other option, a handle, was ap-parently less popular. Greenfield (Massachusetts, 1872) listed no less than twenty-five models,

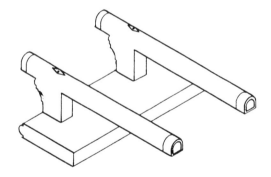

Fig.6:27—Filletster wedge-arm fence

with another fourteen of the screw-arm or wedge-arm type. One could buy almost eighteen of the basic models for the price of the top-of-the-line handled, ebony, ivory trimmed, screw-arm beauty.

A rabbet-type escapement was offered as an option by some makers. Some owners apparently regretted not getting this option, as filletster throats are often found widened unprofessionally. Mathieson (Scotland, 1899 catalog) offered a "skew rabate with shifting fence" in the 1½ in. (38 mm.) size as well as "moving or fore filletster" planes. User modified rabbets fitted with arms and fences are occasionally found, and they were listed by Arrowmammett in their 1859 catalog. John Taber (Massachusetts, 1820-1872) made a convertible rabbet-filletster with a screwed-on side piece (cut away to clear the rabbet escapement) bearing the filletster fence.

There appears to have been a difference of opinion as to the proper direction in which to skew the iron in moving filletsters. The majority have the leading corner of the cutting edge on the right, but many skew in the opposite direction (square setting is even less common). With the right edge leading, the thrust of the wood on the blade tends to hold the plane against the work and reduces the need for side pressure by the user. The disadvantage is that this skew direction tends to push the shaving to the left away from the rabbet cut. The shaving must change direction before escaping on the right side of the stock, which increases risk of choking. There is also the possibility that an outward thrust may splinter the outer edge of the rabbet. The principal advantage of skewing — apparent increased keenness — (covered in Appendix 1) holds for either direction.

The arm filletster is not to be confused with the SASH FILLETSTER, which will be treated later with the sash planes. Suffice it to say here that the sash filletster is designed to cut a rabbet on the far side of the workpiece — the side away from the fence. The nicker and depth stop are therefore on the fence side of the stock, rather than the opposite side. Another tell-tale difference between the two is the fact that the fence of a sash filletster need not fit under the sole, and normally does not. A third type, the combined SASH AND MOVING filletster tries to serve both purposes by providing an arm filletster with depth stops and nickers on both sides of the stock, and longer arms. Since the skew requirements are opposed, at least one of the functions will please the proponents of either skew direction. The majority put the leading edge on the right.

Continental   The French FEUILLERET D'EBENISTE resembles the moving filletster in the French idiom. Some are made with a full side stop, which necessitates changing the escapement to the left side of the body. A steel or brass fence (Fig.6:28) was usually used in the German moving filletster (STELL-FALZHOBEL), for both sole and side fences. A screw arm version (Fig.6:29) has an L-shaped wooden fence sliding on arms fixed in the stock. The nicker is

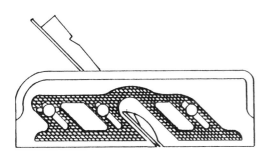

Fig.6:28—Continental full side stop fence

wider than that on the English version, V-tipped and slotted to be held by a wingnut.

Weiss (Austria, 1909) lists two forms not known in England or America. A filletster doubly curved (compass and radius) is called BETTEN-FALZHOBEL, geschweift. A three-arm fenced, twin bench-throated plane with a stepped sole named FUG-und FALZHOBEL uses the left blade to smooth and straighten (joint) the plank, the right one to sink the rabbet. It has, in addition to the moving fence, a second fence to ride the right side of the plank. This may be either an integral fence for a fixed width of the rabbet, or an adjustable fence for varying its width.

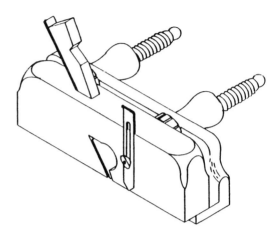

Fig.6:29—German screw arm moving filletster

Japanese   The GYOGITSUKI-KANNA has the shape of their smooth plane, with added nicker and filletster fence.

Chapter 7

GROOVING PLANES

THE PLOW

In the last chapter we covered the cutting away of a square rabbet on the edge of a board. If a groove is required in a piece of wood, along the grain and away from the edge of the board, a rabbet plane will serve, but a different tool is preferred — especially if the groove is to be deeper than wide. Today such cuts are made with a bench saw, a router, or a shaper. Before the development of these power tools, this task was usually accomplished with a plow (Fig.7:1). Among its many uses were grooving stiles and rails to take panels, grooving sides to take drawer bottoms, and hogging away wood to rough out a large molding profile. It was, and is still, a most versatile tool.

It is also, however, a rather ungainly tool to use, store, or transport. Many of its functions are equally well served by such specialized tools as match groove, drawer bottom, or other fixed grooving planes, to be discussed later in this chapter. The plow, though, does have the ability to perform a variety of tasks because of its adjustable fence and depth stop and the range of plane iron widths it can accommodate.

Moreover, the plow has a strange power of attraction. More effort has been devoted to its modification than to most other hand tools. It was available in a bewildering variety of models, in most manufacturers' catalogs. One had a wide choice of woods, of types of fence mounting and depth stop, of styles with or without handle, and quality grades from first through fourth rate. The Greenfield 1872 catalog offered 59 variations of the plow, with the price of the most expensive 38 times that of a simple smooth plane and more than seven and a half times that of the cheapest plow. Their top of the line plow was by far the most expensive of their planes.

Ebony, rosewood, ivory, brass and even silver were used to create objects of beauty that were a status symbol for the successful joiner or cabinetmaker. These were favorite presentation pieces. A special silver-mounted rosewood model with ivory gears driving a screw-arm adjustment and depth stop was presented by the Ohio Tool Co. to one of its foremen in 1857, and survives to be admired today. The magic remains. An ornate plow is the centerpiece of many collections, and an unusual plow often brings the highest price of any tool at an auction.

The standard English or American wooden PLOW, Fig.7:1 (often called a panel plow or a grooving plow in the catalogs, or a FLIT plow in Scotland) consists of a body or stock which holds (by means of a wedge) an iron (bit, blade, cutter), its upper part usually ⅝ in. (16 mm.) wide. The plow iron (Fig.7:2) is strongly tapered in thickness from about ¼ in. (6 mm.) at bottom to less than ⅛ in. (3 mm.) at the top of an 8 in. (20 cm.) length. It normally has a horizontal extension near the top (sometimes called a sneck), to aid in setting.

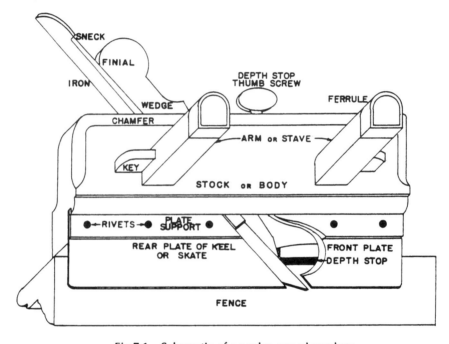

Fig.7:1—Schematic of a wedge-arm plow plane

The plow may be equipped with a graduated set of such irons, the lower ends of which are reduced in width by various amounts to allow cutting grooves of different width. A set usually consists of eight irons, varying from ⅛ to ⅝ in. (3 - 16 mm.). The rear of the cutting end is V-grooved longitudinally.

To support the narrowest iron, while still maintaining sufficient strength to support the widest, is too much to ask of wood. This task is

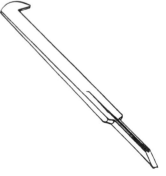

Fig.7:2—Plow iron

106

performed by the rear member of a pair of metal plates (variously called the sole, skate or keel), that are set into a common groove in the bottom of the stock. The front edge of the rear plate is sloped at the bed angle and is beveled to accept the groove at the rear of the cutting end of the iron. This prevents lateral movement of the cutter in use. The front plate of the skate, ahead of the cutter, presses on the wood in front of the cut and helps to prevent tearing (not as well as a full-width mouth would, but smoothness of cut is less important at the bottom of a groove). The rear edge of the front plate is curved away from the cutter to provide clearance for the shavings. Its front edge is sometimes curved upward (like an old-fashioned ice skate blade) to avoid digging in, and unsurprisingly this is called a skate front.

The plow is kept on course by means of a fence, supported on the left side of the stock and projecting about ½ in. (13 mm.) below the skate. The fence rides on the left side of the board being plowed (English or American left-handed plows are very rare). The fence must be set parallel to the skate within the tolerance of the width of the groove being cut, if the skate is not to rub the groove sides. Means of achieving this have kept many inventors busy, as will be seen. Almost invariably a depth stop is provided to ensure uniform groove depth.

DEVELOPMENT OF THE PLOW

Wood absorbs and releases water as humidity changes; coatings can slow but not prevent this. With change in moisture content, the wood expands or contracts across its grain, but it changes very little along the grain. It will invariably crack if two pieces are firmly joined cross grain to long grain for large distances. A so-called six-board chest survives only if some movement is permitted — in the simplest case by nailing instead of gluing.

The usual method of allowing for this movement is frame-and-panel construction. A wide wooden panel is thinned at its edges and held by inserting these into grooves in the inner edges of uprights and cross-pieces of a rectangular frame, as shown in Fig.4:11. The fit is such that room is allowed, in the depth of the grooves, for the panel to expand and contract.

The canopic shrine and other pieces from the tomb of Tutankhamen show that the Egyptians used this type of construction, but no planes of any kind have survived from their era. It is not impossible to make the required grooves in the frame with a chisel, but it must have occurred to many who did so that a better method was needed. Although much frame-and-panel construction preceded the first known plow, we are left to speculate on the development of tools used to perform this task.

Early wooden planes that cut ⅛ in. (3 mm.) grooves are occasionally found. Since these are fragile, a stronger construction with a metal insert to back the cutter would be an obvious step. Trying to keep a narrow grooving plane on track by utilizing a temporary fence attached to the work must have provided strong incentive to find a better way, and the extension of the stock to form a fixed fence may have been an early answer. If you then configure the sole to provide an integral depth stop, you have a fixed grooving plane or FIXED PLOW — these survive to this day as drawer bottom and match groove planes, discussed later in this chapter. Roman irons in the shape of modern plow irons have survived, so that at least fixed plows must have been used by them.

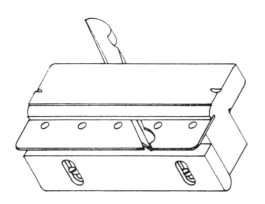

Fig.7:3—Grooving plane with adjustable fence

Making an assortment of fixed plows for different jobs must have suggested that a moveable fence would be useful. Add a moveable fence screwed to the bottom of the stock and we are at the next stage, of adjustable grooving planes. A GROOVING PLANE WITH ADJUSTABLE FENCE (Fig.7:3) was made by Mathieson (Scotland) into the twentieth century.

Two further improvements were required to achieve the plow as we know it. The filletster fence was replaced by a fence mounted on arms or staves (Fig.7:4), and provision was made for the plow to accept blades of different cutting widths. The UNIVERSAL PLOW, as Peter Nicholson called it in 1823, removed the need for separate tools for each groove width. This became the standard in England and the U.S.,

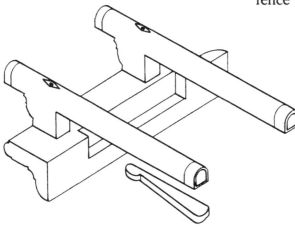

Fig.7:4—Wedge arm plow fence and its key (arm wedge)

108

although some fixed width tools are still used elsewhere.

Greber (1956) illustrates plows from the collection of the Elector of Saxony in the sixteenth century that clearly show a long prior period of development. In this group are the progenitors of the nineteenth century patented three-arm plows and the Yankee plow, as well as prototypes of the present Continental plow. Félibien (1676) illustrates a plane with square arms fixed to the stock. Moxon (1703) copied Félibien's plate (it was converted to a mirror image in reproduction) and (as Goodman noted) he then proceeded to describe a completely different plow in his text, presumably the English plow of the late seventeenth century. His description is repeated below (omitting reference to the non-existent figure).

"The Plow is a narrow Rabbet-plane, with some Additions to it: viz. two square Staves (yet some of them have the upper edges of them rounded off for the better compliance with the Hand). These Staves are set stiff through two square Mortesses in the Stock. They are about seven or eight Inches long and stand straight and square on the farther side of the Stock; and these two Staves have shoulders on the hither side of the Stock, reaching down to the wooden sole of the Plane (for there is also an Iron sole belonging to the Plow). To the bottom of these two shoulders is, Rivitted with Iron Rivets, a Fence (as Workmen call it) which comes close under the Wooden sole, and its depth reaches below the Iron sole about half an Inch: Because the Iron of the Plow is very narrow, and the sides of it toward the bottom are not to be inclosed in the Stock; therefore upon the Stock is let in, and strongly nailed, an Iron Plate of the thickness of the Plow-Iron, for Wood of that breadth will not be strong enough to endure the force the lower end of the Plow-Iron is put to: This Iron-Plate is almost of the same thickness that the breadth of a Plow-Iron is. Joyners have several Plows, for several widths of Grooves.

"The Office of the Plow is, to plow a narrow square Groove on the edge of a Board; which is thus perform'd. The Board is set on edge with one end in the Bench-screw, and its other edge upon a Pin, or Pins, put into a Hole, or Holes in the Leg, or Legs of the Bench, such an Hole, or Holes, as will, most conveniently for height, fit the breadth of the Board: then the Fence of the Plow is set to that Distance off the Iron-Plate of the Plow, that you intend the Groove shall lie off the edge of the Board: As if you would have the Groove lie half an Inch off the board, then the two staves must, with the Mallet, be knocked through the Mortesses in the Stock, til the Fence stands half an Inch off the Iron-Plate; and if the Staves are fitted stiff enough in the Mortess of the Stock, it will keep at that Distance whilst you Plow the Groove: For the Fence (lying lower than the Iron of the Plane) when you set the Iron of the Plow upon the edge of the Board, will lie flat against the farther edge [?] of the Board, and so keep the Iron of the Plow all the length of the Board at the same Distance, from the edge of the Board that the Iron of the Plow hath from the Fence. Therefore your Plow being thus fitted, plow the Groove as you work with other Planes, only as you laid hold of the Stock of other Planes when you use them, now you must lay hold of the two staves and their shoulders [?], and to thrust your Plow forward, til your Groove be made to your depth.

"If the Staves go not stiff enough in the Mortess of the Stock, you must stiffen them, by knocking a little wooden Wedge between the Staves and their Mortesses."

There are two confusing points in Moxon's description (marked by question marks above). He describes the fence as on the "hither" side of the stock. If the fence rests against the "farther" side of the board as he says, the tool would have to be pulled, yet you "thrust the Plow forward". Either Moxon misspoke or the ambiguous "hither" and "farther" mislead us. Usage today calls the "left" side of the plane the one on the user's left as he uses it (that is, facing the heel of the plane). The fence is on the left of the plow, and rides on the left edge of the work.

The English plow may be reassembled with the fence on the right and used left-handed, but it is apparent that this was not intended. The fence normally projects forward of the stock for surer starting guidance, and this is no longer true (in most cases) if it is reversed.

The second point concerns the grip. In The Netherlands the arms are fixed permanently to the stock and project on the left (the fence slides on the arms). These often continue through and project on the right side of the stock as well, and the one in the rear provides a grip for the right hand. Moxon's description implies that this grip carried over in the English planes of his day (or was it that his source was Dutch). English and American plow arms, fixed to the fence and sliding in the stock, could be shifted under the thrust of the right hand. It is better practice (and usual) to thrust with the right hand against the rear of the stock, with fingers around the arms or nuts only as convenient for sure grip. The left hand provides no forward thrust, but only light pressure to keep the fence against the work. It may grip the fence, shoulder, arm, stock, or any combination if care is used not to shift the setting.

Moxon describes friction fit arms. These are not the easiest to adjust. They are subject to variations in tightness, depending on the season (perhaps not as much in the England of that period as in our era of central heat) and would tend to loosen with wear. Friction-fit plows survive made by Madox (England, 1748-75) and Frogatt (England, 1765-90) among other makers. Although they continued to be made in England until about 1770, they are relatively rare as many were post-fitted with wedges. They were also produced in America during the late 18th and early 19th centuries by such planemakers as Tho. Napier (Pennsylvania), Tho. Grant (New York), and Eastburn (New Jersey).

An interesting variant on the friction-fit arm was observed by Robert Graham (1983) in a Tho. Grant plow (New York, late 18th century). The spacing of the arm mountings on the fence was 1/16 of an inch (1.6 mm.) larger than that of the arm mortises in the stock. This slight difference means that as one arm is hammered forward, the fence skews slightly and relieves the side pressure of the stock mortises on the arms — permitting easier movement. With one arm set at the desired distance, as the other is moved to make the fence parallel, the outward pressure of the fence on the arms tends to wedge the arms in the stock and provides a firmer setting. This particular plow had been modified for locking keys, but the indifferent workmanship testified that these were post-fitted (an indication that even this clever variation in the original plow was not long-lasting). The plow resembled those of Robert Wooding, but was made of American beech and it had no depth stop. Other Grant plows using this type of friction-fit arms have been found, as has one by Tho. Napier.

Moxon does not describe a depth stop, and some early American plows do without. The earliest surviving maker-marked English plow, by Robert Wooding (England, 1710-28) is equipped with one, and uses wedges (keys) to fix the fence arms.

THE WEDGE-ARM PLOW

The English WEDGE-ARM plough (to use their spelling) is commonly found with a stock a little over 7 in. (18 cm.) long, although longer ones are known. They are usually about 2.5 in. (64 mm.) high and 1.5 in. (38 mm.) wide (Fig.7:1). The iron is usually bedded at 50°, though sometimes 45°. The fence (Fig.7:4) is carried on arms square on bottom and rounded on top, fitting through holes of the same shape in the stock. They slide freely, and are fixed by a pair of wooden wedges, called KEYS, which slide in tapered horizontal mortises meeting the outer side (occasionally the inner) of the arm holes. The keys are 1/4 in. (6 mm.) or less thick and tighten against the arms by moving toward the fence. Enlargements on their narrow end keep the keys from being removed until the arms are withdrawn.

The ends of the arms are often protected with brass caps or ferrules. The reason for this is evident from the frayed condition of many of the uncapped arm ends, the result of being repeatedly struck to adjust the arms. The shoulders of the arms are downward projections to which the fence is attached. Their outside face is usually decoratively molded. The fence, too, is decorated with deep molding on the outer side and the front, while top and rear are flat (a portion of the inner edge of the top is cut away to provide clearance for the depth stop). These moldings tend to be distinctive to a given maker at a given time. The upper surface of the fence is connected to the arms through their shoulders. This is normally accomplished by machine screws that pass through the fence and shoulder and are threaded into brass pads, often diamond-shaped, on the top of the arms. (The earliest were attached by riveting.)

Five methods of attachment of the metal sole to the stock were studied by Richard Knight (1983) as providing clues as to their chronology. These, listed in their approximate chronological order, are:

i	-Plates riveted to a simple rabbet in the stock.
ii	-As above, inserted into a groove at the rabbet angle.
iii	-Upper edge of the plate forged thicker than the bottom.
iv	-Brass strip riveted with top of plate.
v	-Iron strip brazed to top of plate.

The plows of B. Frogatt (England, 1765-90) include examples of types ii, iii, and iv. The last two persisted through the 19th century, by which time the plates were attached with wood screws rather than riveted.

THE YANKEE PLOW

Early New England planemakers followed rather closely the English designs, but incorporated their own variations (Fig.7:5). They used yellow birch instead of English beech; had longer stocks (9¾ - 10 in. vs. 7¼ - 8 in.; 25 vs. 20 cm.); chamfering of the top front of the wedge mortise; square fence arms vs. rounded tops; and the front of the fence was flat and did not extend beyond the front of the stock as it did on the English style plow. The Yankee plows were also marked by the inletting of the wedge shoulders into dados in the fence (as in Figs.7:5 and 7:6). Other early plows had arms fixed to the flat top of the fence by iron rivets, which permitted some degree of rotation around the attachment and facilitated setting. The dados on the Yankee plow's fence effectively prevented this rotation, presumably to ensure that the fence remained parallel to the skate. What it accomplished more effectively was to make setting the fence more difficult, and incidentally ruled out the "Grant" type of adjustment described above. It is therefore not surprising that friction-fit plows are not found with this feature.

Another distinguishing feature of the "Yankee Plow" (Robert Graham, 1978, 1982) is its use of wooden thumbscrews threaded through the stock to

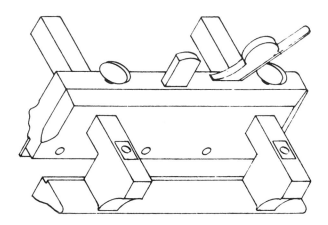

Fig.7:5—18th century Yankee plow

lock the fence. These first appeared on plows by Francis Nicholson (Massachusetts, 1728-53). The longer bodies of his plows allowed enough room for installation of the thumbscrew behind the blade (which was not the case for contemporaneous English plows). There appears to have been a period of experimentation. Two of his plows are known with both methods of locking: arm wedges (keys) and thumbscrews. In one of these the top front of the body had been damaged by hammer blows in setting the blade, in a manner that could not have occurred after the thumbscrews were installed. There is little doubt that his plow, at least, was made originally with key (or arm wedge) fixing and was later converted to the thumbscrew type. Nicholson's work appears to favor the latter

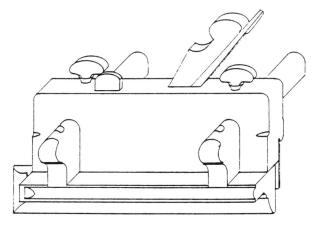

Fig.7:6—Early 19th century Yankee plow

style, although one of his sash filletsters and one his son's (John Nicholson) plows are known with arm keys.

No English plows are known which use the rigid, dado-mounted arm attachment and few use thumbscrews. (One in my collection appears to have been post-fitted with thumbscrews, the rearmost having been installed at an angle for lack of room).

The Yankee Plow design was modified over the years. The body length decreased to about 8 in. (20 cm.), beech replaced birch, the fence acquired the English molded-front form. The arms were changed from square section to the English rounded-top style, and in some cases these round tops were protected against marring by shaped pads concealed under the thumbscrews. The dado shoulder mounting and the thumbscrews were used until the middle of the 19th century by makers such as E. Smith (Massachusetts) and the Copelands (Massachusetts and Connecticut), Fig.7:6, but most makers had by that time accepted the English wedge-arm style. There is, of course, no formal definition of what a "Yankee Plow" is, but most collectors are willing to accept two out of the three criteria of length, dado arm mounting, and thumbscrew fixing as sufficient reason for applying the name.

PLOWS WITH ARMS FIXED TO THE STOCK

Almost all British and American plows have their arms fixed to the fence and moving through the stock. Continental planes, as seen below, use the opposite, with the arms fixed to the body and moving through the fence. There are exceptions, however, and an occasional plow is seen that would be taken for one made in France were it not for British markings. (See Iohn Green plow in the next section under "The Screw-Arm Plow".) In addition, a few are known with arms fixed to the stock but of completely different appearance, the fence quite similar to a conventional English fence. Most of these are bridle plows, to be covered later in this chapter. Alex Mathieson and Sons (Scotland, 1899-1966) patented and made an attractive version using brass tubes fixed to the stock as the arms. These passed through holes in brass fixtures attached to the fence. The upper sides of the tubes were slotted to allow passage of thumbscrews, held in the fixtures, which screws were threaded into captive nuts inside the tubes. Tightening these thumbscrews forced the internal nuts against the tubes, and fixed the position of the fence.

Earlier attempts were made by American planemakers, with less success. Two examples of a design made by Butler (Pennsylvania, -1791-1835) have survived, one in the Mercer Museum of Bucks County, Doylestown, PA. (Fig.7:7). Wooden arms fixed to the stock have rounded bottoms which slide in grooves in a low fence, and under brass fittings screwed to it. Brass thumbscrews threaded through these fittings bear on the arms and fix them. No name has been found for plows of this type: perhaps SLIDING-FENCE PLOW will serve. A unique plane of this type was made completely of whalebone, except for a brass skate and arms of brass rods fixed to the stock and passing through brass fittings on the fence. An alternate plan patented by Chapin and Rust is covered later under "Three-arm Plows".

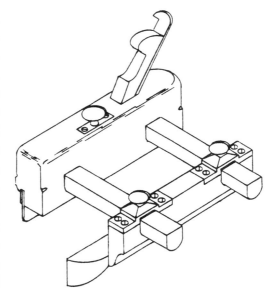

Fig.7:7—Sliding-fence plow

The BRIDLE PLOW (bridge plow, stirrup plow) similarly has arms fixed to the stock which pass over shaped troughs on the fence. Both are clamped to these simultaneously by a wooden or metal bar, the bridle, bearing on the top of both arms and tightened by a central screw. An example made by McGlashan (Scotland, 1837-50) is shown in Fig.7:8. Alex Mathieson & Sons (Scotland, 1899-1966) made a variety of these, including one with brass V-shaped bottoms to the arms to further promote parallelism. Griffiths (England, -1811-1900) made one with a wooden bridle. American bridle plows are rarer. One made by A. Cumings (Massachusetts, -1844-54) was reported by Paul Kebabian (1982) as having V-bottom rosewood arms pegged into holes in the stock, and fixed to the fence by a wooden bridle as in the Griffiths plow. This plane had as another unusual feature a round knob affixed to the right rear side of the stock to serve as grip (much like Fig.7:8). This type is occasionally seen in British bridle plows but seldom in American. Another, a handled plow with a cast iron bridle

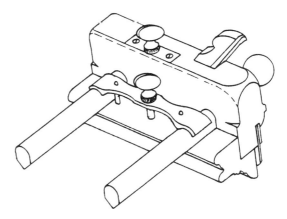

Fig.7:8—Bridle plow

115

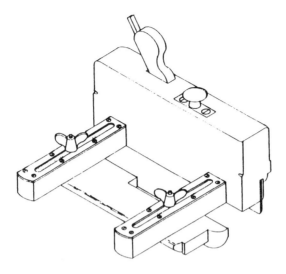

Fig.7:9—Left-handed plow

tightened by two wing nuts and apparently of American make was reported by Alan Bates (1988).

The only example known to me of a left-handed plow by a Western maker is shown in Fig.7:9. Made by Moseley & Son (England, 1878-1914), it uses a variation of the sliding-fence suspension. Slotted arms are attached to the body, and the fence is secured to these by means of studs passing through the slots and tightened by wing-nuts.

THE SCREW-ARM PLOW

The most common form of screw-arm plow in Great Britain and America has a stock similar to that of the wedge-arm but with unthreaded circular holes in place of the arm mortises. The arms are shouldered as before, but are now cylindrical and threaded (threads were not standardized, and it sometimes seems as if every plane-maker had his own size screw-box). Except for the round, threaded arms, the fence assembly is the same as in the wedge-arm plow. Each arm is fitted with a threaded wooden lock-nut (sometimes called a washer), then inserted through the holes in the stock. Each has a threaded knob (usually elaborately turned) on the other side which serves to tighten the fence at the distance set by the lock-nuts.

Though handles are rarely seen on wedge-arm plows, they are fairly common on the screw-arm type. They are closed totes of the type shown in Fig.7:10, usually made integrally with the stock.

Although screw-arm plows were known in Germany in the 16th century, there is no evidence of their general use in England or America until nearly 1800. There are early York (England) plows (such as those by Iohn Green, -1774-1807) which show similarities to the Continental type as shown in Fig.7:23 (full-height fence with arms sliding through and fastened with lock-nuts) and having other characteristics which suggest that they date to the

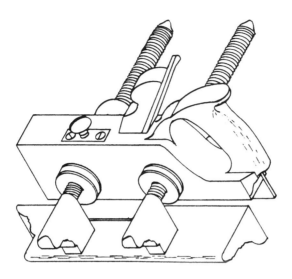

Fig.7:10—Handled screw-arm plow

last decade or so of the 18th century (Richard Knight, 1983). The earliest American screw-arm to surface is one by Thomas Napier, (Pennsylvania, 1774-1811). The sudden popularity of the screw-arm type in the English-speaking world in the first quarter of the 19th century, after it had ignored the Continental versions for over a century, is a mystery. The screw-arm was sometimes called the French Plow in England, and Holtzapffel called it a German plow — both acknowledging that the idea was imported. The scarcity of Continental-type fence mountings by English makers, however, suggests that their preference for fence-mounted arms may have delayed adaptation of the screw arms until someone realized that they could be fence mounted, the same as slide arms.

The Continental type of suspension did not completely vanish in America. Kebabian (1978) shows a plow by A.G. Moore (New York, 1853-61) with screw arms fixed to the body and sliding through holes in an upright attached to the fence.

SCREW-ARM VARIATIONS

An intermediate between the screw-arm and earlier plows is the very rare SCREW-ADJUSTED SLIDE-ARM (Fig.7:11) first noted in a plow by Gabriel (London 1770-1816) in the famous Seaton chest (Rochester Museum, Kent, England). This has a small-diameter screw concealed in a slot in the under side of the slide arms, which is turned by a brass thumb-piece at the end of each arm. It engages a nut buried in the stock. Presumably, by turning each

117

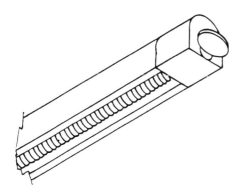

Fig.7:11—Screw-adjusted slide arm

screw the same amount, fence parallelism is maintained. Boxwood scales are sometimes mounted on the arms to aid in setting. Several other specimens by Gabriel have surfaced, as well as others by Stothert (-1785-1841), Griffiths (-1811-1949), and by Moseley & Son (1862-1910), all English.

Another unusual fence adjustment reported by Alan Ferguson (1984, on a sash filletster), has the racks of a rack-and-pinion movement mounted on the underside of the arms, driven by pinions on a common shaft within the stock. Made by Kimberly and Sons (England, 1883-1901), it bears patent number 2461 without a date, and the inventor C. CRISFORD.

A prototype made for Z.J. McMaster (New York, 1839-47) uses a single arm of large rectangular section, fixed to the fence. A metal drive screw, mounted parallel to the arm and threaded through the body, serves to adjust the fence position. The screw is turned, through a pair of gears, by an adjustment knob at the end of the arm (Smith 1992).

E.W. Carpenter (1838, U.S.Patent 594) used threaded arms through threaded holes in the stock. The arms are free to rotate in bearings in the fence but are restrained from lengthwise movement. A knob of conventional shape on the outer end of each arm serves to lock the setting. A variation with no known patents has been found in which the screw-arms terminate in gears, turned in unison by worms on a common shaft (Smith 1981).

Israel White (Pennsylvania, -1831-39) used a brass plate to retain the adjustment knob close to the stock in some of his plows, so that the fence was forced to move as the knob was turned (Moody 1981).

THREE-ARM PLOWS

These are frequently found on the Continent (see Fig.7:22) and will be described in that section, but American-made examples are found from Pennsylvania and other areas settled by Germans. Two outer screw arms are fixed in the stock and pass through holes in the fence. Knobs on the far side of the fence determine the setting, and this is locked by a third, central screw arm threaded through the fence and exerting pressure on the stock.

Israel White (Pennsylvania) received U.S.Patent No.7951X (9 Jan.1834) for a plow (Fig.7:12) whose fence is supported by two round arms and adjusted by a central screw-arm: all three arms pass through holes in the stock. The adjustment knob may be retained by a brass plate screwed to the stock, so that the fence was forced to move as the knob was turned. Fewer than a dozen of the White patent plows have surfaced. (They were numbered serially, with No. 123 the highest known; perhaps others may be found.) An Israel White patented combination filletster (unnumbered) using the same

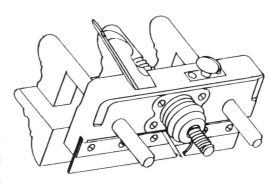

Fig.7:12—Israel White patent plow

suspension method also exists. Both Israel and his nephew, HENRY WHITE, made a variation of this with the central adjustment knob trapped in a fence bridge rather than in the stock (Fig.7:13). Because they mounted the three arms on a common wooden bridge, the appearance is somewhat like that of a bridle plow, but this plane uses a completely different method of adjustment.

Mockridge and Francis (New Jersey, 1835-68) produced similar plows, using a central steel screw and brass nut (as opposed to wood in the White version). Their neighbor Andruss (-1821-41-) also made very similar units. Another neighbor, I. King, used the same design with a brass thumbscrew added to lock the front arm (Hopfel, 1992). William Ward (New York, -1850-74) produced an attractive version with a steel adjusting screw suspended at both ends by brass brackets mounted between the arms. Schaffer (1988) reports a wedge-arm plow that had been modified to the Ward suspension, with the maker's mark W. Williams (New York, 1807-49). Planes such as this invite fascinating speculation and further research.

Fig.7:13—Later variation of the Israel White patent plow

119

The Solon Rust patent plow (31 March 1868, U.S.76051), produced by E.M. Chapin (Connecticut), supports the fence on two slotted, flanged metal guides fixed in the stock and passing through mortises in the fence (Fig.7:14). The fence slides upon these guides, and may be fixed in position by screws passing vertically through the fence, which tighten collars pressing on the under sides of the guides. A wooden screw is threaded through the upper

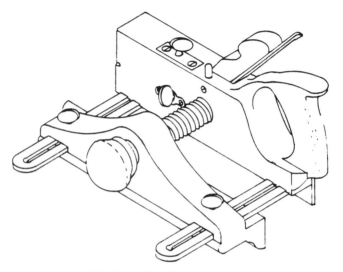

Fig.7:14—The Chapin-Rust plow

part of the fence and passes through a hole in the stock, in which it is free to rotate but is restrained from moving axially. A knob on the other end of the screw provides the means of adjusting the fence setting. This PATENT ADJUSTING PLOW appeared in the Chapin 1878 catalog in five models, all handled, essentially as described in the patent. These plows are also found with solid, rather than slotted guides. An "improved" version replaced the slotted guides with two small-diameter steel rods sliding in steel brackets on the fence, and another threaded steel fitting screwed to the fence top replaced the wooden bridge.

The 1882 Chapin catalog added the "patent V slide arm plow". The metal guides were replaced by wooden arms with V slots in their under side. These fitted V points on a metal bridge attached to the fence, and were secured by a metal bridle tightened by a central screw. This was available in three qualities, also handled. This may be described as a variant of the Alex. Mathieson bridle plow (see Fig.7:8) with an adjusting screw.

Although the patent makes much of the improvement of retaining the adjustment screw in the stock by gluing a wooden washer to its right end, many of the surviving planes use the older method of grooving the end of the screw and securing it in place by means of a vertical wooden pin fixed in the stock and riding in the groove (as seen in Fig.7:14). The patent version must have the adjustment screw mounted well forward to clear the wedge mortise, while the older method permits more central placement as the screw need not penetrate the stock.

One of the more successful versions of the three-arm plow was claimed in England (1887, G.B.2848) by William Kimberly. The fence is supported on metal rods sliding through the stock, and moved by a central screw threaded through the stock and secured to the fence. The screw is turned by a winged fitting on

Fig.7:15—Kimberly sash filletster

the right side of the stock. Unfortunately, this is detachable and not all of them have remained with the tool. Sash filletsters were made with the same suspension, (Fig.7:15) and neither form is particularly uncommon.

The culminating version, in the eyes of many collectors, is the CENTER-WHEEL PLOW (Fig.7:16) patented by Vanbuskirk (30 Nov. 1869, U.S. 97328).

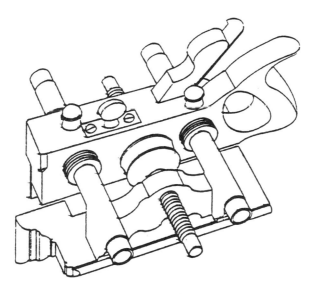

Fig.7:16—Center-wheel plow

In this the fence, supported on two cylindrical arms, is moved by a central screw, threaded left and right hand at opposite ends and rotated by a wheel located between the fence and body. The screw passes through threaded holes, one in the stock and one in a wooden bridge mounted on the fence which also carries the guide arms. Elaborate versions of this were sold by both the Sandusky Tool Co., with a brass center wheel; and the Ohio Tool Co., with a boxwood wheel. An ebony model with six ivory tips, Sandusky No.143, could have been purchased for twenty dollars in 1877. As only two have surfaced to date, their value is difficult to assess, but to judge by the prices at which the more numerous boxwood versions have changed hands recently, the original purchase would have been a good investment.

PLOWS FOR CIRCULAR WORK

The COACHMAKER'S PLOW (Fig.7:17) allows the plowing of grooves inside curved surfaces. The name indicates its origin, but it is used by other woodworkers as well. The skate is short and compassed (curved longitudinally), and the depth stop is curved to match.

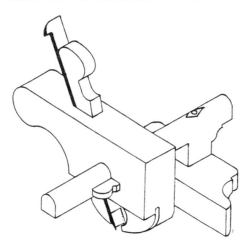

The cutting irons are ground in a special way to provide integral nickers. A rectangular groove is cut along the front edge of the iron for almost its full width. When the iron is beveled, the sides outside of the groove project beyond the cutting edge; they are sharpened as spurs (Fig.7:18).

The CIRCULAR PLOWS are versions with very short skates and equipped with interchangeable fences of different curvature, fences with detachable curved sections, or fences with steel faces bendable by means of screws at either end. These permit cutting curved grooves in flat surfaces with curved edges. One made by I. Sym (England, 1753-1803) is of the last type.

Fig.7:17—Coachmaker's plow

Fig.7:18—Cutting iron for a coachmaker's plow

The wooden fence is sharply curved. Attached to its middle is the center of a face of spring steel with hinges at either end, the free leaves of which are slotted and held to the ends of the wooden fence by cheese-head screws. This permits the steel to take any curvature between flat and the curve of the wood. In addition, the short skate is compassed for use as a coachmaker's plow or even for doubly curved work.

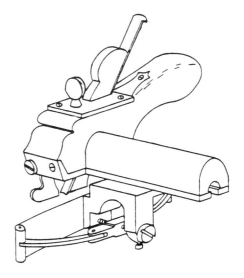

Fig.7:19—Falconer's plow

The extremely rare FALCONER'S PLOW (Fig.7:19) was named for its designer, who received an award for the design in 1846. It has a short, squirrel-tailed stock and very short, adjustable skate. A massive single arm fixed on the stock has a T-slotted bottom along which moves a metal block carrying a spring steel fence. The curvature of this may be changed by a screw adjustment mounted in the block and connected to the ends of the fence by metal arms.

OTHER FORMS

The quest for a practical method of ensuring parallelism of fence and keel resulted in many failures, most of which leave no surviving examples. One last variant will be mentioned. A patent to Samuel Piper (28 June, 1881, U.S.243398) covers a fence pivoted on arms in the manner of a parallel rule, and fixed by a screw on a third arm.

A combination match plane and plow was patented by Lewis Bundy (15 Nov. 1878, U.S.109,174) consisting of a stock with a handle on each end and arms fixed to it. On these arms a plow body and two rabbet bodies were mounted. Only one example has surfaced.

The BOOKBINDER'S PLOW at first glance appears to be a woodworking tool. It has a stock and fence sliding on rods with adjustable spacing by means of a central screw. It has a V-shaped cutter protruding horizontally from the bottom of the stock toward the fence, and is used to trim the page edges of books.

Continental   The plow does not seem to command the same mystique on the Continent as it does in England and America. It is just a variant of the grooving plane and has no simple name of its own. The French word BOUVET (grooving plane) derives from the same root as ox — they both plow furrows. The plow may be listed as BOUVET BRISÉ (broken groover), BOUVET À DEUX PIECES (two-piece groover) or BOUVET À JOUE MOBILE (moveable face groover). To differentiate a tool meant for deep grooving (as our plows) from a fenced rabbet they might add the qualification "à approfondir" — but such a plane might still have a wooden skate. The Plow of Félibien's time (1678) was mentioned above. The form changed but slowly in the eighteenth century. Diderot (1751-77) also shows an open throat, square staves (arms) fixed in the stock, a full height fence sliding on them and fixed by vertical keys. Moxon (1703) stated that each joiner had several plows for different widths of cut. This is difficult to reconcile with his description of the skates as "an Iron Plate of the thickness of the Plow iron", which would be unwieldy for the wider irons. I suspect that the plows of 17th century England were similar to those of France, using iron keels for the narrow irons and wooden soles (like fenced rabbets) for the wider ones. As we have just seen, the French use the same name for both types of grooving tool, modified as needed by "languette bois" (wooden tongue) or "languette fer" (iron tongue).

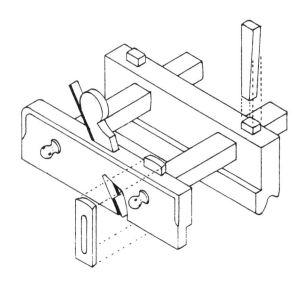

Fig.7:20—Belgian plow

French plows of the 18th century, being user-made, showed much individuality of style. In some, the staves projected through the stock to form transverse handles (which may account for Moxon's description of the grip). Examples of open throat construction persisted into the nineteenth century (some with the blade fitted above the wedge), but closed throat predominated. Toward the end of the 19th century, it became common to mount the staves not in mortises but simply screwed to the stock. A capstan head screw was passed through the stock and threaded into the arm. Such arms (staves) with fences could be purchased separately, and attachment to any plane required only the drilling of two holes. As a result, a wide variety of molding and other planes are found with a moveable fence.

BELGIAN PLOWS (Fig.7:20) use this arm mounting method with the added touch of using the same screw to fix the wooden depth stop and attach the arm. The stop slides in a dovetail slot in the stock. The screw passes through a slot in it, so that when the arm is tightened, the stop is locked. Vertical keys in the fence lock it against the staves, or, in a variant, one wedge forces two horizontal slides against the two arms.

The fixing of arms in French planes by vertical keys (Fig.7:21 front) was followed by a thumbscrew method (Fig.7:21 rear). Initially, the fence was split horizontally through the arm mortises and rejoined by thumbscrews which clamped the two halves on the arms. It was usual to turn the square staves through 45° to give a diamond shape for better grip. Later, metal stirrups were fitted in mortises in the unsplit fence in such a manner as to encircle the staves. These stirrups could be raised, by means of their threaded extensions through wingnuts, to bear against and lock the arms. This method was still in use in the 20th century and has been seen only in French and Dutch plows.

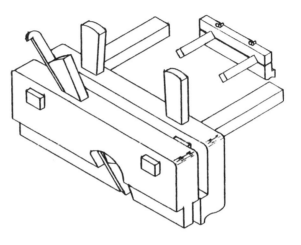

Fig.7:21—French wedge arm plow with alternate style fence (above)

Screw arms were known in the 16th century, but survivors older than the early 19th century are scarce. First to be preferred were three-screw

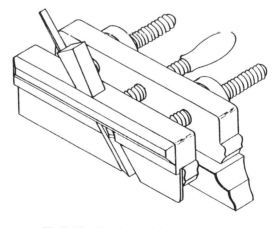

Fig.7:22—Continental three-arm plow

125

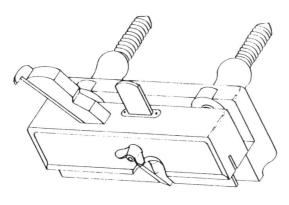

Fig.7:23—French screw-arm plow

methods previously mentioned (Fig.7:22). Two wood screws passing through the fence would be threaded through the stock to set the spacing, and a third, shorter one threaded through the fence would bear on the stock to lock it. Or, the two end screws would be fastened to the stock and passed through the fence into threaded knobs, with the center screw again applying counter-pressure. The final development was as in English plows, using threaded knobs and locknuts, except that the arms were still fixed in the stock and slid through the fence. To permit the two pieces of the plane to approach each other closely, the locknuts between them were commonly sunk into recesses in the fence in French plows (Fig.7:23).

The rare tool commonly called the FRENCH COACHMAKER'S PLOW by collectors is known simply as BOUVET À PLAT or flat groover in France. These have the shape of the old long S or an integral sign. They are described in Chapter 13 — Coachmaker.

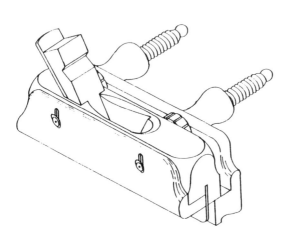

Fig.7:24—German plow

The German plow (Fig.7:24) uses a fence similar to the French, though somewhat thinner and with longer lower extensions which eliminate the need for recessing the locknuts. It has a bench type blade mounting with a top escapement. Like the French, the Germans have no specific translation for the plow. They are listed according to their use such as GLASNUTHOBEL or TÜR-NUTHOBEL (glass groove or door groove plane).

In the Netherlands, the word PLOEG can mean any groover, and the VEERPLOEG is the plow (Fig.7:25). Although the example shown is from the

126

turn of the 20th century, it is in the old style. Decorated and dated examples go back to the mid-18th century. The staves penetrate the stock and serve as transverse handles. Its fence slides on the staves and is fixed by wingnuts raising stirrups as in the French design described above. Earlier the fence was fixed by thumbscrews. An example dated 1770 is in the Garvan collection at the Yale Art Gallery, a collection of artifacts chosen by virtue of their combination of beauty and function.

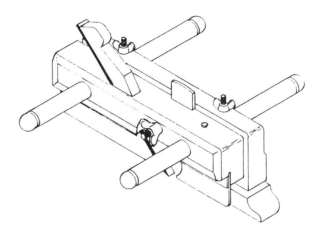

Fig.7:25—Plow : Holland

Seven models of veerploeg were listed by Nooitgedagt (ca. 1890), including two with the old style of extended staves serving as handles. A Belgian (Brusselsche veerploeg) model came with fifteen irons, including molding profiles, much like Stanley combination planes. They also

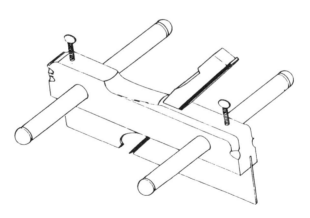

Fig.7:26—Varken : Holland

listed models with French type fence suspension. By 1915, Stolp listed only one model, still in the old style.

A tool unique to The Netherlands is the VARKEN (hog), a grooving plane with a very deep keel and long stout irons — looking like an overgrown plow without a fence (Fig.7:26). It was used to cut very deep grooves previously started by a ploeg, for jobs such as hogging out deep moldings.

Far Eastern   Chinese plows are not designed to take several widths of cutter, but match the cutter width to the (often wooden) keel (Fig.7:27). The stock resembles that of the Chinese smooth plane, but with the sole narrowed by rabbets on both sides. The fence is mounted on a single stave, passing through a mortise in the stock near the front. In contrast to the Western fashion, the fence is short (not much wider than the stave that carries it). The fence may be mounted on either side, and it is not uncommon to guide the cut from the far side of the workpiece. The fence on the right thus does not imply that the plane is pulled: it is pushed in most cases.

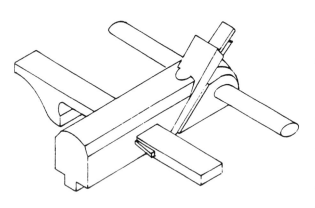

Fig.7:27—Chinese plow

The Japanese, as is the case on the Continent, use the same name for the plow and the rabbet or other grooving planes (SHAKURI-KANNA). As in China, separate stocks are normal for different cutter widths. For the narrower grooves, the keel is of brass, while wider ones are often keeled with hardwood mounted with the endgrain as the wear surface. The iron is fitted with a chipbreaker if the cutting width is one cm. (about ⅜ in.) or wider, with the chipbreaker serving as the wedge. Wide blades are fitted into the stock using a top escapement, as with bench planes, and are wedged against metal pins across the throat. Spur irons are generally used and are held in position by a steel plate. A German style moveable fence may be used, moving on steel bolts fixed to the stock and retained by lock- and wing-nuts. To specify this form of plow, it is called KIKAI-SHAKURI-KANNA (Fig.7:28). Kikai means machine, and the nuts and bolts make the tool a machine in Japanese eyes. Range of adjustment of the fence is rather limited. Another form, MOTOICHI-SHAKURA-KANNA (Fig.7:29), is preferred by the makers of shoji (sliding screens) and is

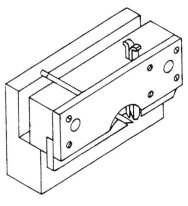

Fig.7:28—Japanese plow

128

used for cutting the grooves in the rails in which they slide. The body is like that of the Osaka grooving plane described in Chapter 4 "Panel Raising". The fence is short (as in the Chinese plow) and is carried on a wooden stave fixed by a wedge or set-screw.

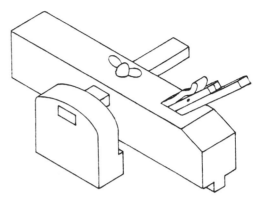

Fig.7:29—Japanese fenced grooving plane

A variant not seen in other countries is the DABO-SHAKURI-KANNA (Fig.7:30) which means pin grooving plane. It is useful for cutting stopped grooves (grooves that do not continue to the end of the board). It has no keel. The mouth is formed by a wooden post wedged in the stock just in front of the cutter. Its full-length fence is supported on two staves.

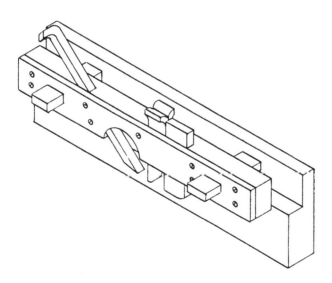

Fig.7:30—Japanese pin plow

OTHER GROOVING PLANES

TONGUE AND GROOVE PLANES

Tongue and groove MATCH planes are used in pairs, one to cut a groove in the edge of a board, the other a tongue in the next board to fit into it. They

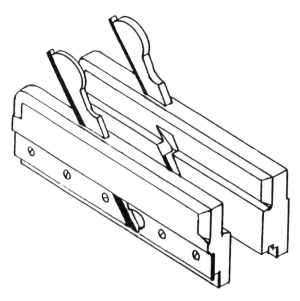

are quite common in the U.S. where this type of joining was widely used in laying floors and decks, for installing sheathing, and elsewhere. Those used by interior finishers were called WAINSCOT planes.

The usual TONGUE plane (Fig.7:31 rear) utilizes a side escapement shape and has a fixed fence. The sole is grooved to the depth of the tongue to be cut. The center of the iron is removed to clear the tongue being cut, and extends on either side beyond the edge of the board worked. The

Fig.7:31—Tongue (rear) and groove (front) match planes

GROOVE plane (Fig.7:31 front) is equipped with an iron keel similar to that of a plow plane and it is, in fact, a fixed plow. The iron resembles a plow iron in section, but is generally not snecked. The integral fence of both planes is often plated — faced with metal — to resist wear, which would cause misalignment of the mated boards.

Match planes were supplied either handled or unhandled. They are marked on the heel with the width of the boards they are intended to work, ½ to ⅝ in. (13 - 32 mm.). Smaller or larger sizes are uncommon. While it would be difficult to skew a groove plane, and none appear to have been made, skew tongue planes are found. These work well and help to keep the fence against the work.

Several forms of combination match planes, which put both tongue and groove functions in one stock, were produced. Most usual is the DOUBLE MATCH (also called DOUBLE GROOVING or MATCH COMBINATION)

(Fig7:32 left) with two throats facing in opposite directions (called "come-and-go" by collectors). This is an old form, pictured by Roubo (1769-75). It is also found in a handled version, with smooth-plane-style closed totes at either end. A less common type has the two functions facing in the same direction, the tongue sole dropped

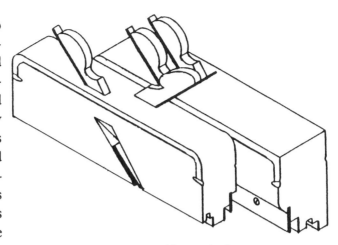

Fig.7:32—Double match planes

below the grooving function (Fig.7:32 right). Porter A. Gladwin (9 June 1857, U.S. No.17,541) patented a form of this type with two irons and two wedges, the tongue blade mounted in a bench type throat. In a later patent (19 Dec. 1876, U.S. 185,442) he added a moving fence which simultaneously changed the tongue and the groove cut, accommodating boards of different thickness. The fence assembly shown at the left of Fig.7:33 provides a fence surface (1) for the tongue function, and another (2) for the groove function. Moving the fence by means of adjustment screws simultaneously changes the position of the tongue on the board being worked, and the distance from the fence (2)

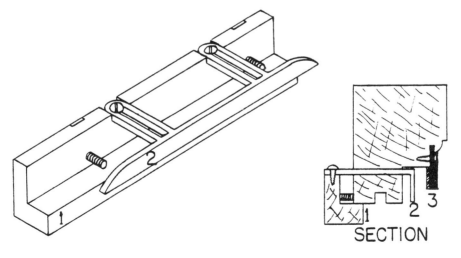

Fig.7:33—Gladwin 1876 patent

131

to the groove blade (3) as seen in the cross-section at the right, producing the proper location of the groove on the mating boards. Both this modification and the earlier form were sold by the Multiform Plane Co. In a third type, more frequently found, of French or German make (see GASTERHOBEL under "Continental" below and Fig.7:42), a removable fillet is fitted to the fence of a tongue plane converting it to a groove plane (using just the outer leg of the tongue iron). An English version (Hathersich, 1820-61) has a jack body with a filletster fence to effect the change. A wooden version of the Stanley No.48 swing-fence model (in which a fence pivots about its center to make the change) has been found.

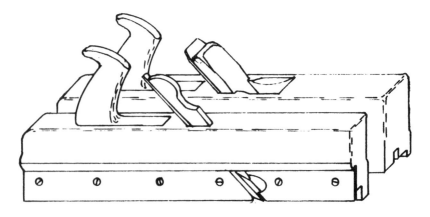

Fig.7:34—Plank match pair

Molding plane size match planes are termed BOARD MATCH to distinguish them from the longer PLANK MATCH planes, Fig.7:34. These are of jack size and shape, with the tongue plane usually being of bench plane type while the groove utilizes a side escapement. They were made in larger sizes, to work boards up to 1½ in. (38 mm.) thick. An unusual form seen in the Mystic Seaport (Connecticut) collection has two fences, which straddle the board.

Since a different pair of fixed-fence planes is required for each board thickness to be worked, it is not surprising that moving fence versions were made, even though much care would be required in setting

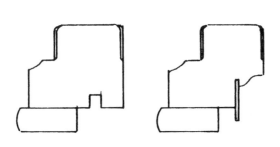

Fig.7:35—Moving plank match pair

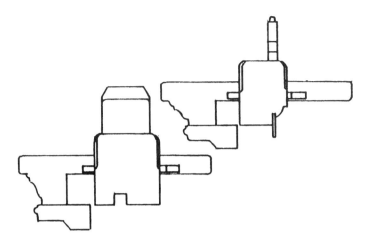

Fig.7:36—Wedge-arm match pair

and locking these to get an accurate mating. Since the width of the tongue is fixed, the size range covered was still somewhat limited. Board match and plank match pairs are found with filletster type fences (moving plank match pair, Fig.7:35), and plank match sets are found with wedge-arm (Fig.7:36) and screw-arm fences.

As the tongue was originally made by cutting two rabbets, one on either side of the board edge, the tongue plane was a refinement developed much later than the groove. The earliest known examples are dated in the middle of the 17th century.

With the advent of milled lumber, it would seem that the need for match planes would decrease sharply. However, they continued to be sold well into the 20th century (through 1958 for the Stanley No.148 metal version). A universal tongue plane, essentially a moving filletster and a skew dado joined on wooden screw arms, was patented by Conrad Jensen (14 May 1872, U.S. 126,707).

While in this country a groove plane is usually regarded as a match plane that has lost its mate, this is not necessarily so. A DRAWER plane (DRAW in older literature) was used to cut the grooves in drawer sides which held the bottom. Here the tongue plane was not needed, but a right- and left-hand pair of groove planes was. These were also made with wooden keels the full width of the cutting edge. One example cut a ⅜ in. (1 cm.) groove and might not have been recognized as a drawer plane were it not for the hand inscription "draw plane" on its heel. A plane of the same profile cutting a ⅝ in. (16 mm.) groove is also known. A handled groove plane or fixed plow made by P. SARGENT (New Hampshire, 1844-56), used in a coach-building factory, had a spur set into the skate for a cleaner groove.

OTHER TYPES

A DOOR plane served to cut the grooves in door stiles and rails to receive panels (Fig.7:37 left). It has a second iron which simultaneously molds the edge. A DOUBLE DOOR plane (Fig.7:37 right) cuts the molding on both sides of the piece, using a previously plowed groove as guide. These are usually made in two pieces, the two being separable on metal screws or wooden screw arms to accomodate doors of different thickness. The Mathieson (Scotland) 1899 catalog lists a FRENCH GROOVING plane, similar to a door plane but of smaller size, for shutters.

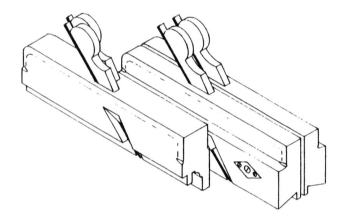

Fig.7:37—Door plane and double door plane

The BURROWES wire screen plane is fairly common and easily recognized by the printed message on its side. It was provided with sliding wire screens sold by E.T.Burrowes for over a half-century ending with the first World War, and was used to enlarge the groove in which the screens slid.

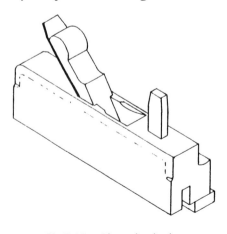

Fig.7:38—Glass check plow

The GLASS CHECK PLOW is found in both bench type (Fig.7:38) and side escapement type stocks and resembles a tongue plane with a filletster fence. It cuts long tongues, and usually has a depth stop to permit cutting these to different heights. The plane is not particularly rare, but no description of its use has been found. The name and shape suggest a use in cutting the two putty rabbets of a sash bar simultaneously, but this supposition remains open to question. An unusual set of three planes has been found that make the same cut — a tongue and a groove — in both boards (Fig.7:39). These appear to be glass check planes with irons modified to the shape shown at the upper right of the figure.

Sandusky Tool Co. made a pair of WEATHERSTRIP planes for fitting metal weatherstrips to window sash. One was a ¾ in. (19 mm.) square rabbet with a fixed metal fence, and the other a ⅛ inch (3 mm.) grooving plane with a slotted steel plate fixed to the left side of the stock with thumbscrews. The fence is the same thickness as the slot made and

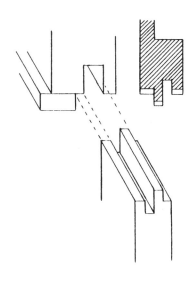

Fig.7:39—Modified glass check plow

adjusts vertically, being kept parallel to the sole by an extension sliding in a wide, shallow dado. The tool appears to be designed to cut a second groove a fixed distance from the first.

Continental　　On the Continent many of the above types are known, although in their own idiom of body style. Match planes with long stocks and transverse handles were favored by house carpenters. The French BOUVETS À JOINDRE are match planes, BOUVET À LANGUETTE or CRÊTOIRE for the tongue and BOUVET À RAINURE for the groove. The come-and-go may be called the CRÊTOIRE À LAMBRIS or simply BOUVET EN UN MORCEAU (one-piece groover). The older planes of this type are frequently open-throated. More recently, as made by Peugeot Frères and others, they are cut as open throats and closed with a batten glued to the upper right side of the stock (Fig.7:40). This leaves a characteristic handhold wider than the bottom of the stock, in contrast to the English style.

A variety of specialized tongue or groove planes were offered commercially in France. A pair for stair builders is characterized by larger distance between fence and cutter in the groove plane (the groove was made in the under side of the tread to accept a tongue in the top of the riser). Parquet floor makers used handled models, and preferred two separate irons in their tongue planes. Parquet installers used only the grooves, but in right- and left-handed pairs. A pair called BOUVETS À EMBREVER (mortising groovers)

135

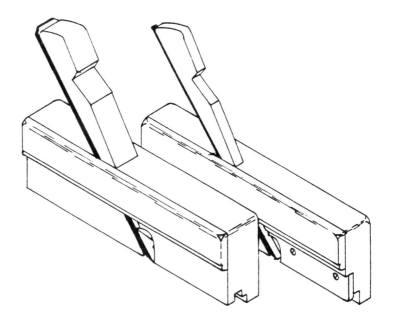

Fig.7:40—French tongue and groove planes

cut a groove in a thinner board, and in a thicker piece two grooves forming a rabbet which accepted the thinner board and had a tongue in its center. This pair was used by casement window makers to attach the batten containing the "gueule de loup" (see Chapter 13 — Sashmaker).

A French plane noted in the Arnold and Walker Catalog #3 uses an interesting method of adjusting the fence position. As the sketch (Fig.7:41) shows, a tapered fence is slid forward or back to change the spacing, then fixed in position with a wing-nut on top of the stock. This device holds the fence rigid

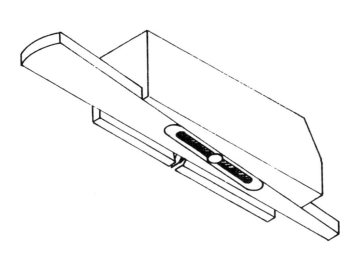

Fig.7:41—Adjustable tapered fence

and exactly parallel to the active sole, but allows rather a limited range of adjustment.

The German FEDERHOBEL and NUTHOBEL (tongue plane and groove plane) have the usual German side escapement shape. A pair used by floor layers (PARKETTNUT- und PAR-KETTFEDER-HOBEL) had trans-verse grips and additional handgrips on their left sides. An unusual FEDERHOBEL zu AUSZUGTISCHEN (tongue plane for pull-out tables) is side-cut-ting, with the iron bedded verti-cally and skewed as in a side rabbet. The lower right side of the stock is grooved and acts as the sole.

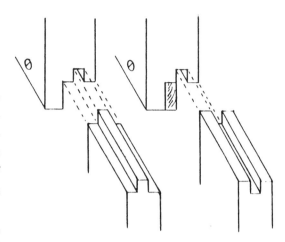

Fig.7:42—Gasterhobel

The German GASTERHOBEL or French BOUVET À JOINDRE TRANSFORMABLE is shown in Fig. 7:42. The form is that of a match tongue plane, having either two irons or a single iron with the center of its cutting edge removed. The outer cutting edge (on the right side of the plane) is of the same width as the groove width desired, while the width of the spacing between the two cutting edges is the width of the tongue. A removable fillet of wood is mounted on the fence (shown shaded in the figure). With this in place, the plane cuts a groove in the edge of a board, as shown at the right. When the fillet is removed, the plane cuts the matching tongue in another board.

CROSS-GRAIN GROOVING

Dado is a term borrowed from Greek architecture and was adapted to mean the lower section of a paneled wall. The skirting was normally tongued to fit into a groove cut in the floorboards. The name eventually came to mean a cross-grain groove, and by association the plane used to cut it was also called a dado.

The wood fibers on either side of a cross-grain groove must be severed before the cut is made if ragged edges are to be avoided. A rabbet fitted with two spurs ahead of the plane iron would serve to do this. However, as the usage of dado cuts increased, a specialized plane was developed (Fig.7:43).

137

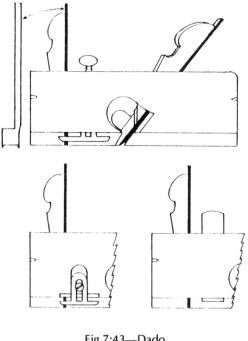

Fig.7:43—Dado

The DADO (cut-and-thrust, or trenching plane) is basically a skew rabbet fitted with a second throat in front of the usual one. This carries an iron mounted vertically or slanted slightly forward, and held by a wedge. The center of this blade end is cut away and the two outer edges ground into spurs, which cut the grain at the exact width of the cut of the main blade that follows.

The stock is normally thicker than the sole, a step on the left side almost always fitted with a depth stop. The top of Fig.7:43 shows a dado with a screw stop. At lower left a brass side stop is shown; at lower right, a wood stop. This may be held by friction or by a wooden screw ("wood screw stop") through the right side of the body. Dado planes are found in sizes to cut dados from ⅛ in.(3 mm.) or less — using a steel skate like a match groove plane — to 1¼ in. (32 mm.) or more (in long planes). Handled planes were sold, but are not common. An occasional dado is found having the depth stop and the larger side of the shavings escapement on the right side. These are shown in the 1899 Mathieson (Scotland) catalog, but have not been seen in American listings, although at least one with the mark of Marten Doscher (New York, 1879-94) is known.

As with the rabbet, the dado plane needs a guide to start the cut — a strip of wood fixed to the workpiece. Since a dado is often cut at a distance from the end of the work, a moveable fence is of limited use. However, fences are occasionally found post-fitted by users, and at least one fenced dado was made by T. Tileston (Massachusetts, -1802-1866).

The dado plane appears to be a relatively recent development, occurring in the mid-18th century. It is not mentioned in print until the Gabriel inventories of 1791-93, but a few made by Madox (England, 1748-75) have survived. His earlier version dubbed the "proto-dado" was a skew rabbet with the cheeks above the sole thickened to carry a dovetailed depth stop on each side, and having a nicker iron mounted behind each.

138

The original use of the dado (floor grooving) is perpetuated in the Scottish FLOORING RAGLET (raglet is a Scottish name for a dado, not to be confused with the reglet). This is a stout dado with a jack handle mounted at an angle on the left side of the stock, for increased hand clearance. The stock is wider than a common dado, again for improved clearance, with the result that the depth stop area of the plane bottom is wider than the true sole. It is also found (rarely) in a left-hand version, and may be equipped with an adjustable depth stop. The common form was pictured in the Mathieson 1899 catalog.

The JACK RABBET has been described with the rabbet planes, but when equipped with two nickers may also serve as a wide dado. Its handle is sometimes offset in the same fashion as the flooring raglet. This version has been called a TRAVERSING plane. An unusual variation by F.B. Marble (Ohio, 1846-65) angled not only the handle but the upper portion of the stock as well. A similar tool used by millwrights to cut or dress notches in timbers was called a DAPPING plane. These were often equipped with handles that could be tilted sideways at various angles for convenience.

The name BANDING plane is sometimes used for a dado. Mercer (1920) used the term to include other wider grooving planes as well. Hotzappfel (1875) applied the name to the luthier's purfling tool used for cutting narrow grooves for inlays. The term was applied in shipyards to the planes used for cutting wide dados for decorative inlay. As a result, the name is not particularly useful.

Continental   The English form of the dado does not seem to have been made on the Continent or in the Far East. It is not listed in their catalogs. In France the function of the dado is served by the RABOT À ENTAILLES, which may be described as a rabbet with two nickers and with the stock widened into two integral depth stops at different elevations. The difference is to allow a fence — of the same thickness as the difference in elevations — to be fixed to the work. In this manner the two depth stops bottom at the same time, one on the fence and one on the work. A metal plated version was used to groove slats for jalousies (JALOUSIE-NUTHOBEL in Germany, RABOT POUR PERSIENNES in France.

Japanese   A specialized dado is used by the makers of shoji, the rice paper-covered latticework screens which are prominent features of Japanese home furnishing. These are made of thin, carefully planed laths woven into a lattice. The joints are prepared by notching the laths half-way across their width at regular intervals, alternating sides. When these are fitted together, a rigid but very light structure is obtained. The notches are cut in many laths at

139

once, as cleaner cuts are attained more rapidly and uniform spacing is ensured. The plane used is the KUDE-SHAKURI-KANNA or joint grooving plane. Two knives serve as nickers in front of the iron. Both these and the main iron are held in slots in the side of the stock and retained by a plate screwed to it. The keel may be of brass or hardwood, its thickness determined by the thickness of the laths to be cut (about ⅜ in., 1 cm.).

Chapter 8

PLANES FORMING ANGLED SURFACES

DOVETAIL AND RELATED PLANES

When boards are edge-glued together to form a wide surface, warping is a risk. This can be countered by attachment of a batten at right angles to the grain direction, but another problem arises. Expansion and contraction occur in the cross-grain direction with humidity change. (There is very little change along the grain.) A pine surface two and a half feet wide can change in size by over a half inch from winter to summer (a 60 cm. width changes by 1 cm.). If the batten is rigidly attached, the panel will inevitably split. For some surfaces — barn doors, for instance — the boards are not glued but half-lapped or tongue-and-grooved, so that the dimensional change can be accomodated in the joints. For other purposes (oil paintings on wood, in particular) this was not acceptable, and another method was developed.

A cross-grain dado was cut in the back of the panel, with its sides beveled inward. A batten with slanted sides was then driven in from one side. This effectively prevented warping, but allowed the panel to slip along the batten to accomodate the dimensional change.

Although a simple slant to the sides of the batten would work, there were advantages to cutting a dove-tail profile on the edge of the batten and mounting it on end, to provide greater rigidity. Such a joint (Fig.8:1 left) is called a sliding or French dovetail (as distinguished from the common dovetail used to join chest corners).

The female member of the joint was originally made by sawing the sides with a tool similar to our stairmaker's saw, held at an angle, and then removing waste with chisel and router plane. A plane was developed to cut the male member of the joint in the sixteenth century or earlier in Germany: one dated 1607 has survived. It was essentially a standing filletster in which the sole and cutting edge slope upward toward the fence. This became the DOVETAIL plane (two Continental examples are shown in Fig.8:1 center and right). They are quite rare in England and the U.S. in spite of having been named in a number of early English listings (no mention has been found in American catalogs). A few by early makers have surfaced (John Rogers, Buck, and I.

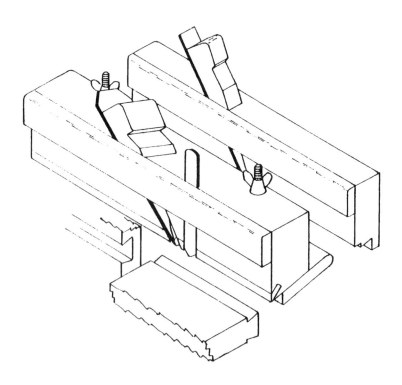

Fig.8:1—Sliding dovetail joint (left); adjustable (center); and fixed (right) dovetail planes

Cox in England, and Wm. Martin in Pennsylvania, all before 1830) as well as an occasional later mark (Kaye, England after 1869). A left- and right-hand pair in one stock was made by T. Clark (Pennsylvania, -1832-). Their scarcity makes it obvious that this type of joint was not as popular in England or America as it was on the Continent or in Japan.

The presence of nickers on some dovetail planes shows that they had uses other than cutting the long-grain joints described above. For example, male dovetails or half- dovetails were cut cross-grain at ends of boards for fitting end pieces (called breadboard ends or clamps), again to prevent warping. Another application is the attachment of shelves to case sides. The so-called housed joint, a simple dado cut in the side to receive the shelf end, provides little resistance against pulling out of the shelf if the case distorts. By cutting the sliding dovetail on the shelf ends and shaping the dado to match, a much stronger construction is gained.

The ability of the sliding dovetail to accomodate long-grain to cross-grain joints is also useful for installing drawer runners. The separation between drawers, in quality work, is provided by dust boards made in frame-and-panel construction and attached to the case sides. The frame rails of the dust board also serve as the drawer runners, providing the supports for the drawer sides. The rails are long grain. They must be solidly attached to the cross grain of the case sides, and this is best done by using the sliding dovetail. They are glued only at the front to the case side. The rear is then free to slide within the dovetails as the case side shrinks or swells, and yet remain solidly connected to the case.

In the best English furniture, the sliding dovetail is stopped. That is, the female dovetail is ended before showing at the front of the piece, and the joint appears as if it were a simple butt. This requires considerably more care than cutting it through: an instance of the ethic of "doing things right" even if the added effort is unseen. The dovetail is unstopped and visible in even the best of American work (by the Goddards, for example). An exposed dovetail is today regarded as a decorative feature.

Another refinement is to taper the dovetail joint slightly along its length, both the male on a shelf and the female in the case side. The shelf must then be driven in from the rear, causing it to wedge snugly. This, too, requires a high degree of skill for proper fitting.

The scarcity of English dovetail planes and the presence of the more frequent (although still uncommon) English-made SHOULDERING plane (Fig.8:2) suggests that these may have been used to cut sliding dovetails. In fact, most U.S. collectors insist on calling these dovetail planes.

The shouldering plane (not to be confused with the shoulder plane) is a side escapement plane with a slanted sole (at a reasonable angle for a dovetail), with the left lower side plated, wedged nicker and blade peeking through slits in the plate. They are usually found with brass plating, or with an angled steel plating covering lower side and sole, and are frequently shorter than the normal rabbet. They could, in fact, be used to cut the male sliding dovetail by using a fence affixed to the workpiece. However,

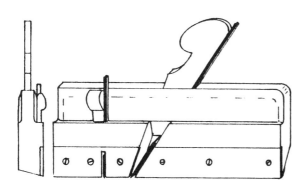

Fig.8:2—English shouldering plane

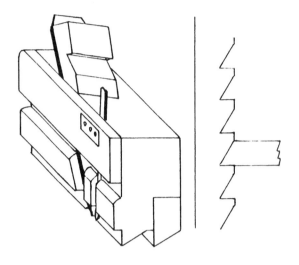

Fig.8:3—Bookcase shelf plane (left)
and the rack cut it makes (right)

they would be equally useful in cleaning rabbets or recesses with limited access in furniture, in cleaning tenons for dovetail half-lap or similar joints, and other uses. They are especially helpful in fitting sliding dovetails, once they are cut. A French plane, the GUILLAUME À ONGLET, is a simple rabbet with slanted sole which would serve like purposes and coexisted with their dovetail planes. The plane is listed by Mathieson (Scotland, 1899) with the sash planes, another indication that it was intended for cleaning rabbets.

A plane easily confused with the dovetail plane is the BOOKCASE SHELF plane (An example is shown in Fig.8:3 left). This was used to cut toothed racks by making a series of triangular grooves. These racks were formerly used to hold the ends of adjustable shelves, which were cut at a slant to fit the grooves, as shown in Fig.8:3 right. The sole of this plane resembles that of a dovetail plane, but there is a level section between the slope and the fence or guide. The guide is removable (to permit starting away from the end of the rack), and is of the same shape as the groove that is cut. Each successive groove is cut with the guide inserted in the previous one

Continental   The dovetail plane is called the GRATHOBEL in Germany (Fig.8:1 right). The STELLGRATHOBEL (adjustable dovetail plane) is found with filletster fence mounted on a slanted sole (Fig.8:1 center), or as a moving filletster with a triangular cut in the sole. In more recent times, metal fences replaced wood (this type is still being made in Germany). They are also found with fences mounted on arms, the fences and arms in the Continental style.

Nooitgedagt of The Netherlands (ca.1890) pictures a double dovetail plane, the ZWALUWSTAARTSCHAAF (swallowtail plane) for cutting either left- or right-handed; the dovetail is called a swallowtail or an eagletail in Europe.

144

The French planes for cutting dovetails are referred to as RABOTS À QUEUE or tail planes — risking confusion with the tailed coach-maker's planes which have a similar name.

There are also special planes for cutting the sliding joints used in

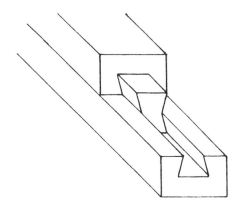

Fig.8:4—Double dovetail for table slides

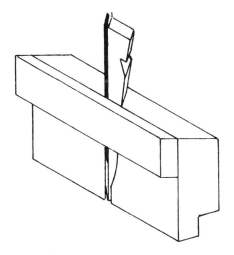

Fig.8:5—French slope rabbet

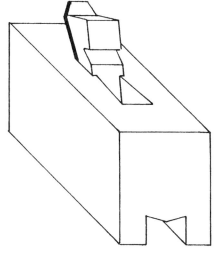

Fig.8:6—French plane to cut table slide

supports for table leaves (Fig.8:4). The female groove is cut first with a rectangular section using a fixed plow. The groove then has its sides sloped with the GUILLAUME DE PENTE (slope rabbet, Fig.8:5), a special form of side rabbet. I am aware of only one American plane of this type, by W. Martin (Pennsylvania, 1773-1801). Having made such grooves in the two outer members of the slide, the center member was cut with two male dovetails back-to-back, using a special form of GRAIN D'ORGE (barleycorn) plane with a fence on both sides and a cutter in the form of a shallow V (Fig.8:6).

The GUILLAUME À ONGLET mentioned above (sloped sole rabbet) was made in pairs with opposite slopes. It was not intended for cutting dovetails, but for trimming surfaces in awkward positions.

Bookcase planes were apparently more popular in France (RABOT À CRÉMAILLÈRE) and Germany (ZAHNLEISTENHOBEL) than they were in England and the U.S. Most examples

145

that we see are imports. They were made in both fixed and adjustable versions, the latter with sliding filletster-type fences.

Japanese   The sliding dovetail is used frequently in Japan, and the Japanese have a variety of planes to cut it. (Surprisingly, the common corner dovetail was not much used there in earlier furniture: even in fine furniture, drawer corner joints were often nailed.) The interior corner-cutting plane SUMI-KIWA-KANNA, mentioned earlier with the rabbets, provides one way of cutting the male member. The Japanese equivalent of the Grathobel is the ARI-SHAKURI-KANNA, in both fixed and moving fence versions. The working surfaces are identical, but the stock and blades are in the Japanese idiom. The female groove is cut by the ARI-KAKE-SHAKURI-KANNA, a Japanese rabbet with the sole at the dovetail angle. A separate fence fixed to the work is used to guide the cut and maintain the proper angle. A sharp-cornered side rabbet previously described (hifukura-kanna; Fig.6:21, Chapter 6) cleans both members.

CHAMFER PLANES

A CHAMFER is a cut made to remove the arris, or sharp corner where two surfaces meet. It may be made with a bench plane and a steady hand or a guide, and was probably done so in the U.S. to judge by the rarity of American chamfer planes. In England and on the Continent, they exist in considerable variety and were named in a number of early lists, though they are not common. Planes which have a stop to determine the width of chamfer cut are called STOP CHAMFER planes. The name is somewhat confusing, since chamfers which do not continue for the full length of the arris are also called stop chamfers.

The most common CHAMFER plane resembles a small, single-iron smooth plane with a full-width, right-angle V cut out of the sole. The width of the chamfer cut may be set by the extent that the cutter protrudes into this V. While it would be possible to use such a plane by starting with blade withdrawn and advancing it with each stroke, this is hardly practical. A moveable member is provided which serves to provide a horizontal mouth at the appropriate point within the V (and making it a stop chamfer plane). The blade is set for the proper cut at this mouth. The cut is started by using one wall of the V as a fence, and continued until the other wall bottoms (Fig.8:7).

146

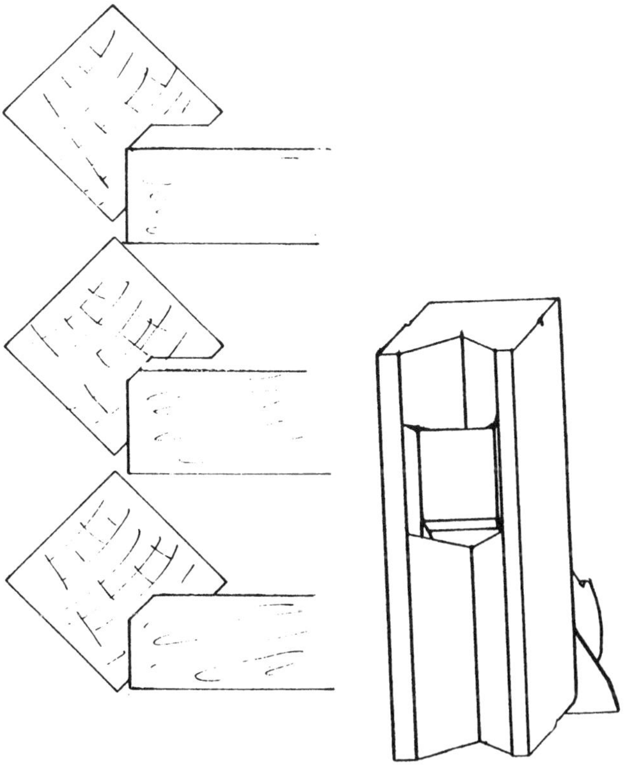

A simple form uses a wooden block, grooved for shaving passage, held between the blade and wedge. More often seen is the type with a SOLE BOX (Fig.8:8). A wooden structure of internal geometry duplicating a bench plane throat slides in a mortise in the stock. It may be moved in a direction parallel to the bed, to place the mouth at the desired position within the V, and secured there by a screw projecting through a brass reinforced slit in the side of the stock. The blade setting may then be made independently of the mouth setting. A less common type made by John Moseley and Son (England, 1862-1900) uses a steel sole box fixed by two screws.

Fig.8:7—A stop chamfer plane (bottom view) and how it cuts a chamfer

A similar form of the wooden sole box plane was patented in the U.S. by James Mander (24 Mar. 1885, U.S.314338) and manufactured by Mander and Dillin, a Philadelphia firm of planemakers. This used a screw on each side of the sole box. As Mander was an immigrant from England, he may have brought the design principle with him. Planes with their mark are uncommon.

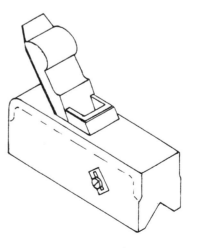

Fig.8:8—Stop chamfer plane with sole box

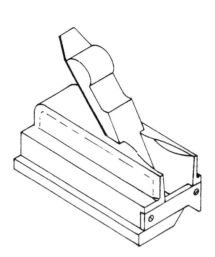

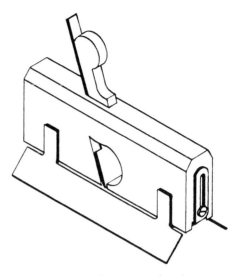

Fig.8:9—Fenced chamfer plane   Fig.8:10—Iron fence chamfer plane

The FENCED CHAMFER plane (Fig.8:9) is an alternate design made in Great Britain. The sole of a smooth type plane provides the horizontal section and the left wall of the V, while the other wall is provided by a fence of the filletster type with a 45° edge. Here the blade setting is fixed, and the width of the chamfer to be cut is set by the position of the fence.

A different implementation of the same idea is seen in a common rabbet plane, with an iron fence extending downward and outward from the sole at a 45° angle on both sides. The fence is supported by two extensions screwed to front and rear of the stock, which permits vertical adjustment and thus the width of the chamfer to be cut (Fig.8:10).

A rare English form of the adjustable chamfer plane has the V sole as a separate member, hinged at the rear of the stock (Fig.8:11). A screw fixes its position and thereby the protrusion of the blade within the V. Another pivots the separate sole on a longitudinal axis, to permit cutting chamfers at other angles than 45°. Still another, made by Greenslade, England, has a gerfschaaf type superstructure with a base which slides longitudinally to set the chamfer width.

Fig.8:11—Hinged chamfer plane

148

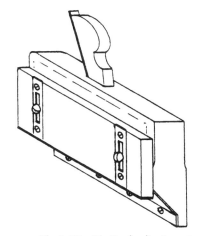

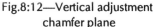

Fig.8:12—Vertical adjustment
chamfer plane

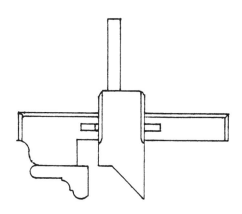

Fig.8:13—Wedge arm adjustable
chamfer plane

The above types of chamfer plane require either the plane or the work to be slanted at the chamfer angle. There are models which permit working with the plane and workpiece level. The simplest is a side escapement plane with a sole slanted at 45° and forming an obtuse angle with an integral fence. A full side stop controls the width of the chamfer Fig.8:12). A variant made by A. Huber (probably late 18th century Pennsylvania; Fig.8:13) uses a wedge arm fence on a rabbet plane having a 45° sole with a level section, and cuts a chamfer on the far side of the work. The flat section of sole stops the cut and thus sets the size of the chamfer. Another unusual plane (Fig.8:14) has a sole at 45° with a filletster fence attached. The fence breaks downward to a vertical section.

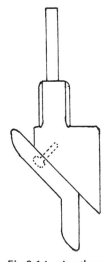

Fig.8:14—Another
chamfer plane variant

A BEVELING plane (Fig.8:15) was patented and produced by M.B. Tidey & Co., New York (4 July, 1854, U.S. 11,235). It consists of two plane bodies hinged on either side of a handled stock, with angle controlled by thumbscrews through a curved brass bridge. It was fitted with a screw arm fence. This very rare plane will cut a right or a left chamfer at any angle. A fixed version described by Franz Wertheim (1869) exists as a fore plane with a stock of inverted Y cross-section. The soles of the two legs of the Y meet at right angles, and each carries an iron.

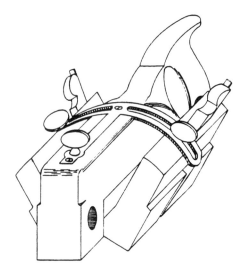

Fig.8:15—Tidey patent double beveling plane

Another way to cut a bevel on the edge of a piece is with a BEVEL ATTACHMENT. This is a fence which is clamped to a bench plane and which can be set to any desired angle. These have been the subject of a number of patents. William H. Blye (10 Apr. 1849, U.S. 6304) hinges a wooden fence on the left side of the plane and fixes its angle with a brass rod pivoted from the stock. This passes through a fitting on the fence and is fixed with a thumbscrew. Michael Garland (30 Aug. 1870, U.S. 106808) improved on this with a device borrowed from a wing caliper. A circular arc attached to the fence is fixed by a thumbscrew on the toe of the plane. H.P.Taylor (5 Mar. 1878, U.S.201068) used a substantial steel plate fixed to the stock with a single screw, with provision for adjusting the angle of a short fence attached to it. Leonard Fairbanks (19 Mar. 1861, U.S. 31707) claimed a bevel attachment fixed to the stock with a C-clamp arrangement. An example of Alexander's plane gauge, which resembles Garland's, was made by Langdon Miter Box Co. (U.S.).

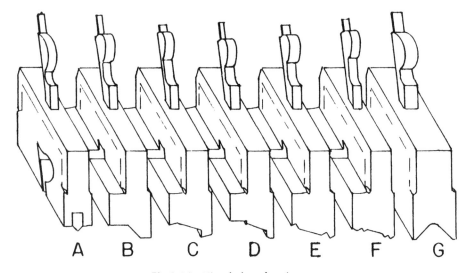

Fig.8:16—Fixed chamfer planes

FIXED CHAMFER planes are less common in England and almost un-known in the U.S. These are usually side escapement planes, and differ from molding planes only in having their soles not curved, but of straight line segments. A selection of these is seen in Fig.8:16. A DOUBLE CHAMFER plane (Fig.8:16A) is a rabbet with a V protrusion from its sole, and fitted with a V-pointed blade which will cut a chamfer on either right or left hand. It is also used to cut a V groove: it was listed by Mathieson (Scotland) as a "Champhering or V plane". The Coachmaker's SIDE CHAMFER plane (Fig.8:16B) has a sole creased in a shallow V with an iron cutting on one side of the V. Early English makers such as Moon (-1799-1851) and Darby (-1790-1785) sometimes made these to cut a 30° chamfer and added a fixed fence (Fig.8:16C).

There are a large number of variations of the simple chamfer plane whose elements are all straight lines, and which are used for decorative purposes on furniture and elsewhere. A chamfer dropped below the surface in a step (Fig.8:16D), is seen in a plane by W. Cresy (ca.1800). The form called "P.G. Molding" by Ohio Tool is a recessed chamfer (Fig.8:16E). A variant of this cuts a broad chamfer with two fillets (Fig.8:16F). A CORNER ROUNDER plane (Fig.8:16G) for cutting a round chamfer has a V-grooved sole with a rounded apex and a cutter with a hollow quarter-round edge to match.

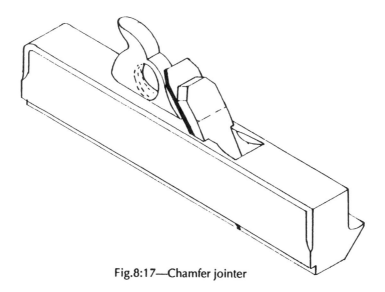

Fig.8:17—Chamfer jointer

A plane used to cut a chamfer on cornice moldings, the SPRING plane, is discussed with the wide molders later. Another tool which may have been used for a similar purpose was reported by Philip Stanley, 1981 (Fig.8:17). It is a jointer with the left side rabbeted as a panel plane and the other extended in a 45° slope The slope may be rested on the bench and the plane will then cut a 45° chamfer on a board fixed to the bench.

Finally, a puzzle left us by Robert Wooding (and a few other early makers). He made a side escapement plane with a flat sole at 45° to the stock, without a fence. Was this used for chamfering, or for trimming rabbets?

Continental   The English type of stop chamfer plane is known on the Continent only as an import. Various fixed chamfer planes are found, and are there classed with the molding planes. Weiss (Austria, 1909) shows a chamfer with fillet at its lower side under the name Einschlagstücken. The French Méplat or Méplat à carré can occur in several shapes similar to the "P.G. Molding" (Fig.8:16E), often with the chamfer at a lower angle.

The V-plane and its cut are called GRAIN D'ORGE (barleycorn) in France. The mating V-shaped tongue and the plane which cuts it are called PAS DE CHÈVRE (goat-step). In large sizes, it is used on small casements (especially in the Alps) as the weather-tight closure in place of the semicircular gueule de loup (see Chapter 13 — The Sashmaker). A smaller version of the V-plane used by floor-layers to ease the entry to the groove of tongue-and-groove flooring is called GUILLAUME À COUP D'ENTREE and may have separate blades for the two sides of the cut.

Japanese   A design similar to the fenced chamfer plane is used in the Japanese KAKU-MENTORI-KANNA or KIRIMEN-KANNA (Fig.8:18). This is a small hira-kanna or common plane with its toe and heel shaped to fit into a T-slot or a sliding dovetail. The female members of the joint are located on a pair of fences, the inner bottoms of which are beveled at 45°. The fences, sliding on the dovetail, are adjusted for the proper separation in the same manner as our stop chamfer planes. They ride on the corner to be chamfered as the plane cuts, and bottom at the desired depth. This double-fence style has the advantage that different sections of the cutting edge may be used, to distribute the wear. A similar plane has the fences beveled differently (although still fitting over a right angle corner). This cuts a chamfer at other than 45°; it is called the monkey-cheek molding plane (ETE-BŌ-MENTORI-KANNA). Since the fences may be reversed on the plane, it will cut either a flat or a steep chamfer and can work in either direction as the grain requires.

The Japanese KEN-KANNA (sword plane) is their smooth plane modified to have a V-shaped sole, with both stock and cutter cut away at 45°. It finds use primarily in wood sculpture.

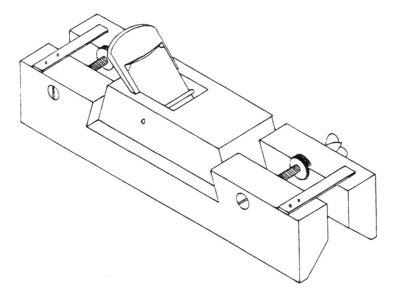

Fig.8:18—Japanese sliding fence chamfer plane

OTHER ANGLE CUTTING PLANES

Note: Planes for cutting the angled sides of panels were treated in Chapter 4 under "Panel Raising Planes".

A molding plane with a V-shaped sole (Fig.8:19) has no common name in English other than V-PLANE. These have various uses. A small one is

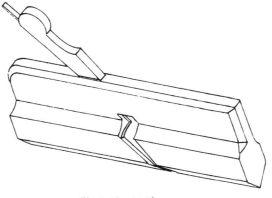

Fig.8:19—V-Plane

sometimes used to relieve the inner edges of a groove joint to facilitate entry of the mating tongue. The partitions in pigeon-hole racks are sometimes beveled at their edges and held in place by V-shaped grooves, cut by the V-plane. Fitted with a movable fence, it cuts a decorative groove in matched boards (see center-board plane) or a groove in paneling as a start for linen-fold carving.

A fenced plow with a V-shaped sole, for straight or circular work, was used in shipyards and called a SHIP HAWK plane. One use was to cut grooves on the sides of a ship, just below the deck level, to provide sharp edges for paint striping. It may also have been used to cut V-grooves in curved ribs for bulkhead panels. These and related tools are covered also in Chapter 10.

The MEETING RAIL plane has a stepped sole with a shallow slope between the steps: it is further described under sash planes. Some other angle cutting planes are used for sash bars and may also be found there.

Chapter 9

PLANES FOR CURVED SURFACES

In this chapter we will be concerned with planes used to prepare functional curved surfaces. Molding planes — planes used to create decorative surfaces — are treated later in Chapters 10 and 11.

PLANES USED FOR LONGITUDINAL CURVED SURFACES

English and American   A bench plane may be used, in a pinch, to plane a convex or rounded surface. It cannot be used on a concave surface, as the flat sole keeps the blade from reaching it. What is needed is a plane with a sole curved at least as sharply as the surface it is to work.

The COMPASS or CIRCULAR plane (Fig.9:1) is usually of smooth plane size and shape except for the curved sole. The English and American planes commonly have coffin shapes (as described under smooth planes) and double irons.

Planes with soles in true circular arcs will function as conventional smooth planes on surfaces of curvature matching their soles, but this is not commonly the case. The surface being worked - a chair arm, for example - is usually of greater radius and often varies in curvature. Although Nicholson (1849) states that soles of different curvature were required for different tasks, most catalogs offered no choice. In fact, the compass plane itself often has a non-circular sole, being more curved toward the toe; presumably

Fig.9:1—Compass plane

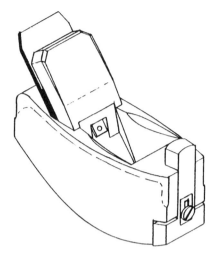

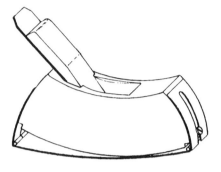

Fig.9:2—Adjustable compass plane   Fig.9:3—Cole patent compass plane

to better accomodate to non-circular surfaces. The compass plane is best suited for working broad surfaces of moderate, simple curvature. Shorter surfaces, especially if sharply curved, or curved in two directions, call for use of a shave (covered in Chapter 12.).

Practice is necessary to get good results with a compass plane. Constant attention must be paid to the changing grain direction of the surface being planed, the iron kept keen, and the strokes made short and firm to avoid chatter. Because the front of the mouth bears most of the pressure, it wears rapidly, accounting for the patched mouths found on many of these planes. Compass planes are occasionally found with a skewed iron, which facilitates cross-grain work.

British compass planes are often equipped with a boxwood adjustable stop that slides vertically in a dovetail on the toe of the plane and is fixed in position by means of a screw (Fig.9:2). This serves to change the effective curvature of the plane, as the stop is set to match the curve being worked. A less common form has an internal stop of wood or iron. Both types are ADJUSTABLE COMPASS planes. Properly set, they serve almost as well as planes having the correct uniform radius.

Planes using other methods of adapting to different curves have been tried, and were probably not too successful, judging by their rarity. A sharply curved compass plane fitted with a spring steel sole (Fig.9:3) was patented by William A. Cole, (6 June 1848, U.S. 5,620), considerably predating the metal compass plane patents. The steel sole was attached to the body at the mouth, but the sole ends could be moved up and down to change sole curvature. Hinged metal strips at each end of the sole were slotted and could be held

156

in position at the toe and heel of the plane by screws through these slots, thus holding the chosen curvature. Examples of this type from several makers (including Baldwin Tool in the U.S., 1841-57, and Fenn, in England, 1826-72) have been found. Wooden adjustable soles have also been reported. One type was made by sawing wedge-shaped slits in a smooth plane just above the sole and fitting adjustment screws. An adjustable wooden compass plane with a concave sole has also been found. The all-metal patented adjustable circular planes became available in the United States during the 1860's, and within a few decades had largely replaced the wooden types.

The UNIVERSAL plane was patented by Stephen Williams of Pennsylvania (28 June 1864, U.S. 43360). It consists of a truncated stock containing the throat, with the rest of the body made up of vertical slices with rounded bottoms. These may be arranged to approximate the desired curvature and fixed in this configuration by means of a peripheral strap. The only examples known to me have the central section made of metal.

One application which calls for an exact match of the plane's circular sole to the surface being worked is the shaping of felloes, the wooden segments that make up the rim of a wooden wheel. The FEL-LOE planes used to shape these exist with both concave and convex soles. It's rare to find a matched pair (Fig.9:4), where the radius of the concave sole is larger than that of its convex mate by the thickness of the fel-

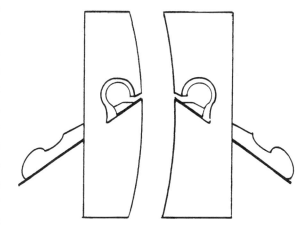

Fig.9:4—Felloe planes

loe. (Another way to cut a felloe is described in the section on radius planes, below.) The concave felloe plane, unmated, would be difficult to distinguish from the lagging plane, described in the next paragraph, except that the latter is usually wider.

The LAGGING plane is of jack size but with its sole concave lengthwise. It was made in different curvatures, and was used to smooth the wooden surfaces of the large pulleys used in belt drives.

The small COACHMAKER'S SMOOTH planes were made in three versions: with soles flat, with soles curved convex lengthwise, or curved concave lengthwise. Still smaller planes such as VIOLINMAKER'S (described with the smooth planes) are also seen in these variations and are found with spoon-shaped or doubly curved soles as well.

Coopers have uses for compass planes, calling them BOWLING planes. Their ROUNDING plane has a concave sole for dressing the outside of the finished cask. A plane with doubly curved convex sole is the STOUP or CLEANING-OUT plane, used to clean the insides of finished barrels. These tools are described more fully in Chapter 13 — The Cooper. Workers in other trades (luthiers, for example) use another name for a plane whose sole is curved in two directions: the ROUND-BOTH WAYS plane. This has a counterpart in a BALL plane made with its sole concave both ways (E.A. Rumayor, 1976) to finish a large wooden globe.

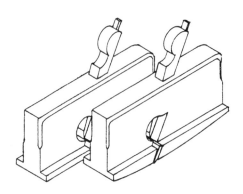

Fig.9:5—T-rabbet and compassed T-rabbet

The compass plane described earlier in this chapter may be considered identical with the smooth plane except for its curved sole. Almost any type of plane can be made with its sole curved longitudinally in the same fashion as the compass plane, and a great variety have been found. I will not describe each of these separately unless some peculiarity of use is known. Their names are simply the name of the straight variety prefixed with the adjective COMPASS or COMPASSED. As an example, the T-rabbet and a T-rabbet with a curved sole are both shown in Fig.9:5. The latter does not command a new name but is simply called a compassed T- rabbet. It trims the sides of a curved rabbet rather than a straight one.

Continental   The French call the compass plane RABOT CINTRÉ CONVEXE, although French wheelwrights call it RABOT À JANTES (felloe plane). These planes may be found in shapes much like the English tool and also with front horn grips. The German compass plane, the SCHIFFHOBEL (literally, ship plane) was made in great variety — scrub, smooth, double iron, toothing — almost always with a front horn. The Gerfschaaf (see Fig.3:4, Chapter 3) of the Netherlands is often found with a compass sole and the smaller GERFSCHAAFJES (Fig.9:6) were made in the same sole configurations as the violinmaker's planes described above.

158

European workshops usually had several compass planes of different sole curvature, until the adjustable metal circular plane replaced them.

An early Bossingschaaf (Holland's panel plane, Fig.4:17, Chapter 4) may be found with a compassed sole. The CO-LUMBELLE (French) or BACKENHOBEL (German) is a compassed plane with the blade exposed on one side and with a slanted sole. It is sketched and its use is described with the cooper's tools in Chapter 13 — The Cooper.

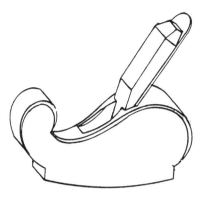

Fig.9:6—Gerfschaafje

Japanese   The Japanese SORI-KANNA or SORI-DAI-KANNA has the shape of a Japanese smooth plane, but with a compass sole. The same name is used for either convex or concave soles. The SHIHŌ-SORI-DAI- KANNA sole is both compassed and round (round both ways).

PLANES USED TO MAKE CYLINDRICAL GROOVES

English and American   The SHIP ROUND is a narrow double iron coffin smoother with a round sole (convex across its width) that was sometimes offered as a companion to the ship hollow (described in the next section), though much less common.

The PUMP, or PUMP LOG plane (Fig.9:7) is a peculiarly American plane. It has an integral fence and a flat sole, the center of which bulges out into a half cylinder. It was made both handled and unhandled and was used to cut semicircular grooves. Two long timbers were grooved using

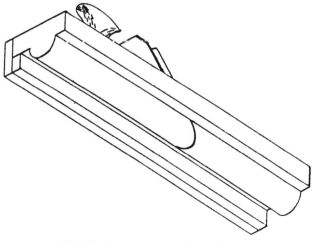

Fig.9:7—Pump, or pump log, plane

159

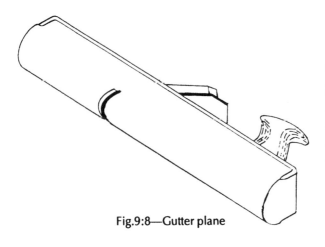

Fig.9:8—Gutter plane

this plane, then bound together (groove facing groove) to form a pipe that served as the barrel of a chain pump. It was also used to make wooden pipes of smaller diameter than could be made by pump log tools, e.g., "salt pipes" to carry brine. Chapin (1874) listed sizes of diameter 1 - 1.5 in. (25 - 38 mm.). FRENCH CASEMENT and the AIR-TIGHT CASEMAKER'S planes are of similar shape but smaller diameter, and are discussed in Chapter 13.

The GUTTER plane (called the SPOUT plane in England) is a jack plane that is rounded across the sole, usually with a single iron, and is used to cut wooden gutters or other wide hollow grooves (Fig.9:8). Many gutter planes are in fact owner-converted jacks, and are betrayed by their non-uniform mouth openings (cutting away the sole while rounding it widens the plane's mouth at the side). Planes made specifically to cut gutters have a uniform mouth. Early examples have an offset handle as do the early jacks. HAND GUTTER planes have no handles and are of the same size and shape as smooth planes, except for their round soles. A similar plane, but with its body curved, was used to form curved gutters and is quite rare. As with many other tools, gutter planes found additional uses beyond their original purpose of cutting conduits for rainwater. They were used, for example, to cut drainage gutters in breweries.

The COOPER'S STAVE plane is similar to the gutter plane, though usually wider and with a much shallower curvature. The convex sole type is used to shape the inside of barrel staves prior to bending. (The concave plane of the same name is mentioned in the next section.) These are user-made and infrequently found, as coopers normally used drawknives and shaves for this purpose. The staves of pails or buckets were sometimes made by shaping long boards to the proper curved profile with these planes, then cutting them to the desired length. The STAVE-HOLLOWING ENGINE guides a stave plane in a jig which serves to ensure a straight cut.

There are a number of different bench type planes with soles convex across their width, as we have seen. These can be arranged in a sequence of increasing radius of curvature. The first member, with flat or but slightly rounded sole, is the roughing jack. Slightly more curved is the backing-out

160

jack, described with the jack planes. The cooper's stave-hollowing plane has about the same curvature range. A short jack with a slightly round sole may have been made by a cooper for hollowing pail staves, or by a shipwright. The degree of curvature alone will not differentiate these two uses, and body style must be relied upon to guess at the plane's original purpose. Clues gained by examination of planes in maritime and cooper's museums may be helpful.

Planes with a degree of curvature between the backing-out jack and the gutter plane are not uncommon, and are frequently classed as gutter planes. My own belief is that a plane of the correct shape with an iron edge radius of curvature of three inches or less may be assumed without undue risk to be either a gutter plane or a hollow used to rough out a cornice molding, but a larger radius should raise doubt as to the plane's original purpose.

Continuing toward smaller radii, ship rounds may cover a range but their body style is fairly characteristic. The pump plane is in the same curvature range, but is fenced.

These points illustrate the fact that many planes are seen whose original purpose may only be guessed at. An unequivocal identification of function should almost always have a small mental question mark appended.

SIDE ESCAPEMENT TYPES

Up to this point, the planes of this section have been of bench type. Let us now examine planes with a side escapement for shavings.

The GUNSTOCKER'S plane (Fig.9:9) is used to finish a channel in the gunstock, which holds the gun barrel. Although this term has been used to refer to any molding plane with a sole covering a full half-circle, such planes are rather too common to have served only this use. They are described in Chapter 10 under the name "full rounds." The tools found in gunmaker's kits are usually shorter than the standard molding plane length, and have the sole continued beyond the full semicircle, until it indents the stock. Not all rifle makers used such a tool, preferring instead to use the end of the gunbarrel itself, filed square, as a scraper; the plane itself is not common (Perch 1986). The unusual sole facilitates shaping the bed to fit the slightly tapered barrel. Planes of

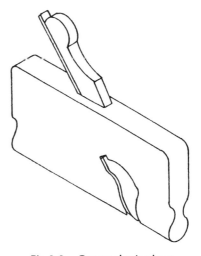

Fig.9:9—Gunstocker's plane

161

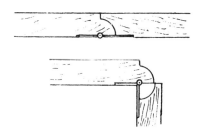

Fig.9:10—Rule joint,
closed and dropped

similar shape but with a smaller diameter, obviously too small for a barrel, are also found. While these may have been used for cutting ramrod grooves, it is more likely that they were made for other grooving purposes. Planes of this type with soles of larger diameter were used to cut wooden bearings for axles, and examples are to be seen in the Wildung collection at the Shelburne Museum, Vermont.

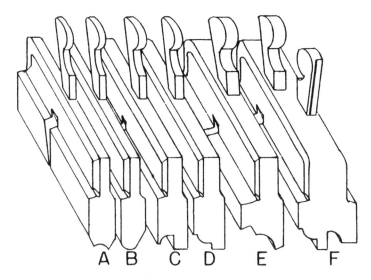

A B   C D   E   F

Fig.9:11—Table planes

TABLE planes are used to cut the moldings used on drop-leaf tables, to improve the appearance of the joint when the leaves are dropped. The table-top has a quarter round projection at the lower edge of the leaf joint. This mates with a quarter-round hollow in the edge of the leaf, as shown in Fig.9:10. These joints may be cut with a special hollow and round pair which cut full quarter circles (Fig.9:11 A and B). Called TABLE HOLLOWS and ROUNDS, they were listed in sizes from ⅜ to ¾in.(10 - 19 mm.) — the size marked being the diameter of the cut in some catalogs, the thickness of the stock to be worked in others. These are easily confused with common hollow and round molding planes. The distinctions are covered in Chapter 10.

Rather easier to use are the TABLE PLANES WITH FENCE (Fig.9:11 C and D). These appear to be a simple cove and a fenced quarter round, but are

162

sized to create the proper mating at the joint. Unlike most planes, the hollow (C) is applied to the edge of the stock rather than the face, and its fence is guided by the under surface. Ohio Tool (Ohio) offered these in sizes of ½ to ¾ in. (13 - 19 mm.) with a somewhat modified profile, cutting rather more than a quarter circle. They also combined a pair in one stock (in the style called come-and-go) as TWIN TABLE planes (Fig.9:11F). Planes are known which appear to be concave table planes with fence, but shaped to be guided by the upper surface of the table rather than the lower. The example shown in Fig.9:11E was made by W. Raymond (Massachusetts, ca.1800). Its use as a table plane is speculative, and the original intent might have been simply decorative.

Some makers included gauges with their table planes to ensure proper placement of the cut. These were of sheet metal shaped to form marking points.

The joint is sometimes called a "rule joint" from the resemblance to the joints of old style folding rules, and the planes RULE JOINT planes. There are true rule joint planes, used to cut the ends of rule sections for their joints. These have a profile like those above, though smaller, and have vertical or high pitched irons. These and other tools are described in a section on rulemakers in Chapter 13.

A pair of planes to cut a similar joint is shown in Fig.9:12. Their original purpose is not known, but one possibility is that they formed a match joint on the meeting stiles of double doors or casement sash.

Fig.9:12—Pair of match joint planes

A side escapement plane with a sole similar in shape to a pump plane, but of smaller diameter, was used in the making of casement windows. Another of similar shape but with much smaller radius was used in making museum cases and is one of a set called AIR-TIGHT CASE planes. The COREBOX plane is a clever device used by patternmakers to make a large groove. All three types are described in Chapter 13.

Perhaps the smallest cylindrical grooving plane was used to groove slips of wood to make pencils. The graphite was placed between two such slips; these were glued together and then planed to form cylindrical or polygonal pencils.

(Continental and Japanese types are included with the cylindrical surface planes following the next section.)

PLANES USED FOR CYLINDRICAL SURFACES

English and American   The name ROUNDER refers to a number of devices for forming dowels. In its simplest form, it is a block of wood pierced by a hole enlarged by a taper at its entrance and fitted with a cutter mounted tangent to its exit. A variety of owner-made versions are found. In use, the end of a stick of appropriate size is roughly tapered and fixed in a vise or otherwise held. The large entrance end of the rounder is placed over the tapered end of the stick and the rounder is rotated much like a large school-box pencil sharpener. As it works its way down the stick, a dowel is formed.

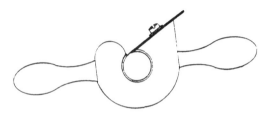

Fig.9:13—Rounder

Several commercial versions were (and are) made. The most common of these has a spiral or snail-shaped stock, pierced with a hole of the shape described (Fig.9:13). This is fitted with a slotted cutter, mounted by screws to a bed surface tangent to the hole. The iron is usually single, but double-iron models were also made. Two lathe-turned peg handles, perpendicular to the hole, were commonly provided for easier hand-over-hand turning. Sets were offered by British manufacturers to cut dowels from ⅝ to 1½ in. (16 - 38 mm.) in diameter.

This simple device has a multitude of names and shapes, depending on the size of the dowel to be cut, or the use to which the product is put. Self-explanatory are DOWELLING BOX (often with multiple holes), FORK-STAFF ROUNDER, STAIL ENGINE (stail is an old name for a long round handle

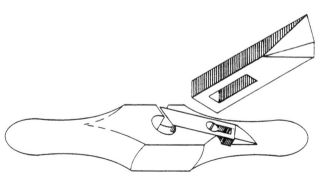

Fig.9:14—Rung tenon rounder

such as a hoe handle), and LADDER ROUND-ER. The form shown in Fig.9:14 has a blade with edge segments at right angles to each other: one pares the end-grain of the work, the other shaves across the grain. This tool may be used to form round tenons on the ends of rungs, as well as to make dowels.

A tool even more like the pencil sharpener is the TAPER ROUNDER (or DOWEL POINTER in smaller sizes). This has the same general shape as the rounder, but the blade edge is straight and mounted parallel to the side of a uniformly tapered hole. This form finds use for push broom handles, chair rungs, and other items requiring a force fit. A small tool of this type has surfaced consisting of a 4 in. (10 cm.) diameter oak body with a 1½ in. (38 mm.) blade. This has an extension to permit mounting in a primitive brace.

A variant of the rounder is fitted with a moveable block which can be adjusted to intrude more or less into the hole, permitting the cutting of different diameters. A better method of selecting the size of the dowel to be cut is used in the WITCHET or WIDGET (these names have also been used for fixed rounders). This tool consists of two blocks, one of which (rarely, both) has a blade similar to the fixed rounder. The size of dowel to be cut is selected by adjusting the spacing between these blocks, and the most common method of doing this is by the use of wooden screwarms to connect them. Each block is grooved transversely in the arc of a circle. At full opening these arcs define the largest cylinder that can be cut. Smaller dowels, of course, are cut by reducing the spacing of the blocks. A particular advantage of the witchet is its ability to change the diameter during the cut, to form gently tapered handles. Among its other names are ADJUSTABLE ROUNDER (England) and TURNING plane (Scotland).

The particularly fine model shown in Fig.9:15 was made by Mockridge and Francis (New Jersey, 1835-1869). The handles of the two wood screws serve also as the grips while cutting with the tool. The blocks are kept in alignment by four square staves sliding in mortises. After setting the size, the position is fixed by four brass thumbscrews opposing the wood screws. Two blades are used, working as in the rounder described above. One acts in the same manner as a lathe tool cutting end grain; the other follows and cuts cross-grain.

The TRAP (Fig.9:16) is a small witchet, the two halves hinged

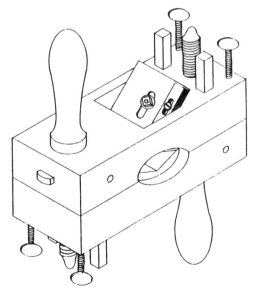

Fig.9:15—Witchet

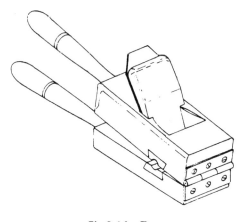

Fig.9:16—Trap

and fitted with dowel handles at the opposite end. Both dowels are held in one hand for easy control of cutting diameter through finger pressure. It was used for rounding fishing rods. These were spun in a lathe, and the trap moved along it with increasing pressure on the handles to taper it. Another FISHING ROD MAKER'S plane has a longitudinal groove in the sole (as in the cock bead, seen later) and a nearly vertical iron. It cuts along the length, rather than around the rod. The high pitch is needed for working the bamboo used in the rods.

The TRENAIL ROUNDER or MOOT was used in British shipyards to make the wooden dowels used in pegging ship timbers. It is similar to the witchet, but usually has integral handles and a plated mouth. Similar dowels, called trunnels in America, were used here for post-and-beam construction. They were not normally rounded, but were roughly shaped by hatchet or knife in the belief that this made them hold better.

A TURK'S HEAD (Fig.9:17) was used to form a tapered end on wooden

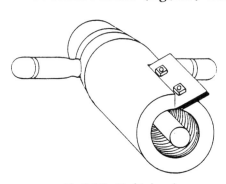

Fig.9:17—Turk's head

pipes. Its round stock is fitted with a wide blade mounted as in a taper rounder. It has, in addition, a central core to fit the hole in the wooden pipe. This ensured that the taper cut would be concentric with the bore so that, after mating with a reamed hole in the matching length of pipe, the bores would line up. Transverse handles on the TURK'S HEAD served to turn the tool.

The FORKSTAFF plane (Fig.9:18) also serves to cut long tool handles, but works along the grain rather than around the shaft. It is found in both smooth and jack sizes, with a hollow groove running the length of the sole. The groove profile is a circular arc, the only curve which will fit at any position around the cylindrical handle. The Gabriel inventories (1791-1793) list the Forkstaff with either a single or double iron. Other makers varied the name to FORKSHAFT or FORKSTAIL. It was still being offered in the twentieth century.

166

In the 18th and early 19th centuries the name Forkstaff and its variants seem to have served for all sizes of bench type hollows. Later different names appeared: OAR, SPAR, and MAST referred to planes of increasing radius of curvature. British oar or spar planes were frequently the size of the smooth plane, with a rectangular sole but with the upper part of the stock rounded in coffin shape. Variants include steel soles and planes with short soles having the rear of the body extended to form a handle called a squirrel tail.

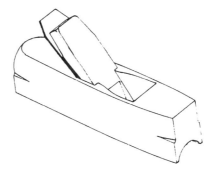

Fig.9:18—Forkstaff plane

In the United States the Forkstaff type planes were collectively known as SHIP HOLLOWS and were normally shaped like the coffin smooth plane (see Chapter 3) and fitted with double irons, although jack sizes were also made. Skew irons are rare. Two such planes are in the Dominy collection (Winterthur): one at common pitch dated 1769, another in satinwood dated 1815 with an almost vertical iron. The mating Ship Round was described above.

The name TAMBOUR plane appears in English catalogs without illustration. It is presumed to be a fenced deep hollow used to cut the tambour strips that make up the roll top for desks. The BLIND plane was used to cut slats for window blinds. As shown in the Barton (New York, 1873) catalog, it is a jack plane whose sole is grooved in a shallow circular arc set between two fences. The fences touch bottom on the bench top when the proper thickness of slat is reached.

A concave form of the COOPER'S STAVE plane is a wide smooth or jack size with sole slightly hollow across, used to shape the outer side of staves. The planes are owner-made and rarer than the convex type, which was described in the previous section.

The smallest cylindrical surface is cut by the very rare MATCHSTICK plane (Fig.9:19).

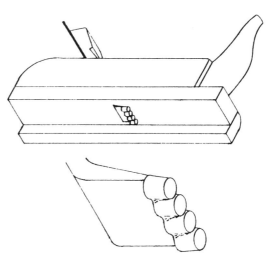

Fig.9:19—Matchstick plane

The cutting iron is configured as a series of tubes, each having a sharpened mouth, and each parallel to the sole. As the matchstick plane is pushed through soft wood, splints of matchstick size emerge.

TABLE HOLLOWS are side escapement planes used to form profiles on drop-leaf tables; their variants and use were described with their mates, the table rounds, in the previous section.

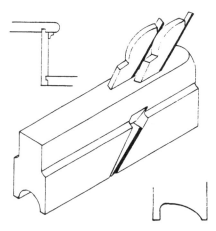

Fig.9:20—Nosing plane
(lower right: French profile)

The NOSING plane cuts a full half circle, and was used to round the overhanging treads of staircases (as seen in the upper left section of Fig.9:20). Some catalogs used the name STEP plane or STEP NOSING plane, as they used the name "nosing" for a type of molding. The bench type nosing plane was not usual in Great Britain or the United States, although I. White (Pennsylvania, 1831-39) made at least one. The more usual side escapement form was listed (for example in the Greenfield 1872 catalog) in sizes from ⅜ to 2 in. (10 - 51 mm.) An improved form (Fig.9:20) is fitted with two irons in separate mouths, each cutting a quarter circle. The irons were skewed in opposite directions, to obtain a smoother cutting action near the vertical sections of the profile.

The WASHBOARD plane cuts a wave-like pattern of hollows and rounds. It was used to form the wooden washboards that were standard laundry equipment before they were replaced by the metal or glass versions. The sole of the plane frequently matches two grooves, while the blade cuts but one, the plane being guided by the groove previously cut.

Continental   The German gutter plane, WASSERRINNER-HOBEL, is found with peg handles front and rear, for easier handling in deep gutters. The smaller plane corresponding to our ship round is the HOHLKEHLHOBEL (differentiated from the side escapement hollow of the same name by adding "spanloch oben", chip opening above). Weiss (Austria, 1909) pictured a plane with a concave lengthwise sole and fence, in the center of which was a round protrusion, as a BETTEN-HOHLKEHLHOBEL, geschweift (beds grooving plane, curved). This would cut a hollow groove around the circumference of a cylindrical surface.

168

German catalogs list the RUNDSTABHOBEL (round staff plane) in both top and side escapement varieties, corresponding to the fork-staff plane and the hollow molder. The bench type (top escapement) was available horned or unhandled, with single or double iron. Different curvatures were offered as rakemaker's planes, ladder- pole planes, wheel spoke planes, etc. A

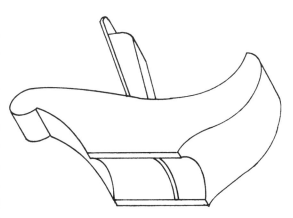

Fig.9:21—Continental spoke plane

"shorter haft plane" with peg handles and sole shortened by cutting back the stock was also made.

The French names RABOTS CREUX or MOUCHETTES and the German Rundstabhobel serve for both forkstaff planes and hollow molders. A hollow with a short sole (Fig.9:21) is favored by Continental wheelwrights, who refer to it by their translation of "wheel spoke plane." As in English, there are a variety of other names.

The names used in France and Germany for rounders or witchets are simple translations of "handle plane" (RABOT POUR MANCHES, STIEL-HOBEL). Commercial forms are much like the American or English. An amusing make-do in the Musée du Bois, Lausanne, Switzerland, is a wood block bored with holes of

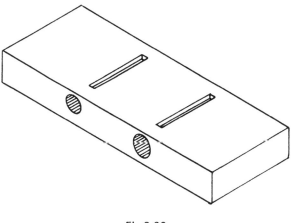

Fig.9:22

various sizes nearly tangent to one face, and slotted to permit entry by the blade of a plane (Fig.9:22). A common smoother is fixed to the block with its blade entering one of the slots and voilà! — a rounder.

169

The French nosing plane, the NEZ DE MARCHE, usually does not cut a true semicircle but a figure more sharply curved on one side than on the other, as shown by an inset in Fig.9:20 (lower right). A 20th century version is in the form of a handled smooth plane.

Japanese   The forkstaff plane is called UCHIMARU-KANNA, and is simply a thicker Japanese smooth plane with a cylindrical groove in the sole, and blade to match. The corresponding round is called SOTOMARU-KANNA.

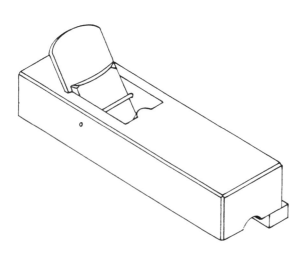

Fig.9:23—Japanese storm door plane (tongue)

Cap irons are common in these Japanese planes, in contrast to their absence with most English or American curved- edge irons. Another refinement rarely seen in our planes is the shaping of the front of the throat to correspond to the blade edge profile, giving easier passage to the shavings.

A profile similar to a casement sash match (see Chapter 13 — Sashmaker) is used on the edges of Japanese wooden storm doors. (These removable doors are put in place as needed for protection of their open architecture from rain and wind.) One edge is given a hollow groove, the other a semicircular tongue to fit into it. The planes used to cut this are INRŌ-MEN-TORI-KANNA. The tongue plane is shown in Fig.9:23. Both members of the pair, to cut the male and female elements, are shaped like the common hira-kanna and have filletster fences. In addition to planes cutting a semicircular pattern, another type makes a cut of trapezoidal section. The latter usually uses two irons (skewed in opposite directions) in the plane cutting the male element, which improves the surface on the steep sides of the cut.

RADIUS PLANES

As there are three directions in space, there are three directions in which a plane's sole may be curved. Hollows and rounds are curved across the sole. Soles of compass planes are curved lengthwise, and planes with soles concave longitudinally have also been described.

This leaves one more type of curvature, that in which the plane's body is curved lengthwise as viewed from the top. These planes move in horizontal arcs. Some tools of this type, to be described in Chapter 13 with Cooper's and Wheelwright's tools, were fitted with a trammel arm so that they could be swung from a center. More commonly, such planes are meant to be guided by a curved surface on the workpiece.

There seems to be no recognized or generally accepted name for this type of curvature in America. A plow plane designed to cut a groove in a circular path has been called a "circular plow", but a "circular plane" is the common name for an adjustable compass plane. The name "circular" therefore seems inappropriate as a general name for the curvature described here. The situation is no better in French or German: Rabot Cintré or Bogenhobel means simply a curved plane, and these names are used for different types of curvature. Either name needs further description to specify the type of curvature.

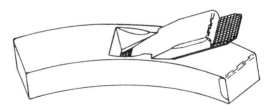

Fig.9:24—Cooper's sun plane

Perhaps because of the trammel mentioned, this type of plane has been called a RADIUS plane. A rabbet plane intended to make a horizontally curved rabbet is called a "radius rabbet" in England. For lack of a generally accepted name, any plane designed to travel in a horizontal arc will be called a radius plane, or radiused, in this book.

An extreme example of a curved body is the cooper's sun plane (Fig.9:24 and described in Chapter 13 — Cooper), in which the body is shaped to ride on the stave ends of a barrel.

The RADIUS RABBET has its body curved in a manner which allows it to cut a rabbet in a horizontal circular curve. If the cut is to be made along a significant portion of a circle, cross-grain cutting becomes necessary, and the tool should be equipped with spurs or nicker irons. A rare form of dado plane

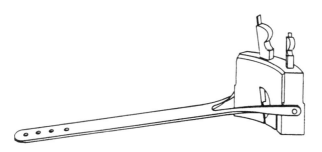

is found with a curved stock attached to an iron trammel (Fig.9:25). One use for such an arrangement has been described as forming decorative grooves around the sides of wheels for circus wagons, the plane pivoting around a pin through a

Fig.9:25—Radius dado on trammel

hole in the trammel. Another plane of this type is seen in the section on wheelwrights in Chapter 13.

An example contrasting a radius plane with a compass plane is seen in an application to the circular hole in a dry sink. You wish to cut a rabbet around its circumference to hold the basin. This could be cut with a compass filletster, working from inside the hole. It would be easier to cut it from the top, using a RADIUS FILLETSTER as shown in Fig.9:26.

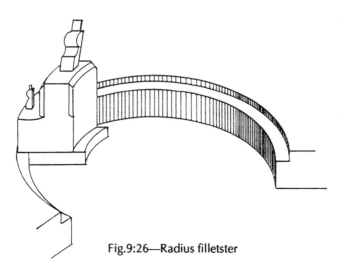

Fig.9:26—Radius filletster

Except for the radius rabbet and trammel planes, the radius planes are usually meant to be guided by an existing curved surface. Even without a fence, the rabbet is guided (once started) by the side of the rabbet it is cutting. A rabbet plane with a curved stock, as shown in Fig.9:27, has the advantage of being usable with either a concave or convex guiding surface, but in spite of this is a rare form. The one shown has two throats, for cutting in either direction; an important consideration because a curved rabbet plane cannot simply be turned around to work a different grain direction, as the common rabbet can. More common is a rabbet with both sides of the stock convex, so that it can work against a concave wall. No English name has been documented for this, but it is commonly referred to as a BOAT-SHAPED RABBET (the French prefer to describe it as a shuttle

172

shape, RABOT À NAVETTE). This can also, for sharper curvature, be made as a common rabbet with the lower stock cut away in the shuttle shape (Fig.9:28). If the curve is sharp, the sole may be rather short. Finally, for planes to work on the outside of a curve, a rectangular body may have an arc cut out of its side leaving a concave fence

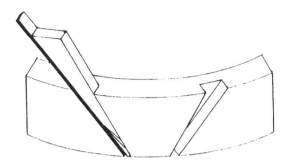

Fig.9:27—Curved stock rabbet

and radius sole. This last type is most often seen in molding planes used to profile the edges of round tabletops or similar objects.

As in the case of compass curvature mentioned above, a variety of molding planes may be found with radiused soles. Unless there is a specific application to be covered, these are not enumerated separately.

A few examples of a plane believed to have been used by wheelwrights to cut felloes (wheel rim segments) have been found. This consists of two stocks joined by wedged staves. Each has a curved section cut out of its sole, one concave and one convex, permitting it to straddle

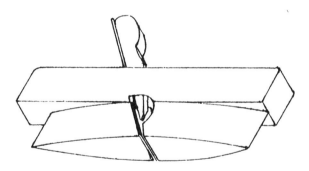

Fig.9:28—Boat-shaped rabbet

the felloe from the side. A nicker and iron in each stock remove wood from the workpiece leaving the felloe. It is assumed that it would be started using a pattern affixed to a board; once the cut is begun, the plane would be self-guiding.

It is possible to incorporate both types of curvature in one plane. A compassed rabbet is occasionally seen with the sides of the sole beveled away at heel and toe, presumably for angled radius cuts. Moldings on arched church windows, fanlights, or any other curved surfaces in quantities too great to be handled by scratch stocks or profiled spokeshaves would call for acquisition of planes made for the specific purpose. If the profile calls for the plane stock to be held at an angle (see "spring"), however, the curve must be radiused as well as compassed. Such sash molding planes are spoken of as doubly compassed, or for circle-on-circle work. Coachmakers, in particular, had a variety of planes with short, compassed soles to handle the curved surfaces they so often worked with, and these include doubly curved forms.

Examples of curvature, both concave and convex, in the three possible directions have been seen, as well as some curved in two directions simultaneously. For an example of a plane curved in all three directions (compassed, radiused and profile) see the wreathing plane in the section on stairbuilding in Chapter 13.

Chapter 10

DECORATIVE MOLDING PLANES — SIMPLE

MOLDINGS - ORIGINS

The simplest form of a molding is a rounding of the arris, or sharp edge where two surfaces meet. This not only gives a more comfortable feel, but the corner is less subject to the scars of daily wear. We may safely assume that this was known to the earliest woodworkers. Simple as a rounding is, it is still subject to variations. If the curve is given an oval or elliptical shape rather than a circular arc, the appearance changes significantly. A horizontal ellipse has the visual effect of thinning the piece, while a vertical one makes it appear more massive. A projecting member such as a table top may have the curve continued onto the under surface to further increase the thinning effect. The striking change in appearance created by these simple moldings inspired further variations.

All of the elements used later in wood molding were known and used by the Greeks in their stone architecture. They showed that linear moldings could add emphasis and richness to the lines of the structure without competing with the sculptural adornment. They brought the proper use of these moldings to a perfection that has been imitated ever since. They also created a large vocabulary to describe the shapes and locations of the elements. Many of these names have been appropriated by planemakers — in some cases with rather confusing results.

The Renaissance reawakened interest in Classic architecture, and architects of the time made pilgrimages to study the surviving structures. One of these was Andrea Palladio, who published his measurements, interpretations and opinions in 1570. His writings achieved wide circulation, were translated into several languages, and were reissued in a number of editions over many years. These included one with notes by Inigo Jones, the architect (1573-1652) and one of the creators of the English Classical style, who was much influenced by Palladio. After the Great Fire of London in 1666, much of the rebuilding of the city was shaped by Christopher Wren (1632-1723), another admirer of the Palladian style.

Greek architecture was not bound by rigid conventions, but it pleased later admirers of the Greek style to create iron-clad rules on proportions and

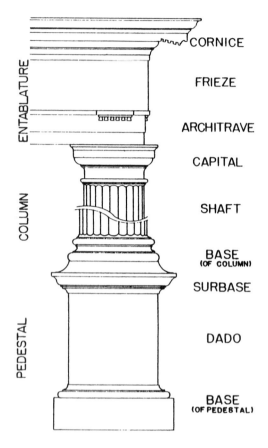

ENTABLATURE
COLUMN
PEDESTAL

CORNICE

FRIEZE

ARCHITRAVE

CAPITAL

SHAFT

BASE
(OF COLUMN)

SURBASE

DADO

BASE
(OF PEDESTAL)

Fig.10:1—Elements of Doric architecture

placement of the elements. They defined the shape and sequence of moldings to be used in each of the Orders. The Greek names, or their Latin forms, entered the architectural vocabulary and remain to this day. The entablature was supported by the columns and in turn carried the roof plate on the sides or the pediment in front and rear. The entablature was divided into three sections. The lower group of moldings was termed the architrave, the upper the cornice, these two separated by a vertical frieze. A molding over a door or window opening, usually carried down the sides as well, is now called an architrave, and a cornice now tops a tall piece of furniture or fills the angle between wall and ceiling.

The Palladian style dominated architecture. It is not surprising that features of it were borrowed by many of the cabinetmakers of the day. The first eight plates of Thomas Chippendale's book *The Gentleman & Cabinet-Maker's Director* (1762) give precise drawings and details of columns of the Five Orders of architecture, with a preface stating that these were the "Soul and Basis" of the cabinetmaker's art. The texts of the Boston architect Asher Benjamin were widely used and helped to shape American architectural thought in the first half of the 19th century. Major portions of these were devoted to description of Greek features. The names of the moldings that the cabinetmakers and house joiners used were in many cases taken directly from the names of the decorative features of the columns.

A round protrusion circling the column and semicircular in cross- section is called a torus. An astragal is a similar but smaller band, flanked by short vertical areas. (Taken from the Greek for vertebra or anklebone, the word has been used in other contexts with somewhat different meaning.) An ovolo (Italian, little egg) is a convex quarter-round between a horizontal and a vertical feature, while a cove or cavetto (from the Latin for hollow) is the corresponding concave depression. A scotia (from the Greek for darkness, because of the shadow it forms) may be considered as a smaller cove smoothly joined to a larger one, forming a groove separating two different levels. A dado is the flat, recessed part of a column base. A quirk is a small channel or groove separating two other features; a fillet a small straight segment. Flutes are hollow grooves, as seen in the vertical features of the column. The ogee is an S-shaped curve formed by joining two circular arcs of equal radius, each one-sixth of a circle, one concave and one convex. The simple ogee (cyma recta) has the convex or round arc nearer the center of the column, the concave or hollow further out; while the reverse ogee (cyma reversa) has the round on the outside. All easy to differentiate on a column, but causing problems when naming the feature in a molding — as we shall see.

Some of the features of the Doric structure of Figure 10:1 (freely adapted from Palladio) are named here to point out the source of many of the familiar names of molding planes. There is a cornice composed of (from the top down) an ogee, fillet, and reverse ogee above the corona or drip edge, and under it an ovolo, fillet, and cove. The capital of the column shows a fillet, cove and wide fillet as abacus or topmost figure, with an ovolo separated by two fillets from a necking of an extended cove (the apophyge) followed by an astragal. The column base has an upper and lower torus separated by fillets and scotia, below which is a wide cove. The pedestal surbase has an ogee, two fillets and a cove above the dado, and the base has a cove and a torus above the plinth.

The word "scotia" was perhaps the most misused of the classical names. The catalogs do not list a plane which cuts the scotia as defined above. Most catalogs list as a scotia a plane which cuts a cove, while several others (including Arrowmammett and Ohio Tool) regard scotia and quarter-round as synonymous. This book will use the term in the architectural sense as a smaller cove smoothly joined to a larger one, forming a groove separating two different levels. Several of the other names have undergone changes of meaning as applied to plane shapes. Torus, for example, acquired a specialized meaning (see beads) and the name "bead" replaced it in the plane vocabulary.

While the classical Greek moldings were made with either circular or elliptical arcs, the early design books — including Chippendale's — used nothing but circular. So did the early moldings. But with the "Greek revival" of the early 19th century the older moldings went out of style and were replaced by profiles described as of elliptical arcs. These were known by the fashionable name of "Grecian" while the older ones were rechristened "Roman". In fact, the new moldings were most often made up by joining circular arcs of different radii, or even straight line segments, to approximate the elliptical arcs.

Moldings were originally cut into the body of the structural member or piece of furniture, but it was soon found that cutting the molding on a separate piece of wood and then attaching it offered advantages. These were called "planted" moldings as opposed to the former "stuck" moldings. If two surfaces meet at an inside angle, applying a finish is difficult. The maid or housewife would not like it because it would gather dust and be hard to clean. A molding was planted, alleviating both problems. Tall pieces such as a chest-on-chest or secretary were made in two parts, separable for moving. The joint between them could be covered or disguised by a molding. Certain joinings might be made more rapidly with nails or screws. A planted molding would hide the telltale heads.

These utilitarian uses of moldings were overshadowed by their decorative function. While today moldings are usually selected from stock lengths at the lumberyard or cut with a standard router bit, they were once considered to be a major part of architectural design. It was common for the architect to send drawings of the profiles he wanted to planemakers, to have his molders custom-made. A "gentleman of taste" would not allow an "improper" molding to be used in his home.

MOLDING PLANES - GENERAL

Purists of earlier years chose not to call tools designed to cut curved profiles "planes", which name they held to be restricted to tools cutting plane surfaces. They were called molding tools. The art of making and using these tools is so closely related to the techniques of the bench plane, however, that the present name is almost universally accepted.

Western molding planes are most often made with a side escapement, although those intended for the wider cuts may utilize the bench style top escapements. Narrow molders have a rectangular cross-section, but wider molding planes will have the top portion of their stocks narrowed to form a handhold. A sketch of this type is seen in Figure 10:2, which also gives some of the nomenclature.

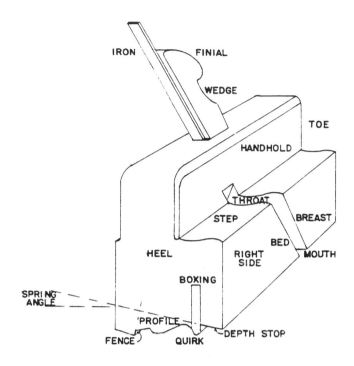

Fig.10:2—Molding plane nomenclature

A tapered mortise is cut from top to bottom through the stock (or body of the plane), and is sized to be completely filled by the wedge and iron. Below the step, the right side of the stock is opened to meet this tapered wedge mortise, thus forming the throat. The rear wall is called the bed, as it is in bench planes, but in molding planes the front wall is termed the breast. The side of the lower end of the wedge is cut away on a slant, to divert shavings toward the escapement.

The molding profile (in English and American planes) is laid out on the sole with two objectives in mind. First, that with the plane in cutting position, no portion of the curve of the iron will be any closer to vertical than necessary (a near vertical segment of cutting edge does not cut as well as a horizontal one); and second, that the overall curve is as nearly horizontal as possible, which helps to make the mouth opening of uniform width. To accomplish this, it is usually necessary when using the plane to hold it at an angle from the vertical. This is called the spring angle. Spring, and the effect of vertical cutting edge segments, are both explored in greater detail in Appendix 1.

179

Beyond the profile on the left, the sole drops to form a fence. This serves to guide the plane by riding along the left side of the piece being worked. On the right side, the stock projects to form a depth stop that contacts the work surface and stops the cutting action when the desired depth is reached.

In use, the plane is held with the fence against the left edge of the workpiece and the stock slanted at the spring angle. The spring angle is usually found from the two scribed lines on the front of the stock (and sometimes on the rear, as well). One line continues the line of the depth stop and the other extends the fence wall upward, the two meeting in a right angle. These are the spring marks. The plane is held at the angle that makes the depth stop line horizontal. In the absence of spring marks, one must rely on the slope of the fence and depth stop to establish the correct angle. With the plane fixed at this angle, the molding is cut until the depth stop hits the work and the blade can cut no further.

Thin sections of the sole, such as the quirk shown in the drawing, are exposed to rapid wear. These points of high wear are usually strengthened by a technique called boxing, in which diagonal slices are taken from boxwood logs and cut into slips with the grain running diagonally across. These slips are inserted into slots that have been grooved into the sole of the plane, the boxwood grain running downward back to front. The partial end grain boxwood resists wear much longer than the beech of the stock would. (In dovetail boxing the boxwood grain direction runs lengthwise.) Occasionally other dense woods such as lignum vitae are substituted for the boxwood. The section on "Boxing" covers various placements of these inserted strips.

Continental   It is unwise to make any categorical statements about the form of the molder in various cultures, as their makers were individuals and not always bound by the customs of their peers. Nevertheless, a few generalizations may be made with the warning that exceptions will be numerous. One significant difference is the absence of spring in molding planes other than English or American.

Figure 10:3 shows three typical Continental molders: Dutch (A), German (B), and French (C). As may be seen, the stocks of French molders are not generally cut away for hand-holds. German molders are often of rectangular cross-section or have a molded groove cut in the right side for improved grip. Those from France are either rectangular or have top wider than bottom — unless the bottom must carry a filletster fence. Of late, Peugeot Frères (France) and others cut an open throat and close it with an applied batten, again giving the wider top. Wedges (Fig.10:4) do not have the English rounded finial, but use a simple angle cut in an otherwise straight front edge. The French may

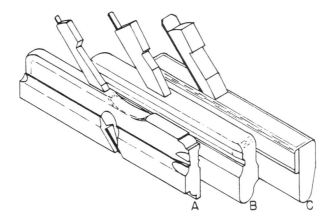

Fig.10:3—Continental molders

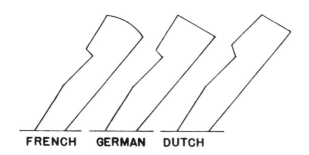

FRENCH   GERMAN   DUTCH

Fig.10:4—Continental wedges

slightly round the top of the wedge; the Germans usually leave it flat. In the border provinces, where sovereignty has passed back and forth over the centuries, there is a melding of national styles. This is particularly noticeable in the bilingual Lachappelle catalog.

Molding planes from The Netherlands have a characteristic curved depression, with rounded edges, in the top of the stock in front of the iron. Two deep gouge cuts, one on each side of a chisel cut, mark the side fronts, and one gouge cut the rear. It has been suggested by Philip Walker (1983) that these are vestiges of the type of stock shown by the English MARY ROSE tools. Their wedge finials are formed by a simple wedge-shaped notch as it is in the French and German, although frequently the finial is narrowed toward the top.

181

Far Eastern   Chinese molding planes take various shapes, not unexpected in largely user-made tools. They are taller than the Chinese low bench planes, often tapering in height toward toe and heel. Open-sided throats, as in early European molders, are found. Wedges are without finial, either unrelieved angles or with rounded projections at top front; and they are often shorter than ours.

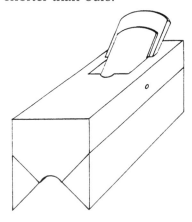

Fig.10:5—Japanese
quarter round plane

Older Japanese molders may be provided with handholds, either Roman style, near the front of the plane, or by thickening the upper stock. The iron is held by a simple wedge placed behind it. Later, top escapement stocks in the form of the common hand plane (hira-kanna) were made with profiled soles. The example in Fig.10:5 is a simple corner rounding plane. It is not unusual to see cap irons in Japanese molders, nor to see the shape of the front of the throat corresponding to the sole profile. These niceties are not usual in Western planes, except for some made by Tolman (Massachusetts, 1820-1860-). Wide molders with complex profiles use irons in separate throats, staggered one behind the other.

Molding planes are also made for the purpose of texturing surfaces. These resemble a Japanese badger plane but have the skew of the throat reversed and slightly patterned cutting edges. They are used cross-grain to simulate, for instance, the marks left by a hewing axe or the pattern of pine bark.

Molding an inside corner is rarely attempted in the West. Molding of the inner edges of stiles and rails is completed before assembly, or the moldings are made separately and planted. There are Japanese planes, however, intended for this purpose. The pistol molding plane (TEPPŌ-MEN-TORI-KANNA) is made with a sole like the quarter rounding plane (Fig.10:5) with the profiled edge between 45° fences, and with the body of the plane behind the blade removeable. (Behind in the Western sense: as Japanese planes are pulled, they would say in front of the blade.) This permits starting the molding near an inside corner, with the molding to be completed using carving tools. They are made in left- and right-hand forms for unsymmetrical moldings. Another form used for shaping concave edges has the left or the right 45° fence cut away in a curve, permitting it to fit inside the curve.

182

MAKING MOLDING PLANES

Molding or other side escapement planes are made by a somewhat different procedure than that used for bench planes. Edward Ingraham has contributed much research on the eighteenth century planes of New England, and has provided a detailed account of his procedure for reproducing these (Roberts 1983).

In brief, a block of seasoned yellow birch is sawn and planed to shape and rabbeted for the handhold. Construction lines are scribed for bed and breast on both sides of the stock, and for the wedge mortise on top; and spring lines are scribed at toe and heel. The latter define the cuts for fence and depth stop. The desired profile is scribed at toe and heel, located by the spring lines. If boxing is desired, the groove for this is plowed and the boxwood slip installed. The sole is roughed out with repeated cuts of a plow, refined with hollows and rounds, and finished with a scraper ground to the correct shape.

If many planes of the same profile are to be made, the shaping of the sole is greatly simplified by first making a MOTHER or BACKING plane (the name COUNTER plane is also seen). This has a sole whose profile mates with the sole of the planes to be made. That is, its shape is that of the desired molding, and it can be used to plane the required profile in one step on the plane blanks. The profile of a mother plane for a side bead is shown in Fig.10:6 (top), with the sole it cuts (bottom).

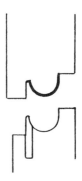

Fig.10:6—
Mother plane
and product

A backsaw is used to cut along the bed and breast lines from the depth stop to the base of the handhold, and the waste is removed by chisel. The wedge slot is outlined on top of the stock by a shallow mortise. A small hole is bored from the center of this to the sawn opening. The hole is enlarged and shaped with saw float and narrow chisel, and a wedge-shaped float finishes the sides. This critical stage is monitored by use of a wedge template.

A soft iron blank and wedge are then fitted to the throat mortise, making the fit tightest at the lower end. With the iron in place, the sole profile is scribed (because of the pitch, the iron profile is more elongated than the vertical section of the sole). It is filed to shape, hardened and tempered, and then honed to match the sole exactly. The plane is then planed clean, the top chamfers are planed and the heel rounded with chisel and file. End chamfers are cut with a chisel and stopped with cuts of a small gouge, and the step is coved with a round plane. The maker's mark is stamped on the toe and the molding size on the heel.

A similar procedure, using power tools where possible, is given by Norman Vandal (1982). Sandusky Tool Co. used machinery to form stock and profile, but the cutting of the wedge mortise was still done by hand.

The irons for molding planes were usually punched from the same 8 x 6 in. (20 x 15 cm.) blanks previously described for other side escapement planes. Even with mass production during the late 19th century, the sole profile was individually scribed on its iron, which was then shaped by punching and grinding before hardening. This underlines the importance of an exact match of iron to sole: the large manufacturers would have found an easier method if they could.

An aside is in order at this point. As a beginning collector, I subscribed to the practice of restoring each tool to the state it enjoyed when it was in use, and routinely sharpened the irons. This taught me that sharpening a molding plane iron is not as simple as it appears. It is not enough to make it sharp, the profile must be preserved. If you are tempted to try it, it is a good plan to work first with a simple profile and judge your success not by the keenness of the edge on your fingernail, but by the performance of the plane.

The tools of some early professional planemakers have been preserved. Special clamps to hold planes while the mouth was cut, and templates used for layout are pictured in Roberts (1983). These were used by Alfred Tovey, who worked for Doscher Plane and Tool Co. and Chapin-Stephens Co. (both Connecticut) at the end of the 19th century. The same text shows the Wolcott Collection of mother planes preserved at Colonial Williamsburg.

BOXING

Common boxwood is known to us as a garden shrub or hedge. This was not a significant source of the wood used in boxing, as it rarely grows beyond a height of 16 feet (5 meters) or a diameter of 10 in. (25 cm.). A close relative, Turkey boxwood, can grow to 80 feet (24 meters), and this was the principal source for planemakers. Both are very slow growing, and the supply of true boxwood has been almost exhausted. It has been replaced as a commercial source by the Caribbean boxwood, from an unrelated tree of the elm family that produces a similar wood. The merits of boxwood are resistance to splitting and wear, a cooperative grain, and a smooth, low-friction surface.

Areas of high wear in many planes are protected by insertion of strips of this wood. Mounted with partial end grain, it survives much longer than beech

184

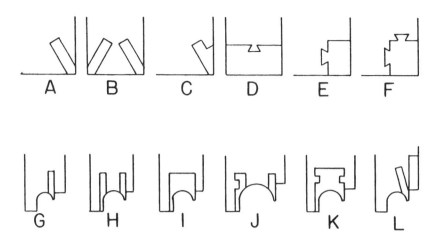

Fig.10:7—Methods of boxing

would. There are a number of ways to accomplish this, as shown in Fig. 10:7. In the simplest, SLIP boxing, a slip of box is glued into a groove plowed in the stock. If the corner of the plane needs the protection, the groove is angled in from the corner to give CORNER boxing (10:7 A) or, if on two corners as in a rabbet plane, DOUBLE CORNER (10:7 B). SHOULDER boxing (10:7 C) uses a more substantial piece of box, held by a groove displaced from the corner and filling a slanted rabbet in the stock. The entire sole may be replaced with boxwood in DOVETAIL BOX FACING (10:7 D), in which the facing is fitted with a sliding dovetail and driven in from one end of the stock. A similar joint is used, particularly on the wear surfaces such as plow fences, in SHOULDER DOVETAIL boxing (10:7 E). The premium method, one which calls for a degree of craftsmanship achieved by few planemakers, removes a rectangular rabbet from the corner and replaces it by a boxwood strip dovetailed on two sides. This is DOUBLE DOVETAIL boxing (10:7 F). Details on how these are cut are given in Chapter 13 — under Planemaker.

Molding planes are called DOUBLE boxed if strengthened at two wear points by separate slips. Examples of single and double boxing types for one of the most common molding profiles, the side bead, are shown in Fig.10:7 G and H. Single boxing protects only the quirk (10:7 G), while double boxing includes the wear surface of the fence (10:7 H). FULL boxing often does not include the depth stop, as in (10:7 I), and some manufacturers call the wider beads full boxed if they are double boxed with the fence slip grooved as in (10:7 J). An alternate to dovetail boxing is HAMMERHEAD boxing (10:7 K). A slipped bead (to be defined later in the section on beads) may be protected by OBLIQUE boxing (10:7 L).

185

USING MOLDING PLANES

The proper use of a molding plane requires an accurate setting of the iron. Not only must the exposure of the cutting edge be correct, but its profile must register exactly with the profile of the sole. The wedge mortise allows for slight lateral and angular adjustments to attain this. To accomplish it the wedge is lightly set, the iron exposure sighted by peering along the sole (good light helps), and adjustments made by taps of a mallet on the tang of the iron or the rear of the stock. When the iron is correctly seated, the wedge is solidly tightened by a firm blow on its top. Until the knack is acquired, setting the iron will take a fair amount of time, and the cut should be checked first on a scrap piece. If any part of the blade edge is not exposed, the cut will stop prematurely when sunk to this point. Simply advancing the iron in this case seldom helps. The shaving thickness elsewhere increases and at best the cut will be rough, at worst the mouth will choke. If no setting gives a smooth cut, the iron has probably been sharpened incorrectly. Another possibility, for an old molder, is that improper storage has caused dimensional change or slight distortion of the sole.

To cut (or "stick") a molding, the workpiece (wood or "stuff") should be of high quality, free from defects and straight of grain. It should be held rigidly, flat on top of the workbench. Narrow molding strips are normally stuck on a wide board, then ripsawed off. (This is a better alternative than nailing the strip to the bench to prevent bowing under the pressure of the plane stroke.) A few molding planes are designed to be used on the edge of the stuff, and with these types the work is positioned edge up. Such planes are, however, the exception, and are specified as "to work the edge" in catalogs.

The plane is held with the left hand on top of the stock in front of the iron, palm down and thumb to the rear, while the right cups the heel (southpaws were not tolerated in those days). The fence of the plane is held firmly against the edge of the stuff. If sprung, the plane must be tilted and rigidly held with spring marks horizontal and vertical as in Fig.10:8. In older planes without spring marks, the slope of the fence and depth stop must serve. The cuts are repeated until the depth stop bottoms, the last cuts covering the full length of the piece to provide a uniform result. A molder in good condition and properly used will create a molding that needs no further smoothing.

Since most molding planes must work in only one direction, grain reversal in the workpiece poses a problem. The use of a right- and left-hand pair to cope with this problem is highly unusual (for an exception, see the section on beads later in this chapter). In architectural work, the use of soft woods

186

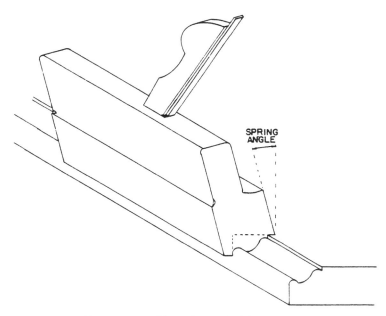

Fig.10:8—Molding plane tilted for spring

of obliging grain was the rule, and handed pairs of molders for this use are rare. In cabinet work, the task of joining cuts in two directions (to say nothing of the task of honing two irons to be perfect mirror images) seems to have been at least as bothersome as coping with awkward grain by using lighter cuts, to judge by the rarity of handed pairs of molders.

NUMBERS ON MOLDING PLANES

Late 19th century planes were often marked with the maker's model number and size designation, both stamped on the heel. Unfortunately, citing the maker and his model number does not necessarily define the plane. Most makers were rather casual about changing their numbering systems. By way of example, a Chapin (Connecticut) No. 200 was a sash coping plane in its 1874 catalog, though formerly a square rabbet in 1859. A half-inch astragal that was No. 91 in the Greenfield (Massachusetts) 1854 catalog, became No. 139 in 1872. This ill wind will blow some good if your catalog collection is extensive and luck is with you, as it may permit you to more closely date your plane.

Sizes, too, can be confusing. A single number usually means the width of the cut (or the "on"). Two numbers give the width and depth (or the "on" and "down"). Some profiles, such as the cove, may be marked with the thickness of the stock to be worked, rather than the cut width. The size on a center bead may be the bead size only or the width of the bead plus fillets. Trust your own measurement.

HOLLOWS, ROUNDS, AND RELATED MOLDING PLANES

In this and subsequent chapters, the molding profile of the plane's sole is shown as a simple outline, the same as would be made by placing the toe of the plane on paper and tracing around it. This outline shows the profile as it would be seen by the user of the plane, facing its heel. The portion of the profile that represents the cutting edge of the iron is shown on the profile by use of a heavier line.

Let us begin the enumeration of the molding planes with those designed to cut a simple concave groove or a rounded edge.

HOLLOWS AND ROUNDS

Hollows and rounds were the most common molding planes, and served a variety of purposes. They could accomplish any task requiring a cut having the cross-section of a circular arc. A special molding for which no plane was available could be approximated with a set of hollows and rounds and perhaps one of the trimming planes described below. In fact, even if the plane creating the desired profile was available, the molding would usually be first roughed out with hollows and rounds before the final cut with the more complex molder — they were much easier to sharpen than the complex molders.

Although most molding planes are named for the profile they cut, the hollow plane (Fig.10:9 left) has a hollow sole and makes a convex cut — a round. (Goodman's attempt to change the convention in *British Planemakers from 1700*, 2nd ed., did not succeed.) The round (10:9 right) has a convex sole and cuts a hollow. The common form of either cuts an arc of about 60°, or

Fig.10:9—Left: hollow; right: round

one-sixth of a circle. The iron is exposed in the throat on the right side of the sole, while the stock is closed on the left and tapers to meet the curved sole. There is no fence. (Hollows and rounds with attached fences are sometimes found, but these are either mother planes or molders modified for a specific purpose.) The arc being circular, the cut may be continued beyond the normal width of one-sixth of a circle by tilting the plane in subsequent cuts — even to complete a full circle in the case of the hollow.

Many makers listed hollow and round pairs with skew irons (often as "made to order") but they were not popular in the United States, to judge by their rarity. Chapin (Connecticut, 1890) charged one third more for pairs with skew irons. As discussed in Appendix 1, little is gained by skewing hollows or rounds, although some felt they performed better in cross-grain work. Skewed irons are more often seen in English hollows and rounds but the skew is usually so small that it often escapes notice. Handled planes for cutting hollows or rounds for functional applications have been described earlier. Hollows and rounds of the type described here, for moldings, rarely had handles.

Hollows and rounds were almost always sold in pairs, each matching the sole of the other. Sets of eighteen pairs were listed by most British makers, as well as half-sets of nine pairs. American catalogs offered twenty-four sizes and a choice of different size sets. Half sets contained all even or all odd size numbers. Size numbers were stamped on the heel, but these were the days before standardization and there was no guarantee that planes by different makers with the same number would cut the same profile. Older plane sizes most commonly differed by sixteenths of an inch of radius in successive smaller sizes, but the system broke in the larger sizes with eighths of an inch between sizes. Dimensions quoted in catalogs could not be relied upon. It frequently happened that the planes' soles differed in size from the listed dimensions. It appears that the users did not pay too much attention to the size numbers of the plane, except to remember which number of their own plane set they used on the last job.

As with many other types, makers sometimes made small changes for specific uses. As examples: Gleave (England) sold pairs of SWING DOOR planes, the hollow having a slightly angled curve, and the round equipped with an integral depth stop. The round cut a hollow in the door frame, the hollow rounded the hinge stile of the door. The TAMBOUR plane is a hollow used to shape the slats that are joined to make tambour doors or the roll-tops of desks. Other variations are covered under French casement sash planes.

Planes that are easily confused with hollows and rounds are sets of TABLE planes, used to cut the profiles at the joining of drop leaves in tables. These

cut a full quarter-circle (Fig.10:10 left and right), and the hollow (Fig.10:10 left) is normally bevelled on both sides of the stock. This and other forms of table planes are covered in Chapter 9 (Fig.9:11).

Precursors of the planes we know as hollows and rounds were known to the Romans, to judge by plane irons which have survived.One of the early uses was in shaping the popular linen-fold design in panels. With the dawn of the Gothic architectural styles using molded beams in the 12th century, they became essential. The names have changed. They were known up to the Middle Ages as inbowing planes or casement planes (Mathieson's 1899 catalog offered "Pair Casements—Hollow & Round"). A convex molding was called a boltel, and so was the hollow plane. An American term, "creasing plane", appears frequently in 18th century inventories and appears to be synonymous with molding plane, though in most cases probably referred to a hollow or round.

The earlier planes varied in the shape of the lower left side of the stock. Some rounds continued the curve of the sole with perhaps an increased radius, others used a relatively short bevel. The length of the bevel increased during the eighteenth century, stabilizing at a slope of about one in three in England, somewhat more in the United States.

Early rounds did not always restrict themselves to short circular arcs or indeed even to circular curves. They are found with blades and soles to cut arcs up to semicircles, or to cut parabolic and other profiles. Small sizes of these are often full face-boxed. Occasionally they are found with rabbet throats.

Naming these variations is difficult, as there seem to be no generally accepted terms. DEEP HOLLOW (Fig.10:15) or FULL ROUND (Fig.10:11) are usually understood. The full round cutting a full semicircle is often called a GUN-STOCKER'S plane in the United States, but they seem to be too common for such a specialized use. The true gunsmith's tool (Fig.10:12) was described earlier in Chapter 9.

Fig.10:11—
Full round

These full rounds had other uses. They could be used for fluting, although the FLUTING plane (Fig.10:13) usually has an integral depth stop on one or both sides and may be fitted with a plow type fence. These were not listed in American catalogs. (The multiple fluting plane will be treated in the section on beads, reeds, and flutes.) The COD plane (Fig.10:14) was described by W.J. Armour (1898). It is a full round with the stock jogged to give greater hand clearance. Sets of these were used by plane-makers to cut profiles to special order, and do not seem to have been adapted by other woodworkers. Full rounds in the Wildung collection at Shelburne (Vermont) include one used by a wheelwright to cut axle bearings and one used about 1812 in making a wool carding machine.

DEEP HOLLOWS, too, are found. One of these, the NOSING plane, was treated earlier in Chapter 9. Sets of hollows to cut one-third of a circle were made by Cox and Luckman (England, 1843-63), and an earlier one by Cox is shown in Fig.10:15.

The SIDE ROUND (Fig.10:16) cuts a quarter-circle, with the sole curving from the bottom to the side of the stock. They were sold in handed pairs to cut on the right or the left side, often marked with a size number on the heel. They provided a useful addition in cutting special moldings in places where common rounds would be awkward. The blade is exposed on both sides of the stock, but is sharp only on the curved arc. The stock is cut away on the straight side to minimize interference, sometimes (rarely) even being hollowed. The extreme case of this is the crow's bill (to use the translation of the name found below in the Continental section). American side rounds are uncommon, most found in this country being by English makers; the only American crow's bill I have seen (Fig.10:17) was made by N. Spaulding (New York, ca.1870).

The corresponding SIDE HOLLOW (Fig.10:18) does not appear in manufacturers' catalogs. It is

Fig.10:12—
Gunstocker

Fig.10:13—
Fluting

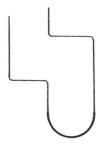

Fig.10:14—
Cod

Fig.10:15—
Deep hollow

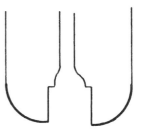

Fig.10:16—
Side round pair

191

uncommon and was usually made by earlier plane-makers or was user-made (although Josiah King, New York, 1835-1869, made them). While it, too, cuts a quarter-circle it has a concave cutting edge which sometimes continues as a horizontal tangent. Side beads that have been converted to this form are often found, leaving the tell-tale remnant of a now non-functional boxing strip.

Although not simple hollows or rounds, two plane types used in conjunction with them in cutting or cleaning moldings should be considered here. The SNIPE BILL (Fig.10:19) has a cutting sole shaped like an ogee, the cutter having a sharply pointed tip vertical on one side and rounded on the other. The sole is almost invariably boxed. These were sold in handed pairs, and used to form quirks or clean the convex sides near the quirks. The SIDE SNIPE has the same sole profile but its iron is sharpened on its vertical side. It is bedded vertically, or leaning slightly forward; and is skewed, after the fashion of a side rabbet. The side snipe was made in handed pairs and also as both in one stock, the two cutting edges facing in opposite directions (Fig.10:20).

Continental   The French RABOTS RONDS and RABOTS CREUX or MOUCHETTES (rounds and hollows) are similar to the English, with bodies in the French style. The rounds often cut somewhat

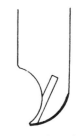

Fig.10:17—American crow's bill

Fig.10:18—
Side hollow

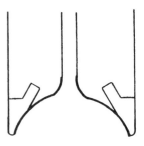

Fig.10:19—
Snipe bill pair

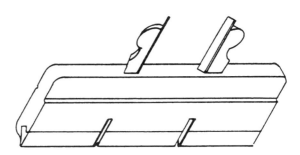

Fig.10:20—Side snipe combination

more than the 60° arc that is usual for the English planes. The German names are HOHLKEHLHOBEL (rounds) and RUNDSTABHOBEL (hollows), with rabbet throats common. In both cases the same names are used for molding planes and bench type planes. In The Netherlands, they are RONDE en HOLLE SCHAVEN. A form of side round almost unknown in England or America is the German RABENSCHNABELHOBEL (Fig.10:21) or the French BEC DE CORBIN (crow's bill) or BEC DE CANE

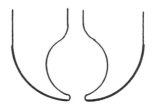

Fig.10:21—
Crow's bill pair

(duckbill). (The latter name is not really descriptive of the shape, but was earlier used to describe a lever door-handle and may have been borrowed from this use.) The narrow tip of the iron is hook-shaped, curving to the horizontal. The iron may also be sharpened on the concave arc, and can then reach underneath a curve to undercut it.

Far Eastern   Molding planes are relatively new to Japan, and are adaptations of Western styles to their plane shapes. The general name is MEN-TORI-KANNA, applied not only to decorative molding planes but also to chamfer and other functional types covered earlier. Most have the shape of the hira-kanna or common plane, except for their shaped soles. They have a top escapement, use cap irons and have a bed angle of 40-45° (larger than their bench planes, smaller than their plows). An example is seen in Fig.10:5. Others have the taller shape of Western molders, and these frequently have open throats with irons inserted from the side. Rabbet style mouths are favored. Surprisingly, the Japanese do not name their hollows and rounds as molding planes (men-tori-kanna), but call them MARU-KANNA or rounding planes. Hollows are UCHIMARU-KANNA and rounds SOTOMARU-KANNA, whether of bench type or with side escapements.

QUARTER ROUNDS

A QUARTER ROUND is one of the most common moldings used today, whether bought as a strip molding to be used at room corners or cut on an edge with a rounding over router bit. Planes designed to cut a simple quarter round are conspicuous by their absence. The side hollow described above would serve, but these are rare. A form of chamfer plane with a V sole rounded at the apex, and a hollow blade, is also very rare. There were other tools used to do a simple corner rounding, but where are the planes?

In fact, a simple edge rounding poses a bit of a problem for a plane. With a side hollow, the cut must be stopped before the plane bottoms, or a step will be left equal in height to the iron exposure. This could be touched up with a hollow, but an easier way was found. Making a virtue of necessity, a plane was designed to create a deliberate step. The profile it made must have been pleasing, for it was generally adapted. It is called a CASING MOLDING in American catalogs (the name "thumb" or "thumbnail molding" is also used in the furniture trade for a flattened elliptical form). Not only the quarter round, but almost all planes cutting a curve which would otherwise be tangent to the surface are made to cut this short vertical step.

One exception (in addition to the side hollow) is found in a few planes which cut a simple quarter round with a fillet at the outer edge. A plane of this type made by Francis Nicholson (Massachusetts, 1683-1753) is profiled, Fig.10:22. No mention of these has been found in English catalogs or texts;

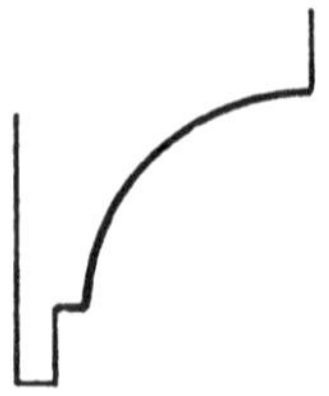

Fig.10:22—Inset
quarter round

however, the profile is shown in French and German catalogs. Were it not for this, the plane might be considered as meant to cut a casing molding by working the edge, rather than the face, of the stuff.

The side hollow with a horizontal extension to the curved cutting edge can be made to cut a simple rounded corner, without a step. The extension is ground with a slight slope that makes the cutting edge fade behind the mouth opening. The plane will then bottom (stop cutting) leaving the curve tangent to the face surface.

The CASING MOLDING plane (Fig.10:23), as mentioned above, cuts a quarter round with a vertical step at what would otherwise be the face tangent point. The name derives from its common use on door and window casings in the nineteenth century. The profile is older than this, however. Examples by Cesar Chelor (Massachusetts, 1753-84) and Jonathan Ballou (Rhode Island, -1770-) survive. Both of these are unsprung. The casing molding plane requires a depth stop to ensure a uniform step height. It is normally sprung at up to 45°, and has no fence. It is awkward to use. The same molding is cut rather more easily by the CASING MOLDING WITH FENCE (Fig.10:24), which is worked from the edge of the board using the under face as the guide. Sizes stamped on the heel of this plane usually refer to the thickness of

Fig.10:23—
Casing molding

Fig.10:24—
Casing molding
with fence

Fig.10:25—
Quarter round,
large step

Fig.10:26—
Boxed quarter round

Fig.10:27—
Quarter round,
recessed

board to be worked, and most commonly are in the range from ⅜ to 1½ in. (10 - 38 mm.).

W. Raymond (Massachusetts, 1762-1836) and others made a quarter round with a large step, comparable in size to the ovolo (Fig.10:25). This may have been used to cut a rule joint, and was shown with them earlier (Fig.9:11 E).

A more common profile is a quarter round with a step and also a fillet at the other end of the quarter circle. This is usually called a QUARTER ROUND in American catalogs but also listed as a PLAIN OVOLO or even as a "scotia". The boxed example in Fig.10:26 was made by W. Loveage (London 1735-51). This molding was widely used to soften sharp edges on furniture, and was supplied in sizes from ¼ to 1½ in. (6 - 38 mm.). The fillet ends in a fence for guidance by the workpiece, the upper step ends in a depth stop.

The term "quarter round" is used to refer to both the simple quarter circle and also to this shape with steps or fillets and so fails to define the shape accurately. The problem is even worse in France, where "quart de rond" may mean any cut used to soften an edge — including various chamfers. Some more specific coinage appears to be called for. A possible solution, which I will employ, is to use "recessed quarter round" to describe the form with two steps (Fig.10:27); "dropped quarter round" for the casing molding (Fig.10:23); and "inset quarter round" for the round with a fillet at the edge (Fig.10:22). Corresponding modifiers are used with "ovolo" for non-circular (e.g., elliptical) curves. The moldings are shown in Fig.10:28.

OVOLO as used in England and the United States means a recessed quarter round. Non-circular forms are also found, and the name may be then modified by adding "elliptical". When circular forms were rendered passé by the Greek Revival in the first half of the nineteenth century, the GRECIAN OVOLO (Fig.10:29) became popular. This is an elliptical curve continuing

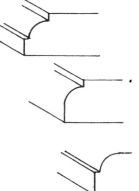

Fig.10:28—From the top: Recessed, Dropped and Inset quarter round

195

Fig.10:29—
Grecian ovolo

Fig.10:30—
Grecian ovolo,
flat form

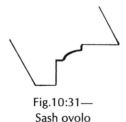

Fig.10:31—
Sash ovolo

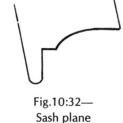

Fig.10:32—
Sash plane

beyond tangency to the face and descending into a quirk. A very similar form had been illustrated in Smith's *Key* (1816) as a QUIRK OVOLO. In U.S. catalogs, the profiles shown for the grecian ovolo differed from these principally in using a flatter ellipse that sometimes became almost linear toward the edge (Fig.10:30). Another distinction was in its relative dimensions: the grecian ovolo commonly stuck "on" twice as far as "down" (the molding was twice as wide as it was deep) in contrast to the more nearly equal proportion in the quirk ovolo. (Further discussion of the distinction between "quirk" and "Grecian" will be found in the section on ogees, below.) Another name for the quirk ovolo used in the 1873 D.R. Barton (New York) catalog is JACK MOLDING. Arrowmammett (Connecticut) in 1857 listed sizes from ¾ to 2 in. (19-51 mm.), and handled versions to 3 in. (76 mm.) (sizes refer to the cut "on": "down" is one-half of this). The plane they called a grecian ovolo is described in the next chapter as a grecian ovolo with fillet.

The common or "square" ovolo was a favorite for 17th century window sash bars. A recessed quarter round with an exaggerated fence was probably meant to cut these. A later style appeared in the second quarter of the 18th century that called for a recessed elliptical ovolo, as seen in a plane by C. Gabriel (England, 1770-1816) that would be called a sash ovolo by a sashmaker (Fig.10:31). A simpler sash plane (Fig.10:32) by J.R. Tolman (Massachusetts, -1849-) cuts an inset quarter round. Sash planes are found in considerable variety and are treated at greater length in Chapter 13—Sashmaker. Planes with an unusually long fence and/or depth stop should be compared with the profiles shown there.

Continental   The French QUARTS DE ROND SIMPLE have been pictured as like our side hollow, but these too are rare. A descriptive French nickname for the recessed quarter round is bonnet de prêtre or priest's cap, but it is more formally called QUART DE ROND ENTRE CARRÉS or quarter round between squares. The German VIERTELSTABHOBEL translates to quarter rod plane. (English and American quarter rounds are sprung while Continental forms, as with all their molders, are not).

The quarter round with a single fillet at the outer edge (Fig.10:33) was earlier called an inset quarter round, for lack of a commonly accepted English name. (An alternate, in the systematic naming proposed in the next chapter, is ovolo with fillet). It is known in France as QUART DE ROND À CARRÉ and in Germany is cut by the DEUTSCHERSTABHOBEL. The latter may have an elliptical shape.

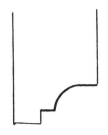

Fig.10:33—Continental inset quarter round

Japanese   The Japanese use a versatile quarter round which is made in the shape of their common hand plane (hira-kanna) with a quarter-circle hollow along the length of its sole, flanked by two 45° bevels (Fig.10:34). Moveable fences of rectangular cross-section are attached to the sole on these bevels. Used in the manner of a chamfer plane, the cut can be varied from a simple rounding of the corner to a quarter-round with one or two extensions of any width desired. They are also found with fixed fences (Fig.10:5). Both are known as GINNAN-MENTORI-KANNA. Bull-nose and compass versions are also used. The same concept is used with other profiles. A form using two blades, one directly behind the other, is used for complicated profiles (NICHŌ-SHIKOMI-MENTORI-KANNA); or two blades

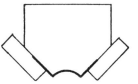

Fig.10:34—Japanese quarter round

offset as in some of our cornice planes (IREKO- MENTORI-KANNA). Their common practice, as mentioned before, is to continue the molding profile up the front wall of the plane's throat.

Another Japanese plane used for free-hand rounding of edges is in the shape of their common smooth plane with a shallow rectangular groove cut down the center of its sole. The BUKKIRI-MENTORI-KANNA has a brass plate installed vertically at the front of its mouth, to minimize sole grooving in this use.

COVES

A COVE or CAVETTO is the reverse of a quarter round, cutting a concave rather than a convex molding. This, too, has been called a scotia. Planes used to cut the simple architectural scotia, which might be described as two coves of different radii facing each other, are quite rare. (One is seen in the next chapter.)

The sole of the cove is convex, a quarter circle between integral fence and depth stop, with spring angle somewhat less than 45° (Fig.10:35). It was listed in sizes from ¼ to 1½ in. (6 - 38 mm.) in American catalogs. Elliptical cavetto, cavetto with one or two fillets, and other variants are found.

Fig.10:36, a plane that might appear to be a cove with fence, designed to work the edge of the board with the fence guided by the bottom surface of the workpiece, is probably a sash ovolo coping plane. (This is treated in Chapter 13 — Sashmaker.) It might also possibly be a table plane, guided by the undersurface of the table top.

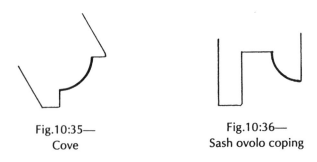

Fig.10:35—
Cove

Fig.10:36—
Sash ovolo coping

Continental   The German cove plane is called a round with a fence — Hohlkehlhobel mit Anschlag — the French, congé. A true scotia is known in Germany as a HOHLE, or cave. A cove between two fillets is shown in the Nooitgedagt catalog (Netherlands, ca.1891) as an Omgekeerde Duivejager. To be consistent with the quarter-round names proposed above this might be called a recessed cove (Fig.10:37). Nooitgedagt also shows the cove analog of the casing molding, a dropped cove (Fig.10:38) as a Vast Rond met 1 bandje.

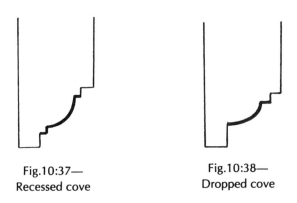

Fig.10:37—
Recessed cove

Fig.10:38—
Dropped cove

ELEMENTS OF COMPOUND MOLDING PLANES

The various forms of the cove and the ovolo, with straight line elements added, may be combined to form any complex molding. An ogee, for example, may be formed by combining a cove and an ovolo. Of the straight line elements, a vertical line in the profile, formed as an edge of the cutter moves downward, is called a STEP. A FILLET is a horizontal straight segment, that usually serves to separate other elements of the profile or to terminate a profile. These may be seen in Fig.10:27, the step at upper right, the fillet at lower left. The fillet is usually incorporated as a part of a compound molding, but where required separately it can be cut with a plow or other grooving plane. A BEVEL or SPLAY is a sloping straight segment, which would be called a chamfer if it stood alone. The profile shown cuts a BEVEL with FILLET (Fig.10:39). A plane to cut a RECESSED CHAMFER (a bevel between a step and a fillet) (Fig.10:40) was listed by the Ohio Tool Co. as a P.G. MOLDING. This and other chamfers were covered previously.

Fig.10:39—
Bevel with fillet

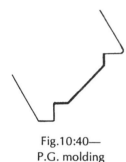

Fig.10:40—
P.G. molding

Certain combinations of these straight and curved elements have been given their own names either because they compose a simple molding plane or occur repeatedly as part of complex ones. Let us review these.

The QUIRK is an indentation serving to separate two molding elements. It may take several shapes, the differences not often apparent in the smaller sizes without close examination. Examples are seen in the beads shown in Figs. 10:43, 10:44, and 10:45. First, a little speculation as to how it came about. We have seen that a quarter round or simple ovolo is usually cut with a step, to separate the curve from the flat surface, and that this was accepted as a preferred profile. In architectural moldings, such a step would be almost obliterated by a few coats of paint. It has been suggested that the quirk was introduced as a way of retaining this design feature after repeated painting, and that it was originally used as an emphasized step. It apparently then proved to be worth doing for its own aesthetic sake. Quirked moldings are popular in fine furniture where there is no risk of concealment of the step by painting.

199

Fig.10:41—Evolution of the quirk

In the sequence shown in Fig.10:41, a rounded edge is followed by a casing molding. This dropped profile could have the step emphasized by letting the molding curve continue a bit past the horizontal. Extend this idea further, and let the curve plunge deeply into the surface before returning as a vertical step. This separation is a quirk, as is any other narrow groove separating two features of a profile. Adding a quirk to the casing molding changes its name to side bead, as is discussed and shown below.

As the depth of the quirk is increased in this sequence, the task of the molding plane becomes more difficult. The sharp point required on the plane sole becomes fragile and must be reinforced by boxing. Even boxing will not survive if the point is too sharp, and the tip of the boxing must be softened by rounding. In some planes, the bottom of the quirk is widened further into a short fillet. Another requirement for cutting the quirk is a sharp projection on the right side of the cutting edge of the iron. For reasons which we will explore in Appendix 1, the maximum slope of the inner, curved edge of this projection defines the maximum useful spring. As we shall see shortly, this means that some planes for quirked profiles are unsprung.

The inner wall of the quirk (the one furthest from the edge of the work) is usually vertical (Fig.10:43), but may be slanted away from the curve (bevel quirk as seen in Fig.10:44) or be hollowed (cove quirk, Fig.!0:45). These variations are more often seen in the Continental planes, and examples are seen below.

BEADS, REEDS, and FLUTES

A bead is a molding, usually of semicircular cross-section, which may be found in different locations with respect to the surface it decorates. Several types, as well as reeding and fluting, are shown in the moldings of Fig.10:42. By far the most common form is the side bead (or quirk bead). The semicircle is cut tangent to one edge of the work. The other end cuts into the adjacent surface and ends at the bottom of a crevice (or quirk). Early 18th century clapboards were frequently decorated with this molding on their lower edges — perhaps only on the front of the house if there was a need to economize. The side bead was also popular as a means of softening the edges of furniture.

The planes used to cut these (Fig.10:43) were listed by major makers simply as BEADS rather than the more descriptive term SIDE BEADS. Their soles were deep hollows, dropped on the left to serve as an integral fence.

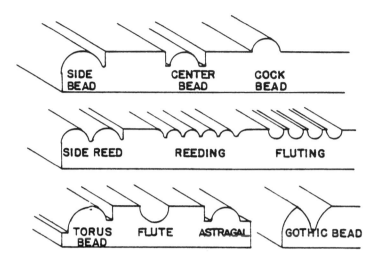

Fig.10:42—Some molding profiles

The quirk was almost always boxed, and an integral depth stop on the right stopped the cut as soon as the top of the bead was formed. The various types of boxing used were discussed earlier (see Fig.10:7). Sizes were stamped on the heel of the plane, and usually referred to the width of bead plus quirk (although sometimes just the bead). Common sizes ran from ⅛ to 2 in. (3 - 51 mm.).

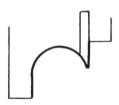

Fig.10:43—Side bead

Beads are almost never sprung, as the full semi-circle poses problems if they are (the vertical edge scrapes, as detailed in Appendix 1). Handled models were offered as an option by several makers, but were apparently not popular and are seldom seen. Another option offered by Chapin (Connecticut) for a short period (around 1876) was a bead with a BEVEL QUIRK (Fig.10:44), in which the quirk did not rise vertically but slanted away from the bead. This is sometimes seen in British beads, and was illustrated by Roubo (1769). Rarely, in large beads, the quirk is returned as a cove, as seen in an example by J. Colton (Pennsylvania, ca.1837-1890) (Fig.10:45).

Fig.10:44—Side bead, bevel quirk

201

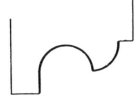

Fig.10:45—Bead, cove quirk

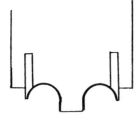

Fig.10:46—Double side bead

Fig.10:47— Return bead molding

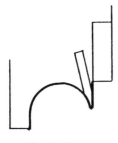

Fig.10:48— Slipped bead

Beads are one of the few forms of molding planes found (although rarely) in pairs to work in either direction, to cope with difficult grain. Left-handed beads are found, and it is reasonable to assume that they were half of a pair. C. Fuller (Massachusetts, 1836-87) made such tools. More often, the two are made as a DOUBLE SIDE BEAD (Fig.10:46) in one stock, with sole cut to form mirror-image beads on either side of a common integral fence. One use of side bead molders made a left- and right-handed pair desirable. The return bead, or staff bead, molding shown in Fig.10:47 was cut by using a side bead twice, on adjacent sides of the sharp edge. With a left- and right-handed pair both cuts could be made in the same direction. A single bead plane would have to be applied to opposite ends of the work and would probably have to work against the grain in one of the passes..

Large side beads are sometimes seen with two irons, much as they were used in nosing planes. Each iron cuts one-quarter of a circle, and the two may have opposite skew to facilitate the cut. Another variation that equipped the two blades with cap irons apparently did not work successfully. As was the case with double-iron rabbets, setting the blade with an unattached cap iron posed problems. Further, the cap iron changed the chip discharge pattern, and many of these planes are found with reworked and widened throats.

Side beads are found compassed (often short, in coachmaker length) and also as radiused planes (that is, with the sole curved longitudinally, as seen from below). The latter form permits beading a circular edge such as a round tabletop. Here a double radius side bead (the double side bead above with both sides radiused) is especially useful to cope with changing grain direction.

A SLIPPED BEAD (Fig.10:48) has the integral depth stop rabbeted away and the rabbet filled with a removeable slip of wood. In building up a complex profile, it was sometimes necessary to cut a side bead next to another molding.

202

The adjacent molding could interfere with the depth stop of the side bead plane, and prevent sinking the bead to its full depth. The slipped bead accommodated such a need, by permitting removal of the depth stop. Only the form shown here, with a slanted boxing strip, is a true slipped bead. A repaired side bead is easily mistaken for a slipped bead, except that the boxing will be vertical. These resulted when the boxing of a normal bead needed replacement and, having difficulty in removing the old boxing, the owner rabbeted away the stock above the depth stop to expose it. After the boxing was replaced, the rabbet was filled with a slip of wood screwed to the stock.

A few oddities might be mentioned. Greenslade (England) made a bead with a revolving circular brass wheel mounted in its throat that carried the profiles of six different bead sizes. It wasn't a success. A double bead arrayed as a "come-and-go" has been seen — the throats face in opposite directions. As this gives identical function on the two sides, it probably was intended for roughing and finish cuts. An early side bead by Jennion (England, ca.1750) had a shallow quirk, which permitted using spring, and also cut a wide fillet beyond the bead (fillet and quirk bead, FQB, in the next chapter).

A TORUS BEAD is perhaps named from its resemblance to the torus at the bottom of a Greek column base (as seen in Fig.10:49). While a torus further up might terminate at the same level on either side, this one appears to have a quirk below and to terminate the arc at different levels on the two sides. At first glance the plane profile (Fig.10:50) appears to be a side bead with a short flat or fillet on the outer edge of the bead. In contrast to the side bead, however, the curve stops short of the vertical at the quirk. Without a vertical to be cut, spring is feasible and is generally used. The far side of the quirk may be beveled. On the side away from the quirk, the bead section is prolonged downward to the vertical in planes made in the United States, while an elliptical curve is favored in England. It was listed by major American makers in sizes from ¼ to 1½ in. (6 - 38 mm.), but

Fig.10:49—
Detail of a
Doric base

Fig.10:50—
Torus bead

is not a common plane. A favorite use for this molding was at the top of baseboards (see Fig.10:42).

A COCK BEAD (seen in Fig.10:42) is one which stands above the surface it decorates. If it is to be stuck (cut in the surface), rather than planted (cut as a separate molding and attached) then the entire surface must be planed away to leave the bead projecting. Needless to say, this is avoided whenever

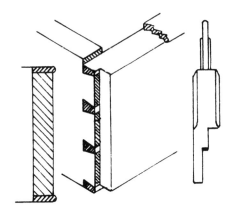

Fig.10:51—Cock beads on a drawer front.
On right: cock bead filletster

possible. A common use for the cock bead is to outline the edges of drawer fronts (Fig.10:51). A strip of wood with one edge rounded is glued to the top of the drawer, forming the bead there. On the sides (because of the joinery there) the edges are rabbeted and a narrower beaded strip is inserted. In the best work the drawer is assembled and fitted to the case, then rabbeted to accept the bead strips with a COCK BEAD FILLETSTER (Fig.10:51 right), a special plane which works from the front of the drawer and cuts a narrow, deep rabbet.

The COCK BEAD plane (Fig.10:52) is not common. It is a molding plane with a semicircular groove in the sole. The iron matches and has horizontal cutting extensions on either side. Usually, the cutting edge reaches the edge of the stock on only one side, so that a rabbet must first be cut if the plane is to function away from the edge of the workpiece. It will, in fact, stick a cock bead, and was probably used in conjunction with other planes in making complex profiles. More often it was used for rounding fillets for drawer fronts as described above. An unusual variation made by Montgomery (Massachusetts, 1847) is a cock bead with two throats and irons at different pitches, for use in soft or hard wood.

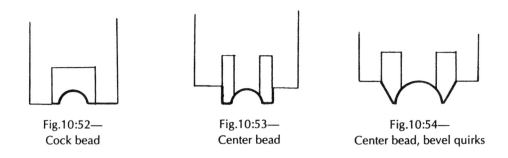

Fig.10:52—
Cock bead

Fig.10:53—
Center bead

Fig.10:54—
Center bead, bevel quirks

A plane similar to the cock bead, but much more common, is the CENTER BEAD (Fig.10:53). It has equal, short, horizontal cutting edges (fillets) on either side of the semicircle, and has the sole rabbeted away to create the depth stop. It cuts a bead rising to the surface from the center of a groove or dado,

204

seen in Fig.10:42. A variant also shown is a CENTER BEAD with BEVEL QUIRKS (Fig.10:54). Boxing was usually employed, and they were offered in sizes from ⅛ to 1 in. (3 to 25 mm.). A form of the center bead is widely used on the tongue side of tongue-and-groove joints as it conceals the joint (the joint appears to be a matching quirk on the other side of the bead; Fig.10:55). Center beads could then be cut in the center of the face of these boards, matching the beads at the joints and giving the appearance of narrower strips of sheathing. As the latter molding is cut away from an edge, an auxiliary fence is required — perhaps a batten fixed to the work. Center beads are frequently found fitted with plow arms and fences (which could be bought separately) or bored with holes that would take them.

The ASTRAGAL (Fig.10:56) is a plane which cuts the same profile as a center bead but which is fitted with an integral fence as well as a depth stop. It differs from the torus bead in having a full semicircular section, with fillets at the same level on both sides, and is not sprung. The astragal, too, is most often used in conjunction with other molders. It was listed by U.S. makers in sizes ranging from ⅛ to 1½ in. (3 - 38 mm.) and is fairly common.

The GOTHIC BEAD (Fig.10:57), named from its shape resembling a Gothic arch, is an astragal that has curved sides rising to a point on the top. It was made in sizes ranging from ¼ to 1½ in. (6 - 38 mm.). Variations are found which cut the gothic bead and one side of an adjacent one (Fig.10:58), instead of a vertical rise to the surface. The Ohio Tool Co. made the gothic bead in one- and two-iron models, and Philip Chapin (Baltimore) listed as a GOTHIC REED a pointed center bead (Fig.10:59). Not surprisingly, the Gothic bead is found most often on church furnishings. Less common are planes that cut multi-

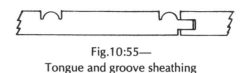

Fig.10:55—
Tongue and groove sheathing

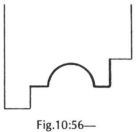

Fig.10:56—
Astragal

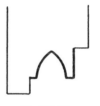

Fig.10:57—
Gothic bead

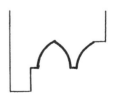

Fig.10:58—
Gothic bead
Gothic return

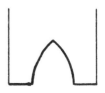

Fig.10:59—
Gothic reed

205

Fig.10:60—Multiple Gothic bead

Fig.10:61—Double side reed

Fig.10:62—Reeding

Fig.10:63— Center reeding

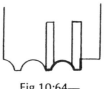

Fig.10:64— Reed and guide

ple Gothic beads, one of which was made by W. Williams (New York, 1807-49) (Fig.10:60).

Several adjacent center beads are called REEDING (see Fig.10:42), and there are a variety of planes used to cut this type of molding. A center bead next to a side bead may be cut by a DOUBLE SIDE REED plane (Fig.10:61). REEDING planes to cut two, three, four or five adjacent beads of ¼ to 1 in. (6 - 25 mm.) size were offered by large U.S. makers. Planes cutting even more are seen rarely. Those with fences are intended to cut reeds at the edge of the work (Fig.10:62) and unfenced versions (Fig.10:63) will cut multiple reeds in the center. To continue reeding beyond this number, repetitive cuts may be made, but extreme accuracy is needed as even slight deviations are very obvious. Several modifications of the reeding plane were devised to simplify this operation.

A plane with two grooves in the sole and an iron which cuts but one was called a REED AND GUIDE (Fig.10:64) in early English catalogs. Having cut one center bead (or a side bead), the first could be used as the guide for the next and this continued as far as required. A variation made by Howarth (England 1872-1939) is a triple reed plane with two irons (Fig.10:65): one cuts the right bead, the other iron the next two. Starting with a temporary fence and both irons, a triple reed is cut. The single iron (#1 in the sketch) is then removed, and the groove it vacates in the plane's sole uses the left bead of the previous cut as a guide to cut the next two beads. Reeding proceeds from right to left. This and several other English variations using removeable fences to facilitate the first cut may be found in a review by Richard Knight (1984).

The BEAD CLUSTER plane (Fig.10:66) cuts several reeds arrayed on the surface of a circular arc. These are not seen in the major catalogs and are uncommon. M. Copeland (Connecticut, 1831-42) made them to cut three reeds, and also known is one by Bewley (England, 1798-1847) which cuts four. These make an attractive molding on furniture uprights.

The opposite of reeding is FLUTING, in which repetitive hollow grooves are cut as a decorative surface treatment. A single flute is cut with the previously described FLUTING plane (Fig.10:13). These are sometimes found with plow arms and fences, usually in the larger flute sizes. They seem to be well suited to cutting the multiple fluting on pilasters (flat simulated columns flanking fireplaces or doorways) which probably accounts for their being called PILASTER planes. Gorlin (1978) reported an unusual single fluting plane with two throats cut through the stock at different pitch angles. The mouth of one is on the bottom, and the other is on the top, of the stock. The wedge and iron would be installed in one of the throats for soft wood; or the body turned 180° and wedge and iron installed in the other throat for hard wood. Multiple fluting planes were made in England, one of which is shown in Fig.10:67. Another form (Fig.10:68) is equipped with removable fences similar to those described above on reeding planes. A wide toted plane has been seen which cuts a multiple alternate REED and FLUTE (Fig.10:69).

The WASHBOARD plane (Fig.10:70) combines reeding and fluting, to cut a wave pattern. It usually has a sole with two wave troughs and a cutter with one, and is used in the same fashion as the above reed and guide. Since wooden washboards were long ago replaced by those made of metal or glass, it is not surprising that this plane is rare.

Planes to cut V-grooves for functional purposes were covered previously in the chapter "Grooving Planes"; however, they are also used decoratively. A CAR BEADING plane (Fig.10:71) sold by Ohio Tool Co. had a steel sole with an angular ridge down the center and a V-iron set at low pitch. One of similar design has survived imprinted S.P.R.R. Car Shop Tool Room. The presumption is that these were used to mold boards used in

Fig.10:65—Reed and guide, another form

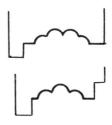

Fig.10:66—
Bead clusters

Fig.10:67—
Center fluting

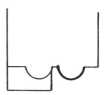

Fig.10:68—
Multiple fluting

Fig.10:69—Multiple reed and flute

sheathing railroad cars, in the same manner as center beads are used to decorate tongue-and-groove planking. (An almost identical profile was previously shown in the double chamfer plane, Chapter 8, Fig.8:16A.) A fenced plow with a V-shaped sole was found in shipyards and was called a HAWK plane. One use was on ship sides, creating grooves to provide sharp edges to paint striping. Wagon builders used V- groove or other narrow molding planes, often with crude stave fences, for wagon planking and called them CENTER-BOARD planes. A similar tool, cutting a wider molding such as a cupid's bow, was called a FACING plane. (The unfenced version of the same name is covered later).

Fig.10:70—Washboard

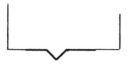

Fig.10:71—Car beading

Continental   Continental beading planes are similar to English, with only minor variations beyond differences in stock styles and the absence of spring. A few names are given here with the caveat that alternate names and forms are at least as common on the Continent as in this country. The center bead may be cut with a small hollow (mouchette in France, Rundstabhobel in Germany) or with fillets on either side (mouchette à joue, Rundeckhobel). A French chamfer plane that leaves a cock bead in the center of the chamfer is called mouchette à joues sur le coin. The French side bead (baguette simple; German: Französischer Stabhobel) usually has a narrow fillet rather than a quirk. The German name for the quirk bead is Einschneidstabhobel. The bead with bevel quirk is baguette sans joue in France, or Stabhobel mit Fase in German. A German variation with a small cove next to the bead is the Perlstabhobel. Nooitgedagt (The Netherlands, ca.1891) listed six variations of the side bead (Kraal) with various quirks. The French name for side reed is baguette double. Their form of torus bead (boudin) is cut with two radii as is the English, and the two sides of the quirk are symmetrical. The German reeding plane is the Stabchenhobel; the fluting plane the Rillenhobel. In France, the reeding plane is called baguette pour applique, and Féron called the fluting plane by the overused name tarabiscot, with a drawing. The astragal is easily recognized in the French astragale, less easily in the German Sockelhobel (pedestal plane) or the Dutch Beuling.

208

Japanese The type of plane used in Japan to cut quarter-rounds was described earlier under hollows and rounds as a bench type plane with fences on either side of the sole sloped at 45° (Fig.10:5). The same shape is used when the sole between the fences is profiled for other types of moldings. These may be made with two blades in separate throats, one behind the other, for complex profiles (NICHŌ-SHIKOMI-MEN-TORI-KANNA).

Repetitive patterns are used for decoration on Japanese woodwork, such as the framework of shoji (room dividers). The HANA-GATA-KUMIKO-KANNA (kumiko is the wooden lattice of the shoji) is made in various patterns. A saw-tooth pattern is found in the SHŌHI-KANNA (pine bark plane). A similar plane NAGURI-MENTORI-KANNA simulates the appearance of hand hewing on beams. Both are hira-kanna, the Japanese hand plane, with profiled soles. As they are used cross-grain, the irons are often skewed and no chip breakers are employed.

COMPOUND CURVES

The combination of a cove and an ovolo to form an S-shaped profile is given a special name — the OGEE. It was an important form in Greek and Roman architecture, little used in wooden moldings until after the Gothic period (12th - 15th centuries), but thereafter one of the most frequently found. Though not an elaborate curve, the ogee has given rise to many variations with some confusion as to their names. Before beginning a description of the specific ogee molding plane types, I would like to clarify the nomenclature.

First there is the question of orientation. To a planemaker, a common ogee is a molding with the concave arc near the edge of the board, the convex arc further in. The reverse ogee is convex at the edge, concave further in. He cuts his plane soles accordingly — on the assumption that they will be used in the usual manner, with an edge of the work as a guide and cutting down from the face of the board. If you choose to use the face as a guide and cut down from the edge of the board, the ogee plane will cut a reverse ogee, as shown in Fig.10:72.

Then there is the question of the length and shape of the component arcs. 18th century ogees were usually formed by joining two quarter-circles, to give a rather bold figure. Later the joining of two sixth-circles, a gentler figure more typical of the Greek form, was preferred. These are hard to distinguish from some versions of the planemaker's Grecian ogee, which are described as being based on elliptical arcs. In practice, Grecian ogees were formed by combining circular arcs of different radii to approximate the elliptical form. The difference may be apparent in the large planes, but it is difficult to distinguish between

209

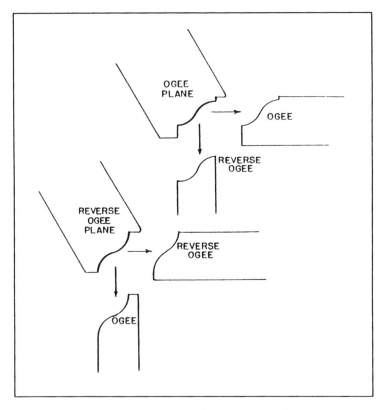

Fig.10:72—Ogees worked on face or edge

an elliptical ogee and a soft Roman ogee in a small one. There is, however, one almost universal convention used by planemakers which makes the distinction clear. The Grecian Ogee, like the Grecian Ovolo, ends with a quirk at the inner end (the end away from the plane's fence).

While in extreme cases the curves known as quirk ogee and Grecian ogee are recognizably different, there is a middle ground which would justify either name (the same is true of quirk ovolo and Grecian ovolo). As we have seen, the term "Grecian" was redefined in the early 19th century to mean curves based on the ellipse rather than the circle, and came to be used in the same sense that "new, improved" is used today by Madison Avenue advertising agencies. I have found no mention of Grecian curves before the Marshes and Shepherd list of around 1840 (reprinted in Roberts, 1980). Before then they were called quirk curves.

The architect specifying these new forms may have called them ellipses, but his draftsmen drew the curves by the usual "four-center" approximation, in which a quadrant of an ellipse was drawn using two circular arcs. This gives a close approximation for all but flat ellipses. The planemaker used his

210

hollows and rounds to make the profile requested. A flat ellipse called for a flat hollow beyond the range available to him, so he made do with a rabbet. By the late 19th century, some Grecian ovolos and ogees were actually bevels terminating in short circular arcs. The distinction, of course, may be splitting hairs. The specific shape was not as important as the overall effect on the way the molding responded with different shadings under different light conditions. The point is that the older quirk ogees or ovolos were often cut in the same shape as the newer "Grecian" forms, and were called quirk curves then. You may choose to honor the original name or use the later redefinition as a Grecian curve.

Catalogs of the late 19th century show examples of complex molders, some with names including "quirk ogee" and another, a few pages later, with the same curve and a name including "Grecian ogee". Many catalogs dropped their quirk ogees when they included Grecian. The ones that include both usually show the quirk ogee as a steeper curve, almost vertical at the midpoint, with ratio of "on" to "down" nearer one to one.

The extension of the ogee into a quirk called for another change in the classical ogee. A symmetrical ogee (concave and convex sections of equal length and radius of curvature) gives an awkward profile if quirked. Even the older quirk ogees, of circular arcs, used a larger radius for the concave part. In fact, even unquirked curves are sometimes seen with unsymmetrical shapes.

Another variation is the tilt of the ogee. Some are cut to meet the edge perpendicularly, others sweep up before hitting the edge. The ogees used in the profile of a cornice plane (see Chapter 11—Cornice Planes), aside from using small fractions of a circle, are lying down (see "lying ogee" below). Then there is the placement of the ogee on the final piece. Is it mounted with the top or the bottom projecting? None of these variations has been honored with a generally accepted name in English (other than "common" and "reverse"). I will offer some coinages later to try to remedy this.

In Germany, some of these distinctions are made. A Karnies, or ogee, may be Stehender (standing) if it projects on top, or Liegender (lying) if the lower curve is further out. The reverse ogee, verkehrt Karnies, is Aufsteigender (climbing out) or Fallender (falling). Either can be Gestreckter (stretched) if stuck on much more than down. If a sharp Roman ogee is tilted to slope up at the edge and sink into a quirk at the inner end it is called a French ogee (französischer). I am not aware of similar terms in French, although they have different names for ogee (DOUCINE) and reverse ogee (TALON).

The PLAIN or COMMON OGEE is almost invariably made with a step at the inner edge of the curve. As discussed under the quarter round, a plane

Fig.10:73—
18th century ogee

Fig.10:74—
19th century ogee

Fig.10:75—
Elliptical ogee

Fig.10:76—Ogee
(Dresden, 1570)

sole without a step would still cut a curve with a step equal in height to the exposure of the cutting edge; small, but quite visible. The step in the sole emphasizes this and gives a more uniform result.

The 18th century form mentioned above is typified by the Gabriel (England, 1770-1816) profile shown in Fig.10:73, while a later form is represented by the A. Howland (New York, 1869-74) in Fig.10:74. This is typical of profiles listed in 19th century catalogs, in sizes from ⅜ to 2¼ in. (10 - 57 mm.) — the size usually meaning the distance from edge to step. The profile is symmetrical with the steepest point reaching about 60° from the horizontal. A similar profile with elliptical arcs is shown in Fig.10:75 and illustrates the subtle difference.

A symmetrical ogee may be canted so that the inner end drops slightly before rising in the step, while the outer rises before meeting the edge. This is illustrated by a plane dated 1570, from Dresden (Fig.10:76). The drop of the inner end was popular with British makers, and was used by Phillipson (1740-75) with an unsymmetrical ogee meeting the edge squarely (Fig.10:77). The Ohio Tool Co. (ca.1910) common ogee used the same profile. Their Grecian ogee in the same catalog had an identical profile except for a deeper quirk. The seemingly clear distinction between a common and quirk ogee is in fact not a sharp one. Let's define the dividing line, for our present purposes, at an angle of 45°.

An ogee stretched to cut "on" more than three times as much as "down" might be called a FLAT OGEE, if you wish to make the distinction. An example by King & Peach (England, ca. 1850) is shown in Fig.10:78. A LYING OGEE appears as if made by joining a bead and a flute (several such are seen in cornice planes). A CABINET OGEE is a wide lying ogee, usually handled and of bench type. Somewhat distorted ogees exist, especially in bench type planes. One of these, by John Nicholson (Massachusetts, 1747-63), most probably intended for forming stair handrails, is shown in Fig.10:79. Other examples are shown under hand rail moldings in the next chapter.

212

Fig.10:77—
Early English ogee

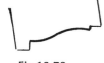

Fig.10:78—
Flat ogee

Fig.10:79—
Stair rail ogee

Fig.10:80—
Reverse ogee with fence

Fig.10:81—
Early quirk ogee

Two different applications called for an ogee with an extended (or deeper) fence. If the depth stop is wide as well, the tool is probably a sash plane used to cut an ogee sash molding. These are discussed more fully in the section on sashmakers in Chapter 13. The other ogee form was used to work the edge of the board — in which case it cuts a reverse ogee, not an ogee. It was so described in the 1890 catalog of H. Chapin's Son, whose style #206½ is seen in profile in Fig. 10:80. However, the Ohio Tool Co. described a similar profile as "to work on edge of board" but persisted in calling it a Roman ogee.

The QUIRK OGEE, as described above, was originally an ogee of circular arcs, one convex with a quirk on the inside and joined to an concave arc of larger radius on the outside. An early Gabriel (England, 1770-1816) has a quarter-circle cove extended by a straight segment on the outside, and joining a convex arc of slightly smaller radius on the inside. The latter continues beyond horizontal until parallel to the side of the stock (which is sprung at 20°, then returns in a quirk (Fig.10:81). Smith's *Key* (1816) shows a similar profile, with a larger difference in arc radii serving in lieu of the straight-line extension. Quirk ogees were offered in several late nineteenth century American catalogs in addition to their Grecian Ogees, in sizes from ⅜ to 1½ in. (10 - 38 mm.).

The Stotherts (England, 1785-1841) and others made ogees with definitely elliptical arcs, as shown in Fig.10:82. Because the curve is steep and the "on" is close to the "down" it would probably be called a quirk ogee today in spite of this. You may prefer to class it with the next group.

GRECIAN OGEES, as drawn in American catalogs of the late 19th century, appear to consist of a larger concave circular arc joined by a short straight line segment to a shorter elliptical concave arc, approximated by two circular arcs. The meeting with the edge may be perpendicular, as in the Ohio Tool (ca.1910) plane of Fig.10:83, or slightly upswept as

213

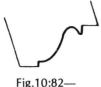

Fig.10:82—
Step quirk ogee

Fig.10:83—
Grecian ogee
(Ohio Tool)

Fig.10:84—
Grecian ogee
(Chapin 1890)

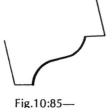

Fig.10:85—
Reverse ogee

in the Chapin (1890, Fig.10:84). They were listed in sizes of ⅜ to 2 in. (10 - 51 mm.). Larger sizes were available with handles, priced per inch of width. Mathieson (Scotland, 1899) called a profile quite similar in shape to these a quirk ogee while their Grecian Ogee is elliptical, symmetrical, and ends in a bevel.

REVERSE OGEES or BACK OGEES were listed in sizes of ⅜ to 2½ in. (10 - 63 mm.). A Chapin profile (style #206, 1890) is seen in Fig.10:85. As this meets the surface at a right angle, there is no technical reason to add a step, but the custom must have been firmly ingrained: they also offered a version with two fillets and a step (style #207, Fig.10:86). A wider, handled version, really a bevel ending in two circular arcs, was listed by Greenfield Tool (1872) to cut a 1 x 3 in. (25 - 76 mm.) or larger profile (Fig.10:87). They also offered a FLAT REVERSE OGEE in these larger sizes with the straight segment horizontal or slightly tilted inward (Fig.10:88). Planes similar to the cabinet ogee but cutting a reverse ogee have also been called cabinet ogees. It seems reasonable to call these CABINET REVERSE OGEES. A profile offered by B. Sheneman & Bro. (Pennsylvania) about 1860 is shown in Fig.10:89.

An unusual plane shown in Fig.10:90 was made by J. Killam (Connecticut, -1850-60). It cuts a sunk fillet and lying reverse ogee at a distance from the edge of the workpiece. The added fence shown appears to be original and not a later addition. It is not known if the profile cut by this molder was the final form, or was to be augmented by another molding cut in the section at the edge untouched by this plane. This possibility is explored further in Chapter 11 under Strip Planes.

As mentioned elsewhere, a plane having an unusually long fence suggests that it may have been used as a sash plane. An example made by E.W. Carpenter (Pennsylvania, -1828-1859-) is shown in Fig.10:91. A LAMB TONGUE sash bar is cut with this profile on both sides of the bar. Variants are seen with other fillet arrangements.

214

An unusual form of reverse ogee has been seen in which the hollow is much smaller than the round (Fig.10:92). The resulting profile gives an appearance not greatly different from a dropped quarter-round or casing molding.

Fig.10:86—Reverse ogee with two fillets

The REVERSE OGEE WITH FENCE was mentioned along with the ogees, since it may be confused with them and will, in fact, cut an ogee if used conventionally. Chapin's style #206½ (1890, Fig.10:80) is meant to be applied to the edge of the board, with the fence guided by the face. The reverse ogee (Fig.10:85), being tangent to the edge of the board, tends to fight keeping the fence in contact with the edge; but by adapting the above method, i.e. working the edge, this problem vanishes. A naming problem remains, with the Ohio Tool catalog (ca.1910) calling it a Roman Ogee with fence. It was listed in sizes ⅜ to 1½ in. (10 - 38 mm.).

Fig.10:87—Wide reverse ogee (Greenfield Tool)

Fig.10:88— Flat reverse ogee

There is an alternate orientation for cutting the reverse ogee which is even easier to use. In this the fence is guided by the bottom face of the board rather than the top, according to the catalog illustrations. I see no reason why it could not be guided by the top face, to create a "falling" reverse ogee. Chapin (1890, Fig.10:93) and Ohio Tool Co. (ca.1910) both listed this form as a Roman Reverse Ogee with fence in sizes of ⅜ to 1¾ in., (10 - 45 mm.). I fail to see why the addition of the adjective Roman differentiates this from the reverse ogee with fence, but cannot offer a name shorter than Reverse Ogee with bottom-guided

Fig.10:89— Cabinet reverse ogee

fence. A similar profile, but with the ogee extended to sink the edge, is seen in Fig.10:94 of a left-handed plane (I presume one of a handed pair) made by the Auburn Tool Co.. New York, 1864-93. Please see next page.

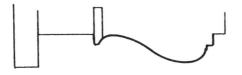

Fig.10:90—Strip plane
J. Killam (Connecticut)

215

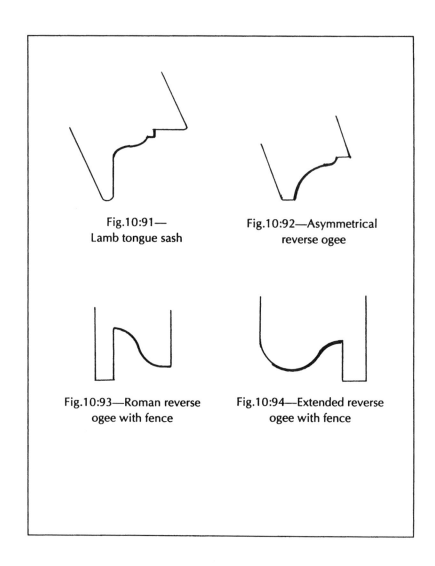

Fig.10:91—
Lamb tongue sash

Fig.10:92—Asymmetrical
reverse ogee

Fig.10:93—Roman reverse
ogee with fence

Fig.10:94—Extended reverse
ogee with fence

Chapter 11

DECORATIVE MOLDING PLANES–COMPLEX

The simple moldings covered in the last chapter may be combined to produce almost any desired profile. In fact, most of the elaborate moldings used on furniture were made in just this manner, by successive application of simple molding planes, or of the narrow two-element complex molders. This creates no great burden when cutting the short lengths of molding needed for furniture. Moreover, a wide plane would be very difficult to push on hard woods. For these reasons wide complex molders are rarely seen with irons at high pitch, since they were designed to cut soft woods for architectural moldings.

Almost all of the simple molders discussed in the last chapter were designed to work near the edge of a wide board, leaving most of the face untouched. The majority of complex molders are of this type as well, and these will be considered first. The exceptions are molders intended to profile the full face of a workpiece, and some special purpose molders. Both of these types are treated in later sections of this chapter.

The sharpening of molding plane irons requires great care. With complex profiles, the difficulty is magnified. Such molders were sometimes made with two, three, or even four irons in separate throats. While this made the sharpening much easier, the proper setting of these multiple irons must have been exasperating to even experienced users. The Scots apparently had the patience, as most of the multiple iron planes bear Scottish makers' names. They were also made in England, the United States, The Netherlands, France, and Japan, though they are not common.

Molders wider than about 3 in. (8 cm.) were often made with bench type bodies. In a few cases these too utilized multiple irons, including some in which the extra irons were mounted with side escapement throats.

Handles are rarely found on side escapement complex molding planes, except for the wider ones. A handle is sometimes added to the step of a wide, sprung molder, mounted so that the grip is vertical when the spring angle is correct. At first glance this seems to be a good idea, but it lessens the side thrust which is necessary to keep the plane's fence against the work.

NAMES OF MOLDING PLANES

The most common profile forms of "complex" molding planes will usually have only two elements. One is the outer feature that may be a fillet, a bevel, a bead, or an astragal. The outer feature would be combined with the second element, one of the ogee or ovolo curves. These types of complex molders have generally recognized names (such as ogee and bevel), and were so listed and named in planemakers' catalogs. Most of the more complex profiles, however, were not.

Molding planes for decorative purposes have been made in an enormous variety of profiles. The naming of these has been, to say the least, inconsistent, and therefore very confusing. Essentially identical profiles have been given different names by different makers, and the same name has been used for different profiles. Examples of this were discussed in the preceding chapter, which covered simple decorative molding planes.

When it comes to planes designed to cut complex profiles, the problem multiplies. Many makers (wisely) ducked the issue and printed page after page of profile illustrations using numbers instead of names. Others adopted the philosophy of Lewis Carroll's Humpty Dumpty, and described their planes by using names that "meant what they chose them to mean". Typical of this approach is the naming of a plane for the architectural feature on which the molding was most commonly used—as "cornice" plane. Catalogs used many such terms: architrave, base and band, bolection, pilaster, etc. The problem here is that one maker would call a flat ogee a "pilaster" plane because it might be used to cut the cap and base of a pilaster; while another would use the same name to mean a fluting plane, as pilasters were often fluted. Finding a name such as this in an inventory or price list leads only to guesswork.

The tradesmen who used the planes, of course, did not need to describe the profile. They knew the use to which they put the tool, and this was the only name they needed. The more elaborate molding planes were probably made to an architect's specification, based on his drawing, and were intended for a specific purpose. If this was for a wainscot cap, the tool was then a "wainscot cap plane". The man who used it needed no other name. In the next town, a completely different profile might be used for the same purpose and have the same name. The next owner of the tool, however, may have used it to mold a small baseboard. For him it then became his "baseboard" plane.

This remains true today. A millwork supply house will offer many varieties of "cornice" or "base", etc., moldings and will show you profiles from which you may choose. One supplier (Center Lumber, Paterson, NJ) offers twelve hundred molding profiles, indexed by application. If you seek a casing, its computer will draw a variety of profiles for you to choose from. They are all "casing" moldings, and are all different.

Given a plane to examine, we may speculate on how it was originally used; in most cases this is little more than a guess. However, the shape of the profile that the plane will cut is self-evident and provides a more useful basis for classification and naming.

A system that generates a unique name for any molding profile encountered, based solely on the profile it cuts, is presented in Appendix 2 and is used to identify the profiles shown in this section. The shorthand code for each profile name (given in parentheses immediately after the name) is also given in that Appendix.

Only the rudiments of the system are needed to find a given profile in the listings, and these are presented below. A few moments spent in becoming familiar with the procedure will help you locate a given profile. Simply identifying the first (innermost) element of the profile will decrease the range to be searched, as all profiles beginning with the same element appear together. Names appear in the alphabetical order of their elements. In many cases this will suffice, and the complete name need not be generated.

SYSTEMATIC NAMING OF COMPLEX MOLDING PLANES : SIMPLIFIED GENERAL PRINCIPLES

- The name is based on the molding profile produced by the plane.

- This profile is divided into its elements, each given a familiar (but here narrowly defined) name. These are given below.

- The profile is named by starting with the element furthest away from the edge of the board being cut, and naming the elements in the order in which they occur moving toward the board edge.

- With one exception, all elements are named, even minor ones. The fillet is not named when it is implied by adjacent elements (see Appendix 2, "Exception to naming all elements").

- The terms accepted as names for the elements of the profile are limited to thirteen. Two are line segments, three convex arcs, three concave arcs, four are double curves, and the thirteenth is the quirk.

PROFILE ELEMENTS

The two line elements:
- the BEVEL for a sloped line.
- the FILLET for a horizontal line.
        (A vertical line, or step, is not deemed an element).

The QUIRK:

> a small crevice between two elements or as a first element. It is usually formed by the continuation of an arc of a subsequent element which carries the curve below the surface, then reverses and returns to the surface.

The three convex elements:
- the OVOLO is a quarter circle or less, or an elliptical arc subtending $90°$ or less. It does not rise appreciably above the level of its inner edge. (The combination QUIRK OVOLO continues the inner end of the ovolo curve downward into the quirk.)
- the BEAD has both ends below the high point of its arc and can extend over a larger arc than the ovolo.
- the ASTRAGAL is a semi-circular arc with both ends at the same level. It has a fillet at its outer end, and usually another fillet at its inner end. The name includes both the arc and the fillet(s) of the profile.

The three concave elements:
- the COVE is a hollow quarter circle or less, with its lowest point at the outer end of the arc.
- the FLUTE is a hollow arc with both ends at the same level.
- the SCOTIA is a hollow arc with its two ends at different levels, both above the lowest point of the arc.

Two common doubly curved elements:
- the OGEE is an S-shaped curve, concave near the edge of the board and convex on the inner side.
- the REVERSE OGEE is similar, but convex near the edge and concave on the inner side.

220

Two double curves with pointed tops:

- the BEAK has a concave and a convex arc joining in a point at the top.
- the GOTHIC BEAD joins two convex arcs in a point at the top.

The above are the *only* elements considered in alphabetizing the name. Other modifiers (raised, dropped, lying, edge, etc.) are defined in Appendix 2 and *do not* affect alphabetic order.

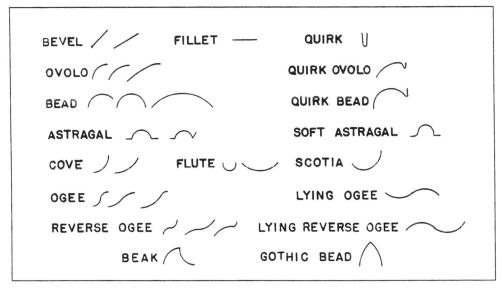

Fig.11:1—Profile elements and combinations

The molding illustrations that follow include, in addition to the profile elements, the depth stop and the fence if they are present in the plane described. These are not part of the profile being cut and are not named or coded. The cutting edge of plane iron is the significant factor and is indicated by the heavy line. The profile is shown from the rear of the plane as it would be seen by a user, or as it would be traced with the front of the plane placed on a piece of paper.

Over 300 complex molding profiles are illustrated and described. These include examples that have appeared in trade catalogs, texts, auction catalogs and displays, and in a number of public and private collections. What is shown is however far from exhaustive. Considering just the thirteen defined elements and taking no more than four at a time, there are more than 28,000 possible molding profiles. It is therefore quite possible to find an example that is not listed here. However, the vast majority of profiles that one is likely to encounter are covered.

COMPLEX PROFILES

ASTRAGAL and dropped ASTRAGAL (AdA) is alphabetically the first of the profiles. The example shown is of an anonymously made 18th century plane that appeared in a Mechanick's Workbench catalog. The profile was described as a component of the moldings used on ornate picture frames.

ASTRAGAL, raised ASTRAGAL, dropped ASTRAGAL with dropped ASTRAGAL (ArAdAdA) is a long name that might be shortened to four astragals, but this suggests a simple row of four and does not do justice to this ornate profile. The example is from a three-iron molder made by Thomas Turner (England, ca.1850).

ASTRAGAL and BEAD (AB) is a profile intended to mold the full width of a surface, as it would not cut unless the blade overhung the right edge. It probably served to mold furniture legs. Two examples have been seen, both by undocumented makers.

ASTRAGAL and BEAD with BEAD and FILLET (ABBF) was seen in an unmarked plane cutting a 2" (51 mm.) molding.

ASTRAGAL and COVE (AC) usually has the two features of equal size. This profile is related to the Quirk Ovolo and Cove (QVC-1 and QVC-2) described later, and the same comments hold. The early example shown is unsprung and was made by John Nicholson (Massachusetts, 1728-53). The same profile was still listed in 1909 by Weiss (Austria). Similar sprung profiles were

made by Jo. Fuller (Rhode Island, ca.1800) and other early makers. Fuller allowed the curve to rise a bit as it reached the edge, making it an Astragal and Scotia (AS). The astragal and cove is not seen in most 19th century American catalogs, but was listed by Preston (England) in 1901 as a "necking and nosing" plane. In sprung planes with astragals or similar arcs, the curve rarely reaches the vertical on the side opposite the fence, but stops parallel to the stock side to avoid cutting problems in use.

ASTRAGAL and COVE with ASTRAGAL (ACA)

has been seen in planes by Levi Little (Massachusetts, 1796-1802), E. Baldwin (New York, 1807-50), and E.W. Carpenter (Pennsylvania, 1828-59-). An earlier unsprung version by Tho. Grant (New York, 1760-70) is shown in the figure, and a similar one was still listed by Weiss (Austria) in 1909. The plane may be slipped to convert it to the Astragal and Cove with Bead (ACB, see below), by inserting a strip of wood inside the fence.

ASTRAGAL and COVE with soft ASTRAGAL

(ACsA) was reported in a user-made plane with offset tote and skew iron. As noted in Appendix 2, the coinage "soft astragal" is used for an astragal softened by rounding the corner between arc and fillet.

ASTRAGAL, COVE and ASTRAGAL with
REVERSE OGEE (ACAR) was a standard profile

for panel or base moldings and was listed in the Roberts 1903 Millwork catalog (U.S.). The sketch shows a plane that would produce this molding, although I have not seen one.

ASTRAGAL, COVE and BEAD (ACB) differs from the Quirk Bead, Cove, and Bead (QBCB) only in the width of the corner fillet. The profile was listed by Weiss (Austria 1909).

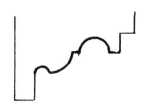

ASTRAGAL, COVE and back BEAK (ACbK) has been seen in an unsprung user-made plane. A similar example, with the beak facing the other way, is seen under Astragal, Scotia, and Ovolo with Fillet (ASVF). "Beak" is an early English name for this shape which has dropped from use but is resurrected here as useful in naming profiles of this type. "Back" indicates that the element is facing in the reverse of the normal direction.

ASTRAGAL and COVE with FILLET and COVE (ACFC) was made in a three-iron version by Alexander Neilson (Scotland, 1820-34).

ASTRAGAL, COVE and OVOLO (ACV) was made in a 3 in. (76 mm.) width by Griffiths (England, 19th century). The outline within the figure shows the boxing of this plane.

ASTRAGAL, FLUTE, ASTRAGAL and COVE (AHAC) is an elaborate profile seen in a plane signed M. Martien (Pennsylvania, ca.1800).

ASTRAGAL and dropped OGEE with ASTRAGAL (AdOA) was made with two irons by Alexander Marshall (Scotland, 1883-1904-). A similar profile with a hollow groove on the inside is shown later (see Scotia, Astragal, Ogee with Astragal, SAOA).

ASTRAGAL and REVERSE OGEE (AR) is seen in molding profiles in the Roberts Millwork catalog (1903) under Nosing, Panel and Base Moldings, but has not been seen in a plane. The profile ending in a fillet is seen below (ARF), and one with a second fillet inside is seen later (Fillet, raised Astragal and reverse Ogee, FrAR).

ASTRAGAL and REVERSE OGEE with soft ASTRAGAL (ARsA) was cut by Speight (England, 1863-). For another profile similar to this see Quirk Ovolo and Reverse Ogee with Astragal (QVRA).

ASTRAGAL and REVERSE OGEE with BEAD (ARB) was made in a two-iron version by Mathieson (Scotland).

ASTRAGAL and REVERSE OGEE with COVE — see Astragal and Scotia-Bead with Cove (AS-BC)

ASTRAGAL and REVERSE OGEE with FILLET (ARF) is shown in the Weiss catalog (Austria, 1909).

ASTRAGAL and SCOTIA (AS) is a form sometimes called (along with other similar shapes) a bolection molding. The example was made by Jo. Fuller (Rhode Island, ca.1800).

225

ASTRAGAL and SCOTIA with ASTRAGAL and COVE (ASAC) was made in a twin- iron version by Joseph Gleave (England, 1832-1913). An unsprung version was made by Kneass & Co. (Pennsylvania, -1818-).

ASTRAGAL and SCOTIA-BEAD with COVE (AS-BC) is a somewhat awkward profile to name. The scotia-bead name (using the hyphen convention, as outlined in Appendix 2) seems preferable to calling the element a reverse ogee. The molder was made by Stewart (Scotland, -1820-50).

ASTRAGAL and SCOTIA with BEVEL (ASL) is seen in a plane by D. Heinselman (probably Eastern Pennsylvania, early 1800's).

ASTRAGAL and SCOTIA with BEVEL and BEAD (ASLB) was listed by Weiss (Austria, 1909). An alternate non-systematic name might end in "bevel quirk bead".

ASTRAGAL and back SCOTIA with FILLET (AbSF) is the name derived from our systematic rules, but I suspect the plane was actually used to cut a Fillet and Scotia with Astragal (FSAseen later) on the far side of a strip. The uncut area near the edge could then be cut with another molder to make a profile of the type covered later under bolection moldings. The profile is from an early Union Factory plane (Connecticut, 1828-1860). A similarly unusual example is shown later in this chapter in the section on strip planes (example QlOE+).

ASTRAGAL, SCOTIA, FILLET and REVERSE OGEE (ASFR) was made by Matthew Crannell (New York, 1862-92). A five inch (127 mm.) wide

version may be seen at Fort George in Ontario, Canada.

ASTRAGAL, SCOTIA, OVOLO with FILLET (ASVF) (or ASTRAGAL and COVE-BEAK with FILLET) was made by Union Factory (Connecticut, 1828-1860) presumably on special order. The heel has the marks 2 and 7/8, the measurements for the cut "on" and "down".

Back BEAK-COVE (bK-C) is shown in the Dutch Nooitgedagt catalog (ca.1890) along with molding planes, but not named. It is unsprung, as all of their molders were.

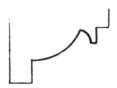

Back BEAK-COVE and ASTRAGAL (bK-CA) is another example from the Nooitgedagt catalog (The Netherlands, about 1890).

BEVEL with BEAD (LB) having a long bevel and a small bead, has been seen in a 3 in. (76 mm.) plane with a pull hole. The **BEVEL and BEAD,** with bead larger than bevel, has the common name "side bead, bevel quirk" (among others) and was shown in the previous chapter as Fig.10:44.

BEVEL, BEAD, back BEVEL, FLUTE, and QUIRK BEAD (LBbLHQB) is a flat form, perhaps intended to mold a chair leg or back. The 1⅜" (35 mm.) profile is by T. Donoho (Pennsylvania -1854-).

BEVEL, BEAD and SCOTIA with BEVEL (LBSL) was listed in the Weiss catalog (Austria, 1909).

BEVEL and BEVEL with BEAD (LLB) was noted in a plane marked T.J. Watson's (owner or perhaps an unrecorded planemaker).

BEVEL, FILLET, OGEE, FILLET, BEVEL, FILLET and BEAD (LFOFLFB) is a long-winded name for a three-iron plane listed by Nooitgedagt (The Netherlands, ca.1890). To shorten this to ogee and bead would not do it justice.

BEVEL and OGEE with BEAD (LOB) was made by George A. Benton (Massachusetts, 1856-68), using a 2⅝ in. (67 mm.) iron.

BEVEL and OGEE-BEAD (LO-B) uses the convention in which the hyphen denotes a smooth transition from ogee to bead. A wide molder with this profile may be seen in Roberts 1978, Fig.66.

BEVEL and OGEE-BEAD with FILLET (LO-BF) is called a "door molding" plane in the Ohio Tool Co. catalog (ca.1910) and offered in sizes ½ - 2 in. (13 - 51 mm.). The same profile in a wider plane (3½ or 4 in.; 89 - 102 mm.) was called a "pilaster" plane.

BEVEL and OVOLO (LV) has been seen with a shallow ovolo in an unmarked plane.

BEVEL with dropped OVOLO (LdV) is called a Kämpferhobel in the Weiss catalog (Austria, 1909).

BEVEL and lying REVERSE OGEE with BEAD (LRB) was made by William Watkins (England, 1845-77).

COVE with ASTRAGAL (CA) is an old form. A plane of this profile **(CA-1)** marked by Tho. Grant (New York, ca.1780) was made without spring. A sprung version was listed in Smith's *Key* (1816). It was called a "cove and bead" by both Philip Chapin (Maryland, mid-19c.) and Arrowmammett (Connecticut, mid-19c.), the latter offering it in sizes of ⅜ - ¾ in. (10 - 32 mm.). It is not listed in most later catalogs. A form in which the cove is extended as a long flat **(CA-2)** was made by Samuel Green (England, 1774-1801). This shape is seen in the apophyge of the column in Fig.10:1; the extended cove may be called a congé. **COVE and ASTRAGAL (CA-3)**, by F. Nicholson (Massachusetts, 1728-53), has the astragal larger than the cove. Griffiths (England, -1811- 1949) made the elements about the same size in a sprung stock. The fillet on the outside of the profile distinguishes this form from the Cove with Bead (CB-2), described below. Although the shape difference is slight, the effect of the additional band of light reflection in use is pronounced.

CA-1

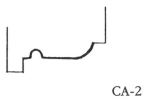

CA-2

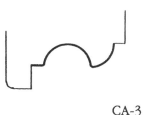

CA-3

229

COVE with dropped ASTRAGAL (CdA) is a variation seen in a plane made by Aaron Smith (Massachusetts, ca.1800); and a **COVE and dropped ASTRAGAL** with a larger astragal and what appears to be bone boxing is seen in a plane sold by E.G. Pierce, Jr. (Vermont, ca.1850).

COVE with soft ASTRAGAL (CsA) a profile by Tucker (England, 1842-84) provides another example calling for the coinage "soft astragal". The Cove and Ogee (CO) is a quite different form, and to apply that name here would be misleading.

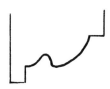

COVE with ASTRAGAL and COVE (CAC) is shown in the Weiss catalog (Austria, 1909) **(CAC-1)** and the same catalog lists the variation **COVE and ASTRAGAL with COVE (CAC-2)** (with a larger astragal).

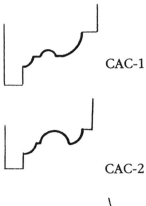

CAC-1

CAC-2

COVE with dropped ASTRAGAL and COVE (CdAC) is a variant of **CAC** (above) with a step after the first cove, made by Speight (England, 1863-90).

COVE, ASTRAGAL and OGEE with ASTRAGAL (CAOA) was made with two irons by Marshall (Scotland, 1883-1904).

COVE with BEAD (CB) survived rather longer than cove with astragal. It was still listed by Ohio Tool Co. in 1910 (and by others) in sizes ⅜ - 1½ in. (10 - 38 mm.) **(CB-1)**. A **COVE and BEAD** with a large bead (A. Mockridge, New Jersey, 1835-41), was sprung at about 20°, with the bead inner arc shortened appropriately **(CB-2)**. (A small cove and large bead would commonly be called a cove quirked bead.)

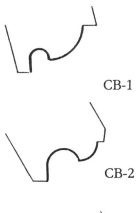

CB-1

CB-2

COVE and dropped BEAD (CdB) by Gleave (England, 1832-1913) is close to a Cove and Ovolo, but has an upward slope after the step (not enough to quality as a quirk). A variation of the profile is the Fillet, Cove and Quirk Bead (FCQB) seen later.

COVE, BEAD and BEAD (CBB) is a variant of the side reed seen in a large molder (iron 3", 76 mm.) made by John Moseley and Son (England, 1819-1914) with an offset, tilted tote. The fence extension made it easier to start the cut.

COVE and BEADS (CBBB) might also be called (but not by using the present system) a cove quirked triple side reed. One by Kirk & Asling (England, 1885-89) is shown; another with a fillet inside and the beads clustered is seen later (see Fillet, Cove and Bead Cluster, FCBBB).

COVE and BEAD with COVE and BEAD (CBCB) is seen in one of a set of triple-iron molders stamped Castel Emmanuel, and presumably was custom-made.

231

COVE and BEAD with FILLET (CBF) was made without spring by F. Nicholson (Massachusetts, 1728-1753). A sprung version was made by B. Sheneman (Pennsylvania, 1846-67).

COVE, FILLET, dropped BEVEL with dropped FILLET (CFdLdF) is noted in a plane by J.V. HILL (England, 1842-63).

COVE, FILLET and REVERSE OGEE-COVE (CFR-C) is another unusual two-iron profile with a serpentine curve made by Gleave (England, 1832-1913).

COVE and OGEE (CO) has been seen in a few English planes, as in the one by Buck (England, 1838-1930) shown here. A form with a distorted ogee is seen coded as Cove and soft Astragal (CsA).

COVE and OGEE with BEVEL and BEAD (COLB) is a variant of Quirk Ogee and Quirk Bead (QOQB) and is seen in the Nooitgedagt catalog (The Netherlands, ca.1890) and the Weiss catalog (Austria,.1909) along with the modification **COVE and OGEE with BEVEL and QUIRK BEAD (COLQB).**

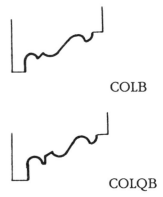

COLB

COLQB

COVE, OGEE with dropped FILLET and BEAD (COdFB) is an Austrian variant of the Quirk Ogee with Bead (QOB), and was seen in the Weiss 1909 catalog. A narrower fillet would have changed the name to COVE, OGEE and QUIRK BEAD (COQB).

COVE and OGEE with FILLET and BEVEL (COFL) is an unusual form cut by McVicar (Scotland, 1850-56).

COVE and lying OGEE with FILLET and REVERSE OGEE (ClOFR) has not yet been seen in a plane, but is listed in the Roberts Millwork 1903 Catalog as a Band molding.

COVE, lying OGEE and OVOLO (ClOV) is seen in the Auburn Tool Co. catalog (New York, 1869) as #159 base molding, cutting down ⅞ or 1 in. (21 - 25 mm.).

COVE and OVOLO (CV) is seldom seen without the fillet, as in the Cove and Ovolo with Fillet (CVF), unless it is in the form of a sash plane (the curve makes a poor fence). It is seen in wide molders. The profile was used decoratively, however, and was more easily cut by the **edge COVE and OVOLO (eCV)** made by the Auburn Tool Co. (New York, 1864-93).

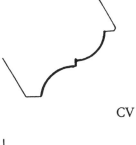

CV

eCV

233

COVE and OVOLO with ASTRAGAL (CVA) was made as a two-iron, wide (2.4 in., 6 cm.) molder by an unrecorded maker.

COVE and OVOLO with FILLET (CVF) was made by Griffiths (England, 1811-1949) (**CVF-1**). This is most often seen as a sash plane, with flatter elements, to cut the so-called astragal and hollow sash bar. A long fence and a number 1 or 2 on the heel are diagnostics. One by Moseley & Son (England, 1832-62) is shown (**CVF-2**). This type is usually English, as other forms of the sash plane were normally used in the United States. (Also see Chapter 13—The Sashmaker).

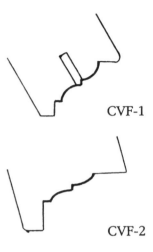

CVF-1

CVF-2

COVE and QUIRK BEAD (CQB) is shown as made by D. Arthur (Scotland, 1793-1844). The profile commonly called a "cove quirk bead" is coded as Cove and Bead (CB).

COVE and QUIRK OGEE (CQO) is shown by Weiss (Austria, 1909). As in many of Weiss's profiles, the quirk is almost wide enough to be called a fillet.

COVE and QUIRK OGEE with ASTRAGAL (CQOA) was made by Hermon Chapin's Union Factory (Connecticut, 1828-1901), probably as a special.

234

COVE, GRECIAN OGEE and BEVEL (CQOL), an augmented Grecian Ogee with Bevel (QOL), was made by J. Stevens (Massachusetts, 1821-22).

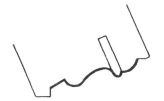

COVE and QUIRK OGEE with QUIRK BEAD (CQOQB) is seen in a molder by Frederick Tucker (England, 1842-84). A similar form with wider quirks (almost fillets) is seen in Weiss (Austria, 1909).

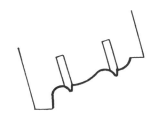

COVE and QUIRK OVOLO (CQV) is cut by a 3 in. (76 mm.) molder by Martin and Shaw (England, 1845-54).

COVE and QUIRK OVOLO with BEAD and COVE (CQVBC) was made as a three-iron molder by James Lumsden (Scotland, 1871-87).

FILLET, raised ASTRAGAL and REVERSE OGEE (FrAR) is cut in 1¼ in. (32 mm.) width by a plane made by Bensen & Crannell (New York, 1844-62).

FILLET and BEAD (FB) is listed by Nooitgedagt (The Netherlands, ca.1890) as "cut bead" in addition to their quirk bead, which they call "sharp bead".

FILLET, BEAD and FILLET (FBF) is another variant of the astragal shown by Nooitgedagt (The Netherlands, ca.1890) and differs from it only in the different levels of the fillets.

FILLET, BEAD, SCOTIA, BEVEL and BEAD (FBSLB) was made with three irons (one with a bench type throat, the other two with side escapements) in an unsprung European plane cutting 2⅜ in. on and ¾ in. down (60 mm. x 25 mm.).

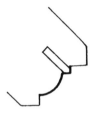

FILLET and COVE (FC) was cut by John Keller (Maryland, -1796-1808-) with unusually high spring.

FILLET and COVE with ASTRAGAL (FCA) has been seen in a 1⅜ in. (35 mm.) molder by Samuel King (England, 1776-1806) and an unsprung version was also listed by Nooitgedagt (The Netherlands, ca.1890).

FILLET, COVE and BEAD cluster (FCBBB) appears on a fully boxed 2 in. (51 mm.) unmarked plane.

FILLET, COVE, FILLET and GOTHIC BEAD (FCFG) is named in the reverse of the normal direction, on the assumption that it was used in one of the fashions described later under strip planes. The profile is also listed under Gothic

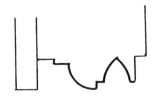

Bead, Fillet, back Cove and Fillet (GFbCF) later. This profile by T. Tileston (Massachusetts, 1802-1866) is quite similar to the one described under Astragal, back Scotia and Fillet (AbSF).

FILLET, COVE and OVOLO (FCV) is called a "covetta and quarter round" in the Mathieson (Scotland, 1899) catalog.

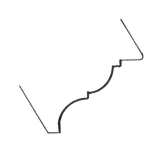

FILLET, COVE and QUIRK BEAD (FCQB) is shown in the Weiss catalog (Austria, 1909).

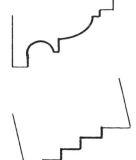

FILLET, FILLET and FILLET (FFF) or triple square has been seen in one of a group of planes marked W. Feast (unknown) — probably custom made.

FILLET, FILLET, FILLET, COVE and ASTRAGAL (FFFCA) is another of the above group.

FILLET, FLUTE, FILLET and BEAD with BEAD (FHFBB) is another of the set of planes marked Castel Emmanuel and presumably made for a special purpose.

FILLET, FLUTE, FILLET, OGEE with ASTRAGAL and COVE (FHFOAC) is another of the complex profiles shown in the Weiss catalog (Austria, 1909).

237

FILLET, OVOLO and COVE (FVC) appeared as an unmarked three-iron plane in an English auction catalog.

FILLET and QUIRK BEAD (FQB) was made by Jennion (England, 1732-69) to add a wide fillet inside a side bead.

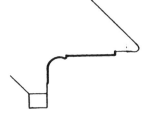

FILLET, REVERSE OGEE and BEAD (FRB) was made by George Speight (England, 1863-90) and another was reported in an unmarked plane.

FILLET, lying REVERSE OGEE and BEVEL with BEAD (FlRLB) is observed in a wide 2⅜ in. (60 mm.) flat profile cut by a Gardner and Murdock (Massachusetts, 1825-42) molder.

FILLET, REVERSE OGEE with COVE (FRC) appeared in a German plane of ca.1570 in the Dresden collection, and is also shown in the Weiss catalog (Austria, 1909).

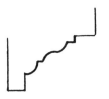

FILLET, REVERSE OGEE with FILLET (FRF) is an old form present in the Dresden collection, (Germany, ca.1570). It is also pictured in Roubo (1769) and often since. The Chapin 1874 catalog called their form (Fig.10:86) "the reverse ogee with square" and offered sizes of ⅜ - 2 in. (10 - 51 mm.). Mathieson (Scotland, 1899) called the same profile a "reverse ogee with double fillet". The sash lamb tongue is also seen with two fillets (see Chapter 13 — Sashmaker).

FILLET, lying REVERSE OGEE with FILLET (FlRF) is seen in a Philip Chapin (Maryland, mid-19th century) broadside in which he called it his "pilaster #2". The same form **(FlRF-1)** is seen in a T. Tileston plane (Massachusetts, 1802-1866). An extreme form was made with sharper curves by E. Blaby (an unrecorded maker). Another, by William Shepley (England, 1799-1810) was flatter **(FlRF-2)**.

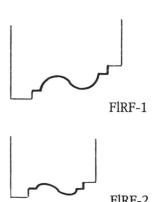

FlRF-1

FlRF-2

FILLET, lying REVERSE OGEE with FILLET and BEAD (FlRFB) is an unusually flat profile seen in a molder by Gardner and Murdoch (Massachusetts, 1825-42).

FILLET and SCOTIA with ASTRAGAL (FSA) names this profile in the reverse of the normal direction. See Astragal and back Scotia with Fillet (AbSF).

FILLET and SCOTIA with BEVEL (FSL) was made with two irons by Mathieson (Scotland) marked #53 but not listed in its 1899 catalog.

FLUTE and BEVEL (HL) was made by J. Searing (New Jersey, - 1821-49).

FLUTE and BEVEL with FILLET (HLF) was made by prison labor under a contract held by T. J. McMaster (New York, 1825-38).

GOTHIC BEAD, FILLET, back COVE and FILLET (GFbCF) is another name arrived at by mechanical application of the system. It leaves an uncut section next to the fence and was probably intended to cut the far side of a strip to produce the **FILLET, COVE, FILLET and GOTHIC BEAD (FCFG)**, see earlier.

NOTE: GRECIAN . . . names are considered equivalent to QUIRK and are listed under QUIRKS.

OGEE with ASTRAGAL (OA) is an old profile not found in U.S. catalogs but listed by Dalpé, a Quebec (Canada) supplier, in sizes ⅜ - 2 in. (10 - 51 mm.). The example shown was imprinted by Tho. Grant (New York, ca.1760).

OGEE, ASTRAGAL, dropped ASTRAGAL and COVE (OAdAC) is another complex profile by George Speight (England, 1863-90).

OGEE with BEAD (OB) was made by many suppliers in sizes ⅜ - 2 in. (10 - 51 mm.). An old form, it was pictured in Roubo (1769).

OGEE-BEAD (O-B) is one of those difficult to classify serpentine forms that led to the hyphen naming convention. They have been called double ogees or hunchbacks. Five variations are shown, but many more are possible. Four lack the usual step and depth stop. These were made by Charles Nurse (England, -1844- 89) **(O-B-1)**, Buck (England, 1838-1930) **(O-B-2)**, and T. Tileston (Massachusetts, 1802-1860-) **(O-B-3)**. A more conventional molder may be seen in the Upper Canada Village collection **(O-B-4)**. Wide planes of this type may have been used to cut the sides of stair handrails (see stairmaker). The last shown **(O-B-5)** is by George Speight (England, 1863-90) and is one of a type reportedly made for wardrobe moldings.

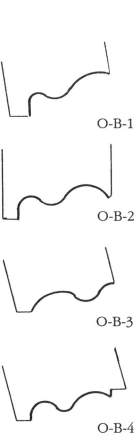

O-B-1

O-B-2

O-B-3

O-B-4

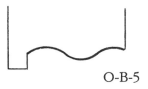

O-B-5

OGEE-BEAD, ASTRAGAL and COVE (O-BAC) is another of the complex profiles favored by George Speight (England, 1863-90).

OGEE-BEAK with FILLET (O-KF) was cut by William Watkins (England, 1845-88) in a 3.6 in. (92 mm.) toted plane.

OGEE with BEVEL (OL) was an option listed in the H. Chapin's Son 1874 catalog (Connecticut) in sizes of ⅜ - 2 in. (10 - 51 mm.). Its style #205 was "plain ogee with bead, bevel or square", but only the bead survived in the 1890 catalog. This profile is found in older planes, including a Tho. Grant (New York, ca.1760). The bevel was also called a splay.

OGEE with BEVEL and BEAD (OLB), commonly called ogee with bevel quirk bead. It is suggested that the form **(OLB-1)** made by S. Tomkinson (England, ca.1780) was used to mold table legs, cutting on both sides and having the ogees meet in the middle to make a symmetrical profile. The usual step and depth stop are not needed for this use, and the 60° or "half" pitch of this plane is consistent with use on hardwood (Gooch 1984). Another form **(OLB-2)** with the initial step is seen in the Nooitgedagt catalog (The Netherlands, ca.1890).

OLB-1

OLB-2

OGEE with BEVEL and FILLET (OLF) The plane on which it was seen is unusual in that it has no step or depth stop.

OGEE and COVE (OC) is not seen in most catalogs. One made by Aaron Smith (Massachusetts, ca.1810) is of the pure form. More often there is a fillet between the elements (see Ogee, Fillet and Cove, OFC).

OGEE with FILLET (OF) can take the form in which the ogee rises to meet the fillet. It is also seen as the **OGEE with dropped FILLET (OdF)**, listed by Philip Chapin (Maryland, mid-19c.). H. Chapin's Son 1874 catalog (Connecticut) listed "plain ogee with square" in sizes from ⅜ to 2 in. (10 - 51 mm.).

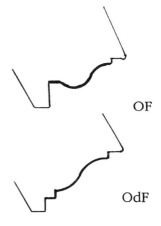

OF

OdF

OGEE, dropped FILLET and COVE (OdFC) was made with two irons by Gleave (England, 1832-68). The same maker produced the unusual **OGEE, FILLET and COVE (OFC)** in which the ogee sweeps up before breaking as the fillet — again with two irons.

OdFC

OFC

OGEE with FILLET and REVERSE OGEE (OFR) is listed as a Band molding in Robert's Millwork 1903 catalog. A plane to cut this would have a quirk or a fillet as its first element.

OGEE and OVOLO (OV) has been seen only in older English planes. One has lost its maker's name through shortening **(OV-1)**. Another **(OV-2),** with the long fence characteristic of sash planes, was made by Sinclair (England, dates unknown) and would cut an astragal and ogee sash bar.

OV-1

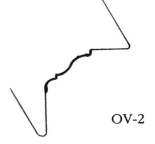

OV-2

OGEE and OVOLO with soft ASTRAGAL and COVE (OVsAC) was cut as a three-iron molder by Alexander Marshall (Scotland, 1883-1904-).

OGEE and REVERSE OGEE with ASTRAGAL (ORA) was made in a bench type plane by Samuel Green (England, -1774-1801). An informal name might be cupid's bow with astragal.

OGEE with SCOTIA and BEVEL (OSL) was made by Edward Preston (England, 1833-83-).

244

OVOLO with ASTRAGAL (VA) was pictured by Roubo in 1769. In contrast to most ovolos, it did not use a step at the inner end of the curve.

OVOLO with ASTRAGAL, dropped ASTRAGAL and COVE (VAdAC) was made by Thomas Goldsmith (Pennsylvania, 1801-37).

OVOLO with ASTRAGAL and COVE (VAC) was cut in a molder by Stewart (Scotland, -1820-50).

OVOLO and BEAD (left VB) is seen in a most unusual plane by T. Tileston (Boston,1802-1867). It is one of the very rare left-handed profile planes. This, too, uses no step and is full boxed in the hammerhead fashion.

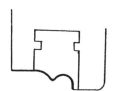

OVOLO and COVE (VC) would be called an ogee if there were no fillet between the ovolo and the cove, so that the fillet need not be named. The profile **(VC-1)** was called a "belection" plane by Philip Chapin (Maryland, mid-19c.), implying a favored use in bolections (discussed later). Usually a recessed quarter round with a cove, it is also seen with elliptical arcs, as in the two-iron plane **(VC-2)** by J.Welch (Scotland, 1845-50). A plane with a smaller cove, **OVOLO with COVE (VC-3)**, by R. Nelson (England, 1823-52) is unusual in that there was no step at the top of the ovolo. Wide forms, such as the 2 in. (51 mm.) cut made by Moore

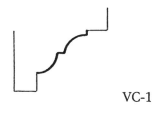

VC-1

VC-2

245

(England, 1824-70) may have been used to field panels. Wide flat profiles such as this are seen in cornice planes (discussed later in this chapter). The Ovolo and Cove in a steep form with an exaggerated depth stop **(VC-4)** is a sash plane, for cutting the astragal and hollow sash in the old way (see Chapter 13—Sashmaker). The example shown is by John Blizard (England, 1805-24). See also Fillet, Ovolo and Cove (FVC); and Ovolo, Fillets and Cove (VFFC).

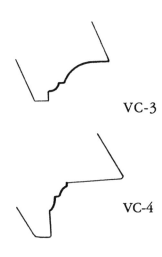

VC-3

VC-4

OVOLO, COVE and ASTRAGAL (VCA) was seen in a plane marked by T. Dickson (unrecorded). A very similar profile is **OVOLO, COVE, BEAD and FILLET (VCBF)**, with the fillet a bit lower. This was one of a pair of planes used to cut a molding listed by Weiss (Austria 1909), shown in Fig.11:4.

OVOLO, COVE, and BEAD (VCB) was made with two irons by Marshall (Scotland, 1883-1904).

OVOLO, FILLET and ASTRAGAL with FILLET (VFAF) was seen in a triple iron molder with two imprints, Malloch (Scotland, 1850- 1912) and John Dobie (Scotland, 1863-1904).

OVOLO with FILLET and FILLET (VFF), is a recessed quarter round with an additional fillet. This example was made by John Sleeper (Massachusetts, -1813-25).

246

OVOLO, FILLETS and COVE (VFFC and VFFFC)
is seen in two planes ca.1570 from the Dresden
(Germany) collection, one with two fillets
(VFFC) and another with three (VFFFC). They
are variations of the Ovolo and Cove with extra
fillets between the elements.

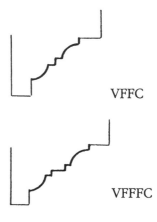

VFFC

VFFFC

**OVOLO, FILLET, OVOLO, SCOTIA and BEAD
(VFVSB)** is another elaborate profile by Gleave
(England, 1832-1913).

**OVOLO, FILLET, QUIRK BEAD and BEAD
(VFQBB)** was also made by Gleave. This would
be called (outside of systematic naming) a quarter round and side reed.

OVOLO and FLUTE (VH) is an unfenced plane
(Dresden collection, Germany, ca.1570) perhaps
intended for use away from the work edge. See
also Ovolo and Scotia (VS).

OVOLO and FLUTE with FILLET (VHF) is seen
in a plane by E.W. Carpenter (Pennsylvania,
1828-59), and may have been a mother plane for
an Astragal and Cove.

247

OVOLO, FLUTE, ASTRAGAL and COVE (VHAC) is reported by Greber (1956) as one of the elaborate profiles made for the Dresden collection, Germany, about 1570.

OVOLO, OVOLO and OVOLO (VVV) or triple ovolo cuts a triple side reed on a slant. The example was made by Gabriel (England, 1770-1816). For a somewhat similar double reed see Quirk Ovolo and Bead (QVB-2).

OVOLO and REVERSE OGEE (VR) is seen in a late 19th century plane by Joh. Weiss (Austria).

OVOLO and lying REVERSE OGEE (VlR) is a shallow molding made by Holbrook (England, 1800-1873). One possible use is in cutting a picture frame.

OVOLO and SCOTIA (VS) is an early molder by John Keller (Maryland, -1796-1808). It differs from Ovolo and Cove (VC) by the upsweep at the edge.

OVOLO, SCOTIA and COVE (VSC) is seen in a plane made by Evans (New York, -1850-85).

OVOLO, SCOTIA, FILLET and COVE (VSFC) is seen in a plane by Isaac Field (Rhode Island, -1842-57). The similar **OVOLO, SCOTIA, FILLET, FILLET AND COVE (VSFFC)** was made with an additional fillet before the cove by George Stokoe (England, -1817- 40).

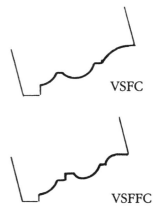

VSFC

VSFFC

QUIRK BEAD, ASTRAGAL, raised FILLET and OGEE (QBArFO) was made by S. Brittain (England). The first two elements, if alone, are called a side reed.

QUIRK BEAD and BEVEL (QBL) was made with two irons by Dunham and M'Master (Auburn, NY, 1821-25). As defined in Appendix 2, a quirked convex arc that continues until it reaches a vertical slope is coded as a bead rather than an ovolo.

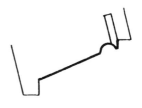

QUIRK BEAD and COVE (QBC) and its variants are popular shapes. The profile sketched is from the Ohio Tool Co. ca.1910 catalog, style #89, and was called a Nosing molding and offered in sizes from ½ to ⁵⁄₄ in. (12 - 32 mm.). Systematic naming differentiates this from Astragal and Cove (AC) in having a less deep quirk, and from Quirk Ovolo and Cove (QVC) in that its circular arc reaches the vertical. It is shown without spring, but an earlier example made with spring by Thomas Goldsmith (Pennsylvania, 1801-37) had the inner side of the bead stopped short of vertical. (See Appendix 1 for the reason.)

QUIRK BEAD, COVE and ASTRAGAL (QBCA)
was a popular complex profile, adding an astragal to a common nosing molding. The first element has a shape that would be called a torus bead were it standing alone. Most examples seen were produced by early makers, prior to 1850, although they were made later in Scotland. The profile shown **(QBCA-1)** is from a wide molder by L. Little (Massachusetts, -1796-1802). **QUIRK BEAD and COVE with ASTRAGAL (QBCA-2)**, having a smaller astragal, is marked Tho. Grant (New York, ca.1760). Another variant, **QUIRK BEAD, COVE and soft ASTRAGAL (QBCsA)** is seen in a plane made by William Tracey (England, -1774-1820). See Quirk Ovolo, Cove and Astragal (QVCA) for a related form.

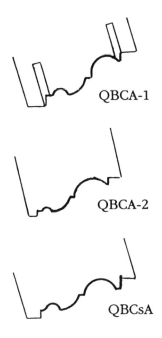

QBCA-1

QBCA-2

QBCsA

QUIRK BEAD, COVE and BEAD (QBCB) was used by a number of British makers. It differs from the common Quirk Ogee with Bead only in the fillet between the first bead and the cove. The profile shown is from a two-iron plane by Marshall (Scotland, 1883-1904-). Almost identical ones were made by his neighbor Ellsworth, and in England by Griffiths and by Gleave. The last was slipped to permit conversion to Quirk Bead, Cove and Astragal (QBCA) seen earlier.

QUIRK BEAD and OGEE (QBO) is seen in a plane by John Moseley and Son (England, 1878-1910).

QUIRK BEAD and QUIRK OGEE (QBQO) was made by J.A. Clarke (England). A smaller ogee would have been called, in this system, a soft astragal.

QUIRK BEAD, lying REVERSE OGEE with COVE (QBlRC) is another possible name for a profile seen below as Quirk Bead, Scotia-bead with Cove (QBS-BC). The scotia-bead form is preferred because the ogee is distorted.

QUIRK BEAD, REVERSE OGEE with FILLET (QBRF) is shown in W.L. Goodman's *British Planemakers* (1978) as a molder by Richard Bywater (England, -1805-12).

QUIRK BEAD, SCOTIA-BEAD with COVE (QBS-BC) is shown in a profile from a Union Factory (Connecticut, 1828-60) plane with hammerhead boxing. An almost identical profile is in the collection at Upper Canada Village, and another was made by I. Sleeper (Massachusetts, -1813-34). A similar profile is seen under Quirk Ovolo and Scotia with Astragal and Cove (QVSAC).

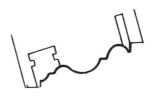

QUIRK BEVEL and BEAD (QLB) was made by George White (Pennsylvania, 1791-84). The quirk was cut by a second iron in a canted throat.

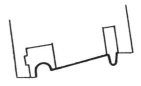

QUIRK COVE (QC), was made by M. Copeland (Connecticut, 1831-42) with a very shallow cove in a wide (2½ in., 64 mm.) stock. The question as to whether this was for molding or some functional use remains open.

NOTE that QUIRK OGEE and GRECIAN OGEE are regarded as equivalent for purposes of indexing in the following section, since in many instances the terms are interchangeable.

QUIRK OGEE with ASTRAGAL (QOA) was a fairly common profile among American makers before 1850, but is rarely found in planes produced after that date, except those by British makers. The profile shown was made by Kennedy (New York, 1825-32) and is typical of many others. One only ⅜ in. (10 mm.) wide was made by J. Stevens (Massachusetts, 1822).

QUIRK OGEE with soft ASTRAGAL (QOsA) is seen in a wide molder with an early Mathieson stamp (Scotland, mid-19th century) although it is not listed in the 1899 catalog. It is of bench type and has a second iron with a side escapement, and cuts a 2¾ in. (70 mm.) molding.

QUIRK OGEE with ASTRAGAL and FILLET (QOAF) was made as a twin iron bench type plane by Manners (Scotland, -1792-1822).

QUIRK OGEE with BEAD (QOB) was listed in the H. Chapin's Sons 1876 catalog, without illustration, in sizes ⅜ - 1.5 in. (10 - 38 mm.) The profile **QOB-1** is from Philip Chapin's broadside (Baltimore, mid-19th century). The **GRECIAN OGEE with BEAD (QOB-2)** was separately listed (in widths up to 2 in., 51 mm.). Wider, handled planes were priced by the inch. This is found in almost all catalogs, being (along with

QOB-1

252

the Grecian Ovolo and Bead, QVB) one of the most widely used profiles in nineteenth century American homes. It served to edge architraves, stiles and rails around panels, and in many places that required a trim somewhat wider than a side bead.

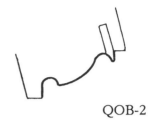

QOB-2

NOTE: The cove quirk ogee profiles may be found under cove and ogee listings, bevel quirk ogee under bevel. Many variations are seen which are obvious permutations of the various ogee and quirk forms, and are not shown here. If the ogee and bead join in a smooth curve, this system prefers to call it a quirk ogee-bead, using the hyphen convention.

QUIRK OGEE-BEAD (QO-B) has the ogee smoothly joined to the bead rather than meeting it in a pointed intersection. An example with a bevel quirk was shown previously as Bevel and Ogee-Bead (LO-B). The illustration **(QO-B-1)** is from a No. 99 molder by A. Mathieson & Son (Scotland, 1853-1910), not shown in their 1899 catalog. The extreme in Grecian ogees is seen in a plane by G. White (Pennsylvania, 1818-24), made before they were called Grecian **(QO-B-2)**, in which the ogee is almost a bevel. A form with a steep ogee is seen in an A. Smith (Massachu-setts, -1816-1822) plane **(QO-B-3).** An example with a bevel quirk was shown previously (LO-B). A similar profile without the central hollow is seen later as the Quirk Ogee-Ovolo (QO-V).

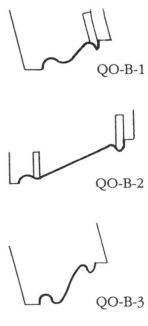

QO-B-1

QO-B-2

QO-B-3

GRECIAN OGEE-BEAD with BEAD and FILLET (QO-BBF) is a subtle variation of the ogee with astragal form. This one was made by Preston (Birmingham, 1833-83).

253

QUIRK OGEE, BEAD and COVE (QOBC) is found in a plane by E. Bassett (unrecorded, late 18th century).

QUIRK OGEE-BEAK (QO-K) has been seen in a number of planes. The simple profile shown is by Barry and Way (New York, 1842-47). Varvill (England, 1796-1830) made a similar profile as a wide, handled plane. The combination of a convex and concave curve done in this fashion was known as a bird's beak or a beak in Gothic moldings. Another possible name is Quirk Ogee with Ovolo, but the present name is more descriptive.

QUIRK OGEE-BEAK with BEAD (QO-KB) is another of the forms in which this unusual curve is seen, this one by King and Peach (England, 1843-64).

QUIRK OGEE-BEAK with FILLET (QO-KF) was made by J.R.Gale (Rhode Island, -1832-36-). It made a 1¾ in. (44 mm.) wide cut and was marked 9/8, referring to the depth of cut. An almost identical profile was cut by Hields (England, 1830-81).

GRECIAN OGEE with BEVEL (QOL) is perhaps the most often seen complex molder. It was commonly used in door casings and base moldings in the late nineteenth and early twentieth century. The profile shown **(QOL-1)** is taken from the Ohio Tool Co. (ca.1910) catalog (style #61¼) where it was offered in sizes from ½ to 2 in. (13 - 51 mm.). The same profile was also listed

QOL-1

254

as a "base" plane (#40) which was the handled version in sizes of 2 to 3 in. (51 - 76 mm.). An almost identical profile was made by M. Copeland (Connecticut, before 1830), who probably called it a "quirk ogee", and by most later makers. William Marples (England) called it simply a "Grecian ogee". There were variants, however. A steeper type is illustrated by the Cunningham plane (Ohio, 1854-), cutting 1¾ in. (44 mm.) down and 2½ in. (64 mm.) on **(QOL-2).** Mathieson (Scotland, 1899) listed these, as well as other Grecian ogees, in two-iron models. One iron cut the ogee, a second cut the other element. There are many other minor variations in ogee shape and quirking that are not illustrated.

QOL-2

QUIRK OGEE with BEVEL and BEAD (QOLB)

was a popular profile in Britain, a variant of the quirk ogee and bead in which the ogee swept up, then broke to a bevel before the bead. It was called "quirk ogee and quirk bead" in the Sheffield list of 1876 (which also showed a QOB). Two varieties are shown in the Mathieson catalog (Scotland, 1899) called simply "Grecian ogee and bead". Surprisingly, their "new pattern" has more nearly circular arcs than the older one. Similar profiles are seen with many other Scottish and northern English makers. The profile is from a three-iron molder by Alexander Currie (Scotland, 1833-44). Okins (England, -1807-35) varied this with a fillet between ogee and bead, seen later as Quirk lying Ogee, dropped Fillet and Bead (QlOdFB). Some varied it with a quirk bead: see Quirk Ogee, Bevel with Quirk Bead (QOLQB). The only related U.S. example seen is shown in the Ohio Tool Co. catalog (ca.1910) as "made to order" and called "G.O.G. quirk and bead", although its quirk was shown as a small bevel

and fillet in the illustration. It is seen below as Grecian Ogee with Bevel, Fillet and Bead (QOLFB). An Austrian version (Weiss 1909) used a cove quirk for the ogee, which is indexed here with the coves (Cove and Ogee with Bevel and Bead, COLB). Flat ogees and other variants are also seen.

QUIRK lying OGEE with BEVEL and FILLET (QlOLF) is a modification of the popular Grecian ogee with bevel (QOL), seen in a plane by William Hields (England, 1830-1881) A variant with raised fillet, Quirk lying Ogee with Bevel and raised Fillet **(QlOLrF)** was made by T. Tileston (Massachusetts, ca.1840).

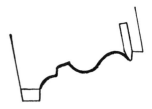

QlOLF

QlOLrF

GRECIAN OGEE with BEVEL, FILLET and BEAD (QOLFB) was previously noted under Quirk Ogee with Bevel and Bead (QOLB) by Ohio Tool Company and called by them "G.O.G. quirk and bead" and "made to order".

QUIRK lying OGEE with BEVEL and dropped OVOLO (QlOLdV) was made by John Lund (England, -1812-32) and by another eighteenth century maker whose name was lost when the plane was shortened. The profile shades into the form with bevel and bead, and is differentiated by the horizontal inner end of the ovolo.

QUIRK lying OGEE with BEVEL and QUIRK BEAD (QlOLQB) was another variant of the quirk ogee and bead, and was also popular in Britain. The profile is by Robert Fairclough (England, 1849-80).

QUIRK OGEE and COVE with ASTRAGAL (QOCA) was seen in an unmarked two-iron molder with a 2¼ in. (57 mm.) width.

GRECIAN OGEE with COVE and BEAD (QOCB) is a variation of the Grecian Ogee with Quirk Bead (QOQB). The example shown was marked by Mathieson (Scotland) but is not seen in its 1899 catalog.

GRECIAN OGEE with FILLET (QOF) was listed by Arrowmammett (Connecticut, mid-19c.) in sizes from ⅜ to 2 in. (10 - 51 mm.) with the ogee curving up to raise the fillet above the low point of the curve. In larger sizes, this was called a "band, base or bed mold" by Philip Chapin (Maryland, mid-19c.). He called a variant with a vertical rise between the ogee and fillet a "Grecian ogee and square". As the term "square" has been used in several senses (even within the same catalog), it is avoided in this naming system and Chapin's nomenclature is replaced by **GRECIAN OGEE with raised FILLET (QOrF).** This profile has been seen with a steep ogee as well. The opposite is seen in an Israel White (Pennsylvania, 1831-39) which has a dropped fillet: **GRECIAN OGEE with dropped FILLET (QOdF).**

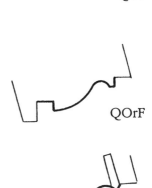

QOF

QOrF

QOdF

QUIRK lying OGEE with dropped FILLET and BEAD (QlOdFB) is an odd variant of the Quirk Ogee with Bead (QOB) made by John Okins (England, 1817-1835). For similar profiles see Grecian Ogee with Quirk Bead (QOQB).

QUIRK lying OGEE with FILLET and COVE (QlOFC) is one of many moldings used as a variation of the common Quirk Ogee with Astragal (QOA). The example is by Moseley (England, 1778-1818), and it is listed by Nooitgedagt (The Netherlands, ca.1890) as well.

QUIRK lying OGEE, FILLET and COVE with QUIRK BEAD (QlOFCQB) adds an element to the above. The profile of a wide plane by Griffiths (England, -1811-1949) is shown.

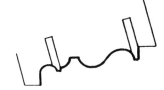

QUIRK OGEE with FILLET and dropped FILLET (QOFdF) is another variant by Gleave (England, 1832-1913). The same profile with a steeper ogee was called a "base, band or bed mold" by Philip Chapin (Maryland, mid 19c.).

QUIRK lying OGEE with FILLET and OVOLO (QlOFV) is still another variant of Quirk Ogee with Bead, this in a two-iron model by Fairclough (England, 1849-80).

GRECIAN OGEE with FILLET and QUIRK BEVEL (QOFQL) was noted in an unmarked handled long molder making a 1 x 2 in. (25 x 51 mm.) cut.

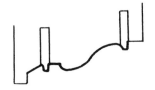

QUIRK lying OGEE with FILLET and QUIRK OVOLO (QlOFQV) is cut by a large twin iron molder made by James Barnes (England, 1829-40). The stock was 14.7 x 4.5 in. (37 x 11 cm.) and had a jack handle.

QUIRK OGEE, FILLET, REVERSE OGEE with ASTRAGAL (QOFRA) is fancy enough for a picture frame. The profile shown was made by T. Tileston (Massachusetts, 1802-1866).

GRECIAN OGEE, raised FILLET, REVERSE OGEE with FILLET (QOrFRF) in a 2⅛ x 1¼ in. (54 x 32 mm.) cut was made by E.W. Carpenter (Pennsylvania, -1828-59-).

QUIRK OGEE and OGEE (QOO) was made as a wide molder by E. Preston and Sons (England, 1894-1934). See also Quirk Ogee with soft Astragal (QOsA).

QUIRK OGEE-OGEE-BEAD (QO-O-B) is yet another serpentine, this one with four reversals of curvature and needing two hyphens for coding. It was made by C. Warren (New Hampshire, 1837-75).

QUIRK lying OGEE WITH OVOLO is indexed as QUIRK OGEE-BEAK (QO-K) and is described there.

259

QUIRK OGEE-OVOLO (QO-V) is a serpentine curve without a generally accepted name, although it has been called a double ogee. The example is by J.M. Taber (Massachusetts, 1820-72). See Quirk Ogee-Bead for similar curves (QOB-1 through 3).

GRECIAN OGEE, OVOLO, with soft ASTRAGAL and COVE (QOVsAC) is an elaborate flat profile cut by a three iron molder made by Alexander Marshall (Scotland, 1883-1904-).

GRECIAN OGEE with QUIRK BEAD (QOQB) QOQB-1, from a plane by George White (Pennsylvania, -1824), is not an uncommon profile. An unsprung version **(QOQB-2)** was listed by Nooitgedagt (The Netherlands, ca.1890)

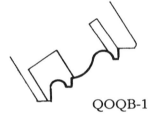

QOQB-1

QOQB-2

NOTE: that QUIRK OVOLO and GRECIAN OVOLO are treated as equivalent for indexing in the following, since in many of the forms the terms are interchangeable.

QUIRK OVOLO with ASTRAGAL (QVA) was pictured in Smith's *Key* (1819). In the Sheffield list of 1870 it was called a "quirk ovoloe & astragal" while an almost identical profile is in the Mathieson (Scotland) 1899 catalog as a "Gre-

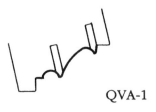

QVA-1

cian ovalo & astragal" — an illustration of naming variants. This shape is not listed in most U.S. catalogs, but appears in an Eastburn (New Jersey, -1802-26-) plane **(QVA-1)** . Steep versions were made by Aaron Smith **(QVA-2)** and T. Tileston (both Massachusetts) in the early nineteenth century. A **QUIRK OVOLO with soft ASTRAGAL (QVsA)** shows a larger bead and a softening of the outer corner of the astragal, as in one cut by Okines (England, 1740- 1835). A related form is seen under Quirk Bead and Quirk Ogee (QBQO).

QUIRK OVOLO with ASTRAGAL and COVE (QVAC) extends a common form by the addition of a cove. The example is from a toted wide molder with a bench type body and a rope hole, made by Moseley (England, 1778-1807).

QUIRK OVOLO with BEAD (QVB-1) is illustrated as seen in a plane by Eastburn (New Jersey -1802-26-). It seems appropriate to call the early planes quirk ovolos rather than Grecian. An even clearer call **(QVB-2)** is a **QUIRK OVOLO and BEAD** with a larger bead, as in the Gleave plane (England, 1832-1913). This cuts a molding like a slanted side reed. **GRECIAN OVOLO with BEAD (QVB-3)** was a very popular profile, listed by H. Chapin's Son (Connecticut, 1890) in sizes ½ - 2 in. (13 - 51 mm.) or larger in handled versions. A stretched version, in which the ovolo was not greatly different from a bevel, was made by E.W. Carpenter (Pennsylvania, -1828-59-) in a wide plane **(QVB-4).**

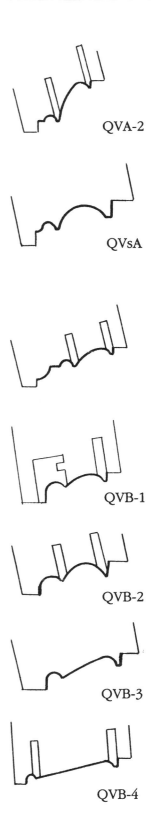

QVA-2

QVsA

QVB-1

QVB-2

QVB-3

QVB-4

QUIRK OVOLO and BEAD with ASTRAGAL (QVBA) is seen in an early J. Andruss (New Jersey, 1821-43).

GRECIAN OVOLO with BEAD, ASTRAGAL and COVE (QVBAC) is seen as a millwork profile for panel and base in the Roberts 1903 *Illustrated Millwork Catalog.*

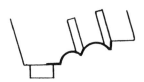

QUIRK OVOLO and BEAD with FILLET (QVBF) was made by Kendall (England, 1765-1814), with a filletster fence permitting changing the size of (or even eliminating) the fillet. A somewhat distorted version of this profile is shown later as Quirk Ovolo-Flute-Bead with Fillet (QV-H-BF).

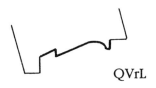

QUIRK or GRECIAN OVOLO and BEVEL (QVL) differs from the Quirk Bead and Bevel (QBL) in that the outer end of the arc does not become vertical. The only form I have seen is the **GRE-CIAN OVOLO with raised BEVEL (QVrL)**, called a "Grecian ovolo with fillet" by Chapin, Greenfield, and Sandusky. To compound the problem, Greenfield used the name "Grecian ovolo with bevel" for the profile shown as with fillet (QVF). Its use is inconsistent not only with logic but with its own usage with the ogees. Therefore the term bevel is used (in agreement with Sellens 1978) for the profile indexed here. Sizes from ⅜ to 2½ in. (10 - 64 mm.) were offered.

QVrL

QUIRK OVOLO and COVE (QVC) is shown in Smith's *Key*, 1819 **(QVC-1)**. It has been called a "belection" or "bilection", "nosing molding", "quirk bilection" in American catalogs, "necking and nosing" or "neck molding" (as well as "astragal and cove") in British listings. It was made in sizes from ½ to 2 in. (13 - 51 mm.). Several quirk ovolos with smaller coves **(QVC-2)**, were made by John Nicholson (Massachusetts, 1739-47), who used no spring. Had these been made later they would have been called Grecian. See the related Astragal and Cove (AC) and Quirk Bead and Cove (QBC).

QVC-1

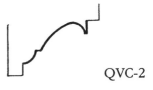

QVC-2

QUIRK OVOLO, COVE and ASTRAGAL (QVCA) adds an astragal to the above form, and was also reasonably popular in the early nineteenth century. The profile by J. Gibson (New York, 1823- 52) is representative.

QUIRK OVOLO, COVE and OVOLO (QVCV) was made with three irons by J. Welch (Scotland, 1845-50).

GRECIAN OVOLO with FILLET (QVF) was called a Grecian ovolo with bevel by Greenfield, Grecian ovolo with square by Chapin, and simply Grecian ovolo by Ohio Tool. The sizes they offered were in the same range as the Grecian Ovolo with Bead (QVB-3) above. If the ovolo approaches the vertical before breaking to the fillet, it is commonly called a torus bead, which was covered in the last chapter.

GRECIAN OVOLO with raised FILLET (QVrF)
is called "Grecian ovolo with square" by Philip
Chapin (Maryland, mid-19c.). A wide version
was made by J.B. Mack (Pennsylvania, -1836-).
Another example was made with a bench type
throat plus a second iron with side escapement
by George White (Pennsylvania, 1819-25).

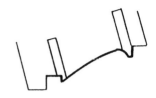

GRECIAN OVOLO, FILLET and BEAD (QVFB)
was sold as a two-iron molder without spring by
Nooitgedagt (The Netherlands, ca.1890).

**GRECIAN OVOLO with FILLET and raised
FILLET (QVFrF)** is called simply "Grecian ovolo
and fillet" in the Ohio Tool catalog (ca.1910) and
offered in sizes of ¾ to 2 in. (19 - 51 mm.).

**GRECIAN OVOLO, FILLET, raised FILLET and
SCOTIA with BEVEL (QVFrFSL)** was made with
three irons by Nooitgedagt (The Netherlands,
ca.1890), without spring of course.

**QUIRK OVOLO-FLUTE-BEAD with FILLET
(QV-H-BF)** is seen in two planes by Randall and
Bensen (New York, 1827-29) and in another full
boxed molder by Wm. Williams (New York,
1807-49).

**QUIRK OVOLO, QUIRK OGEE with ASTRAGAL
and COVE (QVQOAC)** is another unusual
profile by T. Tileston (Massachusestts, 1802-
1866).

264

QUIRK OVOLO, REVERSE OGEE with ASTRAGAL (QVRA) appears in a 1¼ in. (32 mm.) wide molder by T. Tileston (Massachusetts, -1840-). A similar profile was seen earlier as Astragal and Reverse Ogee with soft Astragal (ARsA).

QUIRK OVOLO and REVERSE OGEE with BEAD (QVRB) was listed by Auburn Tool (New York) in an 1869 price list as antae caps, in three sizes (⅞ to ⅝ in., 22 - 29 mm.).

QUIRK OVOLO and SCOTIA with ASTRAGAL and COVE (QVSAC) was cut in an unsprung version by John Sleeper (Massachusetts, -1813-34). The sprung form illustrated was marked by A. Howland and Co. (New York, 1869-74) on a wide form (2¼ x 1 in., 57 x 25 mm.); and made by the same prisoners for Auburn Tool (New York, 1864-93). The plane is listed in its 1869 price list as "antae basse" (sic) in three sizes from ⅞ to ⅝ in. (22 - 29 mm.). The sizes refer to the depth of cut. A similar profile with a vertical end to the ovolo and with the edge between scotia and astragal softened is listed above as Quirk Bead, Scotia-Bead with Cove (QBS-BC).

QUIRK OVOLO, SCOTIA, FILLET and REVERSE OGEE (QVSFR) is an impressive profile seen in a plane by B. Sheneman (Pennsylvania, 1846-67).

REVERSE OGEE (edge) has been seen in a handed pair **(eR** and **left eR)** by Edward Carter (New York, 1854-97). By working the edge rather than the face of the work, it is possible to have the ogee continue as an undercut on the

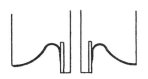

left eR and eR

265

opposite face. This profile forms a pleasing edge on a tabletop, for example. The left- and right-hand pair is most unusual, and would offer an advantage in molding any awkward grain edges of the top.

REVERSE OGEE with ASTRAGAL (RA) is fairly often seen, although the simple version is absent in most American catalogs. Philip Chapin (Maryland, mid-19th century) listed it as "back ogee and bead". Mathieson (Scotland, 1899) offered it in sizes to work stock of thickness ⅜ - 1⅛ in. (10 - 29 mm.). The typical profile shown is that of a T. Tileston (Massachusetts, 1802-66) small molder. A stretched profile, **lying REVERSE OGEE with ASTRAGAL (lRA)** was called a "base and band" molding by H. Chapin's Son (Connecticut, 1874), and listed in large sizes with or without handle. A somewhat distorted profile which might lead you to this name was coded as QUIRK OVOLO-FLUTE-BEAD with FILLET (QV-H-BF).

RA

lRA

REVERSE OGEE with ASTRAGAL and COVE (RAC) is a flat molding by A. Mathieson & Son, Scotland, although not listed in its 1899 catalog.

REVERSE OGEE with BEAD (RB) was illustrated in Roubo (France, 1769), and sold by H. Chapin's Son (1874 catalog) in sizes from ⅜ to 2 in. (10 - 51 mm). The illustration is from a handled wide molder by Hields (England, 1830-81) **(RB-1).** As in the simple reverse ogee, this profile is sometimes seen with a sunk fillet at top of the ogee (see Fillet, Reverse Ogee and Bead, FRB). An unusual variant with a wide, flat bead **REVERSE OGEE and BEAD (RB-2)** was used in a plane

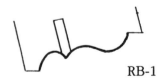

RB-1

RB-2

266

marked W.H. Livingston & Co. (New York, 1840-66).

REVERSE lying OGEE with BEAD and FILLET (RIBF) just fails to meet the criterion for Reverse Ogee with Astragal (RA) (the two ends of the arc are at different levels and it thus becomes a separate entry). It was seen in an unmarked 18th century American plane.

REVERSE OGEE with BEVEL (RL) was offered by Greenfield in its 1872 catalog in handled form. The listing was "reverse ogee, plain, with bead, bevel, or square", but no profile was given. The profile shown has not been reported in an existing plane.

REVERSE OGEE with COVE (RC) has been seen to date, in its simple form, only in German and Austrian planes, the curve shown being from the Weiss (Austria, 1909) catalog. See Fillet and Reverse Ogee and Cove (FRC).

REVERSE OGEE-COVE (R-C) is a double ogee seen in a plane by Jo Fuller (Rhode Island, 1773-1822) and in others. There is no generally accepted name for triply curved profiles of this type, although they occur in several complex profiles shown later. The use of the hyphen, as explained in Appendix 2, was coined for such cases.

REVERSE OGEE and COVE with ASTRAGAL (RCA) has been seen in unsprung versions by Tho. Grant (New York, ca.1760) and in a steeper form in an unmarked plane.

REVERSE OGEE-COVE with COVE (R-CC) was cut by Peter Wilcock (England, 1861-69).

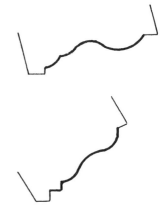

REVERSE OGEE-COVE with FILLET (R-CF) is seen on a plane with the stamp of George Mutter (London, 1766-1812), although the profile may have been reworked to meet a specific need.

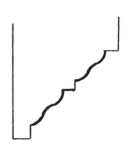

REVERSE OGEE-COVE, FILLET, and REVERSE OGEE-COVE (R-CFR-C) is a combination of two serpentine curves, cut by a Iohn Rogers (England, 1734-65) plane.

REVERSE OGEE, COVE and OVOLO with FILLET (RCVF) was made by Joseph Watson (England, 1820-53).

REVERSE OGEE with FILLET (RF) was listed by Sandusky (1869) **(RF-1)** in sizes ½ to 2 in. (13 - 51 mm.) under the name "reverse ogee with square". Mathieson (Scotland, 1899) specified "fillet on bottom" for the same form. Stretched versions were made by several American makers. Greenfield (1872 catalog) shows a "reverse ogee and square-flat" in a handled version **(RF-2).** Ohio Tool in its catalog #23 (ca.1910) showed a more recumbent ogee (not quite lying) in sizes of ½ to 2 in. (13 - 51 mm.) **(RF-3)**. Philip Chapin (Maryland, mid-19th century) called a similar profile a "pilaster plane". A very flat reverse ogee,

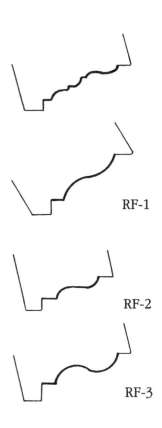

RF-1

RF-2

RF-3

almost a wide fillet with rounded corners, is seen in a plane by W. Preston (England, 1852-88) **(RF-4)**. As in the simple reverse ogee, the profile is often found with a fillet on top (see Fillet, Reverse Ogee with Fillet, FRF). Sash planes used to cut this profile were known as the "lamb tongue" and usually have exaggerated fences. The profile shown **(RF-5)** is of one by Hoffman (Scotland, 1843-72).

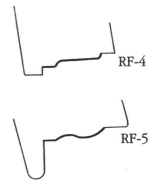

REVERSE OGEE with FILLET and OGEE (RFO)

was made by Jo. Fuller (Rhode Island, -1808-22).

REVERSE OGEE with FILLET and QUIRK BEAD

(RFQB) was found in an unsprung molder by T. Tileston (Massachusetts, 1802-66). The same profile was listed by Nooitgedagt (The Netherlands, ca.1890).

REVERSE OGEE, FILLET and QUIRK OGEE

(RFQO) was made as a wide, toted molder by Samuel Lunt (England, 1824-49).

REVERSE OGEE and OGEE (RO) is sometimes

called a "Cupid's bow". The illustration was taken from a molder by Leist (England, 1845- 96). Although at York pitch (50°), it had been bored for a pull hole, suggesting use on hardwood. It makes an attractive edging.

Lying REVERSE OGEE with back QUIRK (lRbQ)

was made by James Panton (Scotland, 1882-1908) with a depth stop on either side and no

fence. I speculate that it was used as a facing plane of the type discussed later in this chapter under Complex Moldings — Other Types.

REVERSE OGEE with REVERSE OGEE (RR) is a millwork profile in the Roberts 1903 Illustrated Millwork catalog, listed for band molding.

REVERSE OGEE-REVERSE OGEE (R-R) is another unusual profile by T. Tileston (Massachusetts, 1802-66). The absence of a fence would permit moldings of different width but would require an external guide.

REVERSE OGEE-SCOTIA with BEVEL (R-SL) exists in a triple iron French molder.

SCOTIA (S) is listed in most catalogs, but refers to either a quarter round or a cove. The true architectural scotia is seldom seen. A wide form by F. Dallicker (Pennsylvania, mid-19th century) is shown.

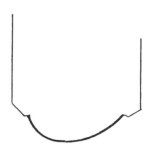

SCOTIA, ASTRAGAL and COVE (SAC) appears in a plane made by L. Marley (New York, 1820-56).

SCOTIA, ASTRAGAL, COVE and ASTRAGAL (SACA) was made by Mutter (England, 1766-1812). The astragals are complete semicircles, so the plane is not sprung.

SCOTIA, ASTRAGAL, COVE, ASTRAGAL, OVOLO and FILLET (SACAVF) is an elaboration of one seen above, possibly intended for picture framing. The profile is from a John Green (England, 1774-1807) molder.

SCOTIA, ASTRAGAL, OGEE with ASTRAGAL (SAOA) is a variant of a profile seen earlier (Astragal, dropped Ogee with Astragal, AdOA) with a dropped groove on the inner face. This one is by Jennion (England, 1732-57) and is also unsprung.

SCOTIA, ASTRAGAL, SCOTIA and OVOLO with FILLET (SASVF) has been seen in an unmarked plane.

SCOTIA with BEVEL (SL) has been seen in a shallow form as made by Heathcott (England, -1829-33). See also Fillet, Scotia with Bevel (FSL).

SCOTIA, BEVEL and OGEE with BEAD (SLOB) is one last profile from the Weiss (Austria, 1909) catalog. The shorthand code illustrates one drawback of an alphabetic coding system.

SCOTIA, BEVEL, OGEE with BEVEL and BEAD (SLOLB) was cut by a three-iron plane listed in the Nooitgedagt catalog (The Netherlands, ca.1890).

SCOTIA and BEVEL with QUIRK BEAD and FILLET (SLQBF) appears on an unmarked plane of Philadelphia, Pennsylvania, style.

SCOTIA with FILLET (SF). Two planes made by H.Tuttle (unrecorded) cut profiles ¾ and 1½ in. wide (19 and 38 mm.). Another is reported in an early 18th century plane with the maker's name obliterated.

COMPLEX MOLDINGS
OTHER TYPES

BOLECTION MOLDINGS

Moldings at the juncture of two surfaces at different levels (as, for example, a stile and a panel) and projecting beyond both are called bolections (with many variations in spelling) (Fig.11:2). In small frame and panel work, it is usual to cut grooves in the stiles and rails into which the panel edges fit (see Fig.4:11). This requires that the panel

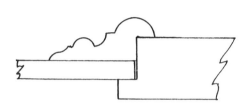

Fig.11:2—Bolection molding on frame and panel

be installed before the final joining of stiles and rails, which can be troublesome in large work.

One option is to rabbet, rather than groove, the frame members. These can then be assembled, the panels dropped into the rabbets and held there with an applied molding. While such a molding may be attached to the edge of the rabbet, it is easier to attach it to the face of the frame, and so the bolection came into being. It is molded on the visible face and rabbeted on the other side to conform to the difference in level between frame and panel face.

Not only was this construction method easier to manage, but it also invited decoration of the applied molding. There is more freedom to create unusual profiles when cutting a molding strip than there is in working large members, a fact that was seized upon by the early joiners. There were more elaborate profiles created for this use than for almost any other. These bolection profiles may be seen in the early woodworking classics or in many catalogs.

Bolections were also used at the top of baseboards or to cap wainscots, and as a part of a built-up complex molding.

Variants of the bolection were used where both sides of the panel would be visible. Instead of a bolection on each side, a single grooved molding was cut to contain the panel, and this was then inserted into the frame. This style, if also grooved into the frame, no longer mitigated the assembly problem but allowed rich decorative possibilities (Fig.11:3).

273

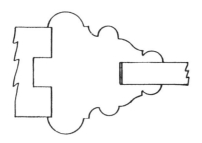

Fig.11:3—Double faced bolection

Bolection moldings were not necessarily made in a single cut. Indeed, some designs included undercuts which made this impossible. Fig.11:4, from the Weiss catalog (Austria, 1909), illustrates a profile cut by a pair of planes. Such patterns require one cut to be made on the face of the molding strip, and one or more on the edge or on the side of a rabbet. An exception is a simple undercut that can be created using the crow's bill plane (described in Chapter 10, Fig.10:21) with the concave edge sharpened. Probably simple bolections were most often cut using planes of the type covered in the last section (such as Grecian Ogee and Bevel, QOL), with one cut made on each side of the molding strip. However, there are bolection types that will cut both sides at once, as we shall see.

Fig.11:4—Undercut molding

ASTRAGAL MOLDINGS

Bolections are not the only applications for applied moldings that require multiple cuts. If the purpose of the molding is to cover the joint between surfaces at the same level, they may be called astragals (not the astragal profile element, but a completely different meaning of the word). As examples: a batten between two sheathing boards, or to cover the meeting of double doors. Most of these have symmetrical profiles, an identical cut on each side of one face. The astragal used on double doors may also have, on the face opposite the molding, a projection fitting between the doors (Fig.11:5).

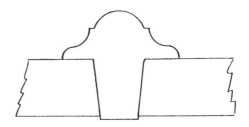

Fig.11:5—Double door astragal

274

STRIP PLANES

The profiles used in these astragal and bolection moldings are related in that the high point of the profile is not at an edge, but somewhere in the middle. The general trend of the profile is downward from that point to either side of the strip. If they are cut using the complex molding planes described earlier in this chapter, two passes will be required, one on each side of the molding strip. Occasionally a plane is seen which was made to cut such a profile in one pass. These are not seen often enough to have earned a generic name, insofar as I know. To fill this gap, the coinage "strip plane" will be used here.

The profile elements on the right side of such planes are "backward" (they face the wrong way), and usually there is no depth stop at the right edge, since there is no surface left uncut for referencing. As in almost every statement made about planes, there are exceptions. Such a profile may be cut on a wide board and then ripsawed off. In these cases, a conventional depth stop is functional and may be present. However, the cut at the right side will penetrate well below the surface referenced by the depth stop.

Another definite indication of a strip plane is the presence of two fences that straddle the strip being cut. Here the fences bottom on the surface of the workbench to act as depth stops, in the same fashion as a reglet plane. (See Chapter 4, Thicknessing Planes).

Naming such profiles poses a problem, and, to the best of my knowledge, no serious attempt has been made to do so. The method used here is to start at the high point of the molding and name the elements of the more complex side from there to the edge, then add the word "OPPOSITE" and name the remaining elements of the other side in the direction toward the other edge. Symmetrical profiles are covered later in this chapter.

The following examples illustrate profiles of this type and the proposed naming:

FILLET and COVE OPPOSITE COVE (FC+C)
is cut by a plane which was sold at auction in 1989. Unfortunately the maker's name had been obliterated. It has two fences, and the high point of the profile serves as a depth stop.

COVE, FILLET and FILLET OPPOSITE COVE (CFF+C) is a somewhat similar profile made with one fence and a central depth stop by Thomas Mackenzie (England 1863-94).

OGEE and BEVEL OPPOSITE OVOLO (OL+V) was made in fruitwood by Jacob & Schick, Strasbourg.

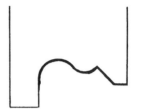

OGEE-OVOLO OPPOSITE-OGEE (O-V+-O) is an unusual profile apparently intended to straddle a strip and bottom on the bench. The right side, however, does not serve as a fence. This was made by T. J. Tolman (Massachusetts, -1850-80-).

The only one of these profiles seen more than once is the **OGEE OPPOSITE FILLET and COVE (O+FC).** This has been reported at least three times. There are two fences in each of two Continental planes (**O+FC-1**). One of these has three irons and is marked Blacas Fres. Vence (a French town); the other has a 2½ in. (64 mm.) iron and is in a museum in Kassel, Germany. The same profile is seen in a plane designed to stick the molding in a wide board, as shown by the single fence and depth stop (**O+FC-2**). This one was made by E. Preston (England, -1833-83-).

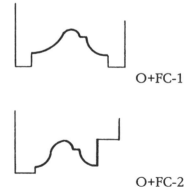

O+FC-1

O+FC-2

A puzzling plane made by N. Camper (Maryland, 1850-80) appears to be meant to cut a profile of this type, but the guidance is minimal. A jack handle in a razee body plus an added transverse handle suggest that it wasn't too easy to push. This is but one example of the

276

many planes which defy definitive description of their use, and which are sure to provoke widely divergent opinions. It is perhaps pushing too hard to provide a systematic name for this profile, as it will undoubtedly be listed simply as a "complex molder" in any catalog. A system intended for profile retrieval in these computerized times, however, must be prepared to cope with oddities such as this. Here the name is of interest only in providing the path to a code designation. With this in mind, the profile would be named **COVE-FLUTE with FILLET and OVOLO OPPOSITE OVOLO   (C-HFV+V).**

A plane made by J. Killam (Connecticut, 1822-60) is an example of a rare type. It appears to cut a conventional Grecian ogee and fillet, but the fence is on the wrong side. There are two depth stops, one on either side of the molding. The profile is cut facing away from the fence and a flat of ¾ in. (19 mm.) is left uncut next to the fence. It may be that this flat was later cut by another conventional molder to form a strip molding, after which the molding was ripsawed from the board. Another plane which could be used in the same manner to cut a fillet, scotia and astragal on the side away from the fence bears an early Union Factory mark (seen in the profile listing under Astragal and back Scotia with Fillet, AbSF). Without documentation this interpretation of the use intended for such planes is, of course, only speculation. An equally likely use was to cut symmetrical facings of the type described below.

We may solve the naming problem for such planes by use of the same "opposite" convention used above. The Killam plane is then **GRECIAN lying OGEE with FILLET OPPOSITE nothing (QlOF+).**

QlOF+

Joh. Weiss & Sohn (Austria) in its 1909 catalog listed a number of planes of this type. Unfortunately, only the molding profile was given so that details of the plane structure are in doubt, although it is reasonably certain that they were made without spring. The planes were grouped with a number of other more conventional types, all having the iron set for hard wood. These include (on the following page):

ASTRAGAL and COVE with ASTRAGAL and COVE OPPOSITE COVE (ACAC+C)

ASTRAGAL, COVE and QUIRK BEAD OPPOSITE COVE (ACQB+C)

BEAD and COVE OPPOSITE COVE (BC+C)

BEAD with FILLET OPPOSITE COVE (BF+C)

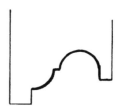

BEAD with FILLET OPPOSITE COVE and BEAD (BF+CB)

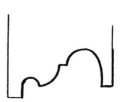

OGEE and dropped ASTRAGAL OPPOSITE FILLET and COVE (OdA+FC)

OVOLO with FILLET OPPOSITE FILLET AND COVE (VF+FC)

278

SYMMETRICAL MOLDERS

Shown below is a selection of symmetrical profiles that have been observed in planes. The list is of necessity illustrative rather than comprehensive and it is expected that other variations will be reported in the future. As is the case with the types just listed, these planes are uncommon and appear but rarely in catalog or auction listings.

Planes to cut symmetrical profiles fall into two types. One will remove wood from the edges of a strip, to form a molding generally higher in the center than at the edges. As with the other strip planes, the moldings they cut could also be cut with conventional planes. As an example, the first profile shown below (DLB) could be cut using a molder that cuts a bevel and bead and using it twice (once on each edge of the strip). This being the case, one must have needed a large quantity of this molding to justify acquiring a strip plane. It is not surprising that they are rare.

The few planes that have been seen are listed below and are named by describing one-half of the profile and prefixing the word "SYMMETRICAL" (alphabetical code D).

SYMMETRICAL BEVEL and BEAD (DLB) was noted in a user-made 11 in. (30 cm.) double boxed molder. Description of the profile as "church window" in an auction catalog is apt.

SYMMETRICAL FILLET, raised ASTRAGAL, COVE and ASTRAGAL (DFrACA) has been seen twice, once as made by Burton (England, early 19th century) as a 2.3 in. (57 mm.) plane and once in a three-iron molder by Thomas Turner (Sheffield, England, 1841-1912). Both were fitted with depth stops.

**SYMMETRICAL OVOLO and COVE
(DVC)** is listed in the Mathieson
(Scotland) 1899 catalog. A perhaps
more descriptive name would be "astragal between coves", but this type
of naming gives too much trouble
with other profiles to be acceptable
for systematic naming. A narrower
version of this profile may be seen in
one form of sash plane, the rare type
that cuts both sides of the sash bar at
once. The sashmaker would call it an
"astragal and hollow".

**SYMMETRICAL OVOLO and
REVERSE OGEE (DVR)** appears in a
fruitwood molder from the Swedish
store (Aux Mines de Suede, Paris).

FACING PLANES

The other type of symmetrical profile is seen in planes intended to cut
casings (the ornamental strips around doors and windows) or similar strips.
This type does not mold the edge of the work, but removes wood from the
center of the face of a board. This task cannot be effected by conventional
molders (except painstakingly by hollows and rounds or related planes). This
type of plane is uncommon enough that a generic name is not widely
recognized, although they have sometimes been called "facing" planes.

As the majority of these profiles would resemble conventional moldings
if the central element were removed, the naming system describes this central
element and adds the word "JOINING" (alphabetical code J), followed by the
names of the outer elements starting at the outside.

ASTRAGAL JOINING COVE and FILLETS (AJCF) was made by E.W. Carpenter (Pennsylvania, -1828-59) in a substantial, toted stock. It cut a 3 in. (76 mm.) profile.

ASTRAGAL JOINING FILLETS (AJF) is another unusual plane by E.W. Carpenter (Pennsylvania, -1828-59).

ASTRAGAL JOINING FILLET and FILLETS (AJFF) is a variant of the above (AJF), seen in a plane having a 2.25 in. (57 mm.) blade width.

ASTRAGAL JOINING OVOLOS (AJV) was cut without depth stops by W. Oothoudt (New York, ca.1840).

BEAD JOINING COVES (BJC) was made by Alexander Currie (Scotland, 1833-44). The same profile, but without either depth stop, was seen in a plane marked by L.Little (Massachusetts, ca.1800). See also Fig.11:9 F.

BEAD JOINING FILLETS (BJF) is a wide center bead made by E. Taft (Massachusetts, ca.1750). Another very similar was made by the undocumented maker M. Daub. This profile is also seen in a wide, fenced version.

281

BEAD JOINING QUIRKS (BJQ) is an unusual plane by E.W. Carpenter (Pennsylvania, -1828-59). The depth stops are below the high point of the profile, so that the full cut could not be made on a flat board.

BEAD-JOINING QUIRK lying OGEES (B-JQlO) was found paired with Gothic Bead-Joining Quirk lying Ogees (G-JQlO). The pair is believed to have been used in church moldings.

BEAD JOINING REVERSE OGEES (BJR) is a wide variant of a center bead made by Mathieson (Scotland, 1822-1966).

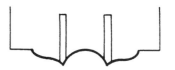

BEAD-JOINING SCOTIAS (B-JS) has been seen in two versions. One was made by A. Clary (unrecorded) as a bench type plane without fence or depth stops, 1⅞ in. (48 mm.) wide **(B-JS-1).** Another has the central curve larger and has two stops and a fence **(B-JS-2).**

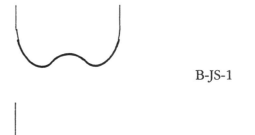

B-JS-1

B-JS-2

BEAD-JOINING SCOTIA-OGEE-OGEES (B-JS-O-O) involves a bead cluster, but the systematic name requires multiple hyphens to show the ten reversals of curvature. The example shown makes a 3.6 in. (91 mm.) cut.

282

FILLET JOINING BEVEL and back BEVELS (FJLbL) was observed in a narrow double-boxed plane by A. Cumings (Massachusetts, 1844-54).

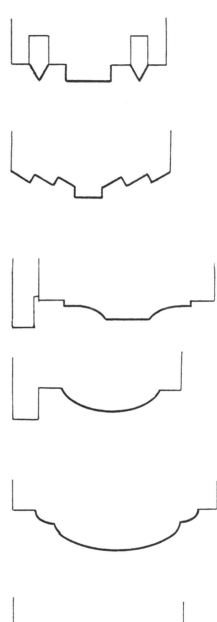

FILLET JOINING triple BEVELS (FJLLL) describes the profile of a tiny, ornately carved plane made in 1760, and now in a Hamburg (Germany) museum. The ¾ in. (1.9 cm) iron is held in an open throat.

FILLET JOINING OVOLOS (FJV) has been seen several times in wide unmarked planes.

FLUTE (wide) (H) was put in this classification rather than with the simple molding profiles because of its 3 in. (76 mm.) width and its fence and double depth stop.

FLUTE JOINING COVES (HJC) was cut three inches (76 mm.) wide by a plane seen in a 1988 auction.

FLUTE JOINING FILLET and back OVOLOS (HJFbV) was cut by a massive, bench type plane with a 3 in. (76 mm.) blade, jack handle, and no fewer than three transverse handles. It was guided by a wedge arm fence. The profile may be described as two beaks back to back, another survival of this old form. (Note that this is the complement of BJC, above).

FLUTE JOINING OGEES (HJO) was reported by Jack Gorlin (1978). He notes that this is the reverse of a popular astragal molding and may have been used to cut a saddle template for mitering this (see Chapter 13—Sashmaker). The plane might also have been a mother plane for a Symmetrical Ovolo and Ogee molding plane (although I have not seen such).

FLUTE JOINING REVERSE OGEE-COVE (HJR-C) was noted in a 4 in. (10 cm.) wide yellow birch molder of 18th century characteristics.

GOTHIC BEAD-JOINING QUIRK lying OGEES (G-JQlO) was cut by an unmarked toted plane 4 in. (102 mm.) wide, with a 2.6 in. (66 mm.) wide iron. (Also see Bead-Joining Quirk lying Ogees, B-JQlO).

UNSYMMETRICAL FACING PLANES

I have seen but one unsymmetrical facing plane, made by Atkin and Son (England, 1843-54). Extending the system to cover this case gave a rather intimidating name, but the type is too rare to warrant special rules to shrink it. The "joining" convention (above) names the more complex side, then the "facing" convention describes the remaining elements from the edge inward. This produced **FILLET JOINING OVOLO, FILLET and back OVOLO FACING COVE and back OVOLO (FJVFbV+CbV).**

HANDRAIL PLANES

Another application for planes which cut the full width of the workpiece is in molding the sides of stair handrails, although such planes are usually of bench type and often have short stocks to facilitate working shallow curves. For a further description, see the section on staircase builders in Chapter 13. A few profiles (Fig.11:6) from 18th century, and earlier, homes are shown here as clues to identification of this form of molder.

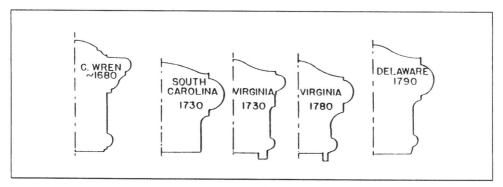

Fig.11:6—Handrail profiles

WIDE MOLDINGS

There is a tendency to call any molding plane wider than three inches (76 mm.) or so a crown molder or cornice plane. While this may be a convenient catch-all name, not all wide molding planes were used to cut cornices. Wide moldings were required elsewhere in the house. The baseboard, a piece planted on the wall where it met the floor, was itself molded in finer homes of the nineteenth century and earlier. Above it was planted a base molding, sometimes tongued into the baseboard. The two could be combined in a base and band molding. A wainscot cap marked the separation of wainscot from plaster. For full plastered walls, a chair rail might run around the dining room at a height to prevent wall marring by chair backs. Each door and window was circled by the architrave, a molding hiding the juncture of jamb and wall (many had a cornice above, as well).

On the other side of the coin, not all cornices were cut with cornice planes. The cornice, in furniture, is a projecting molding usually at the top of the piece. Moldings above or below eye level are more effective if slanted to present their broadest view to the observer. For large furniture moldings, cutting away material to obtain this slant would be a wasteful use of fine wood. A board of finish wood just thick enough to accomodate the profile was therefore backed with a triangular section of secondary wood. The profile was then cut in the hardwood facing. I do not believe that this was done with wide molders, for several reasons. Cutting soft woods is difficult enough, and the harder furniture woods would be much more difficult. The need to maintain exact profiles over long stretches was absent, as only a short length of cornice molding was needed. Most convincing, molding planes cutting profiles wider than two inches (51mm.) or so with blades at cabinet pitch (for cutting hard woods) are conspicuous by their absence.

The envelope of the furniture cornice molding was originally roughed out with plow and rabbets, then finished with successive passes of the simple molders. The procedure is given in detail by Sheraton (1793). Later cabinet-makers built up cornices by cutting several simple moldings on separate strips and then affixing them.

An example of cutting complex profiles in solid wood by succesive use of simple molders is given in Chapter 13—The Planemaker. Planemakers made special planes to ensure that the profiles matched exactly at the front corner of their plow fences, but they did not use wide molders.

Before attempting to sort out the true cornice planes from planes designed for cutting other wide profiles, let us examine some characteristics common to all wide molders. As stated above, examples with irons mounted at angles much higher than $45°$ (as they would be for hardwood) are rare indeed. Pushing wide planes on soft woods is hard enough, and their use on hardwood is impractical for ordinary mortals. They are designed for use on architectural moldings, cut in soft wood. These planes were sometimes made with side shavings discharge, in conventional molding plane shape, and often had two or more blades in separate throats. Some of these were cut to allow shavings to escape on opposite sides of the stock for the two throats, but most vented both on the same side. More often, and invariably for the wider profiles, the planes were made with bench type bodies (shaving escape at the top). These, too, were sometimes made with two irons in separate throats, one diagonally behind the other. The purpose was not to cut one section of the profile at a time (a moment's reflection will convince you that the plane would not work in this fashion) but to simplify the task of honing the blades. Another advantage is that two narrow blades are held more securely, each with its own wedge, than one wide iron.

Why not, then, use two planes — one wide one to cut the far side (having its sole cut away to clear the workpiece), and a narrower one to cut the near section. This possibility was mentioned with the strip planes above, and is taken up again with the cornice planes below.

A jack handle was often supplemented with a pull hole through the front of the stock, or with transverse handles; using wide planes was hard work for two men. A rope, connected to the plane through the pull hole, might be wound around the axle of any available source of power to ease the task.

MACHINE MOLDINGS

It is of interest to look at the wide moldings that were available from millwork supply houses at the beginning of the twentieth century, as the profiles undoubtedly reflected the hand-cut versions that were popular earlier. The catalog of E.L. Roberts & Co., Chicago 1903, provided fifty pages of exact-size profiles of their moldings, in addition to much information on the use of these.

For crown moldings, one had the choice of nine sizes of ogee, six of ogee and cove, nine ovolo and cove. Other profiles for cornice or bed moldings included "sprung coves" (six sizes, Fig.11:7 left) and five in which the cove recurved as a bead at the upper end (Fig.11:7 right). Fourteen smaller profiles of the same type were listed, profiles which would earlier have been cut with a Grecian ogee plane and ripped off at the quirk. An "interior cornice" was listed, a sprung large bead between coves (Fig.11:9 F). "Hook strips" were available which overlapped the edges of this to form a larger complex; these were molded as ovolo, scotia, fillet and ovolo.

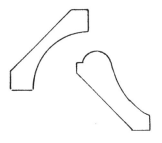

Fig.11:7—Machine moldings

287

Listed as "astragals and battens" were fifteen symmetrical moldings with various simple profiles repeated on each side of the strip. These, of course, were used to cover joints between meeting edges at the same level. More elaborate moldings for use as "panel and base" moldings (for retaining panels in rabbets or to cap baseboards) were available in great variety (a few of these of particular interest have been mentioned in the listing of complex moldings even if the corresponding plane has not been seen).

Two pages of "band" moldings show wide profiles (the term band is a general one that has been used for a number of functions, usually horizontal strips). While some of these were boards molded on but one side of the face, many were of the type called strip moldings above, with both sides molded. Two pages of rabbeted "panel and base" moldings show similar profiles but with a rabbet cut from the back to form a bolection molding. These were used to top a plain baseboard, mount a panel, or stretch other standard forms to make wide moldings.

"Picture moldings" were applied around the walls of the room, usually at about the level of the door and window cornices, to provide a support on which to hang pictures. Three choices were offered, all with three-quarter circles as the upper profile and with a bevel, reverse ogee, or ogee below it. A wide strip molding plane might have been used to cut the faces of these before machine millwork was available,

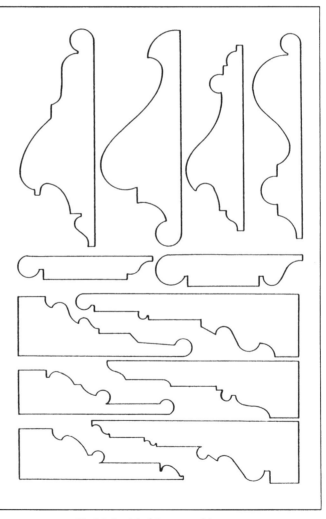

Fig.11:8—Mathieson architraves

288

but a second cut with another plane would be required to complete the circle undercut.

"Casings" (architraves) were available in fifty-six symmetrical profiles and thirty unsymmetrical. A favorite type, to judge by the number of choices, is a rectangular nominal one-by-five or one-by-six piece (finish dimensions 21 by 110 or 130 mm.) with edges left square and having a symmetrical molding sunk in one face. These would have been cut in earlier times with a plane of the type described above as a facing plane, with the symmetrical molders. The unsymmetrical casings shown were of a type that could be made by using a symmetrical facing plane on a wider strip and following this with a conventional edge molder.

This simple style was a departure from the earlier patterns. Unsymmetrical architraves were cut in enormous variety, and any text on interior architecture of the last century will provide examples. Little is to be gained by reproducing a wide variety of these, but a few examples from the Mathieson (Scotland) 1899 catalog are shown (Fig.11:8). Note that (although single plane numbers are given in the Mathieson plates) several planes are needed to cut some of these because of undercuts.

CORNICE PLANES

It might be useful to examine some cornices to gain a clearer picture of the characteristics of the planes used to cut them. An example of a Doric cornice is shown at A in Fig.11:9. A treatment of the top of a window designed by Palladio as an adaptation of this style is seen at B. An almost identical profile was used as a room cornice by Christopher Wren in England, in the late 17th century. The elements of the design are easily recognizable as those used in simpler cornices centuries later.

The profiles and the slanting orientation of the classical moldings were well planned to make use of the play of light and shadow. Other features had utilitarian value. For example, the undercut in the horizontal section served as a drip edge to keep rainwater away from the sides of the building.

The requirements of interior decor were quite different, yet their designs copied the originals closely. A building of any pretension in Colonial America would have elaborately carved cornices at the juncture of wall and ceiling, echoing all of the elements of the Greek designs.

The basic pattern was still in use in the 19th century, although modified to suit lower ceilings. Asher Benjamin (U.S., 1827) recommended that room cornices project into the room at least one-fourth more than their height. This

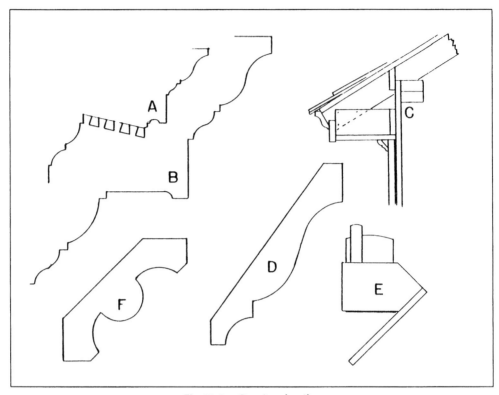

Fig.11:9—Cornice details

was accomplished by increasing the proportion of the horizontal section (plancier) under the topmost or crown molding, which then rose at roughly 45°. Over time, the pattern was simplified until only the topmost (crown) molding remained. Today, of course, only a small vestige (if any) remains.

Exterior treatment, too, used the pattern. The design changed and simplified over time, but the vertical and horizontal surfaces survive as the fascia and soffit in most homes. The uppermost curve is still called the crown molding if present, or, if missing, may be represented by the molded edge of the wooden gutter. The profile below the soffit may be termed a bed molding. A typical cornice construction of 1911 is shown in Fig.11:9C (after Radford, 1911). A machine-cut crown molding of 1903 (E.F. Roberts & Co.) is seen at D.

The cutting of the profile on a board an inch or so in thickness, which is then mounted at an angle, is characteristic of cornice moldings. This was not only to save lumber. Weight was also important to the tradesmen who had to wrestle long pieces into place and ensure that the miters matched.

290

Diagonal elements in the sole profile of a wide molding plane, in particular if these are at 45° or so, are good indicators of the plane's intended use in cutting cornice moldings. The diagonals cut in the flat (as in almost all of the profiles below) become horizontal or vertical elements after the molding is mounted. The profile of D in Fig.11:9, as cut in the flat, has angles of less than 40°. This one was probably intended for outside use, the angle more nearly matching that of the square ends of roof rafters to which it was nailed.

In interior decoration, the cornice moldings were most often mounted at about 45°. Many crowns terminated in a horizontal section at the bottom and a vertical at the top, which meant that a 45° angle had to be cut at the edge of the molding strip. If the molder does this, it is one of the surest signs of the plane's intended use.

As may be seen in D and F of Fig.11:9, both edges of the cornice molding strip must be beveled, front and back, for proper mounting. If this were done before molding, the sharp edge would be an unsatisfactory guide for the cornice plane fence. The profiles shown in Fig.11:11 suggest that several different procedures were possible. Planes such as H or I cut both front bevels, meaning either that the rear bevels were cut later or that care had to be taken in the final cuts because of the sharp edge guiding the fence. Other cornice planes do not cut the front bevel on the fence side, leaving this to be done after molding.

The name SPRING plane appears in old lists with the cornice planes, and it is believed to refer to a bench plane with a re-entrant fence fixed at 45° to the stock, as seen in Fig.11:11 E. One may be seen at Colonial Williamsburg, another signed H. Weigner is in a private collection. The Thomas Napier tool list published in 1786 offers a "spring plane to move any spring", as well as a common one. This plane could have been used to cut the front bevels of cornice moldings, guiding the fence from the rear of the molding strip.

Another generalization serving in identification of crown molders is that they do not use spring. The profile of the plane's sole is relatively flat. The angular adjustment used in common molders is provided for in the angular mounting of the crown molder's product, so that spring is not needed in the plane.

Cornice planes were expensive and highly specialized tools, often borrowed rather than bought; they are not common. One of the largest known was made by W. Raymond (Massachusetts) early in the 19th century, and is preserved at the North Andover Historical Society (Fig.11:10). The stock is 9⅜ in. (24 cm.) wide and carries a blade 7¾ in. (20 cm.) wide. The sole profile is shown at A in Fig.11:11; the molding it cuts is a cove and ovolo when mounted conventionally. It could equally well be mounted upside-down to

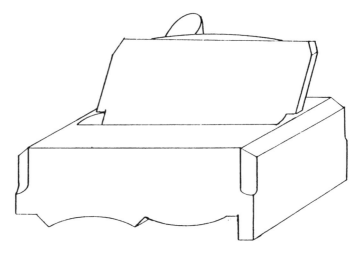

Fig.11:10—W. Raymond cornice plane

give an ovolo and cove. (Systematic names are covered in a later paragraph, not being required for location of a profile in this chapter; but note that they avoid this problem by naming the profile as cut in the flat, without making the decision as to how it is to be mounted.) This profile is frequently seen. The effect, when mounted, is similar to an ogee but adds the accent of the fillet at the transition point between the two arcs.

The profile shown in C in Fig.11:11 is one of the most frequently found. It may be seen

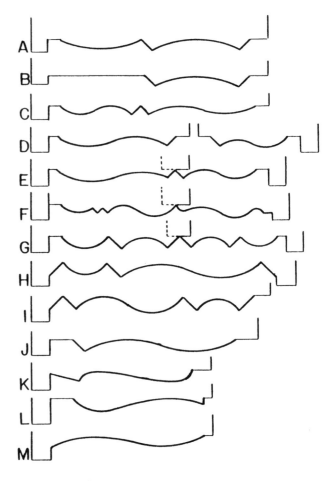

Fig.11:11—Wide molder profiles (names given at chapter end)

in the earliest examples, such as in the plane by Thomas Phillipson (England 1740-75, Fig.11:12) which makes a 2.5 in. (63 mm.) cut; and in one by Henry Wetherel (Connecticut, 1790-97) cutting a 4 in. (10 cm.) profile. As mounted, the molded strip forms an ogee, fillet and reverse ogee, duplicating the crowns of the classical designs of Fig.11:9 A and B. Most of the profiles have the larger ogee on the right, on the side away from the fence, although this makes no obvious difference in the cut. The product is normally mounted with the larger ogee on top.

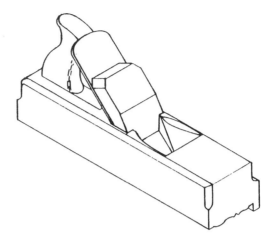

Fig.11:12—Phillipson cornice plane

It is reasonable to assume that large moldings (especially one approaching the size cut by the Raymond plane) were roughed out by smaller planes (plows, rabbets, hollows and rounds) before applying the big one. Their irons were easier to sharpen than the complex blades. The apprentices who had to pull on the rope or transverse handles of these planes must have frequently asked why the molding couldn't have been finished, as well, with the smaller hollows and rounds. A patient master might have explained that the profile had to be exactly uniform if proper miters or coped joints were to be made. The profile on the first piece installed had to mate with the last one when the room had been circled.

Accepting the necessity of creating exactly uniform profiles does not rule out the use of more than one plane. As mentioned in the section on strip planes above, it would be possible to use one plane to cut the molding on the far side of a strip, and follow it with another for the near side. This idea does not seem to have been favored, as no description of such use has been found in print. One molder pictured in Roberts (1978) p.267, might have been so used (profile B in Fig.11:11). It is American, dated 1844, and has a stock 5 in. (127 mm.) wide with a blade about 2¾ in. (70 mm.) wide. The distance between fence and cut leaves room for another, narrower cut with a fenced round to give a profile similar to that of the wide cornice plane at A. This, however, is supposition; it would be interesting to find similar planes or (wishful thinking) a pair.

293

An alternate way of dividing the work was more common. The two sides of the molding were cut with two planes, working from opposite sides of the stock. This produces the same result with planes of more reasonable width, but requires stock of exact width and (since the two planes work in opposite directions) very straight grain. Pairs of "cornish planes" (presumed to be for this use) have been found listed in records of the mid-18th century.

The major tool manufacturers of the late 19th century sold pairs of cornice planes of similar profile but different size, to be used in this way. Both planes of the pairs sold by the Greenfield Tool Co. (Massachusetts, 1851-83) (No.229) and Chapin (Connecticut, mid-19th century.)(No.224) were heel-stamped with the width of the final molding (to 5½ in.). In the absence of a traceable model number, a size stamped on the heel larger then the width of the plane would seem to be a fairly reliable proof of original purpose. The profiles of a pair of these planes are shown at D in Fig.11:11, with the pair superimposed (E) to show the final molding, a close relative of the one shown at C.

Roberts (1983, Fig.103 p.441) also shows a pair of side escapement planes used similarly. Each has a profile like the Raymond plane and the widths of cut are 2.5 and 1.5 in. (64 and 38 mm.). They could be used singly for small crowns, or in concert to give the profile shown at G (which also shows the overlap). This composite provides a profile similar to the ogee and reverse ogee of C, with additional fillets separating the arcs. One more example is shown in F, reported by Karl West, Jr. (1987), a pair of planes found in a carpenter's chest with a tag attached indicating "Need two planes to make a cornice". Both were made by M. Copeland (Connecticut, 1831-42). I think it unlikely that they were made as a pair for this purpose, and prefer to believe that they were adapted to meet the requirement for a wide crown when no suitable plane was at hand. The improviser would leave the note to remind him of the solution to his problem. Either plane would serve alone as a wide molder. Indeed, planes sold as components of different cornice pairs could be used "mix and match" to create acceptable cornices.

Other wide molders quite probably intended for crowns most often combine the elements of ogee, reverse ogee, bead and flute in various combinations. The profile shown at H provides the popular ogee and cove crown (shown at D in Fig.11:9), but the implementation with a fence on both sides is not often seen. This was a massive plane seven inches (18 cm.) wide made in pine, with transverse handles. Note that the bevels at either side of the profile become a vertical at the top of the ogee and a horizontal at the bottom of the cove when the product is mounted. The rear of the strip, the unmolded face, requires complementary bevels on top and bottom to complete the right angle required in the finished molding.

The complement to this profile (in the sense of a mother plane to a daughter) is seen in a plane (I in Fig.11:11) made by J. Gleave (England, 1832-1913) cutting 1.6 in. (41 mm.). The mounted molding would be either reverse ogee and ovolo, or ovolo and ogee depending on its mounting (another reason for avoiding the name of the mounted profile in systematic naming).

The individual planes of Fig.11:11D would serve alone to make a smaller crown. The same molding may be cut with another plane of similar profile but with the fence on the bevel side, as shown at J. An example by C. Warren (New Hampshire, 1837-75) has a four inch (10 cm.) blade, and a number of early New England birch planes are known with this profile. They are also found with lower slopes to the bevel as shown at K, which could mean either that the moldings were intended to be mounted at a higher angle or that another use was intended. Profile K uses a sharply elliptical ogee, one of the variations to be seen in these planes. A similar profile with a higher angle to the bevel, and an ovolo on its right was listed by Mathieson (Scotland, 1899) as a chair rail plane.

With these possible exceptions, the profiles seen so far are reasonably comfortably called CORNICE or CROWN molding planes. Other related planes, lacking the diagnostics, are shown in Fig.11:11 and are more safely called simply wide molders. The CABINET OGEE shown at M is a Chapin (Connecticut, mid-19c.)(No. 225), offered at "$1.00 per inch". This is seen both unfenced and with an applied fence, which may be a later addition. Both this and CORNICE OGEE was offered by the Sandusky Tool Co. (Ohio, 1869-1920), unfortunately without a diagram. It may be that the latter term refers to a profile such as J. In common with other wide molders, the cabinet ogees usually have blades mounted at common pitch (45°) implying use on soft woods. It is possible that they were used by cabinetmakers in shaping secondary woods such as pine or poplar, which were then veneered with the finish wood.

The profile shown at L is from one of the many unmarked planes that require guessing as to their intended use. The two inch (51 mm.) cut is an unsymmetrical lying ogee which ends abruptly with a step on the right. I think that use as a cornice plane is improbable, and that it was intended as a facing plane.

To summarize, a wide molder was not necessarily made to cut a cornice molding. Diagonal elements, particularly at the edge, are good diagnostics for a cornice plane. If the profile makes sense when mounted diagonally, it's a possibility even if diagonals are absent. Since the spring is put in the workpiece rather than the plane, strong spring is evidence that the tool is not a cornice plane.

One last illustration cautions against being too sure in a diagnosis. The profile shown at F in Fig.11:9 was listed as an interior crown molding by E.F. Roberts & Co. (in its 1903 Illustrated Catalog). Profile BJC seen above (with the facing planes) would have cut this molding, but it never occurred to me that it might be used to cut a cornice.

SYSTEMATIC NAMES

The literature of the plane-making period offers no clue to the naming of wide molders. Usage by collectors has been casual, and usually inadequate to gain a true picture of the profile. Some of the reasons have been discussed above. Catalogs have often provided a tracing to supplement the name.

The system used in previous chapters is capable of providing a descriptive name for the wide molders, even if in many cases these are awkwardly long. They are presented here, with their shorthand alphabetical coding.

The letters before each name refer to the profile shown in Fig.11:11.

(A) **BEVEL, BEAD, back BEVEL and FLUTE (LBbLH).**

(B) **BEVEL, BEAD with back BEVEL (LBbL).**

(C) **BEVEL and lying OGEE OPPOSITE BEVEL and lying OGEE (LlO+LlO)**

(D) **BEVEL and lying OGEE, (LlO).**

(F,left) **lying REVERSE OGEE, back BEVEL, BEVEL, back BEVEL and back SCOTIA (RbLLbLbS).**

(F,right) **REVERSE OGEE-lying REVERSE OGEE with FILLET (R-lRF).**

(G, both) **BEVEL, BEAD, back BEVEL and FLUTE (LBbLH).**

(H) **BEVEL, lying OGEE with BEVEL OPPOSITE FLUTE and BEVEL (LlOL+HL)**

(I) **lying REVERSE OGEE, back BEVEL and BEVEL OPPOSITE BEVEL, BEAD and back BEVEL (lRbLL+LBbL).**

(J) and (K) **lying REVERSE OGEE with back BEVEL (lRbL).**

(L) **lying OGEE (lO).**

(M) **lying REVERSE OGEE (lR).**

Chapter 12

OTHER PLANING TOOLS

All of the tools covered up to this point have satisfied the narrow definition of a wooden plane. They have a wooden stock, longer than wide, and a sole which conforms more or less to the shape it is intended to create. The stock (or a steel keel mounted in it) rides on the surface being planed, and serves to control the cutting action of one or more blades rigidly mounted within it. The cutting edge, held more or less perpendicular to the long dimension of the stock, extends from the sole or keel a distance just equal to the thickness of the shaving to be taken. The stock thus restricts the depth of cut. Equally important, the stock (except in the single case of the chisel or edge plane) exerts pressure on the wood in front of the cutting edge, and thus helps to resist splitting and rough cutting.

There are other tools not usually referred to as planes, but which serve a similar purpose in that they are used to remove thin shavings from wood. Those in which the body holding the blade serves to provide control over the cutting action satisfy a broader definition of the word "plane" and deserve consideration here.

SHAVES

The word SHAVE has been used to name so many different tools that, unless clarified with another descriptive word, it conveys little information. Any tool that has a handle on each side, or that has a cutting blade mounted parallel to the long dimension of the tool, appears to be a candidate for the name. Even these simple specifications are not enough to encompass the range, as there are one-handled shaves and ones which mount blades across the sole. The name has even been applied to drawknives, called draw shaves by some trades.

To remain within the scope of the present work, only those shaves will be considered in which a blade is held in a wooden body that provides some degree of control of the cutting action.

Some of the cooper's shaves satisfy even the narrow definition of a plane given above, and differ from common planes only in having their handles on the sides rather than the top. These are described in Chapter 13 — Cooper. The majority of wooden shaves, however, carry their cutting edge aligned with the long dimension of the stock.

The SPOKESHAVE is an old tool. The name was in print by 1510, and sixteenth century indentures show that it was used by coopers of that time. It can, indeed, be used to shave spokes, but the name hardly describes the wide range of usefulness of the tool. W.L. Goodman (1972) suggests that the name may have arisen from a Latin mistranslation. I offer (without evidence) another possibility: that the name was a corruption of the Dutch SPOOK-SCHAAFJE. This was still in use in the Nooitgedagt (ca.1890) catalog, and today translates as "spokeshave". The Dutch word "spook" means "ghost" or "spirit". Was the original name intended to imply an insubstantial or light-duty plane? Interestingly, American spokeshaves were listed by Stolp (the Netherlands) in 1915 with the English name literally translated back to spoke plane, SPAAKSCHAAFJE. Neither the French (BASTRINGUE or WASTRINGUE) nor the German (SCHABHOBEL, LEDERHOBEL) names suggest spokes. The name remains, however — although there is great temptation to shorten it to SHAVE where the meaning seems clear. Shaves will be found in the kit of most woodworkers, especially coachmakers, chairmakers, coopers, stairbuilders, and furniture makers (they were in the top till of Duncan Phyfe's tool box with his most often used tools).

For any task requiring the smoothing of a surface that is curved — especially if it is of changing radius or doubly curved — one of the forms of the spokeshave is generally used. Two examples may be chosen from among many: The cabriole legs of Queen Anne or Chippendale furniture would have been sawn to profile with a turning saw, roughed with a gouge, and then sculpted from there with a shave. The seat of a Windsor chair is formed primarily with shaves; and those having a pommel at the back of the seat for bracing spindles have concave sections of the rounded edge that are difficult to work with any other hand tool.

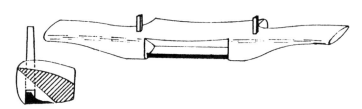

Fig.12:1—Common spokeshave

The common form of SPOKESHAVE (the wooden type, not the metal version that dominates today) is shown in Fig.12:1. The stock is shaped to form a handle at each end. The working part in the center is longer (in the direction of the handles) than wide, and has a short, flat or gently rounded, sole. The cutter is of knife-shaped section, and its two ends are forged into square tangs which are bent upward. These tangs are force-fit into holes in the stock tightly enough to resist shifting in use, yet permitting adjustment of blade exposure by hammer taps. The cutter is set parallel to the sole, and the sole is cut away behind the cutting edge to provide for chip clearance as shown in the section sketch. As the blade is recessed into the sole, the part of the sole in front of the blade presses on the work and serves the same purpose as the mouth of a plane in restraining splitting. Cutting edge length is usually about three inches or 8 cm., although this can vary over a wide range.

The two ends of the stock are thinned by removing wood at front and bottom to form handholds of oval section. Here there is room for much variation in shape, depending on personal preference and the specific needs of the task. In shaves with soles curved across the stock, the depth of cut is determined not only by the blade setting but, as a finer adjustment, the angle at which the tool is held. For this reason, the easiest tools to use are those with handles placed to minimize any tendency for the thrust of wood on the blade to change the tool angle. Upswept handles, where required by the work, need a firmer grasp and are more tiring to use.

Toward the end of the 19th century, the wooden shave was largely replaced in America by the steel versions, and were no longer offered by most Ameri-

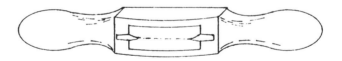

Fig.12:2—Double cutting spokeshave (bottom view)

can manufacturers. Sandusky showed an "improved double cutting" wooden spoke shave in their 1877 catalog (Fig.12:2) as a symmetrical tool, for cutting in either direction. The wooden type, however, remained popular in Britain, the James Howarth 1884 catalog offering six varieties. In spite of the greater ease of adjustment of the metal type, many workers prefer the feel of the wood and they are still being manufactured on the Continent.

Securing the cutter by the force fit of the square-section tangs in holes in the stock works surprisingly well until the holes wear. Many older shaves are seen with remedies in the form of slips of veneer inserted in the tang holes,

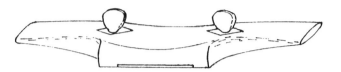

Fig.12:3—Spokeshave with adjustment thumb screws

or with wood screws (with tips cut off) installed to bear on the tangs and acting as set screws. Another method was to slit the stock through the tang hole, and use a screw to close the kerf and pinch the tang.

Refinements in the basic spokeshave include plating the sole of the shave with bone or brass (the small sole area wears quickly), and threading the ends of the tangs to permit blade setting by thumbscrews (Fig.12:3). Single-handled shaves are found for working in confined areas or where the other hand is occupied (see cooper's tools). Long spokeshaves — over a foot (30 cm.) long — are often called WHEELWRIGHT'S SPOKESHAVES. This redundancy emphasizes the tool's misleading name — who else would shave spokes?

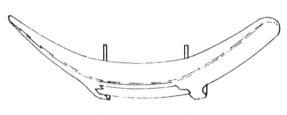

Fig.12:4—Travisher

It is not surprising that a large number of shapes are found, as a shave can be made quickly to fit a specific need. The makers of Windsor chairs use few conventional planes. The seat is shaped, after roughing out, almost entirely with shaves. One made for finishing the deeply scooped or "saddled" seats has a gently curved blade, upswept handles (Fig.12:4), and its own name — a TRAVISHER. (The same name was used by Thomas Hennell, 1947, for a straight-bladed chairmaker's shave with a cap iron). There are many other uses for curved blades. They may be called RADIUS or ROUND shaves or, if the upswept handles recurve, GULL-WING (Fig.12:5).

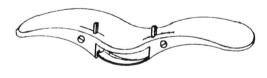

Fig.12:5—Gull-wing spoke shave

Heavier tools with stouter blades are called COOPER'S SPOKESHAVES (Fig.12:6), from that trade's preference for this form. They are sometimes fitted with a cap iron, bolted on the cutter. These (and others) may have the stock behind the blade not completely cut away, but mortised to provide for shaving clearance (as shown in the section) for improved strength. Sometimes called a PAIL SHAVE, a straight-bladed tool was used to finish (cross-grain) the inside of pails or other straight-sided products of the white cooper, before the bottom was installed. It might be called a CROSS shave to distinguish it from a lighter tool

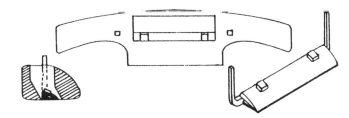

Fig.12:6—Cooper's spoke shave

with the appropriate curvature and upswept handles used along the grain — the BENT shave. These and others are covered in Chapter 13—The Cooper.

Curved shaves were made in other forms. The SHOVELMAKER'S shave has a blade in the form of a half-circle, with ends extended as tangents and forged into tangs (Fig.12:7). The stock has a sole to match, and stub handles. It was used to make other deeply excavated items as well as shovels. A variant seen in chairmaker's shaves at the Shelburne Museum (Vermont) replaces the stub handles with a flatiron grip (Fig.12:8). The BODDA is an Italian form with a blade

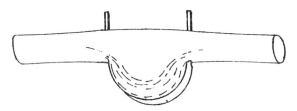

Fig.12:7—Shovelmaker's shave

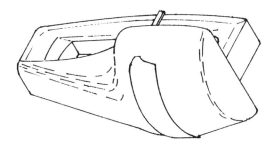

Fig.12:8—Chairmaker's shave

screwed in front of a wooden stock forming a long sole, the stock being grasped by one hand thrust through a leather strap. (See Chapter 13—The Cooper, Fig.13:35.)

Profiles other than simple circular arcs may be cut by bending the spokeshave blade into the desired shape and mounting it on a sole to match. The   HANDRAIL

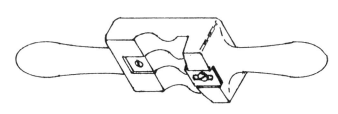

Fig.12:9—Handrail shave

SHAVE (Fig.12:9) may be made to match the profile of a handrail plane, and used to continue the shape around curves. Coachmakers used the same device. These were sometimes made with a double- edged cutter, to work in either direction. One wonders how often it choked with shavings. Some varieties are discussed later in Chapter 13—The Coachmaker.

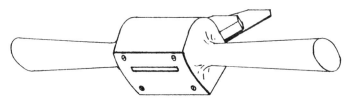

Fig.12:10—Nelson

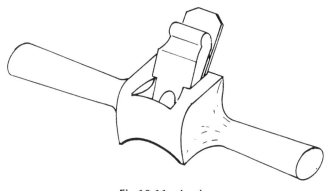

Fig.12:11—Jarvis

PLANE-TYPE SHAVES have a bench throat and plane blade held by a wedge in the same manner as used in bench planes. They are, in fact, planes with a short stock and long side handles. The general shape is that of a spokeshave, but they are more massive with a larger stock to accomodate the blade mounting. Two common types are the wheelwright's NELSON and the JARVIS, both usually having brass plated soles. Since the iron is mounted parallel to the grain of the stock, the thrust of the wedge tends to split it, and the stocks are sometimes strapped with brass on the top to resist this. Both of these tools may be equipped with cap irons. The Nelson (Fig.12:10) has a flat or slightly compassed sole, the Jarvis (Fig.12:11) a hollow one. The French name for the latter — WASTRINGUE DE CHARRON (wheelwright's shave) —

302

shows that English is not alone in using the same name for spokeshaves and plane shaves.

Another shave seen occasionally is the CHAMFER shave. It is a sliding-sole type of chamfer plane (described in Chapter 8) with the exception that the throat lies across the stock rather than along it. It may have side handles as other plane shaves, or be held by the rectangular stock ends (Fig.12:12). A SCOOP-MAKER'S shave or plane in the Shelburne Museum collection (Vermont) (Fig.12:13) has a bench mouth in an egg-shaped

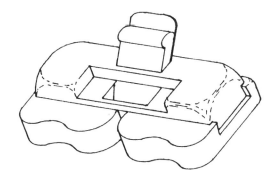

Fig.12:12—Chamfer shave

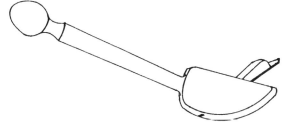

Fig.12:13—Scoopmaker's shave

body. Used in hollowing wooden scoops, it is pulled forward by means of a handle projecting forward from the stock.

Continental and Far Eastern   Continental spokeshaves are difficult to distinguish from English or American, as the range of variation within one country is greater than the national differences.

The Chinese form (copied in other parts of the Far East) is differentiated by the lack of a mouth, the blade not being recessed into the sole.

The Japanese version of the plane shave, the NANKIN-KANNA, has a self-wedged blade and throat like the hira-kanna, but this is placed across the stock as in the Nelson and Jarvis. The Japanese use cap-irons or chipbreakers in a wider variety of tools than is the Western custom, and the nankin-kanna usually has one. They were frequently user-made. They are presently supplied with their stock ends left in the rough or finished with a simple taper, to be shaped by the user to his preference. Note that it is called a plane (kanna), not a shave, and it is in fact a plane similar to a short smoother except for the throat placement.

303

SCRAPERS

A hand scraper is a rectangular plate of steel, often a piece cut from an old saw blade, with edges made straight and square on a honing stone. A hard steel rod, or a special tool called a burnisher, is run along the edge at a slight angle. The edge is minutely distorted by this, a small burr being bent over to form a sharp, hook-like cutting edge (Fig.12:14). In use, the blade is flexed slightly in the fingers, to avoid the tendency to dig in. It is pushed or pulled over the wood surface, held vertically but leaning slightly in the direction of the thrust. Very fine shavings are removed, leaving a surface that many prefer to a sanded one. It is especially useful in following a toothing plane which has been used to level awkward grain.

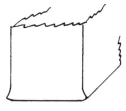

Fig.12:14—
Magnified scraper
edge

For large areas, the finger pressure required to bend the plate is tiring; and if vigorously used, the blade becomes hot enough to burn. This was at first overcome by simply slotting a piece of wood and inserting the blade (Fig.12:15). A tool of this type was shown in Diderot (France, mid-18th century) and an example is in the Dominy collection (Winterthur). More elaborate versions are seen, with handles attached to give a shape not unlike a present-day paint scraper. These evolved into the SCRAPER plane — a plane body with a scraper blade held nearly upright or leaning forward. The sole provided an additional advantage of preventing dig-in if a soft spot was encountered. These are well known in their metal versions, but rare in wood. Somewhat more common is the same tool with its throat transverse, as in a plane shave. In either case, the blade is often thicker than a hand scraper and has a beveled edge which should still be turned with a

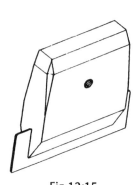

Fig.12:15—
Handscraper

burnisher for best results. A toothing plane is often fitted with a common plane blade, and used as a scraper plane, but the results are not quite as good.

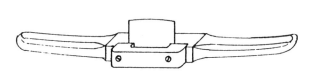

Fig.12:16—Spokeshave-shaped scraper

304

More commonly, scraper blades are held in a stock of spokeshave shape (Fig.12:16). It may or may not have a sole. The blade may be held by means of a metal strap screwed to the stock, or more simply by inserting it into a slit in the stock and pinching this closed with wood screws. This type is almost always user-

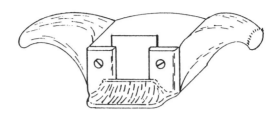

Fig.12:17—Rams-horn scraper

made and may take a variety of forms. The scraper is even easier to make than the spokeshave and a wide variety of shapes are seen; the GULL-WING scraper has handles like those seen in the spokeshave illustrated in Fig.12:5. The RAMS-HORN SCRAPER (Fig.12:17) has two handles fashioned in the shape which gives it its name. More substantially made scrapers are sometimes found with a reversible blade, toothed on one edge.

A SCRATCH STOCK is a tool, almost always user-made, for shaping narrow moldings. It is essentially a profiled scraper held in a stock fitted with a fence. The reverse of the molding to be made is cut in a thin steel plate — a piece of a saw blade is often used. The cutter is usually filed without a bevel, is mounted upright, and will work in either direction. The stock is a scrap of wood shaped to form a handle and slit to hold the cutter, or consists of two similarly shaped pieces screwed together with the cutter between. The stock is shaped to form a guiding fence, and used with its long dimension at right angles to the work edge. As in most user-made tools, it may be found in a wide

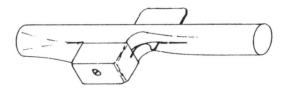

Fig.12:18—Beader

variety of shapes. A common form is the BEADING TOOL, used to cut side beads on curved edges (Fig.12:18). The Windsor beader is a patented wood and metal tool manufactured for the same purpose. Another type, used for cutting narrow profiles, is shaped much like a carpenter's cutting gauge. The cutter is mounted in a mortise at one end of a square rod, and held by a small wedge. The rod slides through a fence which fixes the distance of the cut from the edge. Roubo (ca.1775) pictures one of these. Greber (1956) shows a variant of this in which the fence is replaced by a trammel point, for forming circular moldings. The scratch stock is called a TARIBISCOT in French, LEISTENHOBEL or PROFILSCHABER in German.

A more substantial tool shaped like a shave is used by wheelwrights and coachmakers. It is fitted with a moveable fence, usually made of metal and mounted on the sole The blade is thicker, with a bevel edge, and held almost vertically by means of a wedge. There is no sharp line of demarcation between such a tool and the coachmaker's router that is covered in Chapter 13—The Coachmaker.

As the cutting action of any of these tools is that of a scraper, each cuts slowly but has little problem with grain direction and leaves a finished surface. It is able to work around sharp curves, and is indispensable in making curved moldings of changing radius.

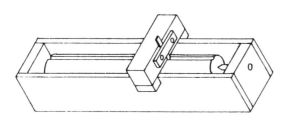

Fig.12:19—Turning box

A form of the scratch stock may be used in a MOLDING BOX, an open-top box that contains the piece to be worked and whose sides serve to guide the two fences of its scratch stock. The workpiece may be mounted on centers (as in a lathe) in such a box and rotated after the cut is finished, to make repetitive cuts on different sides or around the circumference of a round piece. This is called a TURNING BOX (Fig.12:19). It may be fitted with a device to maintain the angle of the workpiece — ranging from a simple wedge to an index plate such as is used in gear-cutting machines. Surprisingly ornate pieces may be formed with this simple tool. It is still used today, with the scratch stock replaced by a power router.

As the need for larger quantities of moldings grew in the mid-sixteenth century, a MOLDING MACHINE was developed — the first step in the mechanization of wood milling. An example dated 1565 was in the collection of Elector August I of Saxony — the German name is PROFILLEISTEN-ZIEHSTOCK. This was in the form of a sturdy scratch stock fixed to the end of a bench, with guides arranged to let a wood strip be fed through it. The bench had a guide strip, on which rode a draw block fitted with a vise or clamp to hold the workpiece. The blade of the scratch stock was profiled, with its bevel on the draw block side. A metal support plate underneath the cutting edge pressed on the under side of the workpiece and forced it against the cutter, being raised by screw adjustments after successive passes.

In use, the workpiece was threaded through the cutting section, the metal support plate raised to put the work in contact with the cutter, and the end of the work gripped in the drawblock. The drawblock was then moved away from the cutter, pulling the workpiece through — by hand for a small molding, with a windlass for a large one. This was repeated with the support plate raised at each pass until the molding was cut to the proper depth. Long pieces of uniform section were thus obtained, simplifying the matching of mitered corners.

Moxon (1703) describes a variant of this, the WAVING ENGINE. This served to cut moldings - for picture frames and other uses - in which the molded profile rose and fell along the length of the piece, as in waves. The molding machine described above was modified as in Fig.12:20 by replacing the support plate with a metal bar having a rounded upper end. A

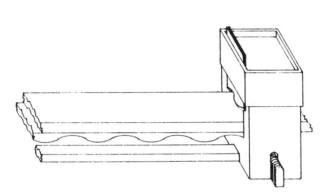

Fig.12:20—Waving machine

long metal rack was provided, with flat upper side and with bottom cut into the wave pattern desired. The rack was attached to the underside of the workpiece, and both threaded together through the cutting head. The metal bar now acting as the support plate was raised, pressing against the under side of the rack, until the work contacted the cutter at the trough of the wave — thereafter the procedure was the same as in the molding machine.

A similar device was used to create a side-to-side, rather than an up-and-down, movement of the molding profile. Such moldings were called "flamed" and in fact predated the waved profiles. Greber (1956) describes a compassed plane with a profiled blade and a box in which it worked. The box had sinusoidal guide rails on either side, which served to move the plane from side to side as it moved down the box.

These machines were important tools for the joiner for three centuries, but are almost unknown today. The rotary milling machines, developed around 1800, replaced them. The lone survival is a modification used to cover wood moldings with a thin layer of brass, still used in France.

307

PLANES TO MAKE SHAVINGS

In the days before matches, a fire was always available in the hearth or cookstove, but a way was needed to carry the flame to a candle or pipe. A glowing coal might serve, but a better way was to use a spill. This is a tightly curled shaving of wood, about six inches (15 cm.) long, which could be set aflame. It burned slowly enough to carry the fire to its destination. Spills were made by a SPILL plane, often found in old woodworker's kits. Almost always hand made rather than manufactured, they provided a way of converting scraps of wood into a useful commodity. Even more than most other user-made planes, these appear in a great variety of shapes. The common characteristic is a sharply skewed blade, to encourage the tight curl. A chip escapement in the form of a small hole also helped and was frequently used.

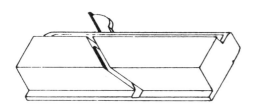

Fig.12:21—Hand-held spill plane

While some were made to be hand-held (Fig.12:21), another type was intended to be held stationary, sole up, while the wood scrap was moved over it. Some were clamped in a vise, others had extensions to fit over a bench edge (two views of one such are shown in Fig.12:22, the lower showing the tool being used). The sole was often made with one or two fences, or V-notched to guide the wood. The cutter might be a bench plane blade held by a wedge in a more or less conventional stock, or in a body like a plane shave. It might also be a thin strip sharpened on one long edge and mounted somewhat as in a spokeshave. The variety of these tools is such that finding two of identical shape is most unusual.

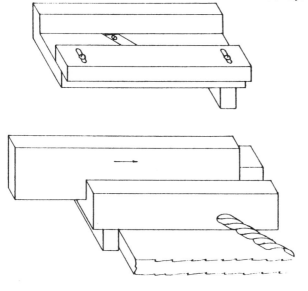

Fig.12:22—Two views, stationary spill plane

308

Spill planes stamped with a maker's name are not common, but they were made commercially by a few British makers (Mathieson listed one in its 1899 catalog). H.J. Brunner of Pennsylvania made them and applied for a patent on his design, but it apparently was not issued. William Drips, Ohio, was granted a patent (26 Aug. 1873, U.S.142,216) on a design meant to be placed on the counter of a cigar shop. Even having a maker's stamp, however, does not necessarily mean that the tool was made as a spill plane, as another type of plane was often converted by its owner to this use.

Planes to make uncurled shavings are also sometimes called spill planes — they might have been so used, but might also have served to make "chips". These were long, thin strips of wood used at one time to weave hats. A CHIP plane makes several at a time. A block of willow or other easily worked wood was first scored with a "widthmaker", a tool with multiple scoring knives. A thick shaving was then taken off using a plane in which the iron was held at a low pitch (about 40°). The scored "chips" emerged at the chosen width and thickness. There is a plane in the collection of Sturbridge Village (Massachusetts) which apparently served as a widthmaker. A tool combining both functions — widthmaker and chip plane — has also been reported.

Thicker shavings were called "spelks" and were sometimes used for weaving baskets but more often used as sides for pillboxes or cheeseboxes. These were made with a SPELK plane (Fig.12:23; sometimes called pillbox or scaleboard plane) . Unlike a spill or chip, the spelk is too thick to allow bending at a sharp angle, and the plane must be designed to accomodate this. For planes used to

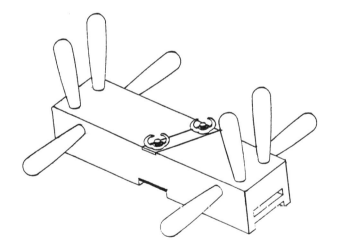

Fig.12:23—Spelk plane

cut the thicker spelks, this is done by mounting the cutter horizontally, retaining it by employing a stouter version of a spokeshave mounting. The sole of the plane is usually grooved to restrict admission to stuff within the cutting capacity of the blade. As the plane moves forward, the cut spelk passes over the cutter with little bending and emerges at the rear through a mortise

309

or a groove in the body of the stock. As may be imagined, much force is needed to operate this type of plane. They are usually equipped with multiple peg and transverse handles. The one illustrated in Fig.12:23 (dated 1764) has eight! These thick strips were woven into fences or heavy baskets, and the thickest served as slats for venetian blinds. After being cut, these were finished and profiled with the BLIND plane previously described in Chapter 9.

More conventional planes were used to cut the thinner spelks. A wide blade mounted at about 30° from the horizontal was held by two narrow wedges, one on either side. This allowed the spelk to slide up the face of the iron and escape through a very narrow throat (Fig.12:24).

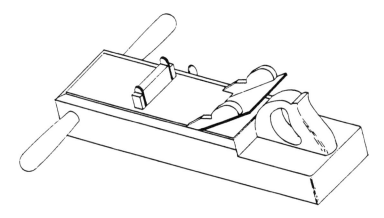

Fig.12:24—Spelk plane

A tool which may be mistaken for a light-duty spelk plane is used in French kitchens (RABOT DE CUISINE). This is mounted sole up, usually on legs with one side notched to brace it against the table edge. It is used to slice dried meats or cheese, or for other kitchen use, in much the same manner as our cabbage slicers. Very similar is the APOTHECARY'S plane, used by pharmacists to slice botanicals prior to extraction with alcohol to make medicinal tinctures.

Continental   Spill planes were used on the Continent as well. The French name is angel's hair plane (RABOT À CHEVEUX D'ANGES); the German, SPEILHOBEL. The chip or spelk plane is most often of Continental make. It was called SCHACHTELHOBEL in Germany or RABOT À TARGES in Switzerland, where it was used to make the veneers used for the sides of cheese boxes. The Joh. Weiss catalog (Austria, 1909) offered two, one to make curled shavings (box sides) and one for straight (tops). A third form was called ESSIGSPANHOBEL, or vinegar chip plane. (Vinegar was formerly made by continuously trickling cider or wine over wood chips, to provide a good access to air required for the fermentation process.)

Japanese   Wide, paper-thin pine veneers find use as wrapping materials or temporary food holders (kyogi) in Japan. These were made with a KYŌGI-KANNA, which might be described as a massive apothecary plane with a wide, thin blade. Straight grain pine boards up to 7 x 24 in. (11 x 60 cm.) are forced over this, yielding thin shavings the full size of the board. The plane (or perhaps it should be called a machine) forms the surface of a table whose legs connect to a frame in which a heavy trammel arm pivots. The arm extends over the workpiece and provides leverage to both press it down and move it over the cutter. The principle was resurrected recently in a Japanese power tool, the super- surfacer, in which a board to be planed is carried by a belt over a stationary blade.

ROUTERS

The ROUTER serves to cut away wood to a fixed depth below a reference surface. The boundaries of the area to be sunk are defined with saw or chisel, then this tool removes the waste. It is particularly useful in assuring uniform depth of grooves or dados meant to accept mating members, but other uses abound. It comes in many shapes, most of which are either user-made or imported. Maker's marks are unusual. The common feature is a sizeable sole to bridge the trench being dug, and an iron that is adjustable to cut at the trench bottom. Routers are not true planes in the sense that they have no mouth to press on the wood in front of the cut, as cutting takes place below the level of the sole.

A common form, the D-ROUTER (Fig.12:25), has a wooden stock roughly in the shape of the capital letter D. The cutter is often fixed to

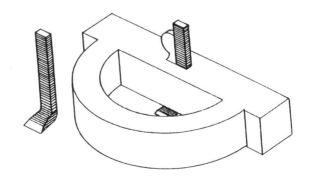

Fig.12:25—D-router (right); D-router iron (left)

the inner, straight edge of the stock (the upright of the D) by means of a stirrup and thumbscrew, or sometimes through the stock with a wedge. The iron (Fig.12:25 left) is a vertical shaft, bent at nearly a right angle at the bottom, and forged into a widened and flattened foot which is sharpened, bevel up, as the cutting edge. The stock in front of the cutting edge is of semicircular outline, with the central region removed to permit seeing where the cutter is working. In variants of this type, the stock may be shaped to form handgrips through extensions of the straight side of the stock, or knobs may be added.

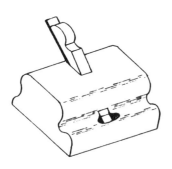

Fig.12:26—Granny's tooth router with straight iron

More common in England is the OLD WOMAN'S TOOTH or GRANNY'S TOOTH (Fig.12:26). These usually have a straight iron somewhat like a plow iron, mounted through the stock and wedge-fixed at 45° or higher. There is no throat, but the stock (a scrap section of bannister rail is a favorite source) has a notch cut away or a hole put through to let the user see the cutting edge. When sinking the background of a relief carving, a wider stock may be necessary to reach the borders of the piece.

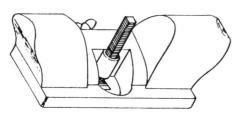

Fig.12:27—Granny's tooth router with "devil's foot" iron

The "devil's-foot" type iron, as in Fig.12:25 left, is also used in the Granny's tooth router (Fig. 12:27). Another common form, more nearly in the shape of a plane and some-times called a ROUTER PLANE, is shown in Fig.12:28.

A BUTT MORTISE plane, as its name implies, is used to cut the pocket in a door frame to accept the hinge. It has the appearance of a narrow plane with a long throat opening (Fig.12:29), but is in fact a router, as it cuts below the level of the sole and has no mouth to press on the work. The long throat opening is needed, for the cutting edge must be visible.

The coachmaker uses a number of specialized routers (covered in Chapter 13—The Coachmaker), but the QUIRK router (Fig.12:30) is mentioned here as one that is more generally useful as a way to cut narrow grooves. These are sometimes found with an unusual cutter shape. A hole is made in the end of a steel bar and the end ground away as an arc intersecting the hole, leaving two cutting edges facing each other. In use, the iron is tipped slightly away from the direction of motion so that the front edge serves as a mouth for the

312

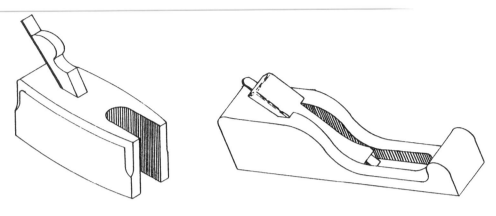

Fig.12:28—Router plane   Fig.12:29—Butt mortise plane

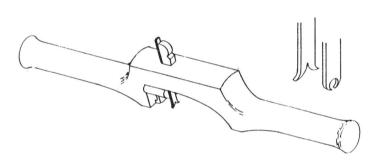

Fig.12:30—Quirk router and cutters

rear cutting edge. Also seen in the figure detail is a bidirectional cutter made by simply splitting the end.

Continental The handled form of router was favored for the French GUIMBARDE and the German GRUNDHOBEL, both of which were made commercially. Older specimens, often of D-router shape, were often elaborately (and sometimes grotesquely) carved. Some appear at first glance, in fact, to be wood carvings, and are revealed to be tools only on a closer look. One such is depicted in a 1612 intarsia on the Konigsberg Joiner's Guild chest.

313

Compassed and radius molding planes have been covered previously, but there are also types that work smaller arcs. Molding planes with radius stocks attached to trammel arms are found, intended for decoration of edges of round surfaces (one such is described under The Cooper in Chapter 13.

Fig.12:31—Corner block

Turn of the century door frames in the U.S. were outlined with wide architrave moldings. It was usual to have these meet at corners not in miters, but by butting a square block, the corner block. This carried a circular molding, echoing that of the architrave (Fig.12:31). A plane has been found which was used to cut these. The circular sole was profiled to mate with the molding desired, and it was used by rotating the plane, not pushing it.

A favorite decoration on church pews and elsewhere was the quatrefoil. This is made by boring a hole, then four more equally spaced around it and intersecting it. The cut surfaces were usually chamfered, and a plane has been found which would do this quickly. A cylindrical stock was turned down at one end to a smaller diameter, to fit inside the holes. A chamfering blade was mounted in the larger diameter. The small end was inserted in one of the holes of the decoration, and twisted to cut the chamfer.

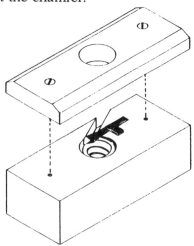

Fig.12:32—Screwbox

While not planes in the strict sense, devices to cut screw threads may be mentioned under this heading. A SCREWBOX is a wooden stock, made in two halves (Fig.12:32), sometimes fitted with peg handles. A hole the size of the outer diameter of the screw pierces one half, the other continues it as a threaded hole. A small V-section cutter, with very sharp edge in the profile of the threads to be cut, is mounted inside the stock, carefully adjusted to be tangent to the root diameter of the thread. Operation is much like a metal screw-cutting die, and it serves to cut the male thread. A metal tap is the usual means of cutting the female thread.

Another tool that was used to cut the female thread was described by Holtzapffel, but seems not to have a common English name. (The French called it TARAUD, and the screwbox FILIÈRE). A wooden screw of the pitch desired, but of smaller diameter, carries a V-cutter near one end located at a crest of the thread (Fig.12:33). The screw passes through a threaded hole in one end of a wooden frame, within which the bored piece to be threaded is clamped. As the screw is turned, the cutter is guided in the desired thread pattern on the inside of the hole in the workpiece. This tool has the advantage that the thread need not be cut in one pass. The thread may be started as a scratch, and the exposure of the cutter increased after each pass until the desired depth is cut. For this reason it is much better for large diameter threading.

The RIPPING plane, too, is not a plane but a version of the cutting gauge. Advertised by Sandusky as "Kinney's Patent Ripping Plane"

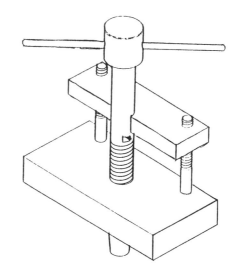

Fig.12:33—Tool to cut female threads

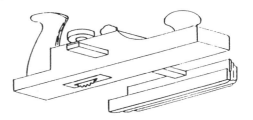

Fig.12:34—Kinney's patent ripping plane

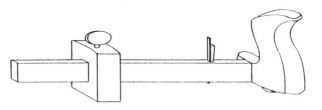

Fig.12:35—Veneer slitter

(15 June, 1880, U.S. 228,766), it has a plane-like stock and a moving fence carried on one arm (Fig.12:34). The cutter is a slotted wheel, sharpened on the circumference, rotating on a horizontal axle (some have been seen sharpened in a wave pattern). It was touted as less apt to follow the grain than a common cutting gauge. A more common cutting gauge with a fixed cutter and jack handle, most often user-made, was sometimes called a SLITTING plane or VENEER SLITTER (Fig.12:35).

315

Chapter 13

PLANES OF SPECIFIC TRADES

In previous chapters, planes were described in terms of the task they performed, with minimum attention to the trade using them. There are certain wood-shaping tasks, however, which are required only in the practice of specific trades. Some background information on these trades is necessary to describe adequately the tools designed to accomplish these tasks. Each section in this chapter concerns one such trade and the planes used therein.

THE COOPER

Wooden tubs were known in Egypt as early as 2700 BC, and the barrel with curved staves was probably developed in transalpine Gaul around 1000 BC. The coopering methods of the recent past were known and used in Roman times. These wooden vessels soon displaced the clay amphorae as the principal shipping containers of commerce. Originally they were made using only axes, adzes and knives, but as coopering became a major industry throughout the world, specialized planes were developed. Every village had its cooper. These tradesmen made casks in sizes from the "bever" barrel to carry the farmer's two pints of beer into the field, to the "Heidelberg tun" that held just under 50,000 gallons.

In the U.S. in 1850 there were over 43,000 coopers, about one for every five hundred inhabitants. Aside from making shipping vessels, they provided many household necessities such as buckets, churns, and watering troughs for cattle. Specialization developed. The white cooper made home and farm items of unbent staves; the slack cooper a variety of containers for dry products; and the most skilled made tight or wet cooperage. Each varied the basic tools to suit his own requirements.

Machine methods of making cask components took over toward the end of the nineteenth century. Still later, the wooden containers were replaced by steel and cardboard, and a huge trade dwindled to the making of containers for beer, wine and spirits and for little else. The art of the cooper — and they were men of great skill — is now kept alive by only a few.

The planes they used, although all designed to accomplish a limited number of tasks, proliferated in type and size. Before attempting to catalog these, let us review the steps in making a "tight" barrel, or barrel to hold liquids. To a cooper, a "barrel" was a cask of specific capacity, and his product was expected (legally required, in some cases) to have a capacity very close to the prescribed volume. This he accomplished by eye, without measuring until the vessel was ready for installation of the heads. He made (in England) pins, firkins, kilderkins, barrels, hogsheads, puncheons, and butts; all of defined content. And, of course, the size of a "barrel" varied according to what was to be put into the barrel and where it was made. For example, Henry VIII of England decreed that ale barrels were to hold 32 gallons, beer barrels 36.

The staves, selected quarter-sawn (or better, rived) white oak, were shaped or "listed" by axe and drawknives. By eye, they were given the proper bulge at the center to produce the proper barrel shape, and the proper angle at their edges to mate with their neighbors. They were "backed" by shaping the outer face to the curvature of the final vessel, and "hollowed out" by scooping wood from the center of the inner face (the ends were left untouched, to allow for shaping after raising). They were then jointed with a long plane, the critical step which determined the amount of bulge in the vessel and the tightness of fit between adjacent staves.

If the barrel was for beer, the staves were 1½ in. (38 mm.) or more thick, and required steaming or soaking before bending. A set was selected to give the proper diameter (the staves were not of uniform width, but sized to make best use of the wood). These were raised within hoops into a conical shape, and this placed like a chimney over a fire of shavings, to soften the staves for bending. In a flurry of activity not made easier by clouds of steam and smoke, hoops were driven on, bending the staves and mating them into a cask of final shape.

The vessel, called at this stage a GUN, now needed grooves around the inner circumference at both ends, to retain the heads. Fig.13:1 shows the end of one of the staves after this operation. First the inner edges of the stave ends were chamfered to begin forming the CHIME. (The term "chime" was used to refer both to this chamfer and to the larger section between croze and stave end.) This was to guard against the possibility that impact during shipment would split out the short grain between

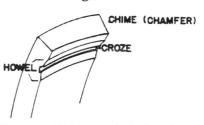

Fig.13:1—Finished end of a barrel stave

317

the stave's end and barrel head, causing leakage. The next stages required a reference surface, exactly level, as a guide for cutting the interior groove that would receive the barrel head. This was done by planing the stave ends. Another plane might be used, in careful work, to smooth the chamfer on these ends. The inner surface of the gun within a few inches of the end needed to be made smooth and exactly circular, for proper mating with the head. To do this, a gently curved surface, the HOWEL, was cut around the inside of the barrel. This paved the way for cutting the groove — the CROZE — around the inside in the center of the howel. Before repeating the process on the other end, a hinged measuring stick was inserted diagonally into the cask (after first installing one head in it): these dips, or diagonals, served to estimate the interior volume. Changing the location of the other croze permitted the cooper to fine-tune the final capacity. After the second croze was cut, the inside was cleaned by planing (unless strong beer, wine or spirits were to be held; these profited from the char left by firing). The vessel was now ready for installation of the heads.

The heads were made by jointing several oaken planks and assembling them with dowels. No glue or adhesive was used, as none was available that would serve under the wet conditions and not contaminate the product. A strip of rush (called FLAG by the coopers) served to caulk the joints. The heads were given a circular shape, planed, and the edges beveled — a longer bevel on the inside — to fit tightly into the croze. The hoops were slackened, the croze supplied with a strip of flag, and the head installed. The procedure was repeated on the other head. The outside of the cask was planed and scraped smooth and the job was done.

The procedure for slack cooperage was somewhat simpler. Thinner staves were used (under ½ in., 13mm.) that could be bent without firing, but these would be excessively weakened by a deep howel and croze, and different head fastening methods were used, as we will see. Performance requirements for the container varied with the intended use. Barrels for nails, for instance, needed strong but not necessarily tight construction; while gunpowder barrels must not leak. The choice for head mounting could be made among several alternatives. These are shown in Fig.13:2. In contrast to the tight barrel head on the left, a shallow V-shaped notch for the croze, a shoulder cut in the staves with a

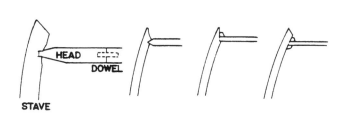

Fig.13:2—Barrel head mounting methods

318

wooden hoop nailed above the head to retain it, or a wooden hoop on either side of the head inside the barrel, were among the methods used.

PLANES OF THE COOPER

STAVE and HEAD JOINTING

The COOPER'S JOINTER (Fig.13:3) is a long, wide jointer without handle, used sole up. It was sold without legs in the United States but was normally fitted with legs by the user; either inserted in the stock or in the form of a trestle. This plane is mounted with the cutting edge on top, and remains stationary as the work is pushed over it (a hazardous operation, as the irons were kept very sharp and would

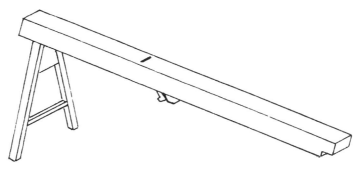

Fig.13:3—Cooper's jointer

plane fingers that strayed too low, as well as the staves). The jointer is mounted at a slant, so that the cooper pushes his piece downward. If the plane is long enough or the workpiece short, the heel of the cooper's jointer rests on the ground against a backstop. A shorter stock or a longer workpiece requires that the heel be raised on a short support to provide more room, while still keeping the sole in a diagonal position. There may be a step cut in the heel for the latter purpose. Shorter jointers (especially as used by other trades) may sometimes be mounted horizontally on legs, or clamped to the edge of a bench.

Made commercially in lengths up to six feet (183 cm.) and four inches (10 cm.) or larger in cross section, even larger ones were made by their users. One found in a New York cooper's shop was nine feet (275 cm.) long and weighed 125 pounds (57 kg.).

The cooper used these for two purposes; to joint the edges of barrel staves, and to joint boards to be joined into barrel heads. Some catalogs list these planes without specifying the use, while others offer COOPER'S HEADING JOINTERS and STAVE JOINTERS. The Chapin 1874 catalog lists both in lengths up to 66 in. (168 cm.) with single or double iron, and either could be had with two throats, fitted with a single and a double iron. Greenfield (1872) offered double iron jointers for head and stave in one stock. Some jointers have four throats in one stock.

The distinction between the two planes is not universally accepted. A stave is jointed before bending, and therefore cannot be planed to a flat edge. The stave must be made wider in the middle than at the ends, to create the bulge of the cask when it is assembled. This is done roughly by axe and drawknife initially, and finished by rocking the stave during jointing. Starting with a level sole on the jointer, this use would soon wear it into a concave (lengthwise) shape. It would then be useless for head jointing, and would be reserved for staves. For this use the concave sole is an advantage. It is possible that the Chapin stave jointers were made with a slightly concave sole (they were slightly more expensive than the head jointers). The head jointer, on the other hand, was believed to be improved by a slight convexity. (A joint in the head pieces which is slightly open in the middle as assembled closes under the pressure of the staves as the barrel is trussed.)

Another distinction was made by Colwell Cooperage (1929). It offered both types of jointers with flat soles, the difference being that the stave jointer had a slightly canted sole (to decrease the angle at which the stave had to be held while planing the angled edge).

Double cooper's jointers are found in different configurations. They may have two throats on the same sole facing away from each other, or two throats on adjacent sides of the square cross-section. Examples of each may be seen at the Farmer's Museum in Cooperstown, New York. One of these shows clearly a convex (lengthwise) sole at one end, concave at the other; providing convincing evidence that this one, at least, served the two purposes of head jointing and stave jointing. The Chapin double jointer mentioned above was equipped with a single and a double iron, suggesting that roughing and finish planing of the same piece was contemplated. The L. & I.J. White Catalog (1909) stated that a pair of cooper's jointers consisted of one with a single iron for heading and another with a double iron as a stave jointer. It is apparent that there was room for differences of opinions among coopers.

Irons for these planes were considerable longer (10-12 in., 25-30 cm.) and wider (3 - 5 in., 8 - 13 cm.) than those of bench planes. As striking the stock is not very effective in removing the iron, some had an extension on one side of the top edge (Spanish sneck) for this purpose.

Shorter jointers (especially those used by other trades) may be clamped to a trestle or bench edge. These may have their heels bored or slotted for clamping bolts, and may be notched at the sole rather than at the top of the stock. A variant seen in England is a two-piece jointer, the pieces joined by a keyed joint which could be taken down for ease of transport (Fig.13:4). A rare form of double-throat jointer cut a V-groove with one throat and a matching V-tongue with the other; this may have been of use in preparing staves for large structures such as water tanks.

Fig.13:4—Two-piece cooper's jointer

Continental   The cooper's jointer shown in the German *Book of Trades* of 1568 is little different from those of the nineteenth century, a stouter stock being the major difference. A description and sketch of a jointer in an Austrian text (Wertheim, 1869) depicts a low pitch angle and states that the iron was mounted with the bevel facing the thrust (as in a metal miter plane). This does not seem to have been general practice, as an Austrian cooper's jointer dated 1823 that sold in a recent English auction had normal bedding. Wertheim gave jointer lengths as 5-8 ft., (150-250 cm.) and shows two legs inserted in the stock and a step in the heel resting in a low jointer prop. Several names are used in German, including Stossbank (push bench), Fugblock, Daubenfüghobel, and Füghobel für Küfer among others.

The French tool is called COLOMBE (pigeon or dove!) and was used in several trades. The cooper's version was specified as COLOMBE DE TON-NELIER, although the coopers themselves used the name JOIGNEUX. This was usually fitted with three inserted legs to mount it at a slant, sole and nose up. If fitted with but two legs, it was nicknamed "escargot" or snail. Féron (ca.1940) sold it equipped with the legs, the rear one sturdily braced. They also listed a similar tool in hornbeam, horizontally mounted, as a COLOMBE D'EMBALLEUR or packer's (boxmaker's) jointer. Lachappelle (1945) listed sizes up to 86 in. (220 cm.) with irons to 7 in. wide (18 cm.). Instead of the Spanish sneck described above, they were also made with the top of the iron bent over to facilitate setting (Fig.13:5).

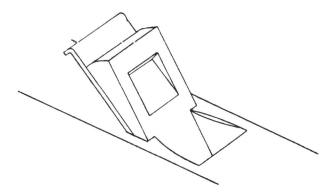

Fig.13:5—Throat detail — French cooper's jointer

Japanese   The Japanese cooper used a jointer in much the same style as in the West, pushing the stave over the Ō-KANNA (big plane, Fig.13:6). The body of the plane is usually a massive slab of keyaki, a wood like red oak but harder, and is usually supported on four legs, sole and toe up. The manner of mounting the iron in the plane, however, was quite different. The iron may be described as like a Western drawknife with the handles cut off, as it is much wider than high and has an ear on either side. It is held by force fit in wedge-shaped slots cut through the sides of the jointer, and adjusted by tapping with a hammer the ears of the blade (which project through the sides of the plane). In contrast to other Japanese workmen, the cooper pushed most of his other planes.

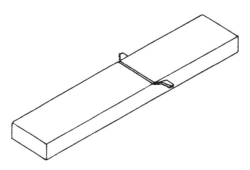

Fig.13:6—Japanese cooper's jointer

FINISHING STAVE ENDS

The LEVELING or TOPPING PLANE, (SUN plane in England), serves to produce a level surface on the stave ends. The common form (Fig.13:7) is essentially a bench plane without handle, with body curved horizontally, to ride on the circular end of the headless barrel. The single iron, 2-2½ in.(51-63 mm.) is usually slightly skewed to cut toward the

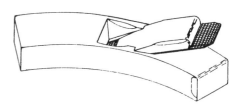

Fig.13:7—Leveling (or sun) plane

chime (the curvature makes the skew appear greater than it actually is). They were made in left- and right-hand styles, to cut in different directions around the rim. Most plane catalogs listed but one size, the one proper for the common barrel, but cooper's supply houses furnished different sizes named for the size cask their curvature matched. Four leveling planes have been found joined together (by some early "efficiency expert", no doubt) to form a complete circle.

322

MOUNTING THE HEAD

A prominent feature of the following planes is the COOPER'S FENCE, the earlier definition of which can now be expanded. As the guiding surface for these planes consists of the stave ends, the fence must be large with respect to the vessel's circumference if stability is to be maintained. It is normally larger than the body of the plane (the word "stock" is avoided here as the cooper's fence was sometimes called the stock). It is a board commonly shaped in a circular arc on the outside, sometimes with extensions to form handgrips. The plane body is attached to the fence, either permanently or with provision for changing the fence-body separation.

The cooper's fence is subject to severe wear. It bears on a narrow surface, often of end-grain oak, and pressure is localized. Most tools, unless reinforced, show severe grooving; this reduces their accuracy. Even fences made of lignum vitae have been seen deeply grooved by wear. It is quite common therefore for these tools to be protected by metal of some sort, from plates crudely screwed on, to metal elaborately inlaid. A device which seems to have caught the American cooper's fancy is to inlay pennies in the wear surface. Often these copper disks, if not too badly worn, may be recognized as the old large Liberty Head copper cents.

An alternate form of the leveling plane, usually used for lighter work, has been called a KEG LEVELING plane (Fig.13:8). It was made by cutting a throat in a stout cooper's fence, inserting peg handles and adding a semicircular piece on the underside to ride on the interior side of the staves. As this piece located the blade on the stave ends, the tool did not need as wide an iron as the leveling plane described

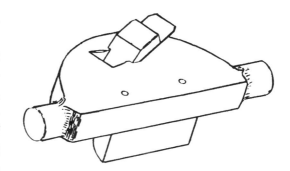

Fig.13:8—Keg leveling plane

above. Keg leveling planes have been seen with rollers to ride inside the barrel as guides, and with adjustable fences to contact the barrel interior on both sides.

The cooper's CHAMFER plane serves to finish the chime, or bevel inside the stave ends of the gun. It is a rare plane, as the chime chamfer was usually cut with an adze and a special drawknife. The tool (Fig.13:9) is usually in the form of a cooper's fence with a bench-type body attached, the sole of which forms about a 45° angle with the fence. The iron and wedge lie horizontally,

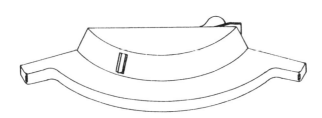

Fig.13:9—Cooper's chamfer plane

Fig.13:10—The groper

perpendicular to the fence, the iron being cut at the 45° angle. In use, the fence is supported on the leveled stave ends (leveled as described above), and the chime is planed as the tool is propelled around the circumference. An alternate form is found in Britain. The GROPER (Fig.13:10) performs the same task but differs in that the throat of the plane penetrates the fence as in the keg leveling plane. Shavings are discharged on top, rather than inside the vessel. A tool like the chamfer plane or groper, the FLINCHER, is used to cut a steeper, hollow chamfer in a cask for dry-tight service, such as herring barrels. In combination with a V-croze (see below), it forms the closure shown in Fig.13:2, second from the left.

The HOWEL (Fig.13:11) was given the same name as the surface it cut. Around 1800 the English changed the name to CHIV, but the former name remained in use in America. The usual form has a body with the sole cut at an angle, both compassed and rounded and attached to a large cooper's fence of semicircular shape. The size of the howel is quoted as the size of the cask on which it is to be used; in the United States some eleven sizes, from three-gallon to hogshead, were available. Aside from having the fence match the rim curvature, having the sole curvature match that of the desired howel surface helps achieve the accurate circular form necessary for a tight seal with the heads. The fence may have a handgrip applied for use by the left hand, while the right grips the body or an applied handgrip on the body.

The body of the plane is

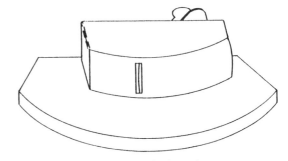

Fig.13:11—The howel

usually attached to the fence with bolts or, in early examples, wooden screwarms. (An adjustable howel was patented by Mathew Moriarty, Bangor, Maine, 16 July 1872, U.S. 129,419). This allowed the spacing between the end of the cask and its groove to be changed, in the former case by placing shims between body and fence. The usual tight-barrel or stock howel has a single iron 2 - 3 in. (51 - 76 mm.) wide. A BEER HOWEL has a larger iron and greater spacing between blade and fence (the internal pressure created by the beer required stronger support for the heads, so the distance between stave end and the bottom of the croze groove could not be too short). Eight sizes were commonly listed, between five gallon and hogshead. Some howels were equipped with a galley handle (Chapter2, Fig.2:9) on the side of the body opposite the fence.

While most howel irons were slightly curved across their width, the GOUGE HOWEL had a sharply curved iron (Fig.13:12) usually under 1.5 in. (38 mm.) wide. This tool was made in sizes from five gallon to barrel, and found use in dry cooperage or in making oil barrels. In England, several variants of the chiv are found. One form simply cuts a smooth round surface on the inside of the vessel at the stave end, and serves to prepare it for insertion of two wooden hoops nailed inside it, one on either side of the head (Fig.13:2 right). The SLOPER

Fig.13:12—Gouge howel iron

(Fig.13:13) has a side escapement with blade exposed at the side opposite the fence. It cuts the chime and leaves a shoulder to support the head, as in Fig. 13:2, third from left..

Fig.13:13—The sloper

Continental   The French name for howel is CHANFRENIÈRE, although the most common type has received the unlikely name of STOCKHOLM (Fig.13:14). This has a shorter fence than English types, covering less than a quarter of the rim, and shaped like a gendarme's hat, with about a quarter of the outer circle extended outward as a handhold. The right handle in the example sketched is a peg inserted in the side of the body opposite the fence. The fence is normally fixed.

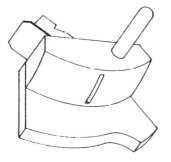

The howel seems to have been less popular in Germany. I have found but one reference to the name for this tool, FROSCHKRANZHOBEL. Nooitgedagt (The Netherlands, ca.1891) lists a TONNENSCHAAF and an OMSNIJSHAAF (gouge howel) with fences similar to that of Fig.13:10.

Fig.13:14—French stockholm

The CROZE can take a number of forms, all designed to cut a uniform groove within the cask. This must fit the bevel of the head tightly enough to form a leak-proof joint, in wet cooperage. The plane was undoubtedly known to the Romans, as some remnants of their casks survive with the croze groove cut. The simplest form of this tool is a compassed fixed plow, but this was used only for light duty vessels. More usually, the croze has a large cooper's fence as a major part. This rides on the leveled ends of the staves, and is equipped with an applied handgrip or is shaped to form one. There are various means of supporting the cutter below the fence, most of which provide some form of handhold within the vessel, while the fence provides a grip for the other hand.

The POST CROZE (Fig.13:15) is designed like an oversize carpenter's marking gauge. A stout fence is mortised to receive a sliding post, fixed by a wedge. The cutter or cutters are mounted in the post, often also held by a wedge. The simplest cutting device consists of large saw teeth with an exaggerated set, to cut a kerf of the desired width. An improvement adds a router blade after the saw teeth, to clean the bottom of the groove. The "hawk-bill" or "lance" post croze uses two nickers and a curved router blade (Fig.13:16). The V-CROZE uses a cutter bent into a V shape, and sharpened to cut a triangular groove (Fig.13:17). The

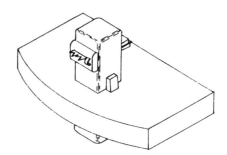

Fig.13:15—Post croze

V-croze is only applicable to dry cooperage. In any case, the cutting device is mounted with provision for a depth stop. A common way to provide this is to enclose the cutter in a box or housing which limits the cut (as shown in Fig.13:18), or includes a moveable member to serve as stop. The TWO-POST croze mounts the box between two sliding posts.

Another form of croze (Fig.13:19), more common in America, has a body shaped as a compassed plow attached to the fence, either rigidly or with provision for slight shifting by shimming. A variety of cutter mountings are used, including box types as above and conventional plane wedge-fixing. The tool fitted with the V-cutter shown in Fig. 13:17, also called a V-CROZE, was sold in sizes up to barrel, for dry cooperage. The LANCE croze, also listed as a TIGHT-BARREL croze uses a hawk-bill cutter like the one shown in Fig.13:16, and was offered in sizes from three gallon to hogshead. A more substantial tool with larger separation between cutter and fence and thicker, plow-type cutters was sold as a BEER CROZE in sizes from five gallon (with $\frac{3}{8}$ in., 10 mm. cutter) to barrel (with $\frac{11}{16}$ in., 17 mm. cutter). The BEER POST CROZE has a similar body mounted on a stout post, as in the post croze; it was available in 1/8 barrel to hogshead sizes. A TANK or HOGSHEAD CROZE, with a massive plane body hung below the semicircular fence by means of three screw arms, has plow type irons and independent nickers that could cut grooves up to 1¾ in. (44 mm.) wide.

A large number of U.S. patents claimed improvements in the croze, mostly concerned with cutter shapes and mountings. Many of these involve metal bodies or cutter mountings and are beyond the scope of this work. An attempt was made to make one croze serve any cask by adjustable arms to vary curvature. This was listed by Sandusky (1877) as Seigfreid's patent croze. One made of glass was patented (John W. Young, 30 April 1874, U.S. 151,188) in an attempt to combat the heavy wear. An unusual post croze had a D handle and a narrow fence which reached across to the other side of the barrel, a type covered in the Continental section below. Another has been

Fig.13:16—Lance croze blade and two nickers

Fig.13:17—Cutter for V-croze

Fig.13:18—Enclosed croze cutter

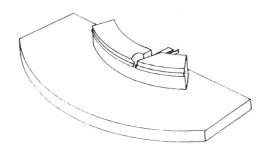

Fig.13:19—Croze, plane type

found with cutters mounted on both ends of the post.

A planemaker or cooper in the Massachusetts area must have been fascinated with combination tools. A number of such have been found, without maker's identification. Three such examples are combined Howel and Croze, Leveling plane and Howel, and Leveling plane and Croze. Combinations from other areas also have been seen.

Continental   The French call the groove the jable, and the plane the JABLOIR. The common form is the JABLOIR MÂCONNAIS that resembles the English post croze except for a shorter fence riding on a much shorter section of stave ends. The outer edge of the fence is shaped to form a handgrip, and the lower part of the post is lathe-turned to serve the right hand. The example shown in Fig.13:20 has a metal wear plate protecting the fence. The cutter may consist of two blades — sawteeth and raker — held in a mortise in the post with a wooden wedge between them. Variants are seen in which

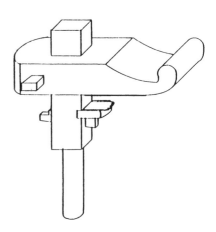

Fig.13:20—French post croze

the post is secured by a thumbscrew tightening a cleft in the fence, rather than by a wedge. Another version, for light work, is the VERDONDAINE or RUELLE (Fig.13:21). This has a long, narrow fence terminated at both ends in handholds, the overall shape a gentle ogee. The JABLOIR À JOUE MOBILE or BOUVET-JABLOIR copies the French grooving plow, and has a circular sole, plow iron and two independent nickers. The wooden keel, three-arm version shown in Fig.13:22 has a semi-circular projection on the outside of the fence for grip or decoration. The German KIMM, or GARGELHOBEL, is often of this form, with three-arm suspension. Some early examples are elaborately carved. Lachappelle (France, 1945) listed as the Frankfurt model

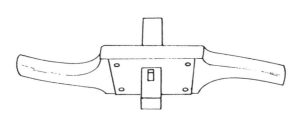

Fig.13:21—French croze for light work

a croze in which a plane-type body was hung below a staff, rather than a coo-per's fence. The staff has a saw-type grip on one end, while the other reached the other side of the barrel (Fig.13:23).

328

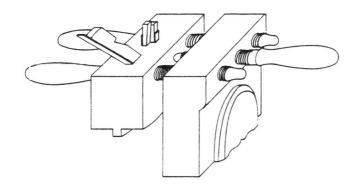

Fig.13:22—Continental three-arm croze

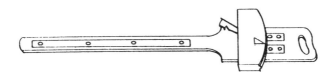

Fig.13:23—"Frankfurt" croze

FORMING THE HEAD

While expert coopers shaped the heads with axe and drawknives, a number of tools were developed which were faster and required less skill. The HEAD CUTTER is not strictly a plane, but a grooving cutter mounted on a bar with a center point adjustable for cutting circles of different diameters. This developed into a tool which simultaneously cut out the disc and, with another blade,

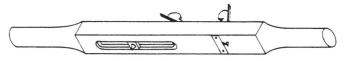

Fig.13:24—Head cutter

cut the chamfer on one side of the head (Fig.13:24). It was suitable only for dry cooperage. A tool which has been called a FEATHER plane mounts a curved knife on a plane stock, and may have been used for chamfering light barrelheads.

Continental   There were a number of tools used in forming the head that are rarely seen in this country except for imports. In addition to the usual cooper's planes, one called a BODENHOBEL in German was used to round the heads. This has a sole concave lengthwise, to match the barrelhead curvature. Lachappelle (France, 1945) shows planes of this name with the curvature not extending the full length of the sole, having flat sections fore and aft. Both simple and steel-plated soles were listed.

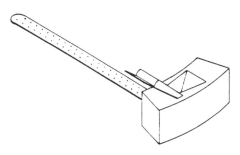

Fig.13:25—Head edge cutter

Another unfamiliar tool was listed as a head edge cutter or BODENBRAMSCHNITTHOBEL in a Weiss und Sohn catalog (Vienna, 1870), and as an EINSCHNEID-HOBEL or RABOT POUR ENTAILLER LES FONDS by Lachappelle (1945). It has a plane body like a short leveling or sun plane fitted with a metal trammel arm (Fig.13:25). The arm is perforated with multiple holes and pivots around a peg in the barrelhead. It is indexed by Greber (1956) without illustration or description, but as he coupled it with the panel raising plane, it would appear that he considered it as a tool to cut the chamfer on the barrelhead. Similar tools served other purposes, one of which is seen below (wreath plane). A sturdier version of Fig.13:24 , fitted with a plane blade, was shown by Kilby (1971) as a RABOT À CHANFREIN (chamfer plane).

Another plane to cut the bevels on the heads consists of a plane stock shaped like a shallow ship round mounted with the sole facing a flat fence (Fig.13:26). The only description of this located to date is of a specimen in the Musée du Bois in Lausanne, Switzerland. They call it a RABOT POUR FONDS DE SEILLES, literally translated as pail-bottom plane. This one had the fence adjustable on three wooden screw arms. A similar tool dated 1847 was made in Germany. There is an example made by John Veit (Pennsylvania, 1857-99), and one with a fixed fence has also been seen. A tool apparently for the same purpose is seen in the Lachappelle catalog (France, 1945) listed with the same two names given for the trammel plane above with the further note "for heads of any size". This is similar

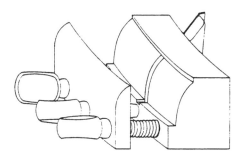

Fig.13:26—"Pail bottom" plane

330

except for mounting the moving fence on a single stave. Both forms would be rather cumbersome for common barrel sizes, and the curvature of the integral fence in the first type indicates that it accomodated heads up to 48 in. (122 cm.) in diameter. A reasonable conclusion is that these tools were intended for beveling the heads of very large vessels, perhaps farm-yard watering troughs or similar tanks.

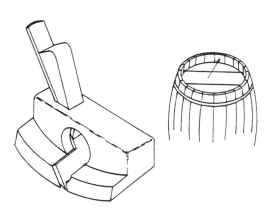

Another plane unknown in the United States is called the COLUM-BELLE in French or BACKEN-HOBEL in German (Fig.13:27). It is a compassed plane with slanted sole, the cutter exposed on one side. It is described as being used for finish planing the inner sides of the staves where they are exposed outside of the head, as indicated by the arrow in Fig.13:27 right..

Fig.13:27—Left: the columbelle
Right: the barrel surface it finishes

An Austrian custom not seen in England or America is the decoration of the ends of the larger casks (Burchard 1984, Townsend 1991). The heads were molded with a KRANZHOBEL (Fig.13:28). As shown in the 1870 Weiss (Austria) catalog and also in Wertheim (Austria, 1869), this is a radius plane with a profiled iron and sole section, fitted with a trammel. Pivoting about a pin placed at the center of the head, it cut a circular molding (perhaps a cupid's bow, or symmetrical double ogee) in the cask head. The literal translation of Kranzhobel is WREATH PLANE, but Kranz is also used in Germany to refer to a circular rim. The FROSCHBRAMSCHNITT (Fig.13:29) also shown in Wertheim, was used to add a molding to the inside of the staves where they projected

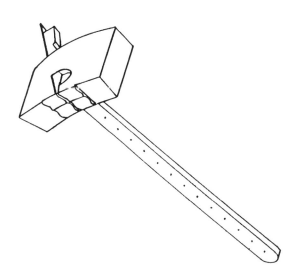

Fig.13:28—Austrian wreath plane

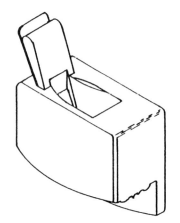

Fig.13:29—German chime molder

beyond the head (again, as indicated in Fig.13:27 right). Its compass sole matched the curvature of this surface. It was fitted with a profiled blade and a fence which rode on the stave ends.

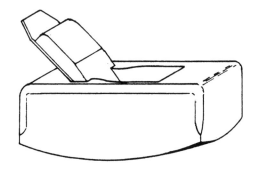

Fig.13:30—Stoup

COOPER'S SMOOTH PLANES

The cooper used several forms of smooth planes for finishing surfaces in quality work. Mathieson (Scotland, 1899) listed as COOPER'S SMOOTH planes tools much like conventional coffin smooth or compass planes (the latter called a BOWLING plane). The same tool with the sole both round and compassed, or round-both-ways, was called a STOUP (Fig.13:30). (The name derives from an old Scottish term for a pail or bucket, later applied to a drinking vessel.) This was used to remove char from, and smooth, the interior of casks. The inside shave, described in the next section, was also referred to as a stoup plane. In some countries, a plane of this type found another use in finishing the chime.

The Brombacher cooper's catalog (1922) listed a COOPER'S ROUNDING plane, a smooth plane with sole concave lengthwise. Similar tools with applied side handles are treated in the next section.

COOPER'S SHAVES

Aside from the cooper's jointers, his stoup and bowling planes, and the other tools described above, most of the cooper's planes are shaped as SHAVES. Unlike spokeshaves, these have bench type bodies with irons held by wedges in abutments; but unlike bench planes, the soles are short, the bodies wide and shaped into handholds on either side of the throat. As this configuration means that the grain of the body runs across, rather than along the throat, the wedge tends to split the stock. The top of the throat is usually reinforced with brass plates to protect against this. Shaves are also made with the grain in the normal direction, with side handles applied to give a similar shape. The Scots name for these shaves, PLUCKER, is limited in the U.S. to one form (Fig.13:32).

The HEADING SWIFT, or HEAD FLOAT in the United States, is a large shave with an iron 2.5 - 5 in. (63 - 127 mm.) across, usually having a slightly rounded edge (Fig.13:31). The handles are usually upturned for better hand clearance. The heads, after being given their circular form, are planed with this tool. The cooper prefers not to work on a bench, and supports the head on a HEADING BOARD. This is a wide plank

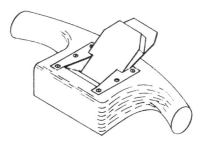

Fig.13:31—Heading swift
or head float

having a wooden ledge across it, or an iron strap forming a pocket into which the head fits. It is used with one end resting on the ground and the other against the cooper's waist. The swift is pushed, planing cross-grain for speed.

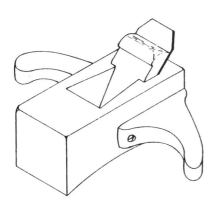

Fig.13:32—Downright,
"Plucker" type

For finer work, it is finished along the grain on the outer surface — although this is awkward to do on the heading board.

The DOWNRIGHT (Fig.13:32) is a similar, slightly smaller shave with a straight-edged iron about 2 in. (51 mm.) across. Used for planing the cask exterior, its sole may be flat or concave lengthwise. In mechanized cooperage, the cask is spun on a lathe for this operation, and a downright with an iron loop at its toe would have been hung from a chain above the lathe. In quality work, the downright would be followed by a scraper plane, the BUZZ (Fig.13:33). Its shave-shaped body holds a 3 - 5 in. (76 - 127 mm.) scraper blade in an upright position, with the edge of the blade turned as in a hand scraper. For inside work, the edge and sole are convex.

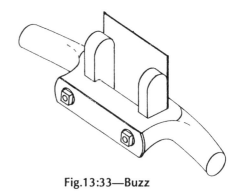

Fig.13:33—Buzz

The INSIDE SHAVE (Fig.13:34) is smaller still, with sole rounded across and shorter handles upswept for clearance. New barrels for non-alcoholic use, and older barrels to be reclaimed, have the interior planed with this tool or the previously described STOUP. This is knuckle-barking work, and some coopers prefer using drawknife type tools instead. A form used in Italy is the BODDA (Fig.13:35), a curved blade fixed to a wooden stock which is held in the hand with the help of a leather strap.

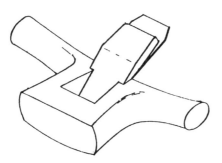

Fig.13:34—Inside shave

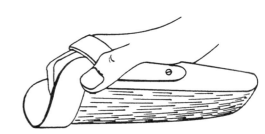

Fig. 13:35—Bodda

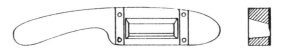

Fig.13:36—Hoop shave

Very old tight barrels and old slack barrels were sometimes hooped with wood rather than iron. The hoops, usually of willow or hazel, were dressed with a HOOP SHAVE (Fig.13:36). This is somewhat like a one-handled spokeshave. The German BANDHOBEL of the eighteenth century is found in carved and decorated form. The body is pierced by an elongated slot, the cutter mounted horizontally with edge at one side of the slot and a metal plate attached to the other side as a mouth. Shavings escape through the slot. One handle sufficed, as the hoop was held in one hand and the tool in the other. The hoop shave appears to be a predecessor of the spokeshave. The HOOP SIZER, another rare tool, served to create a uniform section for the hoop and is found in several forms. The principal is that of the basketmaker's shave (seen in Fig.13:102 in the section on the Basketmaker).

THE SASHMAKER

The wooden frame that supports the glass panes forming a window is the SASH. The sash may be fixed, hinged, pivoted, or sliding, but most have certain structural details in common. The outer frame is made up of two vertical members, the STILES, and two horizontal, the RAILS. In earlier centuries (and sometimes even today), the area framed by these outer members was divided into smaller rectangles, each filled with a pane of glass. The narrow bars that spanned the frame to form these divisions are the SASH BARS. Because these interfere with the main purpose of the window (admitting light), they are made as narrow as possible consistent with having adequate strength.

These members are seen in Fig.13:37, an outside view of a sash. The detail shows a cross-section of one of the sash bars, rabbeted to provide support for the window panes. The glass is held in these rabbets by a few metal glazier's points and a barrier of putty.

The section shows no decorative molding on the inner side of the sash, the one facing into the room. This would not be true except in the most spartan cases, such as a greenhouse or a garden shed. The making of this type of sash poses few problems, and needs only standard joinery techniques and no special planes. It is the molding that adds complications. These can be overcome by use of standard molding planes, but only by slow and tedious work. Avoiding this has been the inspiration for invention of a variety of specialized SASH MOLDING planes.

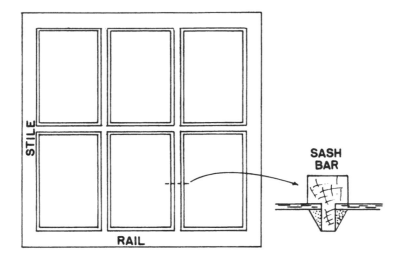

Fig.13:37—The sash

The making of such molded sash was best accomplished in a workshop, rather than at the job site. The men who acquired the skills and the special tools required, and set up such shops, were soon set apart from the ordinary house carpenter and classed with the joiners. Sashmaking was probably one of the earliest areas of specialization for woodworkers.

SASH MOLDING

Some of the variations in sash molding planes are difficult to understand without an explanation of how they were used. For this we are indebted to W.L. Goodman (1983).

The sash bars of early windows were substantial members 2 inches (51 mm.) or more in width. (Let's call the side of the bar seen by looking at it from inside the room the "face", and the distance across the face the "width".) This size had remained unchanged from a time when windows were unglazed and the bars served only to keep out intruders. Although gradually reduced in size, they were still about 1.5 in. (38 mm.) wide at the end of the 17th century.

The first operation in making a sash bar of this period was to cut the putty rabbets (into which the glass was to be inserted), one on either side of the bar. This was probably done with a standing filletster, although a glass check plane (Chapter 7, Fig.7:38) may have been used. This forms the section of Fig.13:38A. The bar was then turned over for molding the opposite corners. The sash specialists, who appeared in the first quarter of the eighteenth century, used a fixture to hold the strips — a "sticking board" — for the molding operations. This is a board with a groove just wide enough to accept the strip between the glass rabbets. The bars, having all been rabbeted, could be inserted into this as shown in Fig.13:38B, for molding one after another with no lost motion for clamping. The molding plane then cut down from the face of the bar, using one side as a guide (Fig.13:38C) then the other (Fig.13:38D).

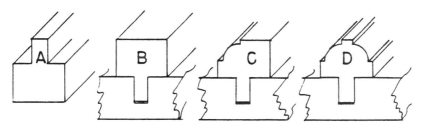

Fig.13:38—Sash bar

The most often used molding profile for the early sash bars was a recessed quarter round, called "square ovolo" in England. Fig.13:39 shows the profile of a pre-1700 English plane made to cut this (without spring). By the second quarter of the 18th century the bar width had been reduced to ¾ in. (19 mm.) or less. There was no longer room for the square ovolo and new profiles were introduced. Simply thinning the profile to an elliptical ovolo as cut by the plane of Fig.13:40 was the obvious answer, but this lost favor in England to the "astragal and hollow", an astragal on the face with a cove on either side as cut by Fig.13:41.

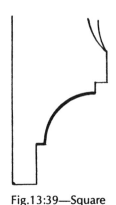

Fig.13:39—Square ovolo sash plane

Fig.13:40— Elliptical ovolo (old style sash plane)

The stiles and rails of the sash were, of course, rabbeted and molded in the same pattern as the sash bars, but only on the one, inner, edge. Sash bars having a flat at the peak of the profile, as in the square ovolo of Fig.13:38D, matched the profile cut on the stiles and rails. As shown in Fig.13:42 left, a coped or miter joint where they joined posed no problem. With the astragal and hollow, or other sash bars without such a flat, this was no longer true. The stiles and rails of the window retained a flat (Fig.13:43), but the sash bars did not (Fig.13:44). (For reasons discussed in Chapter 9 under the quarter round and ogee, the depth stop was set to cut a small step at the top of the profile, as seen in Fig.13:41.) The profile on the bars could no longer reach the forward edge of the frame if a proper joint was to be made (Fig.13:42 right, the point indicated by the arrow). They had to be recessed by the height of the step. (We'll get into how the joint was made

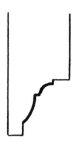

Fig.13:41— Astragal and hollow sash plane (old style)

later.) The cut on the first side of the sash bar, if made with the plane of Fig.13:41, was stopped by the depth stop at the proper depth to ensure a good miter or scribed joint. But in cutting the other side, there was no flat left and the sash bar

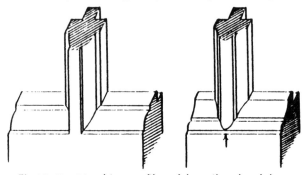

Fig.13:42—Matching profiles of the rail and sash bar

Fig.13:43—Astragal
and hollow rail

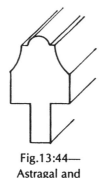

Fig.13:44—
Astragal and
hollow sash bar

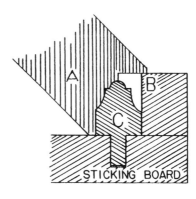

Fig.13:45—Cutting the astragal
and hollow sash bar

no longer had a surface to contact the depth stop. A new device was required.

A "belt and suspenders" method was common. The integral fence of the sash plane (Fig.13:45A) was lengthened so that it bottomed on the sticking board, and the depth stop was extended to reach over to a fence added to the sticking board at the proper height to catch it (Fig.13:45B). The double bottoming assured that the final cut on the sash bar (Fig.13:45C) would be made at the proper spring angle, another requirement for a good miter joint. Higher than usual spring angles were used in the sash molding planes, up to 45° by the London makers and about 30° in the north of England and Scotland; so that the added guidance was useful.

Sash planes of this type were made into the first quarter of the 19th century, one made by John Blizard (England, -1805-26) being one of the latest. Where size-marked on the heel, the size usually refers to the thickness of bar stock to be worked rather than the size of the cut.

As the sash bar thinned, the old method called for sticking "on" less then "down". The cut to be made was deeper than wide, which is not the quickest way to remove wood. It made sense to turn the sash bar on its side, use the face as guide and cut into the side. To cut the astragal and hollow sash bar, the cove and ovolo had to exchange places in the new style plane as seen in Fig.13:46. But now a new problem arose. The flat on top of the molding now served as guide for the plane fence, instead of hitting the depth stop. In profiles without such a flat, this was fine for the frame or for the first cut on the sash bar. In cutting the second side of the bar, however, the last stroke of the cut removed the guiding surface, and a dig-in could be expected.

Fig.13:46

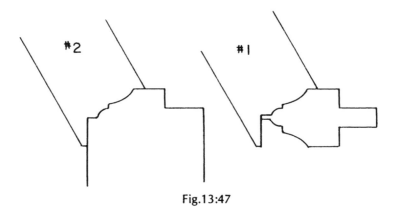

Fig.13:47

This was avoided by making a second plane of the same profile, but which cut just a bit less deeply on the astragal; it stopped short of cutting away the guide. The final cut on the bar left a feather of perhaps $\frac{1}{16}$ in. (1.6 mm.) as shown at Fig.13:47 right. This was enough to guide, but was easily removed by chisel or otherwise. (A plane has been found in a sashmaker's kit that might have been intended for this use; Arnold. & Walker catalog #6, lot 70.) The plane used to cut stiles and rails, since it cut only one side, was unchanged. It was marked #2 (Fig.13:47) and the modified plane #1, and they were sold as a pair. The marking was necessary, as the profile difference is too small to be easily picked up by eye.

While this explanation is convincing for planes without the flat face, the existence of pairs marked 1 and 2 in ovolo, or other profiles which do have the flat, remains a puzzle. W.L. Goodman (1983) reports cutting miles of ovolo molding as an apprentice in a shop which had but one plane per size. Yet such planes were made in pairs in England into the 20th century. The profiles of the #1 and #2 of such pairs are not discernibly different. It is difficult to accept that this was a blind carry-over from the more popular profiles. It seems more reasonable to believe that a second advantage was found (rough and finish cutting?) in the use of the pair of planes that led to their adaption in the other profiles.

A third method of cutting sash moldings was to mold both sides at once, cutting down from the face (much as a nosing plane works). Planes for doing this are very rare, implying that the method was not popular. A single-iron plane of this type would not be suitable for most sash profiles because of the steep edge sections (see Appendix 1). A two-iron plane to cut the gothic profile (Fig.13:48), and a three-iron to cut the astragal and hollow sash bar

Fig.13:48—Gothic profile

340

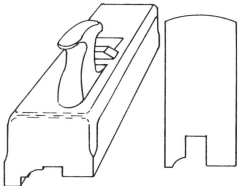

Fig.13:49—American sash plane

Fig.13:50

(Fig.13:44) have surfaced.

All of these methods were abandoned early in America in favor of another, called STICK-AND-RABBET in England but, being the only form used, called just a SASH plane in America. This form was probably developed toward the end of the 18th century. It was advertised as made by Thomas Turner in 1843 and by other English makers since, but was never popular there. One dated 1799 is in the Dominy collection at Winterthur, and others of 18th century New England appearance such as shown in Fig.13:49, are known. These are of the simple form, with a single iron (Fig.13:49 right) cutting both putty rabbet and ovolo profile (Fig.13:50). Such planes were advertised for sale by J.J. Bowles (Connecticut, -1838-43) and by most American makers since.

The TWO-IRON SASH plane uses one iron to cut the rabbet and the other, the molding profile. Sharpening is much easier, and the two irons may be skewed in opposite directions for better shaving clearance. Larger size profiles may be cut with a bench type plane, having two irons held by a single wedge. These are much less common. American catalogs commonly listed ogee, ovolo, gothic and bevel sash profiles (see Fig.13:59 later in this chapter) without choice of size, the sash bar being assumed to be 1.5 in. (38 mm.) wide in the dimension perpendicular to the glass. Other sizes are found, however.

An occasional sash plane will be found with a thin piece of metal screwed to its side, with four sharp points on one end, two on the other (Fig.13:51). Carl Bopp (1978) clarified its use. Laying out a sash calls for precision measurement. With the glass pane size fixed, sizing the sash bars and locating them in the frame left little room for error; and these prickers helped. The four-point side matches the width of the sash bar, with the two central points marking the width of the tongue separating the putty grooves. The pair of points on the other end marks the distance from the side of the bar to the edge of the flat on the

Fig.13:51—
Sash
pricker

341

face. H. Chapin's 1853 catalog (Connecticut) lists gauges and prickers as extras for his sash planes, presumably for the same purpose. Separated from their planes, they would probably not be recognized. We may thank Israel White (Pennsylvania, 1833-39) and the other makers who screwed the gauge to the side of their sash planes, for those that survive.

The ADJUSTABLE SASH plane is made in two pieces, a filletster stock and a molding stock joined by some means of holding a fixed

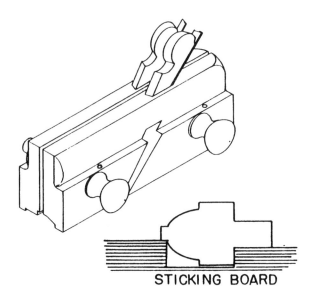

STICKING BOARD

Fig.13:52—Adjustable sash and its sticking board

spacing between them. The object, of course, is to permit cutting bars of different depth for different size windows, the added length being in the flat side of the bar on the room side of the glass. All of the sash planes were also offered in handled versions, but these are much less common. Several forms of boxing were other options.

The simplest adjustment method is simply boring two holes in each stock and joining them by wooden screws and threaded knobs (Fig.13:52). A shim would be placed between the stocks to establish the spacing. In order to keep the two pieces in alignment, two dowels were fixed in one stock and mating holes were drilled in the other to accept them. In the SELF-REGULATING version, the threaded arms were trapped in one stock and passed through threaded holes in the other. This purportedly eliminated the need for the shim. Thin wooden lock-nuts served to tighten the screws once they were set. Other options replaced the wooden screws with steel or brass thumbscrews, or with metal screws trapped in brass pads and turned by a screwdriver.

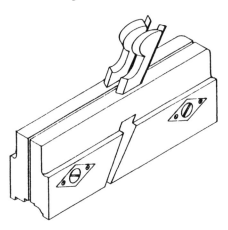

Fig.13:53—Diamond pad self-regulating adjustable sash

342

The latter form with diamond-shaped brass pads was listed as DIAMOND PAD (Fig.13:53), also called self-regulating. More ornately formed brass pads are also seen.

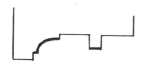

Fig. 13:54—Sash plane for meeting rail

In use, one side of the sash bar would be cut, then it was turned over and inserted into a sticking board. This (somewhat different from the one used with the early English planes) had a groove just large enough to accept the thick section and leave the thin strip between the putty rabbets supported for the second cut (Fig.13:52, lower). A new sticking board was cut whenever the sash plane width was changed.

Another adjustment is possible, to change the thickness of the outside face of the sash bar; that is, the thickness of the strip between the putty rabbets. I have seen this version just once, in a handled adjustable sash plane by T.J. McMaster (New York, 1825-38). Not only is the spacing between the stock cutting the ovolo and the filletster stock adjustable, but the filletster stock may be adjusted vertically as well. This permits selecting the tongue thickness, and thus provides a bit more freedom in sash layout.

An unusual version of the stick-and-rabbet plane was made by A. Kelly & Co. (Massachusetts) around 1850 and is shown in Fig.13:54. The meeting rails of double-hung sash (where upper and lower sash meet) are kept as thin as possible, for the same reason that sash bars are. This plane cuts a groove for the glass (Fig.13:55), rather than weakening the rail by rabbeting.

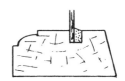

Fig.13:55—Meeting rail sash profile

Continental   Continental versions are similar to the American. Their names are Kittfalzhobel or Fensterhobel (putty-rabbet or window-plane) in German, rabot à fenêtres in French. Both simple and stick-and-rabbet forms were made. A third form was available in The Netherlands. There a sash molding plane and a standing filletster were combined in one stock, in the fashion of the come-and-go match combination. The two cuts had to be made separately.

COPING

Common practice was not to miter the molded joints between stile and rail, but to cope (scribe) them. Cross-grain shrinkage of the wooden frame members causes a gap to appear in a mitered joint, and this is less of a problem if it is coped. With the larger profiles, a SASH COPING plane was used. This has a sole in the shape of the sash molding (the actual shape, not the complementary shape of the sash molding plane). It cuts away a negative profile in the end of the rail (indicated by the arrow), which fits snugly over the stile molding as shown in Fig.13:56. To avoid the tear-out common in cross-grain cuts and for efficiency of operation, the cut was made in a number

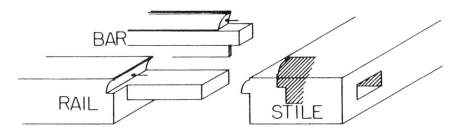

Fig.13:56—Sash components

of pieces at once, after tenoning and before molding. Alternatively, a single rail was coped by using a SIDE TEMPLATE. This is a block of wood shaped to fit over the molding, and with its end cut in the same profile as to be cut by the coping plane. Another template of use to the window maker is the SADDLE TEMPLATE, a grooved block of wood shaped to fit over the molded face of a sash bar and having the coped profile on its ends, so that it served to back up the cut. An alternate form serves to guide the miter cut, for mitered joinings. A saddle template may be shaped for coping at one end and mitering at the other (Fig.13:57).

Fig.13:57—Saddle template

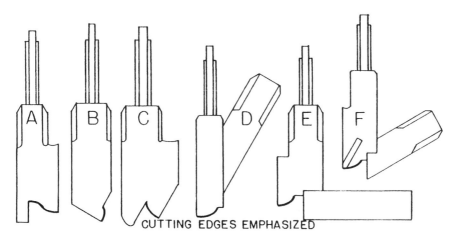

CUTTING EDGES EMPHASIZED

Fig.13:58—Sash coping planes

As the simple sash coping plane (Fig.13:58 A) was used with the side of its stock lying on the sash bar tenon, it was rather awkward to handle. One way to improve this is to mount the blade upright and skewed, so that it was side-cutting as in a side rabbet (13:58 B). This was not too popular, to judge by the rarity of such planes. An improvement was to use spring, raising the stock by 20-30° (13:58 C). More often, a second stock was attached to the coping plane to serve as handhold. This could be at right angles to the working stock (as at 13:58 E) or occasionally at a lesser angle, (13:58 D or F). This type was listed as a DOUBLE SASH COPING PLANE. Each of these sash coping shapes may be found with any of the sash molding profiles of Fig.13:59. An elaborate coping plane was made by Panton (Scotland, 1882-1908), in the general shape of a flooring raglet plane. An unusual combination sash and sash coping plane was reported having the coping function as a detachable stock. This is equipped with steel screwheads, which are slipped into keyhole slots in brass plates mounted on the main stock, to effect attachment.

The sash coping plane fell out of favor toward the end of the 19th century, although it continued to be shown in catalogs until about 1910. The function was taken over by scribing gouges, used with sash templates. Thus, it is not as often found as the common sash planes.

The rare SASH TEMPLATE plane is used to make the sash templates described above. The sole has the profile of the full sash molding, and might be mistaken for a mother plane; but sash planes that cut both sides simultaneously are rare and a mother plane for them would be rare indeed. Further, the plane has a fixed fence whose spacing gives further evidence that

Fig.13:59—Some profiles used for sash bars

it is not a mother plane. A pair has been seen in two forms, one with fence on the left and pitch about 50°, another with fence on the right and the iron at very high pitch. It is supposed they made rough and finish cuts.

Some molding profiles commonly used for sash bars are sketched in Fig.13:59. Their names may vary with location, but the following are typical: (1) Square Ovolo; (2) Ovolo; (3) Astragal and Hollow; (4) Astragal and Quirk Hollow; (5) Astragal and Scotia, or Bilection; (6) Lamb's Tongue; (7) Large Bevel; (8) Bevel Square; (9) Rustic, or Bevel with Shoulder; (10) Gothic; (11) Gothic and Fillet, or Gothic Square; (12) Ogee; (13) Astragal and Ogee. Alternate names are often found. Most large makers offered to make specials to order, so that there is no lack of variation. Continental forms were similar, Weiss (Austria, 1909) adding a Hohlkehle (a fillet replaces the astragal in astragal and hollow), a Verkehrtes Karnies (reverse ogee with a flat), and Fase (rustic with another step at the tip).

A plane similar to a sash plane but producing more delicate members, for use in bookcases or other glazed furniture pieces, is called a GLAZING BAR plane.

For cutting moldings on curved windows such as fanlights, pairs of compass sash planes were used (right- and left-handed pairs were necessary to cope with the changing grain direction). Moldings with face flats were preferred for curved windows, as the guidance problem becomes sticky with others. An un-

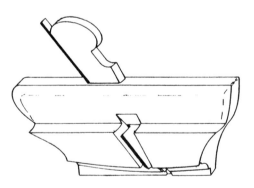

Fig.13:60—Curved sash molding plane

usual pair of sash ovolo planes has been found with sole both compassed and radiused (curved lengthwise and laterally), for an arched top on a bow front. A curved sash molding plane with spring appears similarly curved

346

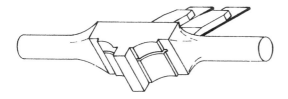

Fig.13:61—Sash molding shave

(Fig.13:60), but is meant for a simply curved profile.

Curved sash moldings were also cut with routers or shaves; in fact, for non-circular curvature this is the method of choice. These may be simple scratch stocks, or more elaborate tools with bench throats mounted in a shave stock. These, too, were in handed pairs, often combined in one tool as in the example sketched in Fig.13:61.

SASH FILLETSTER

In the old method of cutting sash bars, the putty rabbets were made with a filletster before the molding was cut. With the new method (cutting into the side of the bar), it was realized that if the rabbet could be cut on the far side of the bar, it would not be necessary to turn the bar end for end. As one usual practice was to secure the bar for planing by nailing it to the bench (through the tenons), this would be a significant time saver. And so the SASH FILLETSTER was born, probably in the late eighteenth century. It is a filletster fitted with a fence mounted on arms, and designed to cut on the far side. It won immediate popularity, and the number surviving testify that window-making was a significant occupation. A further advantage is gained over the older method, in that both rabbet and molding cuts are guided by the same edge of the bar (the face). Precise sizing of the stock was therefore not quite so critical. (This plane is not needed, of course, when using a stick-and-rabbet sash plane, and therefore American-made examples are uncommon.)

As originally made, the sash filletster was the simplest possible adaptation of the ordinary fence-arm filletster. The depth stop and nicker were moved to the left side of the stock. It retained the skewed iron, usually with left edge leading, and shavings were discharged on the right. The solid left side of the stock had its lower edge rabbeted away to expose the iron. This form is called the "ON THE BENCH" sash filletster (from the direction in which it discharged the shavings) to distinguish it from the later type. At least one maker (Higgs, England, 1780-1817) used a rabbet type throat in this plane. While made by many British makers (indeed, still listed by Mathieson in 1899) it was superseded by another design, and is uncommon. An approximate date for the transition is gained from the fact that Peter Nicholson described only this

347

form in his 1823 work and both it and its successor in 1858.

The rabbet on the left side of the stock of the "on the bench" type tended to conceal the blade edge from the user's view, and it was difficult to observe the cutting action. This was corrected by moving the shavings escapement to the left side of the stock (thus shavings fell "off the bench"), with the right side rabbeted or molded to expose the full width of the iron. This form replaced

Fig.13:62—Kimberly patent sash filletster

the older type almost completely. While it was called the "off the bench sash filletster" for a time after its introduction, this designation is no longer necessary and the name SASH FILLETSTER suffices.

Both forms of sash filletster are equipped with depth stops on the left side of the stock, and usually have nickers on the left side for a cleaner cut. The styles of fence used cover almost the entire range used in plows. Handled versions are rarely seen. Boxing of the inner corner of the stock is common, and double dovetail or full face boxing was used in the better planes. As an example of a sash filletster, one fitted with a Kimberly patent fence is seen in Fig.13:62. COMBINATION FILLETSTERS, combining the function of moving filletster and sash filletster, are also found, and one by Mathieson is seen in Fig.13:63.

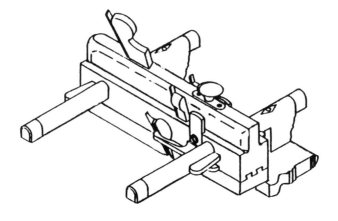

Fig.13:63—Combination filletster

OTHER SASH PLANES

Aside from the above types, other specialized planes were needed to make windows. The MEETING RAIL plane (Fig.13:64) is used to form a profile that

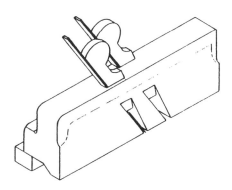

Fig.13:64—Meeting rail plane

makes a weathertight seal between the upper and lower sashes of a double-hung window. The lower rail of the upper sash is cut with a slope which mates with a corresponding slope in the upper rail of the lower sash, as shown in Fig.13:65. This uncommon plane has a stepped sole with a shallow slope between the steps. A fence (integral or filletster type) serves to set the width of the step. It is sometimes fitted with two irons in two throats, and a number of variations in the shape of the mating parts are found; another is seen in Fig.13:66. The tool is known as a COUNTER CHECK plane in England.

The SILL DRIP plane, or THROATING plane in England, is used to cut a groove in the underside of a horizontal member such as a wooden sill. This provides a drip edge and prevents water from creeping back along the under side. These are almost invariably user-made, with the expected wide variations in form. Most are made with open throats. A stock like an old woman's tooth router, with the open throat cut in the sole, is one type (Fig.13:67). Another is an L-shaped stock with the throat in the short leg (Fig. 13:68). Double sill drips, with two irons to cut in either direction, are found. The unusual shapes are solutions, by various individuals, of the problem of cutting a groove on the underside of a mounted sill.

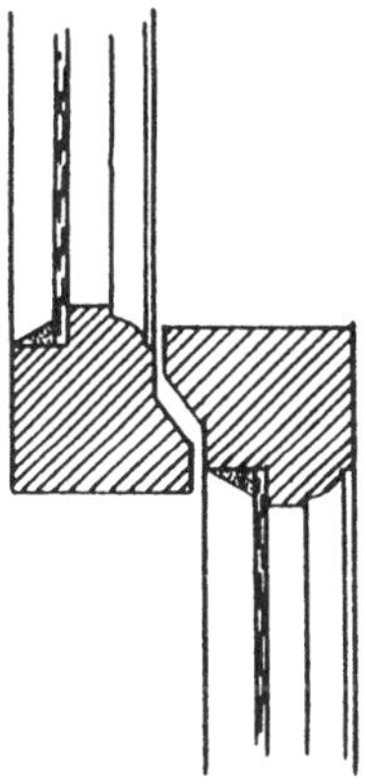

Fig.13:65—Sash meeting rails

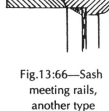

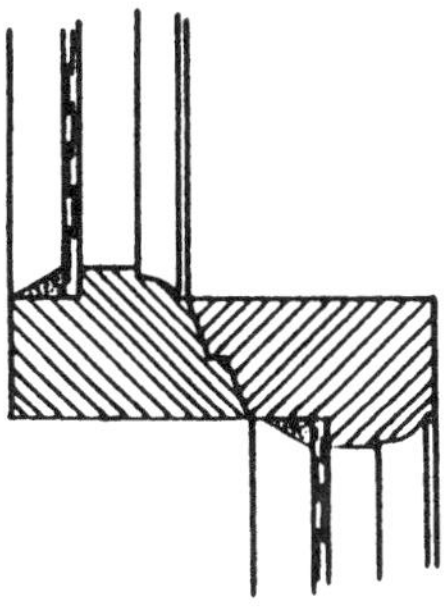

Fig.13:66—Sash meeting rails, another type

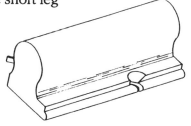

Fig. 13:67—Sill drip plane

PLANES FOR CASEMENT WINDOWS

While double-hung sash predominated in this country in the 19th century, casement windows, usually the inward-opening type, were preferred in France. There are a variety of planes designed for making these which are relatively unknown in the United States. They are reasonably well known in Quebec (Canada), however, where the French preference in sash persisted. The plane-making center of Roxton Pond, near Montreal, provided most of the American examples.

Fig.13:68—Sill drip plane

Double-hung sash have the window stool (commonly called the inside window sill) as a water dam inside the lower sash rail, and water leakage under them is not a problem. Inward-opening casements, however, lack this protection and it is essential that the downwash of rainwater from the outside of the glass be diverted away from the lower rail. The problem was solved by extending the lower sash rail outward, above its seat. It is conventionally profiled in a wide ogee (Fig.13:69) with a plane called an OGEE WATER TABLE plane in Canada (French JET D'EAU or RENVOI D'EAU, waterspout or water return). The underside of the rail is indented with a small groove called a GOUTTE PENDANT (hanging drop) or a quarter-round grooving plane (LARMIER or dripstone, Fig.13:70) which serves the same purpose as the sill drip plane. A later solution was attachment of a similarly shaped drip mold to a lower sash rail of the same thickness as the stiles (Fig.13:71).

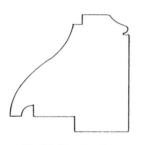

Fig.13:69—Section, lower sash rail, French casement

The SASH MATCH planes are used to form weather-tight seals at the vertical closures of casement windows, and come in several varieties. They have not been found in English or United States catalogs, in spite of the fact that joints of this type were used in America (they are detailed in architectural volumes such as Radford, 1911). The joint shown at A in Fig.13:72 is described in Féron as used for single sash. The lock stile was cut with a semicircular projection, which fitted tightly into a mating hollow in a hinged solid strip. A double sash casement, in the second

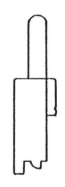

Fig.13:70— French sill drip plane

350

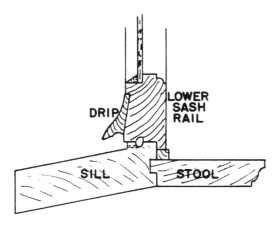

Fig.13:71—Section, casement sash and sill

sketch (13:72B), had the lock stile of one sash rounded in a semicircle. The meeting stile of the mating sash has a matching hollow of the same diameter to receive it. In both types, a force fit is obtained when the casement is closed. As the closure is made in a toggle action, there is a considerable mechanical advantage and little effort is required for the force fit.

As the joint for the double sash uses a male member of di-

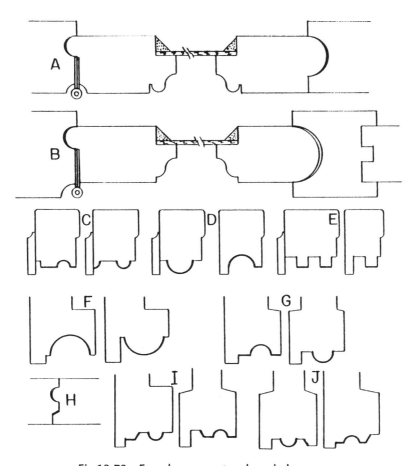

Fig.13:72—French casement seals and planes

351

ameter equal to the stile thickness, the female member must be cut in thicker material to avoid leaving a feather edge. The obvious solution is to cut the hollow groove in a thicker strip, which is then grooved on the opposite side to receive the stile. The pair of planes used for this was mentioned in Chapter 6 with the grooving planes, and is shown at E in the figure.

A similar sealing joint was used at the hinge stiles of the casements. Here, however, a smaller semicircle was used, and it was placed at or near the outer edge of the stile (for inward-swinging casements) to allow maximum room for the hinges. Radford shows a variant which uses a quarter- circle tongue and groove (like the larmier of Fig.13:70). Less careful work might use a simple ungrooved closure, or a joint similar to that cut by the meeting rail plane.

Planes to cut both joints were apparently well known on the Continent, and were offered for sale well into the twentieth century. The first row of plane profiles shown in Fig.13:72 are sketched from figures in the Féron catalog (France, ca.1927). The pair at 13:72C form the hinge stile joint, the pair at 13:72D the lock stile.

The French name for the profile that forms the seal between the edges of the two sashes where they meet, and for the pair of planes that cut it, is "gueule de loup", or wolf's mouth. Both the hollow and round were so called, although the wolf's mouth originally applied to the female member of the joint — the male member was called, picturesquely, the "mouton" or sheep. The second type of joint, at the hinge stile, was called the "noix de croisée" or casement nut, in Féron. The profile of the groove plane of this set (Fig.13:72C, right) shows a second iron for cutting an additional groove in the casing to provide clearance for the hinge (as seen at the left in profile 13:72B). The joint as shown in Radford does not picture this.

The Féron planes are all shown as handled, the plane cutting the female member of the gueule de loup joint having a top escapement for shavings as in a bench plane. Its mate carries two irons in side escapement throats, as in a nosing plane. J.- F. Robert (1985) shows unhandled, unfenced planes for the same purpose. Lachapelle (France, 1925) lists these as for "retouching" the gueule de loup. They also offered a pair in which the round was fitted with an adjustable fence, as in a moving filletster.

The only English language catalogs I have found that offer these planes are from Quebec, Canada, and they list the planes as SASH MATCH. The lock stile joint is made by the "Centre pair" in the Emond (Canada, 1889) catalog, the "Side pair" serving for the joint on the hinge stile. Side pairs (only) were also offered in a double joint model. Both forms were listed in three sizes (1½, 1¾ and 2 in., 38 - 51 mm.), either handled or unhandled. The inch sizes, usually stamped on the heel, give the diameter of the semicircle in the center

352

match pair, and presumably also the thickness of the frame stock. The side match sizes are the distance from fence to edge, again referring to stock thickness. Dalpé (Canada, 1889) offered the same choices except for the two inch sizes.

The profiles of Canadian planes shown in the lower two rows of Fig.13:72 were provided by Bob Westley from his collection, which is now in the Maclachlan Museum (Canada). The pair at F shows a profile slightly different from the French center pair. The single side pair, G, leaves less room for the hinge, suggesting that hinges were to be attached to the face rather than the edge. The DOUBLE JOINT SIDE MATCH pairs shown at I and J are two forms, each with a semicircle and a bevel but differing in the location of these with respect to the fence. (One possibility is that they were for inward- and outward-swinging casements.) The joint they make is seen at H.

THE COACHMAKER

The grace of the horse-drawn carriage tends to make us forget that it needed to be strongly built to endure the punishment from the roads of its day. The design and workmanship had to be of a high order to combine beauty and functionality. A number of specialists were involved: woodworker, smith, leatherworker, wheelwright, decorator, to name a few. The term "carriage maker" at one time referred to the smith who made the undercarriage, but now the terms carriage maker and coachmaker are used interchangeably as names for the trade. We are concerned here with the coach body maker.

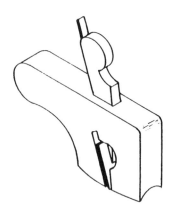

Fig.13:73—English-American coachmaker's plane

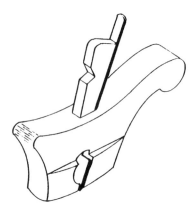

Fig.13:74—French coachmaker's plane

Coaches were designed with "side-sweep", the name the builder used for the curve from front to rear; and "turn-under", as they called the curving in and down below the level of the passengers' elbows. Both contribute to rear wheel clearance, allowing more seat room for a given axle length. Because of these curves, there were few straight lines to be worked. The coach-maker's kit did not need a jointer. Most of his planes were shorter than those of other woodworkers, often about six inches (15 cm.) long. Working gentle curves was facilitated by using a short sole. For sharper concave curves, the soles were compassed.

Short stocks provided poor hand grips. Therefore, where the length of the sole needed to be less than four inches (10 cm.) or so, the rear of the stock was extended in a "squirrel tail" or "beaver tail" to serve as a grip. An example is seen in Fig.13:73. The French developed a body style that has been widely copied, with both front and rear extended, the rear often in a breaking wave design (Fig.13:74). A fine set of these is preserved in the Wildung collection at Shelburne Museum (Vermont), brought from France by their maker and used by him in the Brewster Coach Company in New York City.

American planemakers offered a relatively small selection of coachmaker's planes. In 1880 the firm of H. Chapin's Son (Connecticut) began listing as carriage maker's tools smooth, rabbet, and T-rabbet planes in regular and "circle face" (compassed) styles, as well as other coachmaker's tools such as routers and beaders. The limited selection reflects the fact that most planes of this type found in America appear to be user-made. On the other hand, large English suppliers, (e.g. Marples and Preston) offered a sizeable selection around the turn of the century.

The COACHMAKER'S PLOW was described in Chapter 7 under plows for circular work. It is a tool with a short skate, usually compassed, for working curves. These may take many forms, one of which is illustrated in Fig. 13:75. Working in curves requires coping with changes in grain orientation, and some assistance is needed for this. Some Continental plows are fitted with two nicker blades, mounted with cutting edges quite near to the main cutter. A neater solution was found by sharpening the iron in a special manner as shown in Fig. 13:76. A groove in the front of the iron leaves two extensions when the bevel is made, which are sharpened to serve as nickers.

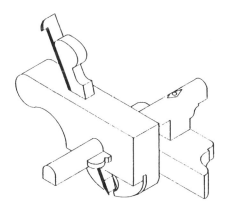

Fig.13:75—Coachmaker's plow

John Philipson's (England, 1897) list of planes needed by a coach body maker included the jack, trying, smooth, three compass, toothing, a set of T-rabbets, door check, two pair of grooving (match) planes (½ and ⅝ in.), and a filletster. These were used by other trades as well, and have all been described previously. The list of tools continued with the following routers: fence, boxing, side, beading and listing. These, described below, handled the sharper curves. They are usually of British make, or user-made.

Fig.13:76— Cutting edge, coachmaker's plow blade

The COACHMAKER'S ROUTERS have wooden bodies 14 - 17 in. (36 - 43 cm.) long with ends rounded as handgrips. Like spokeshaves, the cutting edges are set parallel to, and centered in, the stock. However, unlike spokeshaves, the cutters are shaped like narrow plane blades and are held in mortises by wedges. The usual shavings escape is through a round hole bored through the stock, the "eye" hole.

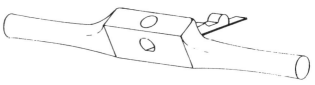

Fig.13:77—Boxing router

The BOXING ROUTER (the coach-maker used the term "boxing" to mean rabbeting or grooving) has a single iron ¼ - ¾ in. (6 - 19 mm.) wide (Fig.13:77). The front of the cutter may be hollow ground to decrease the effective pitch. Used after a rabbet plane, it acts in the same fashion as conventional routers to ensure a uniform depth of cut.

The GROOVING ROUTER is essentially the same but with a narrower iron (⅛ - ¼ in., 3 - 6 mm.). The blade is often turned sideways and wedged from the side, to have its narrow edge face forward, and is sharpened in a hook shape. The tool is usually equipped with an adjustable iron fence, hence the alternate name FENCE router. The fence (similar to the one shown in Fig.13:80) is adjustable over about 5 in. (13 cm.), permitting grooving at a distance from an edge, and the sole is often plated with metal.

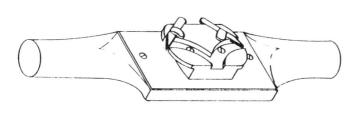

Fig.13:78—The side router, or jigger

The SIDE ROUTER or JIGGER was used to cut the grooves for panels or glazing where the grooving plane would not serve. Flat sections on the stock (usually protected with metal plating) served as fences, and the narrow cutters are held in a metal housing at a fixed distance from these fences. The cutting edges may be on either end of a single iron, sharpened with a hollow grind to give an appropriate pitch; or as

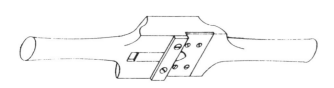

Fig.13:79—Side cutting router

separate cutters mounted at 45° as in Fig.13:78. This tool replaced the earlier pistol router, and in turn was largely replaced by a modern metal tool, the Tectool. A side cutting router sold by Preston (England, 1914) had a single spear point knife as a cutter (Fig.13:79); its use is uncertain.

356

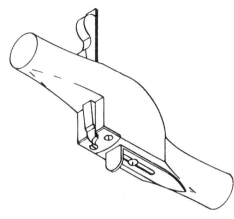

Fig.13:80—Pistol router

The PISTOL ROUTER (Fig.13:80), also for grooving, resembles the fenced router but the handle opposite the fence is jogged upward. This provides a longer flat bearing surface, often plated, to support the hooked cutter. The DOUBLE PISTOL ROUTER (Fig.13:81) may be regarded as two of these in the same tool, sharing the same jogged handle. It permits working in either direction. A simpler way to accomplish this is by splitting the end of the cutter of the simple pistol router, and forming two hooked edges facing in opposite directions (as seen in the quirk router earlier, Chapter 12, Fig.12:30).

MOLDING ROUTERS serve to cut profiles on curved surfaces. An adjustable type is made like a fence router but with a wider cutter. An example used for reeding is shown in Fig.13:82. Often an almost vertical iron ground in the molding profile acts as a scratch stock (the sole is not usually profiled). For beading, rounding, or other corner treatment, a fixed fence DOUBLE MOLDING ROUTER was generally used. A fence, usually formed as part of the sole plating and located between two mirror-image profiled

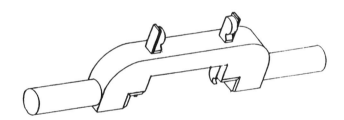

Fig.13:81—Double pistol router

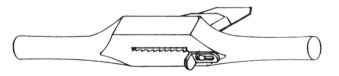

Fig.13:82—Moulding router

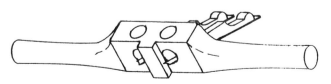

Fig.13:83—Double molding router

cutters, permits working in either direction as called for by the grain. These are found both with flat soles (Fig.13:83) and with the sole echoing the cutter profile, as in a molding plane. A LISTING ROUTER is a form of molding router using small square cutters to cut decorative grooves. QUIRK ROUTERS made like small cooper's post crozes or large cutting gauges are also seen.

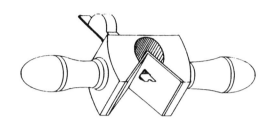

Fig.13:84—Corner router

The CORNER ROUTER (Fig.13:84) is used to put a chamfer or a rounded edge at a corner. This is the router version of a corner rounder plane (Chapter 8, Fig.8:16G), with a notched sole fitting over the corner to be worked. The flat or curved cutter is exposed in the corner of this notch. Another chamfering tool used by coachmakers is a small plane with a sole and cutter angles at 45°, treated earlier (Chapter 8, Fig.8:16B, SIDE CHAMFER plane).

A different type of molding tool, sometimes called a COACH SHAVE, is like a spokeshave with the cutter parallel to the sole. This, however, has a profiled sole and the blade is bent into the matching shape. The cutter is sharpened on both edges so that it will cut in either direction. This style is the same as the HANDRAIL SHAVE seen earlier (Chapter 12, Fig.12:9) except for different profiles, and has also been used by sashmakers.

Two more tools described earlier in Chapter 12 are used by the coach maker. The JARVIS (Fig.12:11) with its deep hollow profile serves for rounding the shafts that draw the vehicle, as well as being of use in making the wheels. The NELSON (Fig.12:10) with its flat sole finds use in heavy chamfering, where there is room for it. Both of these were also used by the wheelwright.

The early coach makers worked to the patron's wishes. Those who could afford carriages would specify their requirements in detail, and the coaches were custom built. If a special purpose plane was required, it was made in the simplest way, not being intended to outlast the current job. Later, large firms arose which made coaches in standard models, bought from a showroom. Repetitive work made a variety of specialized tools desirable. These were more carefully made, with durability in mind. The large variety of planes found with stocks of the coachmaker style reflects this. Further, not only coachmakers favored this style. Furniture makers, stair builders, ship finish carpenters (the cabins had as many curves as the coaches) and others made them. Without provenance, all such tools are apt to be called "coachmaker's". A fancier of these need never fear that his collection will be completed.

It should not be assumed that coachmaker's tools were all made before the era of the horseless carriage. Sets of tools have been preserved that were used to craft the fine woodwork of luxury cars, dashboards in particular. And the "woodie" station wagons, too, needed them.

Continental   Many of the tools of this trade were first developed in France and adopted elsewhere, so this segregation is somewhat arbitrary. The French coachmaker's plow may be found in a variety of user-made forms, from the crude but functional to the ornate. The example chosen for illustration (Fig.13:85) is particularly attractive as well as being functionally effective. The ebonized body has a long tail curving away from the line of the body for finger clearance, and is reinforced by brass strips on top and sides. The blade and iron wedge are in an open throat, permitting work in close quarters. The cast brass fence, supported on a single metal arm, is short enough to work gentle curves.

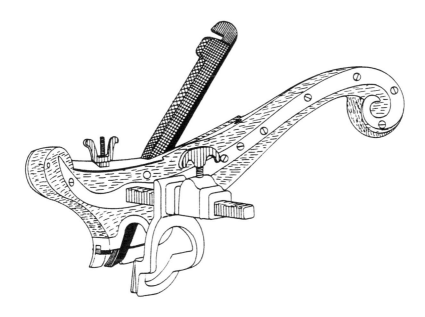

Fig.13:85—French coachmaker's plow

The French coachmaker's router, BOUVET À PLAT (flat groover) is sometimes (and not completely correctly) called in English a French coach-maker's plow. It is not common although it was still being offered for sale in the 20th century. It has a stock in the form of the old long S or an integral sign (Fig.13:86). The cutter is held on one end with the cutting edge in the center of the S, the other end of the stock forming the handgrip. The area

359

beside the cutting edge is plated and serves
as the fence. The cutter and wedge are both
steel and both curved. The tool is used for the
same purpose as the side router. As it will cut
in only one direction and grooving a curve
needs both, it was sold in left- and right-hand
pairs.

French coachmaker's routers (guim-
bardes de carrossiers) are found with functional parts duplicating the English.
User-made tools may take a variety of forms,
some quite ornate. Commercial suppliers
often left the stocks rectangular without

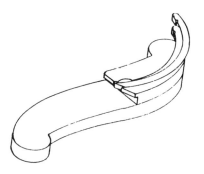

Fig.13:86—French
coachmaker's router

rounding for handgrips, to be shaped by the purchaser to his preference. The
French also use simple scratch stocks (tarabiscots) with profiled scraper blades
held in a cleft stock — which is usually profiled to match the blade.

THE WHEELWRIGHT

Although some worked as specialists in the coachmaking business, the wheelwright was more often engaged in heavier work. He was a tradesman skilled in the demanding art of making strong, light and durable wheels; but was often called upon to make complete wagons or carts, and other equipment for farm use. Most of his planes or shaves found use outside of his specialty, and have been treated in earlier chapters. The jarvis, nelson and his spokeshave shaped the rounds he worked with, and are found in the chapter on shaves. Compass or concave-soled planes served to smooth the felloes that made the wheel rim. A rare tool believed to have been used for shaping these, consisting of two planes joined by staves and having stocks shaped to straddle the felloe was described in the section on radius planes in Chapter 9.

A radius plane on a trammel for trimming the circumference of the finished wheel rim was patented by Reuben Fretz (5 July 1859, U.S. 24623) as a GAUGE plane, and a few examples have survived (Fig.13:87). It is a radius jack rabbet with nicker on the inner side, and the trammel is adjustable in vertical location on the stock as well as in radius. The inventor was told by wheelwrights that they would not buy his tool because it made perfectly round wheels that they couldn't sell; they made wheel radii ¼ in. (6 mm.) longer at the joints. This seems to indicate that the joints, the weakest part of the rim, tended to push inward in use. Inventors, there's a moral here!

The wheelwright, in making wagons or carts, made and used a CENTER-BOARD plane, a molding plane with a fence mounted on arms. This served to decorate the middle of boards used to form the vehicle's sides and ends with a profile, groove, center bead or other stripe.

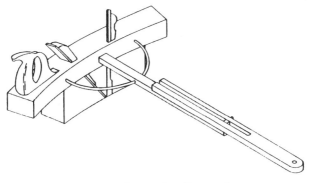

Fig.13:87—Gauge plane

THE PLANEMAKER

Most wooden planes can be made with common woodworking tools. Profiles for the soles of molders or on the fences of plows and sash filletsters can be cut, if need be, without special tools. Any profile can be cut with a full set of hollows and rounds, perhaps with the help of side rounds and hollows, snipe bills and side snipes. With the exception of a few to be discussed below, the planes a maker built for his own use were to speed the work, rather than to make it possible.

It was not unusual for single molding planes to be made on special order, to a customer's drawing; and this was done without special tools. For the common molders, however, it saved time to make a plane with a sole of the same shape as the molding the final plane was to cut. This MOTHER or BACKING plane could cut the sole of its daughter plane much more quickly — and consistently — than could a sequence of common molders. Though it would seem that hollows and rounds could serve as mother planes for each other, their mother planes were equipped with fences.

Molding planes with the handgrip jogged to one side as shown in Fig.13:88 were useful in cutting profiles in tight quarters. They were favored by planemakers, but do not seem to have won favor with other woodworkers. The full rounds of this type (shown at D) were called COD planes by W.J. Armour (1898), and were made in thicknesses from $\frac{1}{16}$ to $\frac{3}{4}$ inch (1.6 - 19 mm.).

Sets of planemaker's tools have survived, including a large collection held at Colonial Williamsburg. Solon Rust began a career as a planemaker with Hermon Chapin (Connecticut) in 1850 and became a master planemaker, with several important plane patents to his credit. His tool chest has been preserved by Ken Roberts. Aside from the mother planes, many of the planes in this chest were common molders that had been modified by additional fences or guides. For example, the planes used to cut the decorative moldings on plow fences and arm shoulders were so equipped.

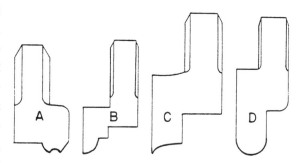

Fig.13:88—Planemaker's molders with offset hand grips

An extensive study of Rust's planes and their probable use has been published by Roberts (1983, 1985), and provides the basis for the following description of the making of a toted plow plane as it was probably done in a mid-19th century American planemaking factory.

The stock blank is sawn out, squared, and marked with templates for outline, handle, armhole centers and other features. The body is sawn to shape, the throat outline laid out (again by template) and cut in the same manner as described for molding planes. A mortise is cut for the depth stop and a recess for its foot. The sole is rabbeted, grooved for the keel, and molded with a cove. Arm holes are bored, and the handle shaped (Rust had a special semicircular shave for smoothing the outside of the grip). The keel and other metal fittings are installed, and the stock is ready for finishing and polishing.

The fences of all professionally made plows were elaborately molded on front and side, the particular profile used being characteristic of the maker and period. If it had been practical to use a wide molder to cut this in one pass, there is little question that this would have been done and that survivors would have been found. Since they have not, and sets of narrow molders specially designed for this purpose are known, it seems likely that the difficulty of cutting wide moldings in hard wood made the wide molder impractical. As we have seen, Sheraton described the use of combinations of narrow planes to cut wide moldings in furniture woods. The Rust and other planes show that planemakers did the same with their beech or boxwood.

The molding is repeated at the front and side of the fence, the two meeting at right angles. Any departure from the front profile in cutting the one on the side creates an unsightly corner, one that would not be accepted by the purchaser. While a skilled craftsman could manage this with simple molders, this would take more time than he would be willing to spend (he was paid by the piece). By adapting special shapes and fences for his planes, the necessary precision could be attained more rapidly.

The cutting of the molding on the end grain at the front involves risk, and is completed before labor is expended on other operations. End grain planing risks split-out at the end of the cut, and requires backing up the workpiece with another piece of wood if this is to be prevented. For this reason, fences were made in batches of a half-dozen or so and end-molded while clamped together with a scrap piece after the last blank. This not only guards against split-out, but provides a longer bearing surface for the molders.

The profile is marked with a template, and the waste stock removed by rabbeting. This must be done carefully as the side of the rabbet later serves as a guide surface for the molders to follow. Figure 13:89 shows at A the completed plow plane fence base, molded at front and side. A stack of fence

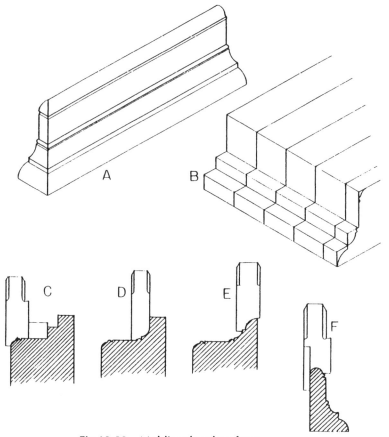

Fig.13:89—Molding the plow fence

blanks (plus the scrap piece at one end) is scribed with the desired profile and rabbeted (B). The steps that follow have not been documented, but seem to be implicit in the forms of the Rust planes. The plane shown at C has a block attached to its right side, which locates the molding with respect to the wall of the rabbet. A second plane is guided by the side of the inner rabbet, as seen at D. Finally, the last cut is made by the plane shown at E, its fence acting conventionally.

The outer ends of the arm shoulders were similarly molded, most often using the same molding profile as the fence.

With end grain molding complete, the fence pieces are thereafter worked individually. This was a good time to cut the stopped rabbet required for depth stop clearance (as may be seen in the fence of Fig.7:4 in Chapter 7). The long side of the fence piece is rabbeted in the same pattern (B) used on the front, and in accurate registry with it. The same sequence of cuts (C through E) is then made on this rabbeted face (which is to be the bottom of

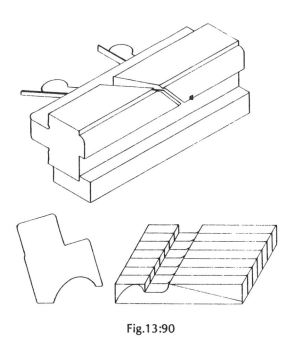

Fig.13:90

the fence). There is one more cut to be made. The outer side of the fence is left with a sharp upper corner on its upper edge. This is rounded with the plane shown at F. Rust's tool chest contains some of these planes in right- and left-handed pairs to cope with uncooperative grain.

The wedge finials of early molding planes provide clues to the time period and the maker, although by the mid-19th century they approached a standardized form. The uniformity of the wedge profile in the planes of a given maker and period suggests that they were formed by special planes. WEDGE NOTCHING planes (Fig.13:90 top) have been found, used to cut the notch in stacks of wedge blanks as shown at the lower right. It seems logical that another plane would be made to complete the profile. These would be difficult to recognize as such, being similar to common molders. The plane whose profile is shown at bottom left of the figure was suggested as a likely candidate by Bopp (1978).

The soles of many planes, especially sash filletsters, were usually boxed. The brunt of the thrust on the iron had to be taken by this boxing, and elaborate dovetailing was used in the better grades to ensure solid attachment. The cutting of these required special BOXING planes, and a high degree of skill. Not all planemakers could accomplish it at commercial rates. A description of the procedure for boxing by the London method was given in 1898 by W.J. Armour (Roberts, 1983), in which nine planes were used. A set of five planes made for this purpose by John Moseley and Son survives, and was described by Salaman (1975). Five is the minimum for accurate double dovetailing, assuming straight grain permitting cutting from either end of the blanks. There are many possible variations in the procedure, one of which is outlined here.

The five planes used are shown in profile in Fig.13:91, with the cutting edges shown as heavier lines. A boxwood blank is squared, and a tongue cut

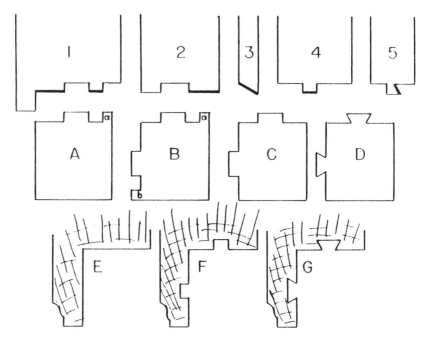

Fig.13:91

with plane (1) as shown at A. A fillet (a) is left to provide a second depth stop, guarding against canting of the plane and overcutting the outer side. The same plane is used, cutting from the other end, to cut the side of the blank into the form shown at B. The fence of plane (1) rides on a surface cut in the first step, which means that the position of both cuts is determined by the same corner of the original blank. Since the second step cuts away a part of the left side of A, the side dovetail tongue is further from the corner than is the top one.

The two fillets a and b, having served their purpose, are now cut away with plane (2). A simple rabbet might do, but the second bearing surface on the other side of the tongue is a precaution against canting and overcutting. This leaves the boxwood blank in the shape seen at C. Plane (3), a shoulder plane of exact angle, undercuts the tongues to form the two male dovetails and finishes the insert to the shape of D.

The plane blank is rabbeted exactly square (E). Grooves must now be cut, the width of the neck of the dovetail, at precise distances from the rabbet corner. This is done with plane (4). The cutting edge is adjusted at exact distances from both sides of the plane stock. One side serves to guide the side cut, the other (nearer) side the top cut. The two grooves shown at F are then undercut with the side-cutting plane (5). This cut has no guidance and calls for the greatest care. Planes 3 and 5 serve also in final fitting. The fit needs to be tight enough to require a mallet to drive it home (it mustn't slip in use), but not so tight as to risk damaging the tiny dovetails.

It seems evident that such painstaking work would not survive in large-scale operation in America. Machine methods using milling cutters replaced the above procedure soon after factory production began.

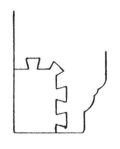

Figure 13:92 shows an even more elaborate dovetailing seen in a sash filletster made by W. Greenslade of Bristol, England, between 1865 and 1881 (Arnold & Walker Catalog No. 6). You might enjoy speculating as to how this joint was cut. It would seem to require a set of planes even more extensive than those pictured above.

Fig.13:92

THE CASEMAKER

The gentleman's glass fronted curio cabinet of the early nineteenth century became the model for large glass museum cases, glassed on all sides, which permitted their contents to be viewed but protected. These were designed to keep as much as possible of the atmospheric dust out. The best of these were known as air-tight cases, which is a bit of an exaggeration. If a large case were in fact hermetically sealed, the pressure change due to even a slight variation in barometric pressure would put a load of several hundred pounds on the glass. The joints used to seal the door openings of the case, however, did restrict the movement of air in and out with air currents and provided

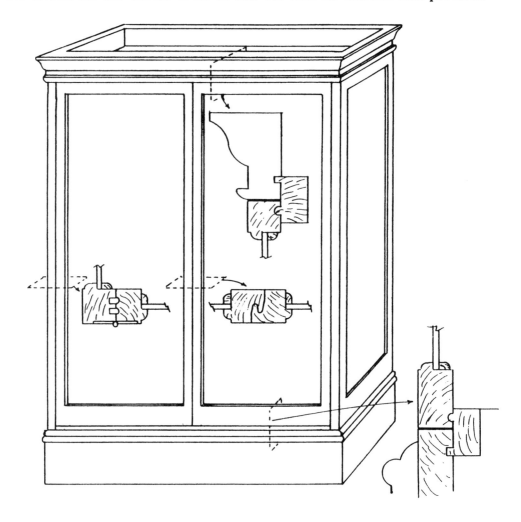

Fig.13:93—Schematic of a case illustrating "air-tight" joints

significant protection to the case contents. Fig.13:93 shows such a case with sections to illustrate examples of "air-tight" joints.

These joints were made with set of profile planes called AIR-TIGHT CASE planes, the use of which was reviewed by Mark Rees (1987). These have profiles somewhat like those of the casement sash match planes, but the tongue and groove is significantly smaller, as is seen in Fig.13:94. Planes A through E, made by Charles Nurse and Co., (England, 1887-1949), comprise a complete set for making a case with single seals. (Here, as elsewhere in this work, all profiles are of the heel view with cutting edges darkened.) One plane (B) cuts a semicircular groove in the hinge stile of the door, shown at K. The case upright, J, needs a matching tongue to fit into this groove as the door swings shut. A plane similar to (A), with added cutting edges to the iron, could form the matching tongue from scratch, but this would be wasteful.

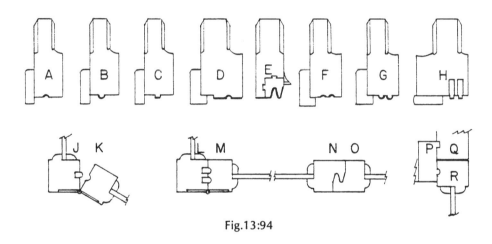

Fig.13:94

In order to conserve the expensive wood used (usually mahogany) it was customary to cut a rectangular groove in the stile with a third plane of the set (C), glue in a fillet of wood and subsequently round it with plane (A) to form the tongue. Thus the first three members of the set cut a semicircular groove, a rectangular groove, and a semicircular tongue. All had fences to ensure proper registration. In this set the fences were removable for replacement at different spacings, but other sets came with integral fences.

These took care of the hinge side of the doors. To seal at top and bottom (the top seal is seen at PQR), the hollow groove was cut on the inside face of the door rails, and a tongue provided on stops at top and bottom of the door opening. Here registration was a problem, as there were no mating edges to serve a guides for the fences. This could be solved with moveable fences, and indeed such planes are found. However, the need for extreme accuracy in setting these fences (if satisfactory mating top and bottom was to be achieved) would have taxed the time and perhaps the craftsmanship of the joiner. A faster and surer method was needed.

The plane C was used to groove the inner side of the case head (Q). A separate piece of wood (P) was prepared with the fourth member of the set (D), forming a stop which, glued into the head (Q), provided the tongue at the correct position to enter the groove in the door rail (R). The spacing is fixed, so that if the door fits its opening properly, the air-tight joints will mesh.

Making a seal at the fourth edge, the lock stiles where the two doors meet (N,O), required another tool, the HOOK JOINT plane (E). This cuts a profile containing both tongue and groove, so designed that the one plane would cut mating surfaces in both doors. This plane requires a depth stop to assure that the join is centered. The best models had two irons and were boxed.

If the thickness of the stiles permitted, a double tongue and groove seal was used, as shown at L and M. Three planes constitute a set for this type of seal: double tongue (F), double groove (G), and double rectangular groove (H). The double seal was apparently not used at head and foot, so a double of type D is not included.

THE ORGAN BUILDER

The pipe organ formerly controlled the supply of air to the various pipes by slide valves with wooden slides, which blocked the passage of air to the pipe until withdrawn by the playing mechanism. These slides had to be of exact and very uniform thickness to operate smoothly and avoid loss of air. Cutting them by hand was a tedious and difficult process. The organ builders, in the mid-18th century, modified the previously described (Chapter 12, molding machine) molding drawbench to do this job. This resulted in the THICKNESSER, called a FILIÈRE by its developer or DICKENHOBEL in German (it has received little attention in the English literature). As in the drawbench, the wood was drawn through the device. A frame held a modified bench plane supported over a rounded metal-clad support. The plane blade was set to be exactly parallel to this. The plane was moved downward by an iron screw for thickness adjustment after each pass, until the desired wood thickness was obtained.

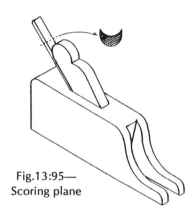

Fig.13:95—
Scoring plane

The slides operated on a common soundboard, and precautions had to be taken to prevent any leakage of air from a sounding pipe finding its way into a silent one. Grooves were cut in the sound-board around each valve, to vent any leakage to the open air. This was done using a SCORING plane (Fig.13:95), a form of router plane. A gouge-shaped iron was held by a wedge in a stock in the same fashion as a molding plane blade. The front of the stock was cut away in a diagonal curve, and a slot from the toe back to the cutter permitted seeing the exact placement of the cut.

Certain of the pipes were reeds. That is, the sound was generated by vibration of a reed, as in a clarinet, rather than by a wind mouthpiece, as in a flute. Elaborate devices were made to guide a cutting edge in a precise pattern, along slideways, to cut such reeds. These are rare, and called ORGAN-REED planes although they might perhaps be classed with precision machines.

The organ pipes were made of a tin-lead alloy, cast in sheets on a flat metal table. These were fairly uniform as cast, but required some correction. This was done with a THICKNESSING plane, a jack body with an upright scraping blade.

THE STAIRCASE BUILDER

The structure of the staircase itself is made with conventional tools, with the exception of special grooving planes and the nosing plane described earlier. The balustrade, however, created need for a variety of special shaping tools.

HANDRAIL planes were used to mold the banister rail (Fig.13:96). The straight sections were cut with a CAPPING plane (such as in Fig.13:97) for the top profile, and another — more usually a pair — shaped the sides (Fig.13:98). Major United States planemakers listed both handled and unhandled types in their catalogs, but offered only ovolo or ogee profiles. Elaborate balustrades were regarded as a major element of the architectural decor in earlier homes. Their rails were shaped either with a series of

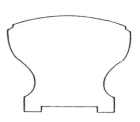

Fig.13:96—A bannister rail profile

common molders, or with planes made to order (perhaps by the user). A few profiles found in early homes are shown in Figure 13:99. It may be that some of the unusual profiles seen in the mid-sized molding planes were made for this use.

A pre-Revolutionary War handrail plane made by John Nicholson (New England) is of jack shape, width 3¾ in. (95 mm.). Usually handrail planes are shorter than jack length.

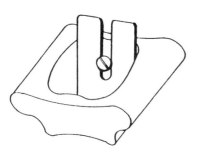

Fig.13:97—Capping plane

At least one jack-size pair was given shorter soles by cutting away the bottom of their heel ends. As with coachmaker's planes, a short sole permits working gentle curves.

A series of planes in the Wildung collection at the Shelburne Museum (Vermont) has stocks no longer than wide, equipped with slotted blades held in place by screws. One, a shallow hollow, cut the top. The second cut a triply curved form for the sides. A fenced hollow rounded the underside, and a double beading plane provided the final decorative feature.

Commercially made handrail planes are, however, more often of British origin. These are short (about 7 in., 18 cm.), with filletster fence to permit making handrails of different height (Fig.13:98). The common profile is two flats at different levels separated by an ogee, but many other profiles are

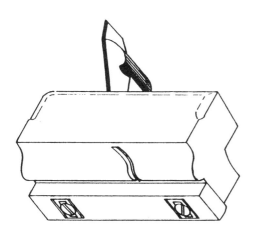

Fig.13:98—Side handrail plane

found. They were normally made in pairs. French "main courante" (handrail) planes, an ogee jack (DOUCINE RIFLARD) and a squirrel-tail ogee (DOUCINE À QUEUE) were listed as stair-makers' planes by Féron (France, ca.1940).

The balustrade was frequently curved at each floor and at landings, and the handrail molding had to be carried around the curve. A variety of tools are found to cope with this. Compassed handrail planes, even compassed and radiused, are found, with short soles and squirrel tails preferred. These planes are not common. Shaves, both of the bench throat and spokeshave type, were made and used.

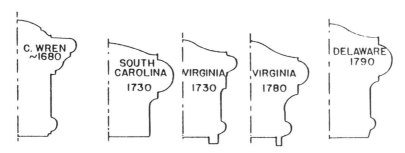

Fig.13:99—18th century profiles

A section of handrail, for example the piece at the lower end which curves from the horizontal upward while at the same time curving outward to reach the lower newel, may be required to curve in both the vertical and horizontal directions at the same time. Such a section is called a "wreath". Molding planes to cope with this problem are rare. Because of the many variations in molding profile and degree of curvature, a set would have limited use beyond the job they were made for. An example of such a HANDRAIL WREATH plane made by Nelson (England, 19th century) is seen in Fig.13:100. More often, a HANDRAIL SHAVE (Fig.13:101) would serve. Even these are ineffective in a tight curve, such as the scroll often used to terminate the rail. These scrolls were (and still are) hand-carved.

While turned balusters pre-dominate now, those in the more elaborate earlier homes were molded. Molding planes of symmetrical profile and suitable width were probably used for this purpose (although similar ones served for chair legs and other uses).

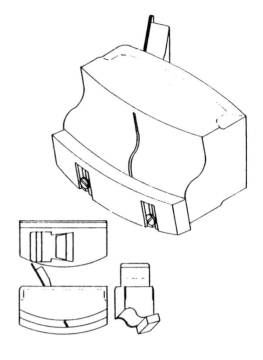

Fig.13:100—Staircase wreath plane

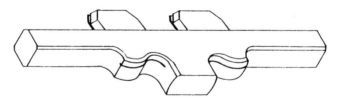

Fig.13:101—Handrail shave

THE BASKETMAKER

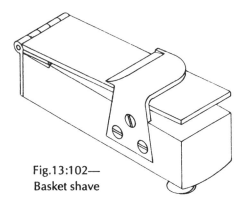

Fig.13:102—
Basket shave

The spelk plane, used by some basketmakers to prepare wooden strips for weaving large items, was treated earlier in Chapter 12. Two tools were used for sizing smaller willow strips to be woven into baskets. The BASKET SHAVE (Fig.13:102) is built on a wooden stock usually 4.5 in. (11 cm.) long. A steel plate covers the top face, and is free to move about a hinge at one end. The cutter is screwed to one side of the stock, and is bent at right angles to bring the cutting edge over the steel plate. The spacing between cutter and plate is set by a thumbscrew through the stock bearing on the underside of the plate. The tool is held in a vise and willow strips are pulled between plate and cutter to make them uniform in thickness.

The second tool is the UP-RIGHT SHAVE (Fig.13:103). The stock is the same size as the basket shave, and has a metal plate screwed to the top face. This has a triangular slot

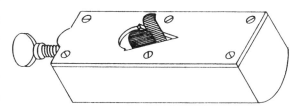

Fig.13:103—Upright shave

cut in it, through which protrude the two cutting edges. These are extensions of a steel bow concealed beneath the plate, the bow acting as a spring to force the two cutting legs against the sides of the V-slot. The spacing between the two cutting edges is controlled by moving the bow horizontally, to the wider or narrower end of the V-slot. This is effected by a thumbscrew at the end of the stock. As with the former tool, the stock is held in a vise while the thicknessed willow strips are drawn between the cutters to bring them to uniform width.

THE RULEMAKER

Boxwood strips for making rules were prepared with bench planes having irons set at very high angles, or vertically, scraping for smoothness. Some makers insured uniform thickness by using such a plane with the cutting edge recessed in a groove in the sole. The sides of the sole bottom on the bench, and serve as depth stops in the same manner as in the reglet plane.

Grooves for the slides of caliper or Gunter's rules were cut by small plows with thin cutters, mounted at high pitch and with either fixed or wedge-lock fences. The ends of the rule blanks were cut, to prepare them for the brass joints, with RULE-JOINT planes. These have soles like the table planes (Chapter 10, Fig.10:2) used to cut a similar joint, but are smaller. They were sometimes made as side-cutters, with vertical, skewed blades profiled on their sides.

THE CHAIRMAKER

A number of specialized molding planes were made for chairmakers, but are hard to recognize without provenance as they resemble molders that might be used elsewhere. Some catalogs list chair foot, chair splat, chair scroll and other "chair" planes without illustration. Speculations on their shape are entertainments that will be left to you.

Planes made and used by chairmaker Samuel Wing around 1800 have been preserved at Old Sturbridge Village (Massachusetts). His 32 in. (81 cm.) lignum vitae jointer has an offset closed tote near the midpoint of its length. A French chairmaker's jointer (VARLOPE pour CHAISIERS) still offered for sale in the twentieth century also had the handle and throat well forward. Another plane known as a CHAIRMAKER'S JOINTER is a short version of the cooper's jointer. Two of Wing's planes have been matched with the bead profile on a curved Windsor chair back found in his shop, implying that it was beaded before bending (Reichman 1986).

Because straight line moldings are not too common in chair design, chairmakers have more use for shaves than for planes. Most of these, including the travisher, double-iron and gullwing shaves, have use in other trades as well and have been treated earlier.

THE PATTERNMAKER

The usual method of casting metal into a desired shape, in a foundry, was to pour the molten metal into a hollow formed in a body of sand. This hollow was created by placing a wooden pattern in an iron frame called a flask, and ramming a special sand into the flask around the pattern. Both flask and pattern were in two sections, allowing the raising of the top half of the flask (the cope) away from the lower half (the drag). Using a layer of "parting sand" caused the sand to separate at the same place as the pattern halves separated. The two halves of the pattern were than carefully removed, and grooves made in the sand to provide channels to guide metal into the hollow and to vent trapped air. Any slight defects in the mold caused by these operations were repaired, the cope and drag were reassembled and the mold was ready to receive the molten metal.

The patternmaker's trade was the creation of these wooden patterns. He was a highly skilled woodworker, able to produce in wood (often mahogany) any intricate detail required by the blueprints for the finished piece. Because metal shrinks after it solidifies from the molten state, the pattern was required to be of the same shape as the finished piece, but larger in the exact ratio by which the metal would shrink. The patternmaker used "shrinkage rules", a different one for each of the metals being cast, to simplify this.

In addition to the planes common to all woodworkers, he owned several types useful to him alone. Wherever two surfaces joined at a sharp internal angle (such as seen inside a box), it was necessary to replace this with a rounded juncture — a fillet — to avoid a weakness in the casting. Most patterns were made in sections, then assembled. Shaping the pieces to produce the required fillets at the joint lines would have been wasteful of time and material. The fillets of the pattern were made by mounting filleting strips in these angles. Such strips were cut from leather, using the FILLETING plane. A short piece of fillet strip is seen in Fig.13:104 bottom.

The surfaces of the patterns had to be true; a cylinder was expected to be a cylinder, not an approximation. Irregularities, even if small enough to be acceptable in the final casting, might disturb the fragile surface of the sand as the pattern was removed. Finishing the great variety of shapes encountered by the patternmaker called for a large number of planes having soles of slightly different degrees of curvature (hollow, round, and compass).

The PATTERNMAKER'S plane described in Chapter 4 was his solution to the problem of storing this volume of tools. A single body and an assortment of detachable soles with matching irons took the place of a bulky set.

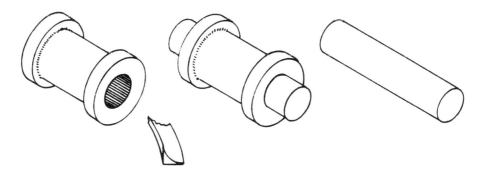

Fig.13:104—Finished casting, its pattern and core (below, scrap of leather fillet)

The casting of a part with an internal void required a special type of pattern. A hollow in the pattern would obviously not be reproduced in the sand mold. What was required was to create the sand mold, then fill the volume of this mold that corresponded to the hollow in the final piece with a solid piece called a core. The core had to be supported by the sand of the mold. The wooden pattern, therefore, was equipped with protrusions which left sockets in the sand mold to hold the ends of the cores. Fig.13:104 shows at the left an example of a finished casting, with the pattern used in the center and its core at the right.

To make these cores required another type of pattern, this time a solid piece having a hollow shape the same as the hollow of the finished casting. This was called a corebox. Foundry sand, together with a binder (molasses was a favorite), was pressed into the corebox to form the core, much as a child would do with his pail at the seashore. The cores were withdrawn from the corebox and baked, which gave them the required strength. They were then inserted in the primary sand mold after the pattern was removed, and just before the two halves of the flask were reassembled.

As the most usual shape for cores was cylindrical, the patternmaker was often called upon to create a hollow in the form of a perfect cylinder. Coreboxes for small cores could be made by boring. Larger ones were made in two sections, each with a perfect semi-cylindrical groove.

A COREBOX plane makes such grooves in wood. They may take several shapes, one of which is seen in Fig. 13:105. They all have the mouth located at a right angle intersection of two cheeks, whether the body is formed from two side walls as in the figure, or is a solid block of triangular section. In the latter case, the plane may have two wooden extensions (wings) attached to the body to extend the cheeks when larger coreboxes were to be made. The

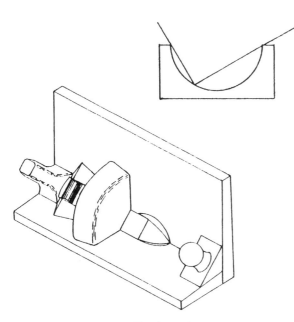

iron may be sharpened in a V-shape to cut in either direction, or slanted to cut just one way.

In the first step of making a corebox, a groove is roughed out in a block of wood twice as long as the desired core, leaving clean, straight, parallel edges where the groove meets the top. The distance between these two edges determines the diameter of the final groove. The corebox plane is then used to remove more wood from the rough groove. As long as the two clean edges at the top of the groove remain uncut, the iron cannot cut beyond the desired profile; and if the sides of the plane (or its wings) are kept in contact with these edges during the finishing strokes, the final shape of the groove is a true half-cylinder. This is a consequence of the geometric principle that any angle inscribed in a semicircle is a right angle, as shown at the upper right in the figure. The block made by this procedure is then cross-cut in half, and each piece has end walls applied. These form the two halves of the corebox.

Fig.13:105—Corebox plane.
Above: geometrical principle

OTHER

Boot soles and heels were formerly attached with shoe pegs, small pointed slivers of wood. A SHOE PEG plane shown in Fig.13:106 was used to make these (P. Kebabian, 1987). This rare tool is a jack-size plane with sole V-grooved twelve to the inch, with an iron to match. The plane might be used to cut multiple V-grooves in the end grain of a hardwood board. A peg-length strip (usually ¹¹⁄₁₆", 17mm.) can be cross-cut off from the grooved end, held in a vise, and again grooved at right angles to the first grooves. The cross-grooving might be done on square blocks sawn off of the original strip; or the whole strip cross-grooved by removing the plane's fence after the first pass and guiding subsequent passes by inserting the unused sole V-grooves in the workpiece grooves previously cut. The cross-grooved blocks (a small section is shown in Fig.13:107) may have a row of pegs split off along a groove, then further split into individual pegs.

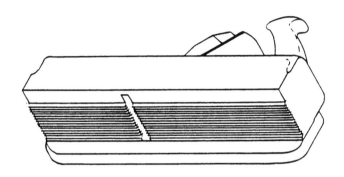

Fig.13:106—Shoe peg plane

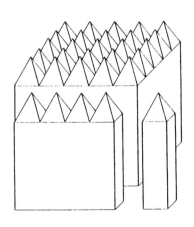

Fig.13:107—Block of shoe pegs

Other industries called for special purpose planes which would not be recognized without a historical record. One example must suffice. The Swanson factory in Albion, Pennsylvania, made boat oars (Sahlman 1984). It employed a full time planemaker to produce planes of sole curvature as required to finish various sections of the oars, eight or more profiles being used on a single oar. His planes were untoted, about 8 in. (20 cm.) long with double irons 1½ in. (38 mm.) wide and fitted with end grain oak or ash inlays in the sole in front of the mouth. The sharply curved planes intended for shaping the edges of the oars were protected with brass strips. An unusual form of rounder has been seen which served to round the ends of oar handles into their hemispherical form. The oar handle was inserted into a round hole, at the end of which a curved blade trimmed it. Outrigger supports served to keep the oar aligned. Planes were replaced by machine tools in the Swanson factory in 1944.

Appendix 1

THE CUTTING ACTION OF PLANE BLADES

In this appendix we will take a closer look at what happens when a plane is used, and the events that occur at the cutting edge as the iron does its job. This may be more detail than you care to have, and is not essential to the classification aspect of this work. However, it does serve to clarify the reasons for certain details of plane structure, and may be of help to those of you who are learning to use these tools. I am indebted to Prof. R. Bruce Hoadley (1980) for his lucid exposition of cutting mechanics.

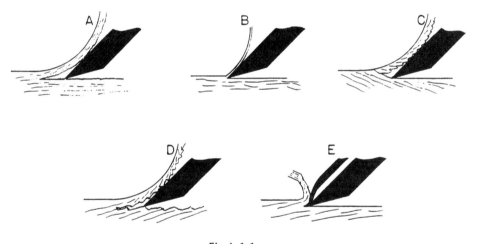

Fig.A-1:1

A blade cutting wood must move wood aside to make room for its passage. The shaving must be bent and levered out of the way as it slides up the face of the blade. If the cut is deep, the force needed to bend the shaving is greater than that required to separate wood fibers, and a split appears in front of the blade (A in Fig.A-1:1). If the shaving is thin, it bends away to let the blade move forward with very little splitting, and a smoother cut results (B).

An early woodworker was immediately aware of grain direction in any piece of wood he picked up, and almost unconsciously placed it in the proper orientation before planing it. If the fibers of the wood are not exactly parallel to the surface, the piece is oriented with the fibers sloping up in the direction of plane motion. By so doing, "planing with the grain", any split that does develop moves up into the wood that will be removed as a shaving (C). The shaving is weakened and less able to force another split. The planed surface is cut, not split, and is smooth. In cutting against the grain, on the other hand, the split enters the surface you are making. The shaving is stronger and better able to widen the split (D) and a rough surface, or "torn grain" results (if, indeed, the plane does not come to a wrist-wrenching halt). Of course, no one does this deliberately, but wood grain does reverse direction more often than one would wish.

The plane body helps to avoid this in two ways. Beside preventing the blade from digging in, the sole of the plane immediately in front of the blade presses down on the wood and tends to restrain splitting. Obviously, the closer to the blade this section of the sole is (the narrower the mouth of the plane) the more effective it is, but the thinner the shaving must be if it is not to choke the plane. Means of adjusting the mouth opening are found in most metal planes and in some wooden smoothing planes, to permit an optimum setting for the purpose at hand. The effectiveness of this factor is lost if the front of the mouth, due to wear or another reason, does not press on the workpiece. This is a major reason for maintaining sole flatness. The Japanese, in fact, remove "a hair of light" from their plane soles between nose and mouth, and perhaps between mouth and heel, to ensure that the front of the mouth exerts maximum pressure.

The wear, or the front wall of the throat, slopes backward but does not match the slope of the bed (to make it so would increase the frequency of choking, or jamming with shavings). As the sole of the plane wears, it is periodically returned to flatness by use of another plane. Because of the difference in slopes, the mouth widens as a result of this, and the cut deteriorates. After too many such treatments, the plane is either relegated to roughing work, or is repaired by inlaying a hardwood patch in the sole in front of the mouth to restore the correct opening.

Another major improvement in performance was introduced early in the 18th century, with the discovery of the benefit of the cap or breaker iron. A shaving riding up the surface of a single iron gains some leverage helping it to initiate a split in front of the cutting edge. The cap iron serves to break or to fold the shaving before it has gained too much leverage (E). With this help, a sharp, well tuned and finely set plane can cope with difficult grain.

It is apparent that the transition from a cutting to a splitting action would be delayed if the pitch were lowered, as the shaving would need less bending to get out of the way. However, the lower pitch requires a smaller angle between the face of the blade and the back. There is less steel in back of the edge to support it, and it would lose its keenness rapidly. Another factor is heat removal. A surprising amount of heat is generated by friction at the edge, and unless this is conducted away the temper is at risk. A small sharpening angle doesn't provide for good heat removal: a razor blade would not hold up well in a plane. The usual compromise puts the pitch angle at about 45 degrees.

In the idealized drawings of Fig.Appendix1:1, we see that the wood touches only the front of the blade. It doesn't appear to touch the back bevel.

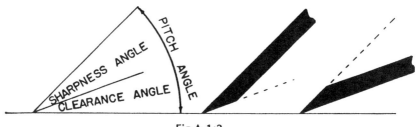

Fig.A-1:2

How, then, does it know whether the sharpening angle is 45° or 20°, and why then the fuss about different angles for hard or soft wood?

The clearance angle is the angle between the bevel on the back of the blade and the wood surface. It is the angle by which the blade clears the freshly cut surface (Fig.A-1:2). This clearance is required, for the following reason. The thrust as the blade moves forward distorts the wood a small amount, until the wood yields to the cutting action. Part of this distortion is a downward compression. As the blade moves on, the freshly cut wood springs back and would tend to lift the plane blade if it had no clearance. Greater downward pressure would be required for a smooth cut, and friction would increase.

The sharpness angle is the angle between the front of the blade and the bevel on its back. (Pitch is the sum of the sharpness angle and clearance angle). The actual angle of the cutting edge is greater than the grinding angle since it is increased by honing (few tradesman honed exactly at the grinding angle as much more steel would have to be removed in doing so, which is a time-consuming process). Thus the sharpness angle is at risk of increasing with successive honings, with consequent reduction of the clearance angle. If the clearance angle becomes negative, the cutting edge of the iron does not touch the wood, and the plane is of little use until the blade is reground.

Although softwoods permit a smaller sharpening angle, they also yield more before being cut and thus require a larger clearance angle. Pitch (clearance plus sharpness) requirement changes little. The verdict of history as well as of recent experiments (e.g., James Krenov) is that a pitch of $45°$ or slightly more is best for bench planes. The historic name for the $45°$ bed angle is common pitch. A bit higher ($50°$, called "York pitch") is used in some bench planes for hardwood and is usual for rabbet or grooving planes. Middle pitch ($55°$) and half pitch or cabinet pitch ($60°$) are frequent in molding planes for soft and hardwood respectively. Angles of less than $45°$ are referred to as low angle or extra pitch, and are seen in some types of planes for softwood and for cutting end grain. It is preferred by the Japanese, who use a rather different planing style.

The bed angle of metal miter planes or low-angle block planes is much lower. However, the actual pitch is in the same range as above because the blade in such planes is mounted bevel up. Thus an iron with a sharpness angle of $25°$ mounted at a bed angle of $20°$ with the bevel up gives the same effective pitch as if mounted at common pitch in a smooth plane with the bevel down (Fig.Appendix1:2). An increase in effective pitch is gained only at the expense of the clearance or the sharpness angle. Other reasons exist for the lower bed angle, the principal one being that the blade is supported by the bed almost up to the cutting edge, and chatter is reduced. With bevel down mounting, bed support ends at the top of the bevel.

In cutting moldings (where the final surface is as left by the plane and further refining by scraping or sanding is not normally done), it was particularly important to have stock of straight and consistent grain. Where grain reversal was inherent in the nature of the work, as in cutting moldings for curved surfaces, the molding planes were used in pairs, one cutting in each direction. Even in straight work a pair of molders can be useful, although these are quite rare — presumably because matching the profiles is quite difficult. As we have seen, side bead planes are the only type commonly found paired, usually cut in one stock as the double side bead.

In furniture hardwoods, grain reversal is much more common than in softwood; indeed, some of the attractive grain patterns are a result of this. Some even have "roey" grain — in which the grain direction changes repeatedly across the width of the board, even within the width of the plane blade.

In dealing with this, final finish is done with a hand scraper or a scraper plane, with a nearly vertical blade. Why is this effective? A vertical blade has little tendency to cause splitting or fiber separation ahead of the edge. The action is not to lift the shaving, but to crush the wood cells, decrease their strength, and scrape them away in very thin shavings. Much more work must be done to remove a given quantity of wood, but a smoother surface is gained.

Molding planes do not have narrow mouths over all sections of their profile, and normally are without cap irons to help with awkward grain. In coping with furniture woods, the last resort is to increase the pitch. As pitch is increased, the action of the edge changes from the cutting type toward the scraping type. At cabinet or half pitch (60°) the shaving tends to yield by a combination of fiber separation and cell crushing. The shavings are weaker and less likely to generate micro-splits. Higher pitch improves finish but also makes the plane much harder to push. Finding the right compromise for specific jobs accounts for the variety of pitches found in the molders.

In cutting across the grain direction, a different type of problem arises. Splitting in front of the blade is no longer the difficulty, as the splits propagate off the sides of the cutting edge. This is not objectionable in roughing, where a diagonal cut is common, but is highly objectionable in cutting a dado (a rectangular trench across the grain). Using a rabbet plane across grain would leave a dado with very ragged sides. The dado plane solves this by placing a nicker blade in front of the main cutter. This acts as a pair of knives which sever the wood fibers at the points where the edges of the main cutter will meet them. The main blade is normally skewed, for reasons to be given below.

Finally, there is end-grain planing, for smoothing the ends of a board or fitting miters. Here the blade must sever the wood fibers rather than separate them one from another. If the cutting edge is not sharp, the fibers will be pushed forward before they yield. Separation from their neighbors will occur and small splits will appear perpendicular to the surface (or at an angle, in the case of miters). Small mouth openings and cap irons do not help in this case, but sharp edges, low pitch, and skew cutting do.

SKEW

There is a way to fool the wood into thinking it is being cut at a lower pitch than that of the plane being used. This is to move the plane along the board with the plane body at an angle to the direction of motion. (This is a good way to start a bench plane cut in any case, to ease the bump as the blade hits the edge). To see why this is so, visualize a single fiber of wood being lifted by a plane blade (Fig.A-1:3). If the blade is set at 45° pitch and is not skewed, the wood fiber is lifted at an angle of 45°. At the same pitch but with the blade skewed, the fiber does not climb straight up the face of

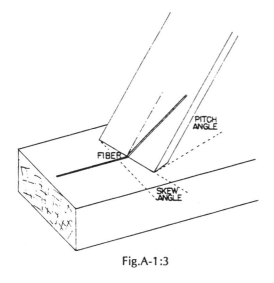

PITCH ANGLE

FIBER

SKEW ANGLE

Fig.A-1:3

the blade but travels along a diagonal. As in climbing a hill, straight up is steepest, traversing diagonally up is less steep — you must walk further to rise the same distance. (To quantify this, the sine of the effective pitch is the product of the sine of the actual pitch and the cosine of the skew angle.) As a result, the effective pitch of a plane at common pitch is 42° if used at a 20° skew angle (a common value) and would be 30° if used at a skew angle of 45°. In the extreme case of a spill plane at common pitch with blade skewed at 55° the effective pitch is 24°, almost as good as could be obtained using an unskewed razor. This decrease in effective pitch is gained with no loss in the clearance angle.

Note that the apparent greater keenness of the blade is not due to a "slicing cut". The blade edge does not move across the fiber as a saw does. In a slicing cut, the minute irregularities of the blade edge (visible under a microscope no matter how well the blade is sharpened) act as saw teeth. It is possible to use a plane to get such a cut, but the action is different: the plane body is aligned with the board and is moved in a diagonal path across it. This is not a usual practice, although a circular motion of a finely set plane is recommended by Krenov for smoothing wood of difficult grain.

Skewing the plane body is acceptable as required for greater apparent keenness, but would be poor practice when using jointers. In planes where skewing the body is not possible (rabbets, panel raisers, shootboard planes, and other such) it is common practice to mount the blade at a skew within the plane body.

Decrease in effective pitch is not the only advantage to be gained by skewing the iron. The skew is normally in the direction which tends to push the fence against the workpiece, and decreases the user's effort to this end. The shavings are directed laterally and choking is less of a problem in rabbets and similar planes. And in cross-grain work, as with a dado, the wood fibers need not be lifted vertically but are peeled back from one end to the other.

The mention of slicing cut, above, prompts some comments on sharpness. There are several kinds. The kind which is best on a carving knife is quite different from the sort needed in a plane blade. The carving knife is used with a sawing motion, and depends on tiny irregularities, like saw teeth, for its cutting action. Meat fibers are more flexible than those of wood, and simply pushing a blade into the meat makes it yield, rather than cut, until the penetration is large. A saw-tooth edge catches individual fibers and tears them apart by pulling sideways as the slice proceeds. This sort of edge is produced by a butcher's steel. The steel bends the metal at the extreme edge of the blade back and forth until it breaks off in minute slivers, leaving a ragged saw-like edge which doesn't have the acute angle needed in a razor or plane blade.

In sharpening to get the razor type of edge, the objective is to remove metal from the bevel with as little distortion as possible. The angle of the blade bevel on the sharpening stone should be constant. If it is allowed to rock, not only is the sharpness angle increased by the rounding of the edge, but the pressure on the extreme tip bends the metal in the same fashion as does the butcher's steel. A certain amount of this is hard to avoid, and a "wire edge" is a frequent result of stoning, which is then removed by stropping. The larger the wire edge, the more is the edge like a butcher's and the less satisfactory it is on a plane iron. Too large a wire edge is a sign that the hardness of the blade is too low, that the temper has been drawn too far.

The plane iron should be sharpened by removing metal from the bevel only. The front of the iron should be laid flat on the stone only to remove any metal bent in that direction as the wire edge. There is a great temptation to tip it "just a little bit" to facilitate this. Doing so changes the effective pitch of the blade. Even if this is your objective, creating

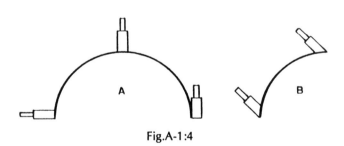

Fig.A-1:4

two perfect planes to meet in a straight cutting edge is more difficult than relying on the flat face of the blade (and it should be perfectly flat) for one of them.

In addition to skew, there is another factor which enters into the apparent pitch; unfortunately in the opposite direction. In molding planes, the curvature of the blade can increase the apparent pitch - to vertical in the extreme case of the curve becoming perpendicular to the sole. In an astragal, the cut at the lowest part of the semi-circle is parallel not to the sole, but to the side of the

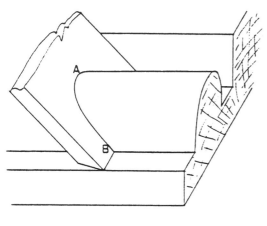

Fig.A-1:5

plane. To make this clear, let us use an analogy due to Holtzapffel (1875) and picture the cutting of a large astragal with rabbet planes. We would cut the lower part with the plane on its side, as on the left of Fig.A-1:4. In cutting a small astragal with a conventional blade, this cannot be done. In effect the lower part of the astragal (at the right in Fig.A-1:4) is being cut as if by a side rabbet. But the blade is not pitched with respect to the side, as it is in a proper side rabbet, but is perpendicular to the surface it is cutting. The action is that of a scraper blade held upright and although skewed (at the pitch angle), this does not help in this case and the effective pitch is still vertical. It is not cutting, but scraping. The sketch of Fig.A-1:5 shows that the blade section at A is cutting like a bench plane, but the part at B is scraping.

Fig.A-1:6

How is it that it can work at all? The saving feature is in the relative thickness of the shaving to be removed. Fig.Appendix1:6 shows an exaggerated cross-section of the shaving. As one moves along the blade toward the bottom of the astragal, the effective pitch is increased but the amount of wood it must remove decreases. At the bottom, the pitch is vertical but the shaving thickness is zero, and a scraper works just fine. The bulk of the wood removal is done by the horizontal sections of the blade edge. The strictly vertical segments of any profile cause no problem. It is the variation of cutting angle as the

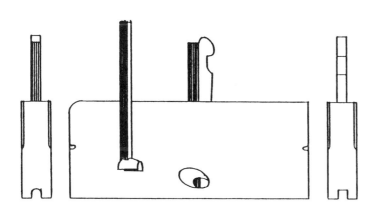

Fig.A-1:7

slope changes that is objectionable.

Holtzapffel (1875), troubled by this, designed several types of cutter to correct the problem. While he reported that they worked satisfactorily, his ideas did not gain general acceptance. A rare type of plane uses one of these. It has a cutter in the shape of a gouge directed almost horizontally, hollow side down. The rear was straight and bent upward to form a normal shank. The example shown (Fig.Appendix1:7, showing a spare blade in front of the stock) is a short molder intended to convert a square ¼ in. (6 mm.) tongue to a semicircle. The same principle has ben seen in planes to cut V-grooves and in a hollow groover.

Molding planes, except for hollows and rounds, are rarely skewed. As an extreme example, an astragal, if skewed, would have effective pitch decreased on one side of the curve, but would suffer an increase on the other side to beyond vertical. As will be seen below, profiles are usually arranged to have equal degrees of curvature on either side of horizontal. Skewing hurts on one side as much as it helps the other, and little is gained. In planes without spring, however, skew can help. It is used in double iron nosing planes, for example.

SPRING

For molders such as the quarter-round there is a way of minimizing the variation of cutting action along the curve. The profile is placed on the sole at an angle, called the spring angle. In use, as shown in Fig.A-1:8, the plane is held at this angle with the vertical. The device was used on some of·the

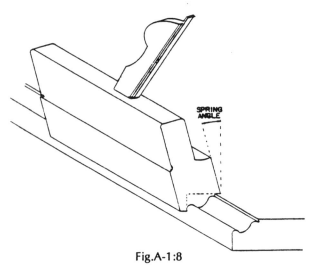

Fig.A-1:8

earliest known molders, including ogees by Robert Wooding (England, 1710-39). Now the equivalent positions of the miniature planes (assuming spring of 45°) are as shown in Fig.A-1:4B. At worst, they are acting like planes with soles at 45°. (The effective pitch, if the blade is at common pitch, is then 55°.

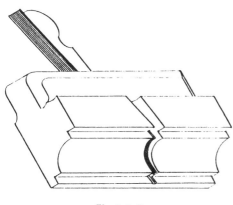

Fig.A-1:9

There are two other advantages gained by using spring. One is the direction of force toward keeping the fence on the work. The second, as was pointed out by Phillip Walker (1977), concerns the mouth clearance. In making the plane, the throat is sawn into the stock with the minimum clearance at the lowest point of the profile. As the sole is cut away to form the profile, the mouth openings of the higher points of the profile are larger due to the wedge shape of the throat. Note that in Fig.A-1:9, a quarter round without spring, the distance from blade edge to the front of the mouth is much greater at the top of the curve than at the bottom. If it is correct at the bottom, it is too wide at the top. This effect is minimized by using spring, to keep the different parts of the profile as nearly as possible at the same level. A quarter round without spring has the top of the curve a distance of one radius above the bottom, while with a 45° spring, the distance is 0.29 of a radius. Thus the mouth widening is reduced to 29% of that of the unsprung plane.

While a spring angle of 45° has been used in some of the examples above for simplicity of argument, this is larger than is common in practice. The reasoning is complicated by the fact that the plane is cutting downward, and not in line with the stock, being guided by the fence. Another reason is that a large spring is a bit awkward to use in practice. Spring angles of 30° or less are more usual.

None of the above implies that spring is essential to good performance. It is almost never seen in Continental planes, and in many common profiles (astragal, bead, etc.) it cannot be used and the planes work well. But the advantages are sufficient that, where possible, it is almost always used in the English-speaking world.

It remains to be explained why astragals and beads do not use spring. At first glance, it is natural to assume that the cutting action progresses in line

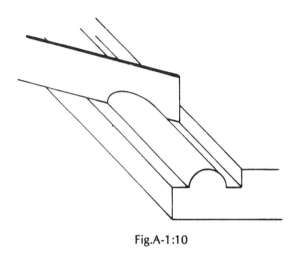

Fig.A-1:10

with the body of the plane, as it would if unsprung; and that, of course, the far side of the curve couldn't be cut. Not so. The progress of the cut is vertical, as the fence does not permit movement along the line of the body. In fact, a sprung astragal would cut the profile, but not very well. The real reason is that the spring, as outlined above, improves the effective pitch on the near side of the curve. It makes it worse on the far side, where the effective pitch is beyond vertical (pitch greater than 90°).

Perhaps this will be clearer if we look at an example in which the spring has been carried to the extreme of 90°. The plane body is then positioned on its side, but its motion is still vertical. Take away the plane body and consider the position of the blade (Fig.A-1:10). It is held at a horizontal angle equal to the bed angle of the plane, say 45°. The left side of the astragal is then cut well, with an effective pitch of 45°. The top of the curve is scraped, effective pitch of 90° and skew angle of 45°. The right side of the astragal is not cut or even scraped well: the blade is leaning forward (effective pitch 135°).

For further discussion of spring see Kean (1988, 1989) and other references cited therein.

Appendix 2

SYSTEMATIC NAMING OF MOLDING PROFILES

The brief description outlined in Chapter 11 should suffice, in most cases, for location of any given molding profile described there. This more complete exposition offers additional detail should questions arise, and a rationale for the choices made in development of the system.

BACKGROUND

The present naming system was generated to fill the need imposed by ordering the presentation of a large number of molding profiles in rational and retrievable fashion. We might begin by consideration of the limitations of any naming system for this area.

A given name, even if commonly accepted, still does not completely specify the profile. Several quite different ogee curves were seen in the section on ogees (Chapter 10, Figs 10:73 through 10:79), and intermediate forms will be found. To attempt to give a descriptive name to each would complicate the names so much that few would use them.

If you wish enough information to be able to duplicate a profile, you will need a drawing or a complete specification that would permit a draftsman to draw it. It is too much to expect to get all of this information from a name, unless you like paragraph-long names. A practical system will provide a name that describes a family of closely related profiles, rather than one specific plane.

An ideal system would permit giving a unique name to any shape encountered, providing a key to its location in a list. It would generate names that are consistent with those in current use for the common molders. The system described here does not pretend to meet this ideal. It does, however, approach it to a useful degree, and has proven itself to be workable. It worked for the author in the sense that any new profile seen could be immediately given a name and a location to be checked to see if it had already been listed. I hope that it will serve you for the same purpose.

The requirement for generating names consistent with those in common use proved to be more easily specified than done. It would have been simpler to abandon the common names entirely, because most of these are ill-defined and used in different senses. Practically, however, few would care to learn a completely new set of names for the elements of the profile. The price paid for this objective is the acceptance of arbitrary definitions of how the specific name is to be used.

Many of the common names seem to be clear enough but can grade imperceptibly one into the other. The sequence shown in Fig. 10:41 evolves from a simple round through a profile having the common name "casing molding" to finish as a "quirk bead". Continuing the sequence through similar gradual changes would finish as a "Grecian ovolo". Since a gradual change in shape can convert a molding of one name to one of different name, there is no sharp dividing line between these molding names. What is an intermediate form to be called? Where in the listing should one look to find it? If we are to limit the choice among several possible element names and force selection of one, arbitrary definitions are required. These are provided here.

In order to accomodate some of the more unusual forms, it was necessary to make a few coinages. These were accepted reluctantly, and only after concluding that they were a lesser evil than use of the awkward or ambiguous names generated without them. In most cases, the names will appear familiar, or at least recognizable. The present system of naming is thus reasonably satisfactory in going from name to profile.

However, the opposite direction, going from profile to name, is thornier. Unfortunately, this is the direction you will take in trying to locate your plane's profile in the list. For the majority of molding profiles found, it should be relatively easy to generate a unique name under which your tool is listed. For some, an apparently reasonable name fails because of an arbitrary dividing line between the use of one element name as opposed to another. And for a very few profiles, it is in fact possible to justify more than one name. An attempt has been made to provide cross-references in such cases.

Offsetting this difficulty is the fact that a complete name is not required to locate your profile. In the vast majority of examples, the name begins with the name of the element that the plane cuts at the greatest distance from the edge of the work (the few exceptions are taken up later). Having selected the name for this first element from the list below (or, indeed, recognizing it as the common name), this can be located in the alphabetical list of Chapter 11. All profiles beginning with this element are grouped together, and scanning a relatively small number of adjacent profiles should locate your quarry, if it is in fact listed. (If it is not, either the Astragal Press or the author would be delighted to learn of it.)

ELEMENT NAMES

The names to be used for profile elements are restricted to thirteen. (The elements were pictured in Fig. 11:1.) Only these names are considered in determining the order of presentation. They are fully capitalized in the listing. Each is given a single capital letter for use in a shorthand version of the name (given in parentheses after each name in Chapter 11; this is used in some cases to identify profile sketches). Several other terms may be used as modifiers in the extended names. These are in lower-case letters, and are coded as lower-case letters in the shorthand. They are ignored in the alphabetization. The entries in Chapter 11 are arranged alphabetically in the order of their element names (full names, not shorthand codes)   The first alphabetically is the astragal, and all profiles that begin with an astragal are listed before any others. The listings within this astragal area are in alphabetical order of the names of the succeeding elements.

All but one of the major element names are taken from common usage. Where necessary, ambiguous common use is countered with somewhat narrower definitions.

LINES

The two linear elements are the FILLET and the BEVEL. The fillet is horizontal, and the bevel is at an angle. A bevel or a fillet that is a smooth extension of an arc, as in the extreme Grecian ovolo of Fig. 10:30, is not cited. A vertical line in the profile is not regarded as an element. (These are not associated with a corresponding section of the plane blade, but are generated as a corner of the blade moves downward through the work.) It may be shown by one of the two modifiers "raised", meaning a step up (in moving toward the edge of the work), or "dropped", a step down. These are optional in the shorthand coding, and do not affect alphabetical order.

QUIRK

A QUIRK is a narrow crevice at the innermost end of a molding, or between two other elements. In the most common form it is formed by the extension of the arc of a subsequent element beyond the horizontal, such that it penetrates the surface, then turns sharply upward to return to the surface. This return is normally a vertical step. The juncture of the two sides of the quirk (although intended to appear as a sharp edge) must be broadened in practice if the plane sole is to survive wear in this area. This broadening varies from a slight rounding to a narrow fillet to a broad fillet. All will be considered as part of the quirk unless the width of the fillet is more than half the length of the vertical rise. In this case, the element will no longer be considered a quirk and will be coded as a fillet.

In some cases, especially in Continental molders, the return is not vertical but either a bevel or a cove. Common usage is to call these "bevel quirks" or "cove quirks". Consider a series of profiles in which the cove grows in size, from a form clearly a "cove quirk bead", to another form clearly a cove and bead. There is no sharp dividing line, no discontinuity. Rather than force a judgement call or add one more arbitrary distinction, all such profiles will be coded as COVE and BEAD and not as a quirk. Similarly, the term "bevel quirk bead" will not be used: it is coded as BEVEL and BEAD.

ARCS

In general, the difference between a circular and an elliptical arc will not be recognized in naming. The difference between an extreme elliptical ovolo (which can approach a bevel in appearance, as in Fig. 10:30) and one nearly circular, is more pronounced than the difference between the usual ellipse and a circular arc. Coding such differences in type of curvature creates unjustified complication. Although a distinction may be made between elliptical and circular arcs in the full name (e.g. quirk ovolo and Grecian ovolo) the arcs are considered equivalent in shorthand coding and in alphabetical placement within a list.

CONVEX ARCS

Three names apply to convex arcs. A quarter circle or less (or an elliptical arc subtending $90°$ or less), commencing with a nearly horizontal or a downward slope, is an OVOLO. A half circle or less, with both ends of the arc below the high point of the curve, is called a BEAD. A full half-circle with both ends at the same level, with a fillet at the outer end of the arc, is named an ASTRAGAL.

The bead and the astragal are forms commonly used at the outer edge of the molding. In general, the name "astragal" implies a fillet on both sides of the arc, and neither fillet need be cited in the name. However, the fillet on

396

the inner side of the astragal may be replaced by the adjacent element, and the name astragal is retained. As one example, the OGEE with ASTRAGAL (in chapter 11) shows the elements meeting without a distinct fillet. As another, the OVOLO with ASTRAGAL has elements meeting as in a quirk. This joining is not coded as a quirk, however.

A variant of the astragal uses a slight curvature in place of a sharp corner at the juncture of arc and fillet. This has the same effect in use as the astragal, and is seen often enough to require a coinage (to name this as an ogee is misleading). This is called here a "soft ASTRAGAL". The modifier "soft" does not change alphabetic order, and the requirement that both ends of the element be at the same level remains.

The commonly used name QUIRK OVOLO is so named in this system, but is alphabetized and shorthand coded as two elements, quirk and ovolo. It is an ovolo which extends the upper end of its arc inward, turning downward and penetrating the surface, then returning to the surface leaving a narrow crevice. The distinction between quirk ovolo and quirk bead requires another arbitrary definition. Common use prefers the term ovolo either if the curve is non-circular or if it does not reach the vertical at its outer end. To avoid this gray area, the system restricts the term QUIRK BEAD to a circular arc tangent to a vertical at its outer end.

Since both GRECIAN OVOLO and QUIRK OVOLO are firmly established in common naming, both will be used in the extended names, and in borderline cases either may be chosen arbitrarily. However, both are short-hand coded as quirk and ovolo, and are considered as identical in establishing order of presentation ("Grecian" is alphabetized as if it were "quirk"). The name "Grecian", both in common use and as used here, implies a quirked elliptical curve.

In another problem area, the transition from astragal to quirk bead can also be a gradual one. Here the Greek usage is employed. If the inner end of the arc is above the outer end, it is not here called an astragal, but is coded as a quirk bead. As defined above, the term "ovolo" (unless quirked) will be restricted to curves that start nearly horizontally or with a downward slope. A convex shape starting with an upward slope (not sharply enough to be called a quirk) and continuing for a quarter-circle or more will be called a bead. Again to avoid ambiguity, let us define the distinction between "bead" and "quirk bead" (or "quirk ovolo") by saying that a quirked element has an upward slope of 45 degrees or more at the beginning (innermost end) of the arc.

CONCAVE ARCS

Three names are used for concave elements. A COVE is a quarter circle or less with its lowest point at the outer end of the arc. If the low point falls between the ends, the arc is a FLUTE if both ends are at the same level, a SCOTIA if the ends are at different levels. This restores the original meaning of scotia, which has been used in some catalogs to mean a cove, and in others to mean a quarter round.

DOUBLE CURVES

An OGEE smoothly joins two arcs, a convex one inside and a concave nearer the edge. The REVERSE OGEE inverts this, the convex toward the edge. (Although this is two words, it is treated as one in alphabetization.)

The modifier "lying" used before the name "ogee" or "reverse ogee" is perhaps self-explanatory. A typical "lying" ogee (or reverse ogee) is one formed by smoothly joining a bead (whose ends are at the same level) and a flute (as defined above), as opposed to a common ogee formed by joining an ovolo and a cove. Slight deviations from this form are accepted. As the modifier is not considered in alphabetization and is in fact optional, a precise definition would be wordier than is justified.

As in the case of the ovolo, both terms QUIRK OGEE and GRECIAN OGEE are used in extended names but both are coded as quirk and ogee, and considered identical for alphabetical sorting.

POINTED CURVES

These forms occur rarely, but are awkward to name by using the previous elements and are given their own codes. The GOTHIC BEAD consists of two convex arcs joining in a point at the top. A second, related form was in common use in early England, but its name has dropped from use. The form occurs often enough to warrant resurrecting the name. This is the BEAK, a convex and a concave arc joining at a point near the top. The convex surface is nearer the work edge.

BACKWARD ELEMENTS

In a very few cases, an element will appear in a profile "backwards", in the reverse of its usual orientation. An example would be an ovolo that is horizontal at its outer end, rather than its inner. This may be indicated by prefixing the element name with lower-case "back". This does not change listing order.

PRINCIPLES

FIRST PRINCIPLE — NAME THE PROFILE OF THE MOLDING THAT THE PLANE PRODUCES.

In common usage, all molding planes (except for hollows and rounds) are named for the profile they create. The system, then, is directed to naming these profiles. As shown in Fig.10:72, in some cases the manner of using the plane may change the profile it cuts. Here it is important to define the method of use.

The great majority of molding planes are intended to be used to shape the edge of a board that was held flat on a benchtop. The plane's fence is guided by the board's left edge. It cuts down, into the face of the board, until the plane's depth stop touches the face and it can cut no further. (This is shown in Fig.10:8.)

A few planes are intended "to work the edge", as the catalogs say. The work is supported narrow edge up, and the plane is guided by the face of the work and cuts into the edge. Such planes usually have unusually deep fences. These are also named for the profile they cut, and given the same name as the ordinary type of plane which cuts the same molding; but the lower case word "edge" is added to the name. An example is shown with the COVE and OVOLO in Chapter 11.

Such use permits an undercut which would be impossible with a plane working the face. The only example encountered was shown as a REVERSE OGEE (edge) in Chapter 11. As this name shows, the profile may be regarded as rotated as necessary to conform with an element definition.

The following exposition refers to naming a molding as cut by either of these types of plane. In either case, a portion of the face of the work is uncut, and there is no problem in identifying the "innermost" profile element, the one next to the uncut region of the face of the work. Strips that were completely molded were usually made by using these planes in one of two ways. Either the profile was cut on a wide board and ripsawed off, or both sides of the face of the strip were molded in two steps, by the same or different planes. In either case, the "innermost" element is evident.

A very few planes were made to mold the entire face of a strip in one pass. Extension of the naming system to cover this type will be taken up later.

SECOND PRINCIPLE — EACH ELEMENT OF THE PROFILE IS IDENTIFIED AS ONE OF THE THIRTEEN PERMITTED.

The only element names used in this system are those defined above, and summarized below. Every element is named, even the smaller ones. Modifiers selected from the list given below may be used to provide additional information.

EXCEPTION TO NAMING ALL ELEMENTS

In some cases a fillet is understood, and is not named. Those implied in the name "astragal" were covered earlier. As another example, an ovolo and cove must be separated by a fillet. If they were not, the curve would have been called an ogee. The systematic name is thus ovolo and cove, not ovolo, fillet and cove. Since this is common usage, a fillet is understood as being present between any two elements that would otherwise join smoothly. The fillet is not cited in the name. Similarly, a cove and ovolo is understood as having a vertical step between them (else it would be called a reverse ogee). It need not be named "cove and dropped ovolo".

THE HYPHEN CONVENTION

In a few cases two of the named elements in fact are joined smoothly (without a point or corner). This only occurs in profiles with multiple curvature. The name ogee and ovolo implies a vertical step between them, in accord with the above practice. Rarely, the elements may be smoothly joined to give the curve having two reversals of curvature (sometimes called a double ogee). One is seen in the QUIRK OGEE-OVOLO in Chapter 11. The present system names the curve an OGEE-OVOLO, the hyphen between the names meaning a smooth joining. The ogee or reverse ogee is stated first. (The curve cited could otherwise support the name "quirk bead-reverse ogee"). An exception may be made when doing so requires a grossly distorted ogee. The only such case encountered is the last profile of page 282.

THIRD PRINCIPLE — THE SYSTEMATIC NAME IS DERIVED BY CITING THE INNERMOST ELEMENT FIRST, THEN THE REMAINING ELEMENTS IN THE ORDER IN WHICH THEY OCCUR MOVING TOWARD THE BOARD EDGE.

Common usage is not consistent, but in the majority of cases, a two-element molding is named by giving the name of its inner element, then the name of the element at the edge of the work. This principle makes systematic names for the simpler profiles agree with currently used names (example, Grecian ogee with bevel).

If the innermost element is a minor one, for instance a small fillet, it is frequently ignored in common usage. If the present system is to avoid requiring a nebulous judgement call as to when an element is a minor one, it is necessary to name *all* elements, regardless of size (barring the exceptions given on the previous page). As the first element determines the alphabetical order of presentation used herein, it is especially important that a first element, however small, not be neglected in coding your profile. They are included in the names used here, even though this is not common practice.. Reminders of this fact are used in the form of cross-references where necessary.

OPTIONAL SIZE INDICATION

The most frequently found complex forms are those which combine two simple forms, usually a simple element augmented on the outside by a smaller feature. Several catalogs named these as the inner, larger element "with" the smaller (for instance, ogee with bead). Others used the connective "and". It seems a pity to waste two names for the same meaning. The present system will use "with" to imply that the second element is smaller; "and" if it is not. Thus a cove with a small bead will be called "COVE with BEAD", while "COVE and BEAD" implies that the bead is at least as large as the cove. Neither term is considered in determining alphabetical order. This is a minor refinement and should cause no problems with judgement calls, as the order of listing is unaffected.

LEFT-HANDED PLANES

The very rare left-handed molder (with its fence on the right side of the plane) is named simply by prefixing the name of the profile cut, or its profile code designation, with the lower-case word "left". Being in lower case means that this term does not affect alphabetical order.

EXTENSION TO OTHER FORMS OF MOLDINGS

STRIP PLANES

A few planes were intended to cut the full surface of the workpiece. The clearest indication (but a rare one) is the presence of two fences, one on either side of the stock. Lacking this, the purpose is clear if the cut is deep at the right side of the sole, the blade overhanging the stock. Problems arise in applying the above system to this type, as the elements cut by the right side of the plane iron are "backward" and naming becomes awkward. This may be dealt with simply by choosing the highest point of the molding and designating the element at this point as the "innermost". The molding may then be named as if it were two separate moldings of the ordinary type. Choose the more complex side, and name the elements of this starting with the "innermost" and naming the rest in sequence toward the edge. Add to this the word "OPPOSITE" and name the remaining elements, starting with the element on the other side of the innermost and naming the remaining elements in sequence toward the other edge. For symmetrical moldings (those unchanged by turning end for end), this may be simplified. The profile is divided at the center, and one half is named conventionally. The name is prefixed with the word "SYMMETRICAL".

While description of the process becomes wordy, it is in fact simple and should become clear by examination of the examples in the "Other Types" section of Chapter 11.

FACING PLANES

These planes are designed to create a molding by removing wood primarily from the center of the workpiece, rather than the edge. These are most often intended to create symmetrical profiles, used in door casings and similar applications. They are named by naming the central element, adding the word "JOINING", and then naming the remaining elements of one side from the outer edge inward. (The naming of these elements from the edge inward has been found to give simpler names requiring fewer "back" elements).

Unsymmetrical facing planes are rarely encountered. They are named similarly: the central element, "joining", the more complex side from the outer edge inward, "facing" the remaining elements named from the edge in.

CORNICE PLANES

Cornice planes are intended to create profiles that are mounted at an angle, and when named (which is rare) are given the name of the profile as it appears when mounted. Because there are many cases where the use intended for the plane is unclear, it seems prudent to avoid such judgements and to code the profile as if it were to be used in the flat.

These types of planes are relatively uncommon, and are listed separately to reduce search complications. However, the instructions given above need no extension to serve for naming these planes.

SUMMARY

DEFINITIONS

The following list repeats one given in Chapter 11, giving somewhat greater detail. It may be useful for quick reference.

ASTRAGAL: a convex half-circle with both ends of the arc at the same level, with a fillet on the side toward the edge and usually one on the other side. The innermost fillet may be replaced by an adjacent element. A soft astragal meets one or both fillets in a curve rather than a right angle.

back: prefix for an element that faces the wrong way in the profile, as if it belonged to a molding on the opposite edge of the workpiece.

BEAD: a round projection rising above the level of the junction with a previous feature and covering a half-circle or less.

BEAK: a convex and a concave arc meeting at their upper ends in a sharp corner.

BEVEL: a flat section slanted with respect to the board surface.

COVE: a hollow element, quarter circle or less, ending at the lowest point of the curve (which may be circular or elliptical).

dropped: not an element, but used to mean the feature is dropped to a level below the end of the one last named by a short vertical step.

edge: denoting a plane meant to be guided by the face of the board, and cutting into the edge.

FACING: see naming of facing planes above.

FILLET: a flat section, parallel to the board surface.

FLUTE: a hollow groove, the ends of which are at the same level.

GOTHIC ARCH: two convex arcs meeting at the top in a point.

GRECIAN OGEE: a quirk ogee with elliptical curves.

GRECIAN OVOLO: a quirk ovolo of elliptical curvature.

hyphen (-): This is not a named element, but is used to indicate a smooth juncture of the two elements it joins as opposed to their separation by a fillet or step.

JOINING: see naming of facing planes, above.

left: describing a molding plane having its fence on the right side.

lying: describing an ogee (or reverse ogee) which could be made by smoothly joining a flute (as defined above) and a bead having both ends at the same level.

OGEE: an S-shaped curve, hollow or concave near the edge of the board and round or convex further in.

OPPOSITE: (see "other forms" above). Used in coding special types of plane, for cutting bolections or astragals.

OVOLO: a convex arc subtending $90°$ or less, upper end close to horizontal or sloping down.

QUIRK: a narrow groove separating two elements, usually a vertical step returning a curve to the surface.

QUIRK BEAD: a quirk and a circular arc reaching the vertical at its outer end.

QUIRK OGEE: a quirk and ogee of circular or nearly circular arcs. The name is used here for profiles, regardless of type of curvature, observed in early molders before the term "Grecian" became popular.

QUIRK OVOLO: a quirk and circular or nearly circular arc. The name is also used here for profiles, regardless of type of curvature, observed in early molders made before the "Grecian" usage became popular.

raised: not an element, but a term used to indicate the feature is raised above the last named by a short vertical step.

REVERSE OGEE: an S-shaped curve, convex near the edge of the board and concave further in.

soft ASTRAGAL: astragal with rounded joining of arc and fillet.

SCOTIA: a hollow groove with ends at two different levels, and dropping below the level of the lower end.

SYMMETRICAL: See naming of symmetrical strip planes, above.

CODE

Each name for the profiles in Chapter 13 is followed by a shorthand alphabetic code, which is used is some cases to identify or refer to drawings of the profiles. These are more useful than sequential numbers, which resist rational additions. The code is simply a shorthand notation for the significant features of the name. Decoding these is not necessary for their use, but for the curious, the upper-case letters refer to the profile elements defined above:

A=Astragal, B=Bead, C=Cove, D=Symmetrical, F=Fillet, G=Gothic bead, H=Flute (Hollow), J=Joining, K=beaK, L=beveL, O=Ogee, Q=Quirk, R=Reverse Ogee, S=Scotia, V=oVolo, + = Opposite or Facing

A few modifiers, represented by lower-case letters, are occasionally used. These may be considered as optional, as they are ignored in alphabetization. They do, however, add detail. These are:

b=back, d=dropped, e=edge, l=lying, r=raised, s=soft, left=left-handed plane

In some cases, sketches are shown of several variants of a named profile. These are indicated, in the code identifiers, by a suffixed hyphen and ordinal number.

Used in the extended name but not coded are the connectives "and" and "with". These give indications of relative size; "and" implying that the element that follows is at least as large as the earlier one, "with" that it is smaller. These are optional and do not affect listing order.

AN INDEX BASED UPON THE PHYSICAL SHAPE OF THE PLANE

BACKGROUND

The conventional index at the end of a book provides a means of locating the page on which a given topic is treated, IF one knows its name. Faced with an unfamiliar plane, knowing neither its name nor its function, the usual type of index is of little use to you. If you are not to be forced to thumb through the book page by page in order to find the information you seek, a way must be provided to furnish you with a name or a number.

The preceding Appendix outlined a naming procedure for the profiles of complex molding planes. It provides a name, which in turn permits locating the profile sought in an alphabetical list.

The location of other plane types requires another system. The one to be described will provide not a name, but a number, which can be used to index the entries. It is designed to be of use to one with little prior knowledge about planes, and to accomodate planes yet to be discovered.

A procedure is given through which a two-digit number may be assigned to any plane, based solely on the shape of the plane's cutting edge and its body; no knowledge of function is required. Having determined this number, you will find all planes of this class listed together in the Numerical Index. Where there are a significant number of entries of the same class, and where a sole profile would be of help in identifying the plane in question, these will be found in the Cutter and Sole Profile listings, which are also arranged in numerical order of their codes.

In most cases determining the two-digit code will be all that is required to facilitate your search, as it narrows the list of planes to be scanned to a manageable number.

However, as will be seen in the tables that follow, the names and profiles are assigned additional numbers appended to the two-digit class code, after a decimal point. Borrowing the principle of the Dewey decimal classification, this notation can be extended to give a unique code to any individual tool.

These decimals have been assigned in a systematic manner, planned to permit rational assignment of a numerical code to planes not covered here, as they surface. Gaps in the number sequence occur because of this. (further details are available from the author should you desire information applicable to inventory record keeping).

CLASS CODES

All wooden plane types described herein have been sorted into classes labeled with their two-digit class number. This number is determined solely by the physical appearance of the tool, in accordance with the definitions below. The shape of the cutting edge provides the first digit, and the body shape provides the second.

Where a tool satisfies more than one of the definitions, the higher numerical code is used. For this reason, the definitions are given in reverse numerical order; the first applicable definition provides the correct digit.

FIRST DIGIT: SHAPE OF CUTTER EDGE

(If there are multiple cutters, see Note 1 below: for vertical edges see Note 2: for edge projections, see Note 3.)

DIGIT	CUTTER EDGE DESCRIPTION
9	More than one curve plus one or more straight sections. (Elements may be connected or separated.)
8	More than one curve, without straight sections.
7	Reverse curve or S-shaped curve (one that changes direction of curvature at least once), with or without straight sections.
6	One concave (hollow) curve plus one or more straight sections.
5	One convex (round) curve with one or more straight line sections.
4	One concave curve without straight sections.

407

3   One convex curve without straight sections.

2   Two or more straight segments, either meeting at an angle
           or separated (includes serrated edges).

1   A single straight edge (not necessarily horizontal). A very
           slight rounding of the cutter corners is allowed.

0   Reserved for tools that have interchangeable cutters of
           different shapes (see Note 4).

NOTE 1: MULTIPLE CUTTERS. Some planes have nickers or spurs (knifelike edges which sever the wood fibers in front of the main cutter, at its edges). These are not considered in coding. Others have two or more main cutters. If these work in concert, both cutting at the same time, the coding is the same as if the profiles were combined in one blade. There are combination tools, however, which are really two planes in one stock. Only one of the blades works at a time. In these cases, the profile with the higher numeric code is used.

NOTE 2: SCRAPING EDGES. Some blades, especially those mounted at an angle to the sides of the plane body, are beveled on a vertical edge to provide clearance. They may even be sharpened on the side, although this edge does not actually cut in use. Such edges are not considered in coding.

NOTE 3: QUIRKS. Many molding profiles include a narrow crevice separating adjacent features, called a quirk. The part of the cutter that forms this is an edge projection that may be either rounded or flat on the bottom. This section, however, is small and subject to change in resharpening. It is treated as if it were a point, and is not considered in coding. Quirks are usually found in molding planes: a few of the simpler molding profiles are included in the numerical index.

NOTE 4: An example of this class is the patternmakers plane, which has interchangeable soles and matching cutters.

SECOND DIGIT: SHAPE OF PLANE BODY

(Names fully capitalized below are defined in the DEFINITIONS section which follows. As with the first digit, numbers are listed in descending order. The first definition found which is satisfied by your tool gives the correct digit.)

DIGIT	BODY TYPE
9	Unconventional shapes: that is, not satisfying the definition of USUAL SHAPE, SHAVE TYPE, PLOW or ROUTER, and not having a COOPER'S FENCE.
8	Having a COOPER'S FENCE.
7	SHAVE TYPE.
6	PLOW or ROUTER.
5	SIDE ESCAPEMENT type, CURVED.
4	SIDE ESCAPEMENT type, FUNCTIONAL sole.
3	SIDE ESCAPEMENT type, SIMPLE sole.
2	BENCH type, CURVED.
1	BENCH type, FUNCTIONAL sole.
0	BENCH type, SIMPLE sole.

For those readers familiar with plane terminology, the only definitions needed are CURVED (path of plane in use is curved, not straight) and FUNCTIONAL sole (having a fence and/or a depth stop): a SIMPLE sole has neither. More complete definitions are given below.

For planes having movable fences or depth stops, see Note 5. For planes with hollow simple soles see Note 6.

DEFINITIONS

BENCH type planes are planes of USUAL SHAPE (defined below) whose shavings exit the plane body through the top (or, in one case, through the rear), not from the side.

COOPER'S FENCE: A massive guiding surface, intended to ride on the ends of the staves of a headless barrel to guide a cutter working inside of the barrel. Further description and illustrations may be found in Chapter 13, the Cooper.

CURVED planes are those whose body or fence is designed to move the cutter along a curve rather than in a straight line. The curve may be either in a vertical or horizontal plane.

FUNCTIONAL sole: One having a FENCE, a DEPTH STOP, or both (terms defined in next paragraph).

An extension of the plane body downward, beside and below the cutting edge, that provides a surface which remains in contact with the edge of the workpiece and guides the course of the plane, is called a FENCE. An extension of the plane body outward, beside and (usually) above the cutting edge, which serves to stop the cutting action of the plane after it has reached a certain depth, is a DEPTH STOP. These are illustrated in Fig.5:9.

PLOW: A plane whose cutting edge is located at a distance from the wooden body of the tool. The back of the cutter is braced by a vertical metal plate mounted in the plane's body, parallel to the plane's motion.

ROUTER: A tool with a cutting edge located at a distance below the bottom of the wooden body. The cut is made below the level of the surface on which the tool rides.

SHAVE TYPE tools have their cutting edge aligned parallel with the longest dimension of the tool.

SIDE ESCAPEMENT planes are of USUAL SHAPE (defined below), and permit the shavings to escape from the side of the body.

SIMPLE sole: The wooden body of a plane with this type sole does no more than support the cutter and prevent it from taking shavings that are too thick. It has no extensions which serve to guide the course of the tool in its path along the work, or to stop its cutting action when a certain depth has been reached.

USUAL SHAPE: The most common form of a wooden plane body starts with a block of rectangular section, longer than wide or high. It carries a main cutter which is secured in the body, usually by means of a wedge. The cutter protrudes slightly below the sole, or bottom of the body. The opening for this, called the mouth of the plane, runs from side to side, rather than along the length of, the body. It may or may not extend over the full width of the

410

body. The sole of the plane conforms to the shape of the exposed cutting edge, over the full width of the mouth. For convenience in handling in certain applications, there may be material removed from the original block shape by cutting away parts of the top or sides, or there may be additions such as handles. As long as the sole of the tool in the vicinity of the mouth is untouched, the function of the tool is unchanged and so is its class number.

Planes of USUAL SHAPE are divided into BENCH TYPE and SIDE ESCAPEMENT type, defined above.

NOTE 5: FUNCTIONAL SOLES. Metal or wood adjustable attachments are considered as equivalent to the integral fences or depth stops they replace if they extend the full length of the body, and the coding is as a functional sole. Attachments which extend for less than three-fourths of the sole length are not considered as making the sole functional.

NOTE 6: NON-FUNCTIONAL SOLES. Some planes, in particular those with concave cutting edges, have non-functional sole extensions beyond the blade sides. A nosing plane (profile 44.41 in the Cutter and Sole profiles) and one form of the cock bead plane (44.40) have similar profiles. In the former case, the flats at the edges of the sole have no function, while in the latter they serve as a depth stop. The differentiation requires a knowledge of the function, which is at odds with the premise that coding requires no such knowledge. For this reason, any sole segment not obviously non-functional suffices to require coding the sole as functional. For the present purpose, a tool improperly coded (e.g. panel plane coded as 10) because this provision was ignored will be cross-referenced at the improper code.

PROCEDURE

Having determined the proper two-digit class code of the plane you seek, locate this CLASS number in the following Numerical Index. If there are a significant number of planes of the same class, and if a sole profile would be of assistance in identification, their profiles will be found in the Cutter and Sole Profile listings at the end of this Appendix. This will provide a decimal extension of the class code, which will locate the name of the plane in question in the Numerical Index.

NUMERICAL INDEX

QUICK REFERENCE, CODING

FIRST DIGIT
(Cutter)

1 straight edge
2 multiple straight
3 convex
4 concave
5 convex + straight
6 concave + straight
7 contains an ogee
8 multiple curves
9 multiple + straight
0 interchangeable cutters

SECOND DIGIT
(Body)

0 bench type, simple sole
1 "   ", functional sole
2 " , ", curved
3 side escapement, simple sole
4 " ,   ",   functional sole
5 "   ",   curved
6 plows and routers
7 shave types
8 having cooper's fence
9 unconventional shapes

CLASS 10 : Straight cutting edge, bench type, simple sole.

10.0 : Small surfacing planes (less than 6",15 cm.long) are described in the section "SMALL PLANES" of Chapter 4, p.55. These include Violin, Thumb or Modeling, Toy, Whip and Carriagemaker's Smooth.

10.1 Surfacing planes 6-30 inches long (15-76 cm.). These are further subdivided into bench planes (10.11 through 10.14), to be found in Chapter 3, "BENCH PLANES—INDIVIDUAL TYPES". American names commonly used for planes included in various size ranges are:

    10.11   6-14 in. long (15-35 cm.): Smooth
    10.12 14-18 in. " (35-46 cm.): Jack
    10.13 18-22 in. " (46-56 cm.): Fore or Trying
    10.14 22-30 in " (56-76 cm.): Jointer

    10.15 "Strike Block" has been used for various forms, described in that section of Chapter 4, p.62
    10.16 Planes in Class 10.1 with skewed irons:
Shootboard (Fig.4:10). Skewed Jacks are also seen.

10.2 Very Long planes are found in the section of that name in Chapter 4, p.55

    10.21 Floor plane p.55

10.3 Low blade mounting angle (less than 45°).

10.4 High blade mounting angle (more than 50°).

10.5 Abbreviated sole

10.6 (Blade exposed at side of plane)

NOTE: Panel and Coach Door planes are found under code 11 (see Note 6 above).

CLASS 11 : (Straight edge, bench type, functional sole)

11.0 (Depth stop): Panel, p.68; Slipped Panel, Fig.4:12

11.1 (Double depth stop): Door Check, p.69; Osaka Grooving, Fig.4:19; Tenoning, p.70

11.3 (Double fence): Reglet, p.61; Slat, p.61; Spelk, Figs.12:23 and 12:24; Japanese Rounding (Bukkiri-mentori-kanna),p.197; and Shoji Slat plane, Fig.4:6

11.4 (Fence and depth stop): Panel Raiser, Fig.4:15 left; Badger Panel Raiser (p.72); Chinese Plow, Fig.7:27

11.6 (Fence or sole at other than 90°)

11.653 Hinged adjustable chamfer, Fig.8:11

11.7 Spring plane, Fig.11:9 E

CLASS 12 : Straight edge, bench type, curved cutter path.

12.0 (Sole convex lengthwise): Compass, Fig.9:1; Violin Smooth (compass), p.55; Cooper's Bowling plane, p.158; Adjustable Compass plane, Fig.9:2; Felloe plane, Fig.9:4 left; Universal plane, p.157; Gerfschaafje, Fig.9:6

12.2 (Concave lengthwise): Felloe,Fig.9.4 right; Lagging plane, p.157; Coachmaker's Smooth (concave) p.355; Cooper's Plucker, Fig.13:32; Cooper's Rounding plane, p.158; Cooper's Head plane (Bodenhobel) p.330

12.3 (Flexible sole): Cole patent, Fig.9:3

12.6 (Radius): Sun or Leveling, Fig.13:7

12.8 (Trammel planes): Cooper's Head Edge cutter, Fig.13:25; French Head Chamfer cutter, p.330

CLASS 13 : Straight edge, side escapement type, simple sole.

13.0 Rabbet, Fig.6:4; Shoulder planes, Fig.6:13

13.1 Stop Rabbet, Fig.6:19; Bullnose Rabbet, e.g.Fig.6:12

13.2 Beaver Tail or Coachmaker's Rabbet, p.354

13.3 Ship (Bridge) Builder's Rabbet, Fig.6:5

13.4 Jack Rabbet, Fig.6:5 bottom : Banding, Traversing planes, p.139

13.5 Sole wider than stock
    13.51 T Rabbet, Fig. 6:11 center
    13.52 L Rabbet, Fig. 6:11 left

13.6 (Edge vertical)
    13.60 Side Rabbet, Fig.6:15
    13.61 Side Snipe, p.192
        13.615 Side Snipe Combination, Fig.10:20
    13.62 French Slope Rabbet, Fig.8:5 (see also code 13.72)

13.7 (Slanted sole)
    13.70 Shouldering plane, Fig.8:2
    13.71 Planemaker's Boxing plane, Fig.13:91 #3
    13.72 French Side Rabbet, Fig.6:20

13.8 (With spur blade) Dado, Fig.7:43; Shoji groover,p.140

CLASS 14 : Straight edge, side escapement type, functional sole.

14.0 (Integral depth stop)

    14.01 Shoulder Rabbet, p.92

    14.02 Raglet, p.139

14.1 (Double depth stop)

    14.11 Planemaker's Boxing plane, Fig.13:91 #4

    14.15 Blind Grooving (Rabot à entailles), p.139

14.2 (Fence)

    14.20 Standing Filletster, Fig.6:23 right; Spill plane, Fig.12:21

    14.22 Continental Long Filletster, Fig.6:25

    14.23 Double Continental Filletster, p.101

    14.24 Weatherstrip plane, p.135

14.3 (Adjustable fence)

    14.30 Moving Filletster, Fig.6:26

    14.31 Arm Filletster; wedge, Fig.6:27, screw, Fig.6:29

    14.32 Belgian Plow, Fig.7:20; French Plow, p.124

    14.33 Sash Filletster, Fig.13:62

    14.34 Combination Filletster, Fig.13:63

14.4 (Double fence): Spill, Fig.12:22

14.5 (Fence & depth stop)

    14.50 Halving, Fig.6:23 left

    14.51 Panel raiser (side escapement), p.70

    14.52 Halving, to work far edge, Fig.6:24

    14:53 Planemaker's Boxing plane, Fig.13:91 #2: Casemakers Grooving plane, Fig.13:94 C; Casement Sash Grooving plane, Fig.13:72 E right

    14.54 Plows with wooden skates: French, Fig.7:21; Japanese Plow, Fig.7:29

    14.55 Cock Bead Filletster, Fig.10:51 right

14.6 (Sloped sole) Side Chamfer, Fig.8:16 B

14.7 (Sloped sole or fence)

    14.70 Dovetail (no depth stop), Fig.8:1 center

    14.71 Adjustable Chamfer, Fig.8:14

    14.72 Bookcase plane variant, Fig.8:3

    14.73 Planemaker's Boxing plane, Fig.13:91 #5

14.8 (Sloped sole or fence, fence and depth stop)

    14.80 Panel Raiser, side escapement, p.74

    14.81 Chamfer, Fig.8:16 C

    14.82 Dropped Chamfer, Fig.8:16 D

    14.83 Dovetail, Fig. 8:1 right

        14.831 Dovetail left- and right- combination, p.142

14.84 Bookcase, Fig.8:3

14.85 Adjustable Chamfer planes

    14.851 Vertical Adjustment Chamfer, Fig.8:12

    14.852 Iron Fence Chamfer, Fig.8:10

    14.853 Wedge Arm Chamfer, Fig.8:13

14.86 Bevel Sash plane, English style, Fig.13:59 #7

14.9 Side Cutting Rabbet, Fig.6:16

CLASS 15 : Straight edge, side escapement type, curved path.

15.0 Compass Rabbet, e.g., Fig.6:11 right or Fig.9:5 right; Felloe plane, compass, Fig.9:4 left; Columbelle, Fig.13:27

15.1 Felloe plane, concave, Fig.9:4 right

15.2 Boat-shape (Navette) Rabbet, Fig.9:28; Door Rabbet, Fig.6:9

15.3 Compass Fillister, p.172

15.5 Radius Rabbet, Fig.6:10

15.6 Radius Filletster, Fig. 9:26

15.7 Dado, radius, on trammel, Fig.9:25

    15.71 Gauge plane, Fretz patent, Fig.13:87

CLASS 16 : Straight edge, plow or router type.

16.0 Unfenced Plow; Varken, Fig.7:26

16.1 (Fixed or filletster fence)

    16.10 Board Match Groove,Fig.7:31 front; Weatherstrip plane, p.135

    16.11 Plank Match Groove, Fig.7:34 front

    16.12 Stair builder's Match Groove, p.135

    16.13 Drawer plane, p.133

    16.15 Filletster Fence Plow, Fig.7:3

    16.16 Filletster Fence Match Groove, Fig.7:35 right

NOTE: Match combination planes are coded as 24

16.2 Plows with two arms fixed to fence

    16.20 Friction-fit arms, p.110

    16.21 Wedge Arm Plow, p.111, Fig.7:1

        16.215 Wedge arm Match Groove plane, Fig.7:36 right

    16.22 Thumbscrew (Yankee) Plow, Figs.7:5 and 7:6

    16.23 Screw-adjust Arm, Fig.7:11

    16.24 Screw-arm, Fig.7:10

    16.25 Rack-and-pinion adjustment, p.118

16.3 Plows, two arms fixed to body

    16.31 Continental Wedge Arm Plows; p.124

CLASS 21 : Multiple straight edges, bench type, functional sole

21.0 Glass Check, bench type, Fig.7:38

21.1 Plank Match Tongue, Fig.7:34 rear; Gasterhobel, bench type, Fig.7:42

21.2 Combined Jointer and Rabbet (Fug-und-Falzhobel) p.104

21.4 Panel Fielding, Figs.4:13 B,C; 4:14, 4:15 right

21.5 Bevel Sash, bench American style, p.341

> 21.60 V-groove plane, p.132
> 21.61 Table slide plane, Fig.8:6
>
> 21.71 Japanese storm door plane, trapezoidal, female, p.170
> 21.72 Japanese storm door plane, trapezoidal, male, p.170
> 21.73 Panel Raiser, Fig.4:13 D
> 21.74 Panel Raiser, Fig.4:13 E

21.8 (Serrated edge) Shoe-peg plane, Fig.13:106

CLASS 22 : Multiple straight edges, bench type, curved cutter path

A variety of planes may have curved soles, for example: V-Compass, Compass Toothing, Radius Panel Raiser. These are not separately described, but may be identified by finding their straight-sole counterparts.

CLASS 23 : Multiple straight edges, side escapement type, simple sole

23.4 V-plane, Fig.8:19

23.5 Gunstocker's plane, for octagonal barrels, p.161

CLASS 24 : Multiple Straight edges, side escapement type, functional sole

> 24.01 Tongue plane, side-cutting (Federhobel zu Auszugtischen), p.137
> 24.10 Casemaker's Double Groove, Fig.13:94 H
> 24.11 Double Grooving, Fig.13:72 E left, p.136
> 24.12 Planemaker's Boxing (No. 1 in figure 13.91)
>>   24.150 Board Match Tongue, Fig.7:31 rear
>>   24.151 Match combinations, Fig. 7:32
>>   24.152 Gladwin Patent Tongue and Groove, Fig.7:33
>>   24.153 Gasterhobel (side escapement type), Fig.7:42
>
> 24.40 Bevel and Fillet, Fig.10:39
> 24.41 PG Molding, Figs.8:16 E, 10:40
> 24.42 Meeting Rail plane, Fig.13:64
> 24.43 Panel Raiser, side escapement, p.74

24.50 Bevel Sash (American style), p.341

24.51 Bevel Square Sash(American style), p.341

24.52 Rustic Sash (American style),p.341

24.60 Carbeading, p.208

24.61 Double Chamfer, Fig.8:16 A; V-groove plane, p.152

24.62 Bookcase Shelf plane. V-type, p.144

24.63 Ship Hawk plane, p.154

24.64 Double Door plane (bevel), Fig.7:37 rear

24.65 Tidey patent plane, Fig.8:15

24.71 V-tongue plane, p.152

24.72 Chamfer with two fillets, Fig.8:16 F

24.75 Jensen patent Universal Tongue plane, p.133

CLASS 25 : Multiple straight, side escapement type, curved cutter path

Ship Hawk plane, p.154, compassed

CLASS 26 : Multiple straight, side escapement, edge below body

Bookbinder's Plow (V-blade), p.123; Modified Glass Check, Fig.7:39

CLASS 27 : Multiple straight, shave or scraper

Toothing Scraper

CLASS 28 : Multiple straight, cooper's fence

V-Croze, p.236; Sawtooth Post Croze, Fig.13:15

CLASS 29 : Multiple straight, unconventional shape

Corebox (V cutter), Fig.13:105; Screwbox, Fig.12:32; Tapping machine, Fig.12:33; Two-blade witchet, Fig.9:15; L-blade Rounder, Fig.9:14; Plasterer's plane, p.61

CLASS 30 : Convex edge, bench type, simple sole

30.0 Roughing plane, p.38 et seq.

30.1 Backing-out Jack, p.44,160; Stave Hollowing, p.160;

30.2 Coachmaker's, p.355, and Violin (p.55) Smooth Rounds

30.3 Ship Round, p.159; Japanese Round, p.193

30.4 Gutter, Fig.9:8; Hand Gutter, p.160

CLASS 31 : Convex edge, bench type, functional sole

     31.70 Japanese Storm Door (Female), p.170

     31.71 Pump Log plane, Fig. 9:7; also the smaller Casement Sash Match, female, French bench type, Fig.13:72 D left

CLASS 32 : Convex edge, bench type, curved cutter path

     French Cooper's Head Champer Plane, Fig.13:26; Stoup, Fig.13:30; Round-both-ways plane, p.158; Violin Spoon Smooth, p.55; Filletster, round, concave, p.168; Scoopmaker's Shave, Fig.12:13

CLASS 33 : Convex edge, side escapement type, simple sole

33.0 Round, Fig.10:9 right; Coachmaker's, Fig.13:74

33.1 Table Round, Fig.9:11 B

     33.20 Full Round, Fig.10:11

     33.21 Cod plane, Fig.10:14

33.3 Gunstocker's, Fig.9:9

     33.50 Side Round, Fig.10:16

     33.52 Side Round, crow's bill style, Fig. 10:17

33.6 Burrowes Weatherstrip plane, p.134

CLASS 34 : Convex edge, side escapement type, functional sole

     34.00 Sill Drip, Figs.13:67 and 68

     34.01 Planemaker's jogged side Round, Fig.13:88 B

     34.05 Double Sash Coping (ovolo), Fig.13:58 D

     34.20 Table Round (fenced), Fig.9:11 D

     34.21 Cove plane, Fig.10:35

     34.23 Door Joint Groove plane, Fig.9:12

     34.25 Double Sash Coping (ovolo), Figs. 13:58 E,F

     34.30 Sill Drip plane (larmier), p.350

     34.35 Swing Door (female)

     34.40 Mother plane for hollow, p.183

     34.45 Sash Coping, ovolo, Fig.13:58 C

     34.46 Sash Coping, gothic (see Fig.13:59#10 and 13:58)

     34.50 Sash Ovolo Coping plane, Fig.10:36

     34.53 French Sill drip, Fig.13:70

     34.63 Sill or Drip Mold, Fig.13:68

34.64 Fluting (pilaster), Fig. 10:13

34.71 Casemaker's Round Groove, Fig.13:94 B
34.72 Casement Sash Match (female),Fig 13:72 F,G(right)
34.75 Multiple Fluting, Fig.10:68
34.8 Wedge Notching (planemaker's) Fig.13:90 top

CLASS 35 : Convex edge, side escapement, curved cutter path

> See the uncurved forms for identification. Examples, a round (Fig.10:9 B) may be curved to a Compass Round, a Navette Round or a Radius Round.

CLASS 36 : Convex edge, edge below stock

> Organ Builder's Scoring plane, Fig.13:95

CLASS 37 : Convex edge, shave or scraper

> Inside Shave,Fig.13:34; Travisher,Fig.12:4; Shovelmaker's Shave, Fig.12:7; Gull Wing Shave, Fig.12:5; Scratch Stock, p.304; or Scraper, p.305 (both convex)

CLASS 38 : Convex edge, cooper's fence

> Howel, Fig.13:11 and Howel combinations, p.328; Flincher (curved blade) p.324

CLASS 39 : Convex edge, unconventional shape

> Bodda, Fig.13:35; Chairmaker's Shave, Fig.12:8; Quatrefoil Cutter (curved cutter), p.314

CLASS 40 : Concave edge, bench type, simple sole

> Stave Rounding, p.167; Violin Hollow, p.55; Japanese Hollow, p.170; Handrail Capping plane, Fig.13:97: see also p.167

CLASS 41 : Concave edge, bench type, functional sole

41.0 Ship Hollow and related planes: p.167
> 41.01 Blind plane, p.167
> 41.12 Japanese Corner-round Molding. Fig.10:5
41.4 Nosing (bench type),p.168; Forkstaff plane, Fig.9:18
41.7 Japanese Storm-door plane, male, Fig. 9:23
41.8 French Nosing plane, Fig.9:20 lower right

422

CLASS 42 : Concave edge, bench type, curved cutter path

Ball Plane, p.158; Compass Corner Rounding, (Japanese) p.182

CLASS 43 : Concave edge, side escapement type, simple sole

43.0 Hollow, Fig.10:9 left

43.1 Table Hollow, Fig.9:11 A

43.3 Deep Hollow, Fig.10:15

      43.40 Swing Door (male), p.189
      43.45 Snipe Bill (simple curve on edge), p.192
      43.46 Crow's Beak, inside cut, p.274

43.5 Side Hollow, Fig.10:18

    (Nosing plane, see Class 44)

CLASS 44 : Concave edge, side escapement, functional sole

44.0 Mother plane for round, p.189

44.1 Corner Rounding, Fig.8:16 G

      44.20 Gothic Sash (new style),Fig.13:57 #10 and p.339
      44.21 Gothic Sash (old style)   "   "
      44.25 Casing Molding, Fig.10:23

44.3 Gothic and fillet sash, Fig.13:57 #11

      44.40 Cock Bead, p.204; Fishing Rod maker's (both Fig.10:52)
      44.41 Nosing plane, Fig.9:20
      44.43 Center Bead (narrow quirks), p.204

      44.50 Casemaker's tongue rounding, Fig.13:94 A
      44.52 Reed and guide, Fig.10:64
      44.53 Side bead, Fig. 10:43
        44.535 Double side bead, Fig 10:46

      44.80 Tambour, p.167
      44.81 Nosing, French (side escapement type), p.170
      44.82 Grecian Ovolo, Fig.10:29
      44.85 Wedge finial former (planemaker's) Fig.13:90

CLASS 45 : Concave edge, side escapement, curved cutter path

Compass Hollow, Radius Hollow, Coach Compass Hollow, and other types with curved paths

CLASS 47 : Concave edge, shave or scraper

Scratch Stock, beading, Fig.12:18; Jarvis, Fig.12:11; Coachmaker's Beading Router, p.357

CLASS 50 : Convex+straight edge, bench type, simple sole

Japanese Corner-rounding plane, p.76; Japanese Hewing pattern plane, p.182

CLASS 51 : Convex+straight edge, bench type, functional sole

51.00 Japanese Corner-rounding (another type), Fig.4:21
51.01 Cove Raising plane, p.73

CLASS 52 : Convex+straight edge, bench type, curved path

Concave Round (German Bettenhohlkehlhobel),p.168

CLASS 53 : Convex+straight edge, side escapement, simple sole

V-plane (Fig.8:19) with rounded point

CLASS 54 : Convex+straight edge, side escapement, functional sole

54.0 Dropped Cove, Fig.10:38

54.80 Casement sash match, double, Fig.12:72 I left
54.81 Casement sash match, double, Fig.12:72 J left

54.90 Mother plane, Bead, Fig.10:6

CLASS 57 : Convex+straight edge, shave or scraper

Sash Molding Shave,Fig.13:61

CLASS 60 : Concave+straight edge, bench type, simple sole

Corner Rounding, Coved Panel Plane, Fig.4:13 A

CLASS 61 : Concave+straight edge, bench type, functional sole

61.60 Japanese Corner Rounding, Fig.10:34
61.61 Reed and Guide (bench type), p. 206
61.63 Japanese Storm Door (male), Fig.9:23

61.70 Quarter Round (Japanese) Fig.10:34
61.71 See cornice planes, e.g., B in Fig.11:11

CLASS 64 : Concave+straight edge, side escapement, functional sole

64.00 Planemaker's Plow Fence tool, Fig.13:89 E
64.01 Quarter Round, Figs. 10:26, 10:27
    64.051 Sash Ovolo, Fig.10:31 (new style)
    64.052 Sash Ovolo, Fig.10:32 (old style)
    64.053 Sash, Gothic Square, Fig.13:39

64.10 Table Hollow (fenced), Fig.9:11 C
    64.105 Twin table plane, Fig.9:11 F
64.11 Casing molding plane, fence, Fig.10:24

64.20 Gothic Sash, American style, Fig.13:59 #10
64.21 Gothic and Square Sash,. Fig.13:48

64.30 Door plane, ovolo, Fig.7:37
64.31 Door lip plane, Fig.9:12
64.35 Sash ovolo, American style, Figs 13:52, 13:53

64.40 Cock bead (for edge),p.204; also Planemaker's tool, Fig 13:89 F
64.41 Casement sash match (male), Fig.13:72 D right
64.42 Torus bead, Fig.10:50

64.60 Cock bead, Fig.10:52
    64.610 Astragal, Fig.10:56
    64.611 Casement sash match male, Fig.13:72 G left
    64.612 Casement sash match male, Fig.13:72 F left
    64.620 Casemaker's (D in figure 13:94)
    64.621 Casement Sash plane, male, Fig.13:72 C left
64.65 Reed and guide (wide fillets), Fig.10:64

64.70 Center bead, bevel quirks, Fig.10:54
64.71 Bead, bevel quirk, Fig.10:44

64.80 Casement sash match, double, male, Fig.13:72 I right
64.81 Casement sash match, double, male, Fig.64:80 J right

CLASS 65 : Concave+straight edge, side escapement, curved path
    Compass Sash planes, for example

CLASS 66 : Concave+straight edge, edge below body
    French Grooving plane, p.134

CLASS 67 : Concave+straight edge, shave or scraper

Varieties of Scratch Stock,p.305; Coach Molding Router, Fig.13:82; and Sash Molding Shave, Fig.13:61

CLASS 70 : Ogee edge, bench type, simple sole

Forms of Stair Rail Capping plane, p.372

CLASS 71 : Ogee edge, bench type, functional sole

71.0 Water Table plane, p.350

71.11 Cabinet Ogee, Fig. 11:11 M, and p.295
71.12 Wide molder, Fig.11:11 L

71.20 Cornice plane, Fig.11:11 J

71.60 Washboard plane (bench type), p.168
71.61 Stair rail Capping plane, p.372

CLASS 72 : Ogee edge, bench type, curved path

Compass Handrail, p.373, and Handrail Wreath plane, Fig.13:100

CLASS 73 : Ogee edge, side escapement, simple sole

Snipe Bill, Fig. 10:19

CLASS 74 : Edge with ogee, side escapement, functional sole

74.00 Reverse Ogee, Fig.10:85
74.01 Reverse Ogee "to work edge", Fig.10:80
74.02 Reverse Ogee to work edge, "new style", Fig.10:93
74.021 Extended form, p.215
74.03 Sash Coping plane, Lamb Tongue, Fig.13:58 A

74.11 Ogee, p.209
74.12 Grecian or Quirk Ogee, p.214
74.14 Casemaker's Hook Joint, Fig.13:94 E
74.15 Sash plane, Lamb Tongue (old style), p.338
74.16 Sash plane, Lamb Tongue, p.339

74.20 Sash plane, Lamb Tongue with shoulder, Fig.10:91

74.35 Sash plane, Lamb Tongue (American style), p.341

74.61 Washboard (multiple), p.168
74.62 Saddle template plane for lamb tongue sash, p.345

CLASS 77 : Edge with ogee, shave or scraper

Forms of Sash Shave,p.347; and Handrail Shave,p.374

CLASS 82 : Multiple curves, bench type, curved cutter path

Chime Molder, Fig.13:29

CLASS 83 : Multiple curves, side escapement type, simple sole

Crow's Bill plane with both curves sharpened

CLASS 84 : Multiple curves, side escapement, functional sole

84.00 Center Fluting plane, Fig.10:67
84.01 Casement Sash Match, female, Fig.13:72 C
84.02 Casemaker's Double Round Groove, Fig.13:94 G
84.03 Flute and Guide plane, p.207
84.05 Saddle template plane for Gothic bead, p.344

84.10 Casemaker's Double Male. Fig.13:94 F
84.11 Double Side Reed, Fig.10:61
84.12 Gothic Reed, Fig.10:59
84.13 Multiple Gothic Reed, Fig.10:60
84.14 Planemaker's molder for plow fence, Fig.13:89 C

84.20 Cove quirked Bead (Cove with bead), Fig.10:45
84.21 Planemaker's molder for plow fence, Fig.13:89 D
84.25 Sash plane, Quirk Astragal and Hollow, Fig.13:59 #4
84.26 Sash Coping plane, Astragal and Hollow, p.345

84.3 Triple Fluting plane, p.207

84.40 Reeding, Fig. 10:62
84.41 Bead Cluster, Fig. 10:66

84.70 Ogee with Bead, p.241
84.75 Sash plane, Astragal with Ogee, Fig.13:59 #13
(see also complex molding planes)

CLASS 85 : Multiple curves, side escapement,curved cutter path

Cooper's Wreath plane, Fig.13:28

CLASS 86 : Multiple curves, edge below stock

Matchstick plane, Fig.9:19
Kinney patent Ripping plane, Fig.12:34

CLASS 87 : Multiple curves, shave or scraper
Molding Router, Fig.13:82 and related tools

CLASS 89 : Multiple curves, unconventional shape
Basketmaker's Upright Shave, Fig.13:103

CLASS 91 : Multiple curves+straight, bench type, funct. sole
Molded Panel Raiser, Fig.4:13 F. See also Cornice planes, Fig.11:11 and other complex molders

CLASS 92 : Multiple curves+straight, bench type, curved cutter path
Corner Block plane, p.314

CLASS 94 : Multiple curves+straight, side escapement, functional sole
94.0 Saddle Template plane for Square Ovolo Sash, p.344
    94.10 Double Reed Plane, p.206
    94.11 Multiple Reed, p.206
    94.12 Double Side Reed, bevel quirk, p.206
        94.130 Gothic reed, Fig.10:59
        94.131 Sash plane, cutting both sides of Gothic Square, p.340
        94.132 Gothic Bead, Fig.10:57
        94.133 Gothic Bead, Gothic return, Fig.10:58
    94.14 Bead Cluster, Fig.10:66

    94.20 Multiple Reed and Flute, Fig.10:69
    94.25 Sash, Astragal and Hollow, new style, Fig.13:46
94.7 Double Door plane, ovolo, p.134
94.8 Sash, Astragal and hollow (American style), p.342
    (see also complex molding planes)

CLASS 97 : Multiple curves+straight, shave or scraper
Various Handrail shaves, scrapers, or scratch stocks

CLASS 99 : Multiple curves+straight, unconventional shape
Circular molding cutter (for corner blocks), p.314

CLASS 00 : Patternmaker's sole planes, Multiform planes

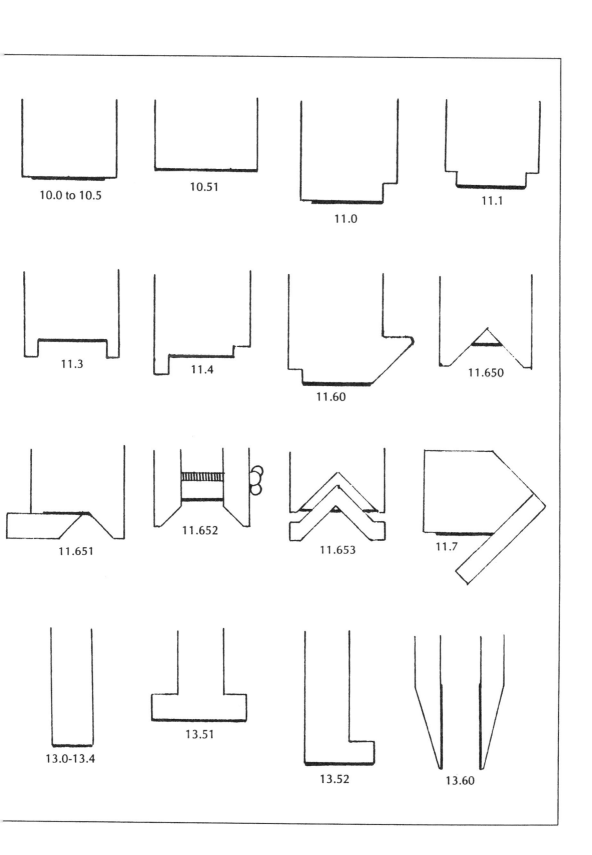

10.0 to 10.5

10.51

11.0

11.1

11.3

11.4

11.60

11.650

11.651

11.652

11.653

11.7

13.0-13.4

13.51

13.52

13.60

429

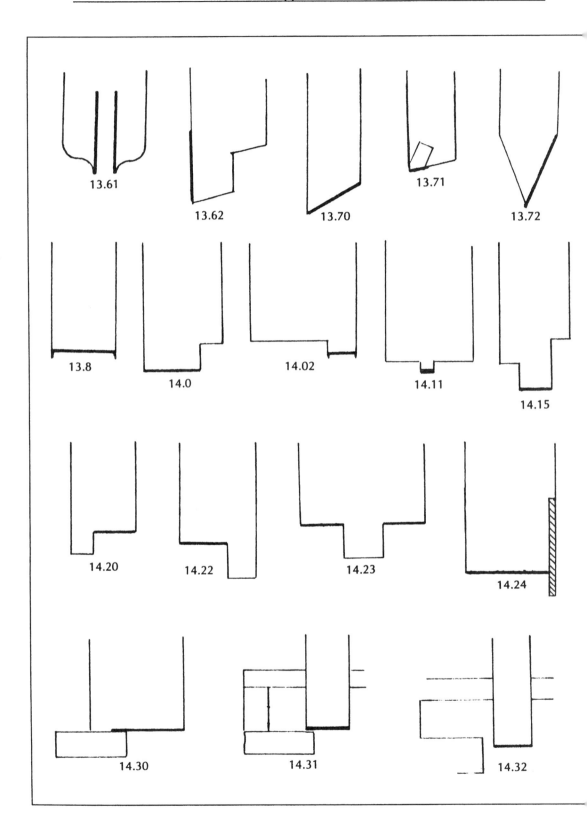

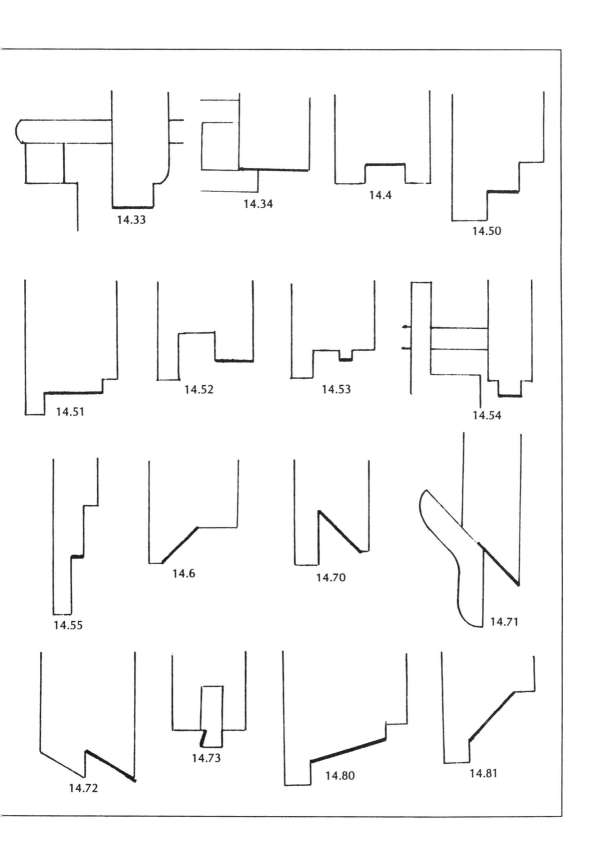

14.33

14.34

14.4

14.50

14.51

14.52

14.53

14.54

14.55

14.6

14.70

14.71

14.72

14.73

14.80

14.81

431

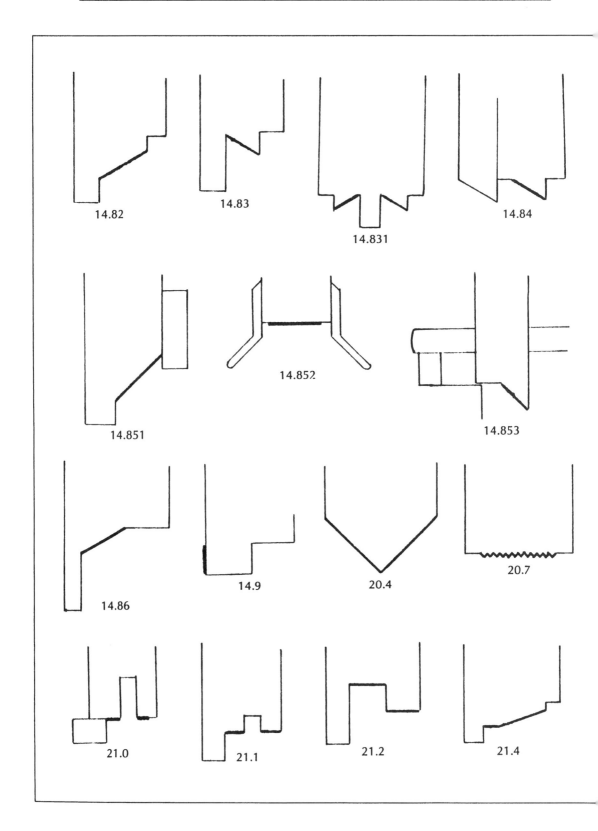

14.82

14.83

14.831

14.84

14.851

14.852

14.853

14.86

14.9

20.4

20.7

21.0

21.1

21.2

21.4

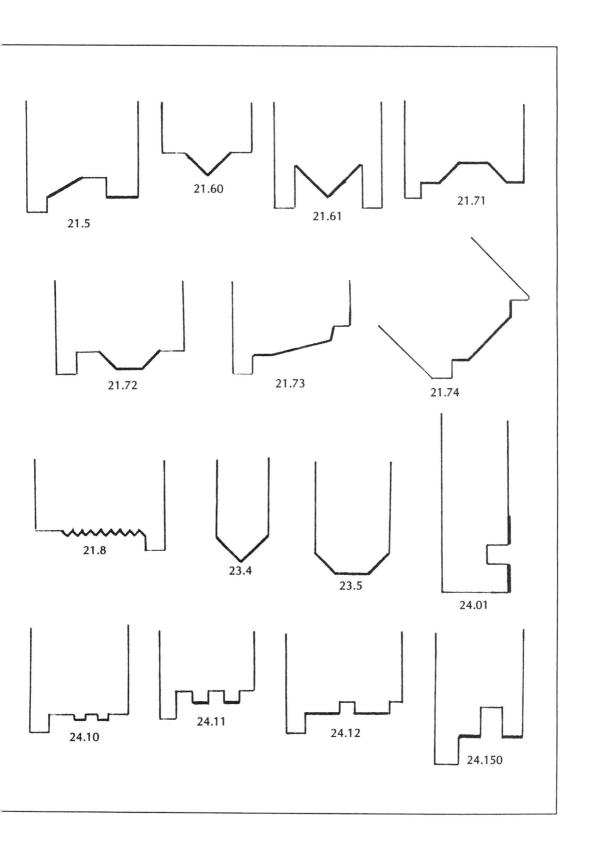

21.60

21.5

21.61

21.71

21.72

21.73

21.74

21.8

23.4

23.5

24.01

24.10

24.11

24.12

24.150

433

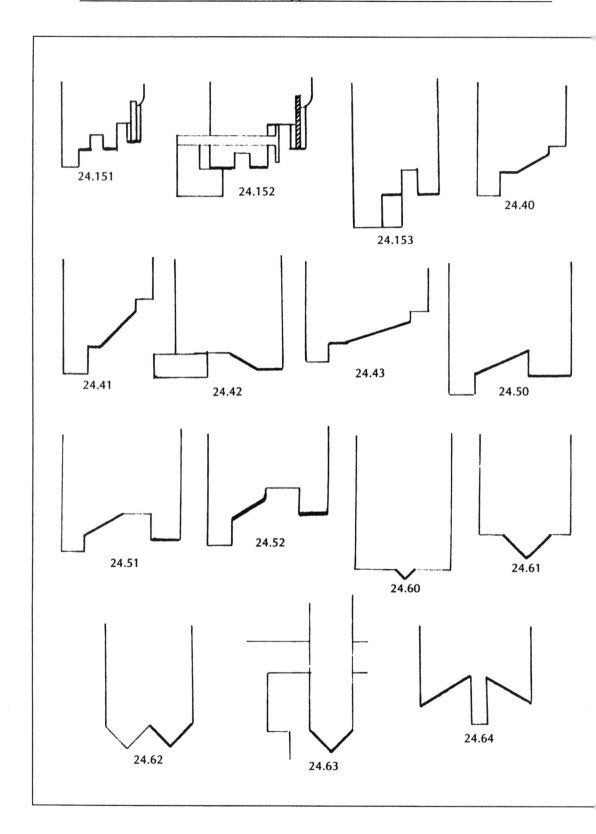

24.151

24.152

24.153

24.40

24.41

24.42

24.43

24.50

24.51

24.52

24.60

24.61

24.62

24.63

24.64

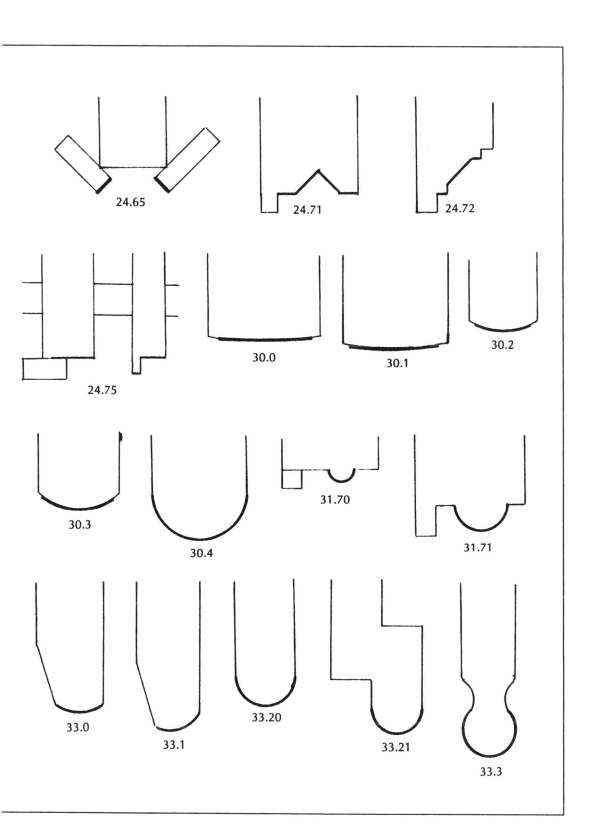

24.65

24.71

24.72

24.75

30.0

30.1

30.2

30.3

30.4

31.70

31.71

33.0

33.1

33.20

33.21

33.3

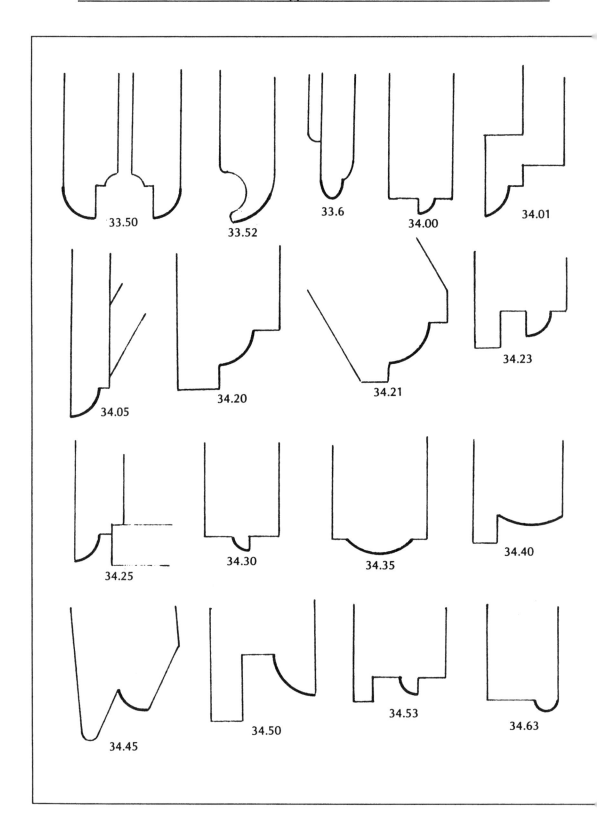

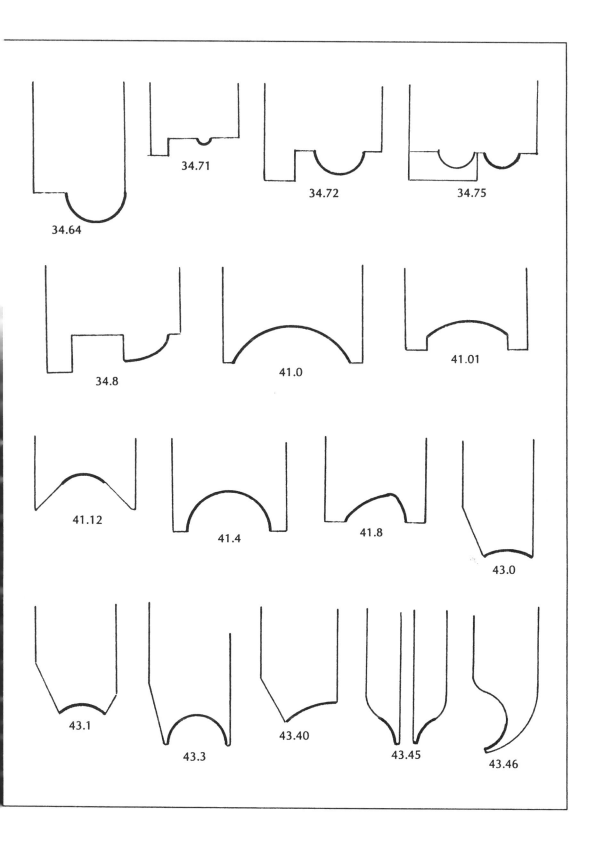

34.71

34.72

34.75

34.64

34.8

41.0

41.01

41.12

41.4

41.8

43.0

43.1

43.3

43.40

43.45

43.46

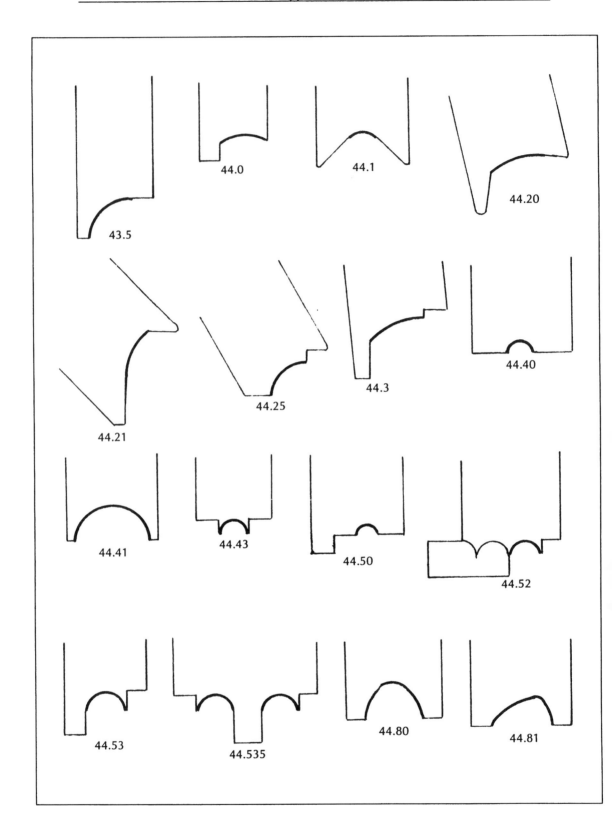

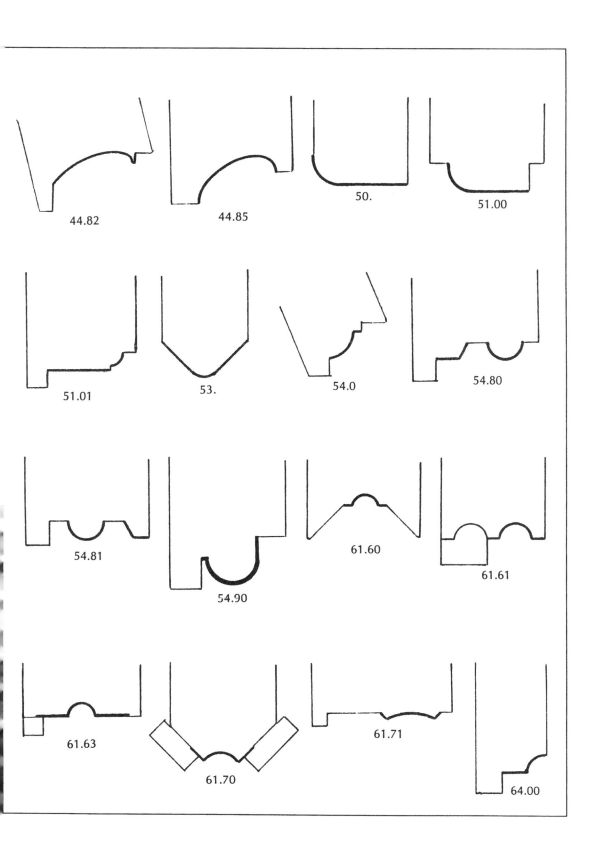

44.82

44.85

50.

51.00

51.01

53.

54.0

54.80

54.81

54.90

61.60

61.61

61.63

61.70

61.71

64.00

439

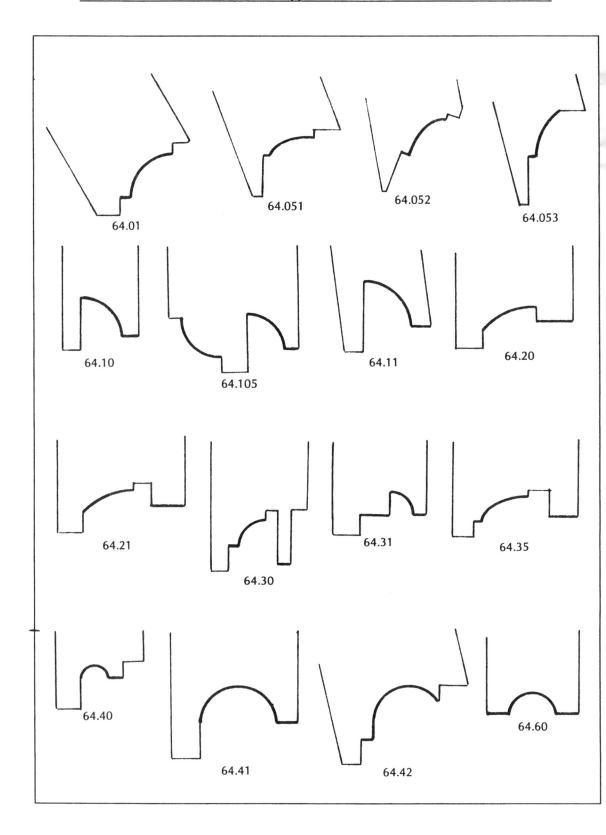

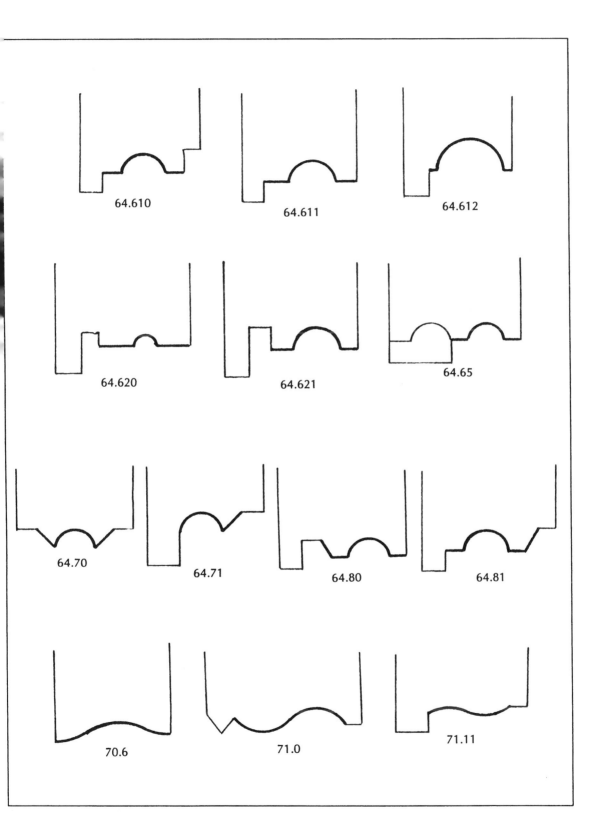

64.610

64.611

64.612

64.620

64.621

64.65

64.70

64.71

64.80

64.81

70.6

71.0

71.11

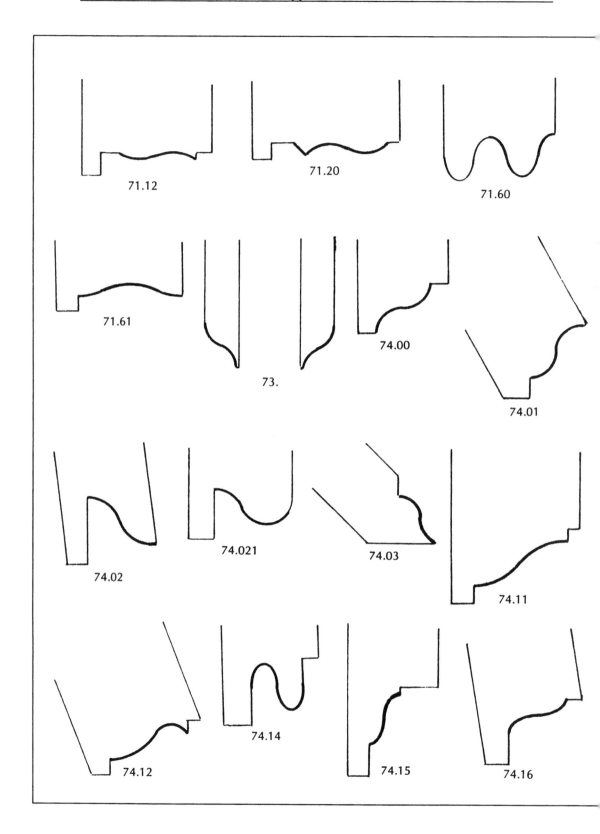

71.12

71.20

71.60

71.61

73.

74.00

74.01

74.02

74.021

74.03

74.11

74.12

74.14

74.15

74.16

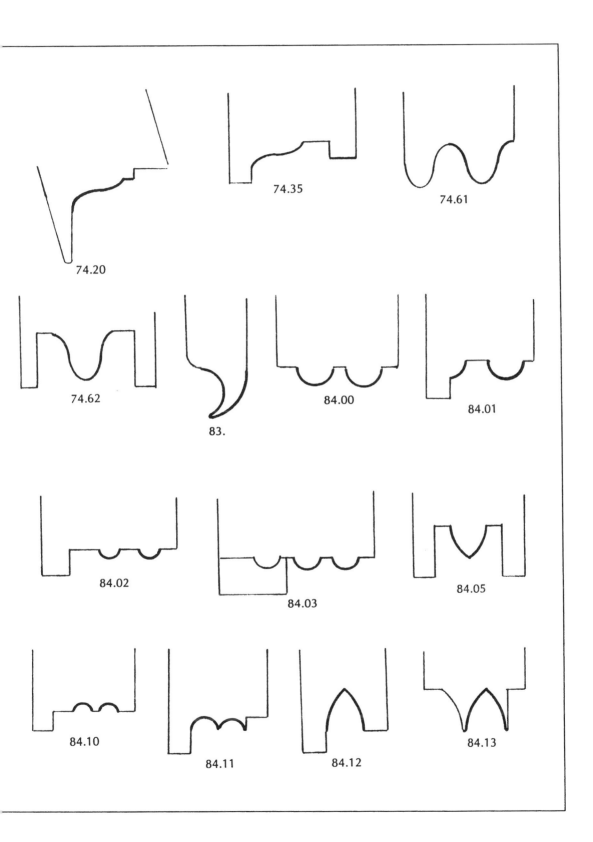

74.20

74.35

74.61

74.62

83.

84.00

84.01

84.02

84.03

84.05

84.10

84.11

84.12

84.13

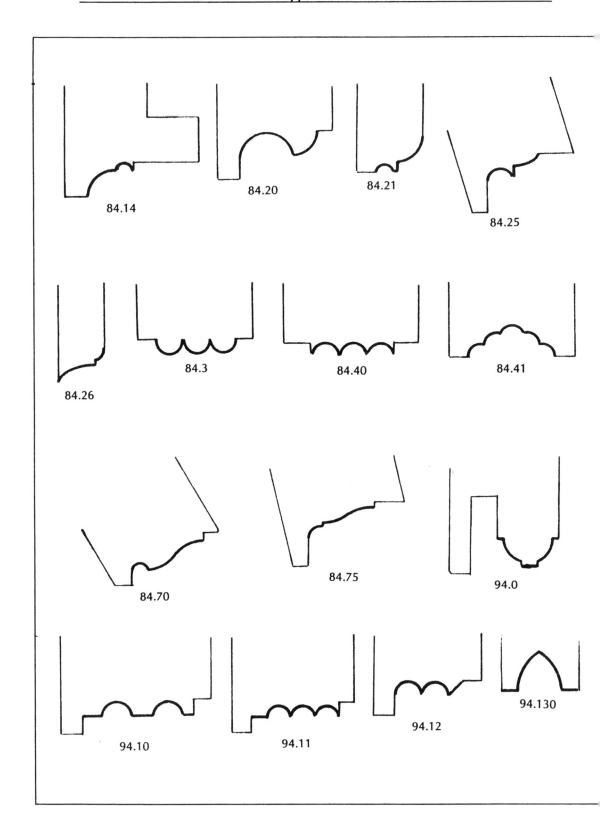

84.14

84.20

84.21

84.25

84.26

84.3

84.40

84.41

84.70

84.75

94.0

94.10

94.11

94.12

94.130

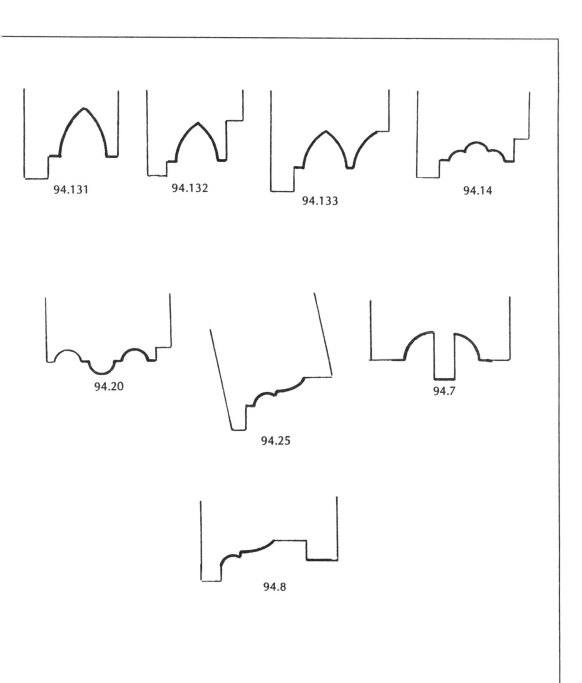

94.131

94.132

94.133

94.14

94.20

94.25

94.7

94.8

Glossary

Adjustable mouth: A front of a plane mouth formed by a separate piece, adjustable to change the mouth opening.

Adz: A wood-cutting tool shaped like an axe but with a cutting edge perpendicular to the handle

Amphora: A large jar, used as a shipping container by the ancient Greeks.

Apophyge: The portion of a classic column molded into a concave sweep separating column from base or capital

Architrave: In classical orders, the lowest molding on the beam spanning columns; later used for the ornamental moldings around doors or other openings.

Arris: A sharp edge, the meeting of two plane surfaces.

Astragal (molded strip): A strip covering the juncture of two architectural surfaces lying in the same plane.

Astragal (molding element): A convex half-circle with one or two fillets.

Awkward grain: Wood grain that changes direction, posing planing difficulties.

BPII: Common abbreviation for *British Planemakers from 1700*, second edition (See Goodman,1978, in Bibliography).

Backing plane: Another name for mother plane.

Balk: A roughly squared timber.

Balustrade: The railing system of a stairway or balcony.

Band molding: A horizontal member or molding marking a division in a wall

Base molding: A molding used to trim the upper edge of a baseboard.

Batten: A narrow strip of wood used to cover a joint or fill a rabbet.

Bead (element): A convex molding. Systematic definition on p.396.

Beak (element): Concave and convex curves meeting in a sharp edge.

Bed (of a plane): Surface on which the iron rests (See Fig.2:1).

Bed molding: One covering the joining of a vertical and a higher horizontal surface.

Bedding angle: The angle made by the back of a plane iron and the sole of the plane.

446

Belection: Variant spelling of bolection.

Bench plane: A plane used to create large flat surfaces: smooth, jack, fore, jointer, etc.

Bevel: The surface made in grinding the plane iron to produce the cutting edge.

Bevel (element): A tilted straight segment of a molding.

Bevel (double): Formed by grinding away both faces of the plane iron in forming the cutting edge.

Bevel (single): Bevel on only one face of a plane iron.

Blister steel: Wrought iron converted to steel by heating with carbon.

Bolection: A molding covering the junction of two surfaces at slightly different levels.

Boxed: Having strips of boxwood inserted at areas of high wear, to improve durability.

Boxing: The strips of boxwood used to improve wear resistance, or the process of installing these.

Boxwood: A hard, tough, close-grained yellow wood used in premium planes or in boxing.

Breadboard ends: Wooden strips installed across the grain and covering the end grain of wooden structures such as table tops, to prevent warping.

Bridge mounting: A plane blade mounting that fills a mortise completely with wedge and iron, and provides a separate opening for shavings escape through the top of the plane.

Burl: Wood of tangled grain, taken from hemispherical growths on trees.

Cabriole: A curved form of furniture leg used in Queen Anne and Chippendale styles, named for its resemblance to an animal leg.

Canted: Tilted or slanted.

Cap iron: A second iron fixed to the front of a plane iron to break the shavings and thus cause a smoother cut.

Capstan head screw: A screw having radial holes in its head (as in a capstan), permitting turning by rods inserted therein.

Cask: A barrel-shaped wooden vessel of any size.

Cavetto: A cove molding.

Chain pump: A liquid pump consisting of disks mounted at intervals along an endless chain threaded through a pipe.

Chamfer: A flat surface made by removing, at an angle, the sharp juncture of two plane surfaces.

Chatter: A surface defect, small transverse ridges caused by vibration of the plane blade during cutting.

Cheeks (of a plane): The sides of the throat.

Choke: To block the mouth of a plane by shavings which did not escape.

Closed tote: A plane handle that has an opening for the fingers.

Coffin shape: A plane rectangular in the side view with sides curving inward toward toe and heel.

Column: An upright, slender cylindrical structural member.

Compassed: Having the sole convex longitudinally.

Coped joint: One in which the end of one section of molding is cut away in a negative of the molding profile, so that it fits snugly over the molding to which it is to be joined. See Fig.13:56.

Cormier: The wood of the service-tree, sorbus domestica, used in France for premium planes.

Cornice: A molding which crowns a structure, or which fills the angle between wall and ceiling.

Cove (element): A concave molding, ends vertical and horizontal.

Cross-grain: In the direction at right angles to the tree trunk.

Cross-section: The view that would be obtained by cutting across the object viewed.

Crotch: A wood section obtained from a tree branchpoint.

Cut: see nicker.

Dado: A rectangular groove cut across the grain of the wood, or the plane that does this.

Depth stop: A device to stop the cutting action of the plane at the desired depth.

Double hung sash: Windows with an upper and lower sash, movable vertically.

Double iron: Usually, an iron with a cap iron. Also used for planes with two cutting irons.

Dovetail: A joint in which a tenon of inverted wedge shape (as a dove's tail) is inserted into a matching slot. See Fig.8:1.

Dowel: A small cylindrical pin, used to reinforce a joint.

Draw-pinned: A mortise and tenon or similar joint with holes through each member slightly offset, is pulled tightly together with a taper pin and secured with a dowel through the holes.

Drawknife: A sturdy knife blade fitted with handles at both ends.

Ears (of a plane): The projections at the side of the throat which form abutments to retain the wedge.

Edge-glued: Glued edge to edge, as boards to form a wider board.

Edge-planed: Planed on the long-grain edge.

Embossed: Design impressed by sinking its surroundings.

End grain: The grain exposed by cutting in the direction across the original tree trunk.

Escapement: The exit port in the plane for shavings escape.

Eye (of a plane): A curved chamfer at upper edge of the cheek.

Face (of an iron): The flat, unbeveled side.

Fanlight: A semicircular window, often located above a door.

Fascia: A flat band, such as the board mounted vertically under the eaves.

Felloe: One of the curved wooden segments making up the rim of a wheel.

Fence (of a plane): A member serving to guide the plane by riding on an edge of the workpiece.

Field: The sunken peripheral areas of a raised panel.

Fillet (element): A straight horizontal area in a molding.

Filletster fence: A movable fence, usually screwed to the sole of the plane. See Fig.5:19.

Finish carpenter: One who completes non-structural elements such as moldings, cabinets, shutters, etc.

Flitch: A section of log made by parallel lengthwise cuts.

Float: A tool for shaping wood, like a very coarse single-cut file.

Flute (element): A hollow groove.

Frame-and-panel: A method of constructing broad surfaces by enclosing a panel in a frame of vertical stiles and horizontal rails.

GAWP: Common abbreviation for *Guide to American Wooden Planes*. See Pollak, 1987, in Bibliography.

Galley: A seagoing vessel propelled by oars.

449

Galley grip: Plane handles projecting from the side of the plane. See Fig.2:9.

Gothic bead (element): Two convex curves meeting in a sharp edge at the top.

Grain: The direction in which wood fibers are oriented, or the surface appearance related thereto.

Groove: A rectangular furrow along the grain of a board.

Heartwood: Wood from the non-living core of a tree, between the pith and the sapwood.

Heel (of a plane): The after end, which faces the user.

Hinge stile: The vertical structural member of a door or casement sash to which the hinges are attached.

Honing: Sharpening a cutting edge by rubbing on a fine-grain whetstone.

Horn grip: A front grip on a plane resembling a section of a cattle horn (See Fig.2:7C).

Hornbeam: A tough, close-grained wood from trees of the carpinus family, favored by Continental planemakers.

House carpenter: One who normally works at a building site rather than in a shop. The term includes the rough carpenter who completes the structural work and the finish carpenter who provides final details.

Housed joint: A joint in which the end of one board is inserted into a groove (usually a dado) in another.

Hyphen convention: Part of the systematic naming scheme. See p.400.

Imprint: A maker's name (and sometimes location) stamped (usually) on the toe of a plane.

Incuse: Letters sunk into the wood, rather than raised by sinking their background.

Iron: The principal cutter of a plane, usually of iron with a steel face.

Joiner: A woodworker skilled in joining wood members to make attractive and durable structures.

Jointing: Planing the edges of boards perfectly square and straight, in preparation for gluing these edges together.

Kerf: The slit made in wood by the passage of a saw.

Key (of a plow): The wedge fixing a slide arm of the fence in position.

Lamb tongue: Term used for an ogee profile in sash moldings. See Fig.13:59 #6.

Left side (of a plane): The side to the left of the user.

Lignum Vitae: A dark, very heavy and durable wood sometimes used in place of boxwood.

Linenfold: A form of carving on panel surfaces resembling draped linen.

Lock stile: The vertical structural member of a door or casement frame, opposite the hinge stile, in which a lock may be installed.

Long grain: The direction along the wood fibers, parallel to the original tree trunk.

Long screw: A device for positioning a cap iron on an iron. See Fig.2:14.

Longitudinal: In the direction from toe to heel of a plane.

Luthier: One who makes stringed instruments, such as violins.

Make-do: A tool created from materials at hand for the immediate purpose.

Millwork: Wooden elements shaped by a planing mill or other power woodworking machinery.

Miter joint: A joint formed by mating two members, each of which has its end cut at an angle or angles.

Molding planes: Planes designed to cut decorative, rather than functional, surfaces.

Mortise: A recess cut in a wooden member, into which a projection on another (the tenon) will fit.

Mother plane: A plane used to cut the profile on the sole of a molding plane.

Mouth: The slot in the sole of a plane through which the cutting edge protrudes.

Nicker: A secondary cutting blade, intended to sever wood fibers at the edges of the cut to be made by the main cutter.

Ogee (element): A curve which is concave near the work edge, and convex further in. See Fig.10:72 et seq.

Ovolo (element): A convex curve of $90°$ or less, circular or elliptical.

Paneling: A surface treatment for walls or ceiling of a room, made of wooden panels supported in wooden frames.

Patched mouth: A plane mouth repaired by inlaying a piece of wood or harder substance at its front.

Peg grip: a plane grip formed by inserting a shaped peg in the stock. See Fig.2:7 left.

Pilaster: A decorative feature simulating a pier or pillar partially embedded in the wall, often flanking a fireplace.

Pitch: The angle at which the face of the plane blade meets the work.

Planing beam: A stout beam used by Far Eastern woodworkers to support work being planed. See Fig.3:8.

Planted molding: One formed on a separate piece of wood which is then attached (as opposed to a stuck molding).

Plated: Covered with metal to increase wear resistance.

Plow: A tool to groove along the grain, or the act of using this.

Post-and-beam: A form of building construction in which the structural members are large vertical timbers (posts) spanned by similar horizontal beams. An alternate to stud framing.

Pull hole: A horizontal hole through the front of a plane into which a rope or dowel may be inserted for pulling by an assistant.

Pump log tools: Large augers and reams designed to drill lengthwise holes through logs, to make water pipes or chain pump pipes.

Purfling: A narrow inlaid border, on a violin or other instrument.

Quirk (element): A narrow groove separating other molding elements.

Rabbet: A rectangular step cut in the edge of a board.

Radiused: Curved in the horizontal direction.

Rag: A splintered edge left by a coarse saw or a common plane cutting cross-grain.

Rail: A horizontal structural member of a door, sash, or panel.

Razee: A plane with the top rear surface of the stock lower than the front. Mounting the hand grip here provides a more direct thrust.

Rebate: British term for rabbet.

Reservation: The central, raised section of a raised panel.

Reverse ogee (element): A curve convex at the outer edge, concave at the inner.

Right side (of a plane): The side to the right of its user.

Rip saw: A saw designed for cutting along the grain.

Rising grain: A section of wood subject to rough planing because the wood fibers slope upward toward the nose of the plane.

Riven (Rived): Split, rather than sawn, from the log.

Roey grain: Difficult to plane because rising and falling grain alternate across the width of the work.

Root diameter: Diameter measured at the bottom of the threads of a threaded member.

Rough carpenter: One who erects the structural members of a building and is not involved in the finishing details.

Roughing plane: A plane designed for rapid removal of unwanted wood, without concern for the surface finish.

Router: A tool which removes wood at a distance below the surface on which its sole rides. The name is also applied to some coachmaker's shaves.

Sapwood: The outer layers of wood which carried sap while the tree stood, as opposed to the inert heartwood.

Scotia (element): Used here to mean a hollow with ends at different levels.

Scraper: A steel blade used nearly perpendicular to the surface being worked, removing very fine shavings.

Seasoning: Storing wood to permit equilibration of its moisture content with the moisture level in the air.

Seaton chest: A tool chest made by Benjamin Seaton, containing a complete, almost unused set of cabinetmaker's tools purchased in 1796: now in the Eastgate Museum, Rochester, Kent, England

Serpentine: A curve with more than one reversal of curvature from concave to convex.

Sheath (a surface): To cover with boards.

Ship's prow grip: A plane front grip fancied to resemble the prow of a Viking ship (See Fig.2:7B).

Shoji: A light wooden frame covered with translucent paper, used as sliding partitions in Japanese homes.

Shootboard: A board with fences designed to support a workpiece and guide a plane finishing its edge, end, or miter.

Shooting: Jointing the edge of a board.

Short grain: A region of a wooden article in which the dimension along the grain (in the direction of the wood fibers) is too short for maximum strength.

Side escapement: An exit for plane shavings located on the side of the stock.

Side grip: Handles formed by extending the upper stock outward along the sides and piercing these projections. See Fig.2:9.

Simple curvature: A curve that remains either concave or convex, without reversal.

Sinusoidal: Wave-like, with multiple crests and troughs.

Six-board chest: A simple chest formed by joining two boards for sides, two for front and back, one each for top and bottom.

Skew iron: A plane blade intended to be bedded at an angle (other than a right angle) with the side of the plane,

Slide arms: Horizontal staves fixed to the fence of a plow and sliding through holes in the stock or, in Continental plows, fixed to the stock and sliding through holes in the fence.

Sliding dovetail: A tenon larger at its end than its root, sliding into a groove shaped to accept it. See Fig.8:1.

Slipped: Having a removable strip of wood filling a rabbet in the stock.

Snecked iron: A plane blade with a projection at its upper end, to provide a striking point to assist its removal from the plane.

Soffit: The underside of an overhead projection, usually one under the eaves.

Spring: The design of a molding plane to optimize the cutting action, which requires that the stock be held at an angle to the vertical while in use.

Sprung: Made with spring, as defined above.

Spur: A small nicker, to sever wood fibers in front of the main cutter.

Squirrel-tail: A handle formed by removing the lower rear section of the plane body, leaving a projecting rounded grip.

Stave: One of the arms used to support a plow plane fence.

Stave (cask): One of the curved wooden pieces forming the sides of a cask or barrel.

Step: The horizontal surface left when a part of the plane body is cut away to form a narrower handhold. See Fig.10:2.

Stile: One of the vertical structural members of a door, sash, or panel.

Stock: 1) The body of a wooden plane. 2) The wood being worked. 3) The fence of a cooper's plane such as a croze or howel.

Stop: An adjustable member used to limit the depth of cut (depth stop) or to establish the effective curvature of an adjustable compass plane.

Stop chamfer: A chamfer that terminates before the end of the member, leaving a short section of untouched arris.

Stopped: A cut (such as a chamfer or dovetail) that does not continue to the end of the piece is said to be stopped.

Strike button: A metal or hardwood insert to protect the plane body from the mallet blows used in setting the blade.

Strip Planes: Planes designed to mold the full width of a wood strip.

Stuck Molding: A molding cut in the material of the structure, rather than applied as a separate piece.

Stud framing: A construction method using many 2 x 4 or similar members (studs) as opposed to fewer heavier members (post and beam).

Stuff (British): The wooden stock being worked.

Stuffed (metal planes): Having hardwood pieces installed in the metal outer body.

T-slot: A groove with the bottom of its sides widened, to form a slot having a section like an inverted T.

Tear-out: A rough surface caused by the wood splitting ahead of and below the level of the plane blade, usually due to rising grain.

Tenon: A projection formed at the end of a wooden member, intended to fit into a socket (mortise) cut into another member.

Throat: The passage for the shavings produced by the plane.

Timber: A squared length of wood for structural use.

Toe (of a plane): The front face, furthest from the user.

Tooth: Surface roughness produced with the intent of improving glue adhesion.

Tote: The handle or grip of a plane. Also spelled Toat.

Tote (closed): A tote which surrounds the gripping fingers.

Tote (jack): An unpierced tote which slants forward slightly.

Trammel: A bar which restricts to a circular path the motion of the article to which it is attached.

Transverse: At right angles to the long dimension.

Transverse grip: A grip formed by dowels or staves mounted across the plane body.

Trench: A groove, usually along the grain.

Tropical woods: Rosewood, cocobola, ebony, lignum vitae or other similar dense woods grown in tropical regions.

Trying: Planing after roughing and before smoothing, to attain surfaces that are plane and square to each other.

Twisted grain: Wood grain in which fiber direction changes repeatedly.

Up-and-down mill (sash mill): A sawmill with reciprocating vertical sawblades.

Veneer: Thin sheets of wood, usually fine woods used to cover supports of secondary woods. Now very thin, formerly hand-sawn in thicknesses of about ¼ in. (6 mm.).

WPINCA: Common abbreviation for *Wooden Planes in Nineteenth Century America*. See Roberts in Bibliography.

Wainscot: A facing (sheathing or paneling) applied to the lower part of a wall.

Wedge: The tapered wooden member used to fix the plane blade in the stock.

Wedge angle: The angle between front and back of a plane wedge.

Wheelwright: One skilled in making wooden wheels, and often in related tasks such as making farm carts.

Workpiece: The wooden article in process of being converted to a finished product.

ZB: Common abbreviation for the zigzag border often found surrounding the maker's imprint on a plane.

French Glossary and Index

Acier: Steel

Astragale: Astragal (p.208).

Baguette: Bead

Baguette double: Side reed (p.208).

Baguette pour applique: Reeding plane (p.208).

Baguette sans joue: Bead with bevel quirk (p.208).

Baguette simple: Side bead (p.208).

Bastringue: Spokeshave (p.298).

Bec de cane: Side round, duckbill (p.193).

Bec de corbin: Side round, crow's bill (p.193).

Bonnet de prêtre: Quarter round (p.196).

Boudin: Torus bead (p.208).

Bouvet: Grooving plane (p.124).

Bouvet à-

  -approfondir: Plow (p.124).

  -embrever: Double groove or mortise groover (p.135).

  -joindre: Match plane (p.135).

  -joindre d'une piece : Match combination, come-and-go.

  -joindre transformable: Combination match plane (p.137).

  -joue mobile: moving fence rabbet or plow (p.124).

  -languette: Match tongue plane (p.135).

  -plat: French coachmaker's router (pp.126, 359).

  -rainure: Match groove plane (p.135).

  -vis en bois: Screw-arm plow.

Bouvet brisé: Plow (124).

Bouvet en deux pièces (or en deux morceaux): Plow (p.124).

Bouvet en une pièce (or un morceau): Combination match pair (p.135).

Bouvet-jabloir: Croze (p.328).

Brocheuse de charron : Wheelwrights rounder

Carré: Square.

Carrossier: Carriage builder.

Chanfrein: Chamfer or chamfer plane.

Chanfreinière: Howel (p.325).

Charme: Hornbeam.

Charpentier: Carpenter.

Charron: Wheelwright.

Chemin de fer: Plasterer's plane (p.61).

Chêne vert: Holm oak.

Cintré: curved (used for any of the three directions).

Clé: Plane wedge or key.

Coin: Plane wedge.

Colombe: Cooper's jointer (p.321).

Colombe d'emballeur: Boxmaker's jointer (p.321).

Colombelle: Cooper's finish plane (pp.159, 331).

Conduit: Fixed fence.

Congé: Cove (pp.198, 229).

Contre-forme or contre-rabot: Sash coping plane.

Cormier: Servicewood (p.27).

Corne: Horn.

Corniche: Cornice or edge (see e.g. doucine pour corniche)

Corps: Body or stock.

Couleuvre: (grass snake) Long filletster (p.101).

Coupe-fil: Nicker.

Coulisse: Sliding fence or depth stop.

Crêtoire: Tongue (of tongue-and-groove) (p.135).

Crêtoire à lambris: Combination match pair (p.135)

Demi-varlope: Fore plane (pp.40, 47)

Dents de bouvet: Rabbet with double stops (p.97).

Doucine: Ogee molder (p.211).

Doucine à queue: Coachmaker's or stairmaker's ogee (p.373).

Doucine pour corniche: Ogee plane to work the edge of the board.

Doucine riflard: Ogee in jack plane shape (p.373).

Ébène: Ebony.

Ébéniste: Cabinetmaker (p.8).

Enlève-carré: Adjustable narrow groove plane.

Fer: Plane iron.

Feuilleret: Filletster (p.100).

Feuilleret à plate-bandes: Panel raiser.

Feuilleret d'ébéniste: Moving filletster (p.103).

Feuilleret cintré: Radius filletster.

Feuilleret en contre-parement: Half-lap to work far edge.

Feuilleret en parement: Half-lap plane.

Filière: Screwbox (p.315)

Filière: Inventor's name for thicknesser (p.371).

Front: Toe of plane.

Fût: Plane stock or body.

Fût à rogner de relieur: Bookbinder's plow.

Galère: Carpenter's smooth or jack plane (pp.41, 52).

Galère à poignée entaille: Razee jointer (p.47).

Goutte pendante: Sill drip plane (p.350).

Grain d'orge: V-groover (pp.145, 152).

Gravoir: Simple post croze.

Gueule de loup: Casement sash match plane (p.352).

Guillaume: Rabbet plane (p.96).

Guillaume à-

   -adoucir: Rabbet plane for fitting (p.97).

   -coup d'entrée: V-groove, for flooring (p.152).

   -deux fers: Come-and-go double rabbet (p.97).

   -ébaucher: Roughing rabbet (p.97)

   -élégir: T-rabbet plane.

   -navette: Rabbet with curved cheeks.

   -onglet: Shouldering plane (pp.144, 145).

   -plate-bande: Panel raiser (p.74).

   -queue: Coachmaker's rabbet (p.96).

   -reculer: Finishing rabbet (p.97).

 Guillaume convexe: Compass rabbet.

Guillaume de bout: Chisel plane or stop rabbet (p.97).

Guillaume debout: Rabbet with blade at high pitch (p.97).

Guillaume de côté: Side rabbet (p.97).

Guillaume de pente: Slanted side rabbet (p.145).

Guillaume double: Rabbet with iron and cap iron.

Guimbarde: Router (p.313).

Guimbarde de carrossier: Coachmaker's router (p.360).

Hêtre: Beech

Jable: Croze groove (p.328).

Jabloir: Croze plane (p.328).

Jabloir à joue mobile: Croze in plow shape (p.328).

Jabloir maconnais: French post croze (p.328).

Jet d'eau: Ogee for casement drip mold (p.350).

Joigneux: Long filletster (p.101): also cooper's jointer (p.321).

Joue: Plane cheek or side.

Languette: Keel of plow (p.124).

Lame: Plane iron.

Larmier: Sill drip (p.350)

Lumière: Plane throat.

Main courante: Handrail (p.373).

Menuisier: Joiner or finish carpenter.

Méplat à carré: Chamfer plane (p.152).

Mouchette: Hollow plane (pp.169, 192, 208).

Mouchette à filets: Center bead with bevel quirks.

Mouchette à joue: Side bead.

Mouchette à joues: Center bead (p.208).

Mouchette à joues sur le coin: Centerbead on chamfer (p.208).

Mouton: Male casement sash match (p.352).

Navette: Shuttle; **à navette**: shuttle-shaped or boat-shaped.

Nez: Nose or toe of plane.

Nez de marche: Nosing plane (p.170).

Noisettes de luthier: Violinmaker's planes.

Noix de crossée: Casement plane for hinge stile (p.352).

Noix pour fenêtres: Sash coping plane.

Oeil: Eye: plane throat.

Oblique: Skew

Palissandre: Rosewood.

Pas de chèvre: Plane to make V-tongue (p.152).

Plate-bande: Panel raiser (p.74).

Poignée: Handle or tote.

Poirier: Pearwood.

Quart de rond à carré: Side hollow and fillet (p.197).

Quart de rond entre carrés: Quarter round (p.196).

Quart de rond simple: Side hollow (p.196).

Rabot: Plane.

Rabot à-

  -corne: Horn plane (p.51).

  -dents: Toothing plane (p.61).

  -élégir: Door check plane (p.75).

  -entailles: A form of dado (p.139).

  -navette: Shuttle-shaped rabbet (p.173).

  -queue: Dovetail plane (p.145) (also used for tailed plane).

Rabot à- (or Rabot pour-)

  -chanfrein: Chamfer plane (p.330).

  -cheveux d'ange: Spill plane (p.310).

  -crémaillère: Bookcase plane (p.145).

  -débillarder: Round-both-ways plane.

  -dégrossir: Roughing plane (p.41).

  -fenêtres: Sash plane (p.343).

  -jantes: Felloe plane (p.158).

  -manches: Witchet, rounder (p.169), or forkstaff plane.

  -moulure: Molding plane.

  -planir: Smooth plane (p.51).

  -plates-bandes: Panel raiser.

  -raplanir: Smooth plane (p.51).

  -targes: Spelk plane (p.310).

461

Rabot cintré: Curved sole plane (p.171).

    -convexe: Compass plane (p.158).

    -concave: Plane with sole concave lengthwise.

Rabot creux: Hollow plane; also plane with sole concave lengthwise (pp.169, 192).

Rabot de cuisine: Kitchen plane (p.310).

Rabot de fond: Radius plane for barrelheads (see Head cutter)

Rabot de jabloir: Croze plane.

Rabot double: Plane with cap iron (p.51).

Rabot galère: Carpenter's plane with side grips (p.45).

Rabot plat à carré: Square smooth (p.51).

Rabot plat à navette: Coffin coach smooth (p.51).

Rabot pour entailler les fonds: Trammel plane to chamfer cask heads (p.330).

Rabot pour fonds de seilles: Plane to chamfer cask heads (p.330).

Rabot pour jeunesse: Youth's plane.

Rabot pour persiennes: Jalousie plane (p.139).

Rabot racloir: Scraper plane.

Rabot rond: Round plane (p.192).

Rabotin: Plasterer's or stonemason's plane (p.61).

Râcle à osier: Basketmaker's plane.

Réglable: Adjustable.

Renvoi d'eau: Large ogee for drip mold (p.350).

Riflard: Jack or fore plane (pp.41, 47).

Ruelle: Light duty croze (p.328).

Sabots de luthier: Violinmaker's planes.

Scotie: Scotia.

Semelle: Plane sole.

Stockholm: French howel (p.325).

Talon: Reverse ogee (p.211). Also heel of plane.

Tarabiscot: Scratch stock (pp.305, 360). Also fluting plane (p.208).

Taraud: Screw tapping tool (p.315)

Tige: Arm of plow.

Tonnelier: Cooper.

462

Tranche-fil: Nicker.

Varlope: Tryplane or jointer (pp.40, 47).

Varlope à feuillure: Panel plane (p.75)

Varlope à onglet: Miter plane (p.67).

Varlope pour chaisiers: Chairmaker's jointer (p.376).

Verdondaine: Light duty croze (p.328).

Wastringue: Spokeshave (p.298).

Wastringue de charron: Wheelwright's shave or jarvis (p.302).

German Glossary and Index

Abfalz-Putzhobel: Putzhobel with rabbets on both sides of sole.

Abfashobel: Chamfer plane.

Abplatthobel: A form of panel raiser (p.75).

Absatz-Simshobel: Chisel plane, stop rabbet plane.

Anschlag: Adjustable fence.

Ausgründhobel: Plane to sink a broad recess.

Backenhobel: Cooper's compass badger plane (pp.159, 331).

Bandhobel: One-hand shave (p.335).

Bestosshobel: Old name for horned jack plane.

Betten-Falzhobel, geschweift: Compass and radius filletster (p.104).

Bettenhohlkehlhobel, geschweift: Concave fenced round (p.168).

Boden: Cask or barrel head.

Bodenbramschnitthobel: Cooper's head chamfer plane (p.330).

Bodenhobel: Barrelhead plane, flat or concave lengthwise (p.330).

Bogenfalzhobel: Radius filletster.

Bogenhobel: Curved plane, radius or concave (p.171).

Breite: Width.

Daubenhobel: Cooper's stave plane, a compass round.

Daubenfüghobel: Cooper's stave jointer (p.321).

Deutscher Stabhobel: Quarter round molder (p.197).

Dickenhobel: Thicknesser (p.371).

Doppel- (prefix to plane name): Having a cap iron.

Doppeleisen: Double iron, iron with cap iron.

Doppelhobel: Smooth plane with double iron (p.50).

Doppelsimshobel: Rabbet with double iron (p.97).

Doppelzwiemandl: Zwiemandl with double iron (p.52)

Eckenhobel: Chisel plane.

Eckensimshobel: Stop rabbet plane.

Einlasseckenhobel: Butt mortise plane to inlet window corner braces.

Einmannhobel or Einmannshobel: Large head swift.

Einschlagstück: Chamfer with fillet (p.152)

Einschneidhobel: Barrelhead chamfer plane (p.330)

Einschneidstabhobel: Bead or cock bead (p.208).

Eisen: Iron, plane iron.

Eisenbreite: Width of cutting iron.

Eisensohle: Sole plated with iron.

Endhobel: Levelling or sun plane.

Essigspanhobel: Vinegar-chip plane (p.311).

Falzhobel: Filletster (p.101).

Falzschiffhobel: Compass rabbet plane.

Fase: Chamfer, bevel (p.346).

Fasenhobel: Chamfer plane.

Fassonhobel: Molding plane.

Fausthobel: Hand plane, short bench plane (p.50).

Feder-und-Nuthobel: Match combination plane.

Federhobel: Match plane, tongue (p.137).

Federhobel zu Auszugtischen: Side-working tongue plane (p.137).

Fensterhobel: Sash plane (p.343).

Fensterkarnieshobel (or -karnis-): Sash plane, lamb tongue.

Flammenhobel or Flammhobel: Plane for "flamed" moldings (p.307).

Flammleistenhobel: Flammhobel.

Fluchthobel: Long filletster (p.101).

Französischer Stabhobel: Side bead (p.208).

Froschbramschnitt: Chime decoration (p.331).

Froschkranzhobel: A form of howel (p.326).

Fuchsschwanzgriff (Foxtail grip): Saw-handle grip.

Fug-und-Falzhobel: Plane that both joints and rabbets (p.104).

Fügbank: Jointer (p.47).

Füghobel: Long filletster.

Füghobel für Küfer: Cooper's jointer (p.321)

Gaisfusshobel: Meeting rail plane (Austrian spelling).

Garbhobel: Cooper's compass plane.

Gargelhobel: Croze (p.328).

Gargelkamm: Croze.

Gargelreisser: Croze.

Gasterhobel: German style match combination plane (p.137).

Geigenhobel: Violin plane.

Geissfusshobel: Meeting rail plane.

Gerade, Gerader: Straight or square, not skew.

Geschweifte: Curved or tailed.

Gesims-: Austrian equivalent of Sims-.

Gesimshobel: Simshobel, rabbet plane.

Gestreckter Karnies: Stretched ogee (p.211)

Gewindebohrer: Device for cutting female threads (Tap).

Glasnuthobel: Glass plow (p.126).

Glasnutstellhobel: Adjustable Glasnuthobel.

Glätthobel: Cooper's finishing smooth plane.

Grathobel: Dovetail plane (p.144).

Gratnuthobel: Dovetail groove plane.

Griff: Handle.

Grundhobel: D-router (p.313).

Gusshobel: Metal spokeshave.

Guss-stahl: Cast steel.

Hagebuche: Hornbeam.

Halbbank or Halblanghobel: Fore plane (p.47).

Harthobel: Plane of high pitch, for hardwood.

Haushobel: Household plane.

Hinternusshobel: Sash coping plane.

Hirnholzhobel: Miter plane (p.67).

Hobel: Plane.

Hobeleisen: Plane iron.

Hobelgestell(e): Plane sold without iron.

Hobelkasten or Hobelkörper: Plane body.

Hobel für Krallentäfer: Beading plane for tongue & groove boards.

Hohle: Scotia (p.198).

Hohlkehl: A sash profile (p.346).

Hohlkehlhobel: Full round (p.168), molding or ship round (p.193).

Hohlkehl mit Anschlag: Cove (p.198)

Holzdrahthobel: Matchstick plane.

Holzspindeln: Wooden plow arms.

Jalousie-Nuthobel: Dado with two unequal fences, for notching venetian blinds (p.139).

Jalousiebrett(li)hobel: Molding plane for blinds. (li),diminutive

Jalousiehobel: Venetian blind plane (p.139).

Jugendhobel: Youth's plane.

Kämpferhobel: Bevel & quarter round (p.229).

Karnies: Ogee (p.211).

Karnies-Falzhobel: Ogee grooving plane, or fenced reverse ogee.

Karnieshobel: Ogee plane.

Karnieshobel, verkehrter: Reverse ogee plane.

Kehlhobel: Molding plane.

Keil: Wedge.

Keilwinkel: Sharpening angle of plane blade.

Kernkastenhobel: Corebox plane.

Ketschhobel: Carpenter's jack plane (pp.41, 45, 52).

Kienspanhobel: Spelk or pillbox plane.

Kimmhobel: Croze (p.328).

Kittfalzhobel: Sash plane or sash filletster (p.343).

Kittfalzschiffhobel: Compassed sash plane.

Klappe: Cap iron.

Konischzieh-hobel: Taper rounder or trap plane.

Kontrahobel: Sash coping plane.

Kopfhobel: Cooper's compass smooth plane, for barrelheads.

Korbflechterhobel: Basketmaker's shave.

Krallenhobel: Bead plane.

Krallenhobel mit Fase: Bead with bevel quirk.

Krallenhobel mit Rabenschnabel: Bead with cove quirk.

Kranzhobel für Küfer: Cooper's wreath plane (p.331).

Kreuzlochschraube: Capstan-head screw.

Küfer: Cooper.

Länge: Length.

Langhobel: Long plane (p.47).

Lederhobel: Spokeshave (p.298).

Leistenhobel: Scratch stock: old name for molding plane (p.305).

Liegender Karnies: Lying ogee (p.211).

Lisenenhobel: Reeding plane.

Maul: Mouth of plane.

Messing: Brass.

Nase: Nose.

Nusshobel: Sash coping plane.

Nuthobel: Match groove or plow plane (p.137).

Nut-und-Federhobel aus 1 Stück: Match combination, come-and-go.

Nut-und-Federhobel aus 2 Stücken: Match tongue and groove pair.

Parkettfederhobel: Flooring tongue plane (p.137).

Parkettnuthobel: Parquet flooring groove plane (p.137).

Perlstabhobel: Side bead with cove quirk (p.208).

Plattbank or Plattbankhobel: Raising plane (p.74).

Plattel: Fillet.

Plattelhobel: Halving plane.

Pockholz: Lignum vitae.

Profilhobel: Kehlhobel, molding plane.

Profilleisten-Ziehbank: Molding drawbench.

Profilleisten-Ziehstock: Molding machine (p.306).

Profilschaber: Scratch stock (p.305).

Profilschabhobel: Coachmaker's molding router.

Profilschweifhobel: Scratch stock.

Putzhobel: Finishing smooth plane (p.50).

Putzhobel, hohl: Smooth plane, sole concave lengthwise

Putzhobel, längs zugespitzt: Coffin smooth plane.

Putzhobel, rund: Compass plane.

Querbolzen: Bar across throat to hold wedge.

Rabenschnabelhobel: Crow's bill plane, for undercut moldings (p.193).

Radkehlhobel: Wheel molding plane.

Rauhbank: Foreplane (p.47).

Rechenstielhobel (rake-handle plane): Forkstaff plane.

Rillenhobel: Reeding plane (p.208).

Ritzhobel: Schlichthobel, smooth plane.

Rohrhobel für Büchsenschäfter: Gunstocker's plane.

Rohrziehhobel: Basketmaker's plane.

Rückwandhobel: Wide standing filletster (for cabinet backs).

Rundeckhobel: Cock bead plane (p.208).

Rundhobel: Round plane, also used to mean compass plane.

Rundstabhobel: Hollow plane or ship hollow (pp.169, 193, 208).

Schabhobel: Metal spokeshave or scraper (p.298).

Schabzahnhobel: Toothed scraper.

Schachtelhobel: Spelk plane (p.310).

Schawrangenhobel: Ausgrundhobel for routing shutter recesses.

Scheineckeneinlasshobel: Einlasseckenhobel.

Schiffhobel: Compass plane (p.158); also used for a plane with sole concave lengthwise.

Schindelnuthobel: Shingle grooving plane.

Schlagknopf: Strike button.

Schlagleistenhobel: Plane to make symmetrical moldings, by cutting from both sides of a strip.

Schlicht- (prefix): Smooth.

Schlichthobel: Smooth plane (p.50).

Schlichtschiffhobel: Compass smooth plane.

Schlichtsimshobel: Finish rabbet plane (p.97)

Schlichtzwiemandl: Two-man carpenter's smooth plane (p.52).

Schneidkluppe: Screwbox.

Schräg, Schräger: Skew.

Schraubenanschlag: Screw-arm fence.

Schrobber: Schropphobel, scrub plane.

Schropp- (prefix): Scrub or roughing.

Schropphobel: Scrub or old form of jack plane (p.40).

Schroppschiffhobel: Compass scrub plane.

Schroppzwiemandl: Two-man scrub plane (p.41).

Schrupphobel: Schropphobel; scrub plane (p.40)

Schürfhobel: Schropphobel; scrub plane.

Schürfsimshobel: Roughing rabbet plane (p.97)

Schweifhobel: Spokeshave, wooden.

Seitenhobel: Wangenhobel; side rabbet or T-rabbet.

Seitenkehlhobel: Side-cutting molding plane.

Senkkopfschraube: Flathead screw.

Simshobel: Rabbet plane (p.97).

Sockelhobel: Astragal (p.208).

Sohle: Sole of plane.

Spanloch: Throat of plane.

Spanloch auf der Seite: Side escapement.

Spanloch oben: bench mouth, top escapement.

Speichenhobel: Spoke plane.

Speichenzapfenhobel: Spoke tenoner.

Speilhobel: Spill plane (p.310).

Spindeln: Plow arms.

Spundhobel: Match groove, or wider groove plane.

Stäbchenhobel: Reeding plane (p.208).

Stabhobel : Hollow plane or forkstaff plane.

Stabhobel mit Fase: Side bead with bevel quirk (p.208).

Stabhobel mit zwei Platteln: Bead with two fillets, or torus bead.

Stabziehhobel: Trap plane.

Stahl: Steel.

Steilhobel: Plane with blade at a steep pitch.

Steilsimshobel: High pitch rabbet plane (p.97).

Stellfalzhobel: Moving filletster (p.103).

Stellgrathobel: Dovetail plane with moving fence (p.144).

Stellschraube: Long screw (see Fig.2:8).

Stemmhobel für Küfer: Sun plane.

Stielhobel: Rounder (p.169).

Stossbank: Cooper's jointer (p.321).

Stossblock: Strike block.

Tischler: Joiner.

Türenhobel: Door molding plane often an ovolo.

Türnuthobel: Door groove plane, or plow (p.126).

Türnutstellhobel: Turnuthobel, adjustable.

Überschiebhobel: Sash coping plane.

Vergatthobel: Hirnholzhobel, miter plane (p.67).

Verkehrter Karnies: Reverse ogee (pp.211, 346).

Viertelstabhobel: Quarter-round plane (p.196).

Vorschneider: Nicker.

Wand: Sliding fence or depth stop.

Wandhobel: T- or side-rabbet.

Wandsimshobel: Navette rabbet plane.

Wangenhobel: T- or side rabbet.

Wangenwiderlager: Abutment holding wedge.

Wassernashobel: Sill drip plane.

Wasserrinnerhobel: Gutter plane (p.168).

Wasserschenkelhobel: Ogee water table plane.

Wolfsrachenhobel: Casement sash match plane, for fitting.

Zahnhobel: Toothing plane (p.61).

Zahnleistenhobel: Bookcase or toothed-rack plane (p.145).

Zahnschiffhobel: Compass toothing plane.

Ziehhobel or Ziehklinge: Scraper.

Ziehklingenhobel: Scraper plane.

Zimmerleute: Carpenter.

zum Verstellen: Adjustable.

Zundhölzchenhobel: Matchstick plane.

Zwiemandl: Carpenter's two-man plane (p.52).

Zwillingsbank: Twin-throat jointer.

Dutch Glossary and Index

Bandje: Fillet (p.198).

Band-Kraal: Torus bead.

Beitel: Iron, cutter.

Beitelbed: Plane bed.

Bekopening: Mouth of plane.

Beukenhout: Beechwood.

Beuling: Bead or astragal (p.208).

Beuling zonder geleider: Center bead.

Blindploegen: (Shutter plane) casement sash match plane.

Blok: Plane body or stock.

Blokschaaf: Plane shaped like an English smooth plane.

Blokschaaf met hoorn: Horned smooth plane (pp.40, 51).

Boorschaaf: Rabbet (p.97).

Bossingschaaf: Panel plane (pp.74, 159).

Breedte: Width.

Diepte: Depth.

Dieptesteller: Depth stop.

Duivejager: Quarter round.

Extragaal: Bolection.

Geleider: Fence.

Gerfschaaf: Scroll or whale plane (pp.40, 51, 158).

Gerfschaafjes: Violin planes (p.158).

Glassponningschaaf: Halving or sash rabbet plane.

Greep: Grip, tote

Grieksch rond: Grecian ovolo.

Groefschaaf: Groove plane, match groove.

Grondschaaf: (Ground plane) router.

Handgreep or Handvat: Tote.

Hol: Hollow.

Holle Schaaf: Hollow plane (p.193).

Hoorn: Horn.

Hout: Wood.

Inleg-Ojief: Fillet, ogee and bead.

Insnij (of a quirk): having a narrow fillet for bottom.

Insnij-Kraal: Fillet and bead.

Insnij-Ojief: Grecian ogee.

Insnij-Ojief met schuine kant: Grecian ogee with bevel.

Keerbeitel: Cap iron.

Koolschaaf: (cabbage plane) kitchen plane.

Kraal met ronde poot: Bead with cove quirk.

Kraal-Ojief: Ogee, bevel & bead.

Kraal-Ojief met bandje: Ogee with astragal.

Kraalbeuling: Grecian ovolo with astragal.

Kraalschaaf: Bead plane.

Kuiperschaaf: Cooper's plane.

Leuningschaaf: Handrail plane.

Messing: Tongue.

Neus: Nose.

Ojief: Ogee.

Omgekeerd Kraal-Ojief: Reverse ogee and bead.

Omgekeerde Duivejager: Fillet cove and fillet (p.198).

Omsnijschaaf: Gouge howel (p.326).

Overzijboorschaaf: T-rabbet.

Overzijschaaf: Side rabbet.

Palmhout: Boxwood.

Papegaaibek: (parrotbeak) Flat quirk bead.

Ploeg: Groover (p.126).

Ploegschaaf: Match plane.

Poot: Quirk.

Puntschaaf: V-groove plane.

Raamschaaf(je): Sash plane.

Rechte boorschaaf: Square rabbet.

Reischaaf: Jointer (Rei- from "ready", Rij- from "drive") (p.48).

Rijschaaf: Jointer (misspelling used in catalogs for Reischaaf) (p.48).

Roedeschaaf: Bevel and fillet plane.

Roffel: Jack plane (pp.40, 45, 51).

Rond: Round.

Rondeschaaf: Round plane (p.193).

Schaaf: Plane or shave.

Schaafbeitel: Plane iron.

Schaven: (verb) To plane; (noun) Planes (plural of "Schaaf").

Scherpe (of a quirk): Having a sharp bottom.

Scherpe kraal: Quirk bead.

Schrobber: Scrub plane (p.40).

Schuine boorschaaf: Skew Rabbet.

Slagknop: Strike button.

Spaakschaafje: Spokeshave (p.298).

Sponningschaaf: (groove plane) moving filletster.

Spookschaafje: Spokeshave (p.298).

Strijkblok: Strike block (pp.62, 67).

Tandschaaf: Toothing plane (p.61).

Tonnenkroos: Post croze

Tonnenschaaf: Howel (p.326).

Varken: Deep, unfenced plow plane (p.127).

Vast rond met 1 bandje: Fillet and cove (p.198).

Vast rondje met beuling: Grecian ovolo and cove.

Veer: Tongue or spline.

Veerploeg: Plow plane (p.126).

Verkeerd ojief: Reverse ogee.

Verstellbaar: Adjustable.

Voorlooper: Foreplane (pp.40, 48, 51).

Voorsnijder: Nicker.

Wig: Wedge.

Zonder: Without.

Zool: Sole.

Zwaluwstaartschaaf: (swallowtail plane) dovetail plane (p.144).

Japanese Glossary and Index

Ai-jakuri-kiwa-kanna: Moving filletster (p.76).

Akagashi: Japanese red oak.

Anazuki-kanna: Grooving plane for sliding screen tracks.

Ara-shiko-kanna: Roughing plane (p.41).

Ari-kake-shakuri-kanna: Shouldering plane (p.146).

Ari-shakuri-kanna (or ari-kanna): Dovetail plane (p.146).

Bōzu-kaku-men-tori-kanna: Molding plane with sole removed behind the blade, to work between rounded corners.

Bukkiri-men-tori-kanna: Plane with rectangular groove in sole, used for rounding (p.197).

Chibi-kanna: Finger planes (p.56).

Chū-shiko-kanna: Intermediate roughing plane (pp.45, 53).

Dabo-shakuri-kanna: Plow (p.129).

Dai no koba: Side of plane body.

Dai no shitaba: Sole of plane.

Dai-naoshi-kanna: Scraper for plane sole (p.61)

Daigashira: Heel, in Western sense; or front, in Japanese.

Dōgu: Tool (literally, the way of the tool).

Ete-bō-men-tori-kanna: Chamfer for odd angles (p.152).

-ganna= -kanna (alternate transliteration).

Ginnan-men-tori-kanna: Corner rounding, quarter-round or similar bench type molding plane (p.197).

Gyogitsuki-kanna: Moving filletster (p.104).)

Haguchi: Throat of plane.

Hana-gata-kumiko-kanna: Planes for surface texture (p.209).

Herashi-kanna: "Taking-off plane": a coarse roughing plane (p.41).

Hifukura-kanna: Pointed bottom side rabbet (p.98).

Hinnagata-kanna: Polishing plane.

Hira-bōzu-kanna: Plane with no sole behind blade (pp.58, 76).

Hira-kanna: Common plane (p.52).

Inro-men-tori-kanna: Match planes for storm doors (p.170).

Ireko-men-tori-kanna: Wide molder with two blades (p.197).

-jakuri- = -shakuri: (alternate transliteration).

Jō-shiage-kanna: See Jō-shiko

Jō-shiko: Finishing smooth plane (p.53).

Jyogituki-aikanna: See Gyogitsuki-kanna: moving filletster.

Kaeshi-ba-kanna: Plane with blade bevel-up (p.67).

Kai jiri: Nose in Western sense, heel in Japanese.

Kaku-mentori-kanna: Chamfer plane (p.152).

Kanna-ba: Main plane blade.

Katagi-shakuri-kanna: Movable sole dovetail; see Ari-shakura-kanna.

Ken-kanna: V-sole bench plane (p.152).

Kenyo-sumi-maru-kanna: Ginnan-men-tori-kanna with parts of fence removed, for molding inside curves.

Kikai-shakuri-kanna: Japanese style plow (p.128).

Kirimen-kanna: Adjustable chamfer plane (p.152).

Kiwa-kanna: Badger plane (p.75).

Kokutan: Ebony.

Koppa-gaeshi: Front wall of mouth.

Kude-shakuri-kanna: Groove plane for shoji joints (p.140)

Kumiko-kezuri-kanna: Reglet for shoji lattice strips (p.61).

Kushi-gata-shakuri-kanna: Comb-shape rabbet plane.

Kyōgi-kanna: Spelk machine for food wrappers (p.311).

Mado-waku-shakuri-kanna: Window frame grooving plane. See Osaka-shakuri-kanna.

Maru-kanna: Bench type hollow or round (p.193).

Men-tori-kanna: Molding plane (p.193).

Mizo-kanna: General name for grooving plane (p.98).

Mizo-nimai-shakuri-kanna: See shakuri-kanna (rabbet).

Mizotsuki-kanna: See Mizo-kanna (p.98).

Moto-ichi-shakuri-kanna: Japanese fenced plow (p.128).

Naga-dai-kanna: Jack length plane used for jointing (p.45).

Naguri-men-tori-kanna: Hewing-pattern molder (p.209).

Nankin-kanna: Spokeshave (p.303).

476

Nichō-shikomi-men-tori-kanna: Two-blade molding plane (pp.197, 209).

Nimai-wakitori-kanna: Side rabbet (p.98).

Ō-kanna: Japanese form of cooper's jointer (p.322).

Omote-najimi: Bed of plane.

Oni-arashiko-kanna: Scrub plane.

Osae: Abutment of plane.

Osaemizo: Groove holding main blade.

Ōsaka-shakuri-kanna: Shoji rail grooving plane (p.75).

Seme-kanna: Bench plane with sides slanted to expose blade (p.75).

Sendan: Rosewood.

Shakuri-kanna: Rabbet or grooving plane (pp.98, 128).

Shiage-kanna: Final finishing smooth plane (p.53).

Shihō-sori-dai-kanna: Doubly curved concave or convex plane (p.159).

Shōhi-kanna: Plane to form pine-bark texture (p.209).

Shokunin: Dedicated and skilled craftsman.

Sokotori-shakuri-kanna: Rabbet for shaving groove bottoms.

Sori-dai-kanna or Sori-kanna: Compass or concave plane (p.159).

Sotomaru-kanna: Round bench type or molding plane (pp.170, 193).

Sotomaru-sori-kanna: Spoon bottom plane.

Sumi-kezuri-kanna: Edge or chisel plane.

Sumi-kikai-shakuri-kanna: Plow with no keel behind blade.

Sumi-kiwa-kanna: Badger with side slanted for dovetail (pp.76, 146).

Sumi-maru-men-tori-kanna: Ginnan-men-tori-kanna with part of fence removed, for molding inside curve.

Sumi-maru-yoko-zuri-kanna: Plane for coved panel (p.76).

Tachi-ba-kanna or Tachi-kanna: Scraper plane (p.61).

Teppō-men-tori-kanna: Plane with sole removable behind blade (p.182).

Tsuki-kanna: Push plane (p.12), or Chinese type smooth block plane.

Uchimaru-kanna: Hollow bench type or molding plane (pp.170, 193).

Uchimaru-sori-kanna: Bench compass hollow.

Uragane: Cap iron.

Uraganedome: steel pin across throat of plane, to hold cap iron.

Uwaba: Top of plane body.

Waki-kanna: Side rabbet plane (p.75).

Waki-tori-kanna: Form of side rabbet (p.98.

Wakitori-hibukura-kanna: See Hifukura-kanna (narrow side rabbet).

Yari-kanna: Spear-shaped knife used for planing (p.12).

Yoko-zuri-kiwa-kanna: Badger plane with nicker (p.76).

Bibliography

- **Sources of periodicals cited:**

The Chronicle — Journal of the Early American Industries Assn. (EAIA), Box 2128, E.S.P. Station, Albany, NY 12220-2128

The Fine Tool Journal — Vernon U. Ward, Pittsford, VT 05763

Gristmill — Journal of the Mid-West Tool Collectors Assn. (M-WTCA), 808 Fairway Dr., Columbia, MO 65201

Plane Talk — Plane collectors' journal, Astragal Press, Box 239, Mendham, NJ 07945

Tool Shed, Collectors of Rare and Familiar Tools Society, (CRAFTS), 38 Colony Court, Murray Hill, NJ 07974

Tools & Trades — Journal of the Tool and Trades History Society, 60 Swanley Lane, Swanley, Kent BR8 7JG, United Kingdom

Newsletter — of the Tool and Trades History Society (above).

- **Text acronyms:**

BP II — *British Planemakers from 1700,* Second Ed., W.L. Goodman

EAIA — Early American Industries Assn.

GAWP — *Guide to American Wooden Planes and Their Makers,* Pollak, Astragal Press, Mendham, NJ 07945

M-WTCA — Mid-West Tool Collectors Assn.

TATHS — The Tool and Trades History Society, U.K.

WPINCA — *Wooden Planes in Nineteenth Century America,* Vols. I & II, Roberts (1978, 1983)

Albright, Frank (1972) *Toothing Planes:* Chronicle XXV #1 pp.30-31

Amman, Jost & Sachs, Hans (1568) *The Book of Trades:* Reprint Dover Publications, NY 1973

Armour, W.J. (1898) *Work, the Illustrated Weekly Journal for Mechanics:* Reprinted in WPINCA II Chapter II

Bates, Alan (1988) *Bridle Plows Revisited—One Last Time:* Plane Talk XII #1 p.73

Bates, Alan G. (1986) *Thomas Napier:* Published by the EAIA and M-WTCA

Bealer, Alex W. (1976) *The Tools That Built America:* Bonanza Books, NY

Bealer, Alex W. (1980) *Old Ways of Working Wood:* Barre Publishing, Barre VT

Benjamin, Asher (1827) *The American Builder's Companion, 6th Ed.:* Reprint 1969 Dover Publications, NY

Benjamin, Asher (1830) *The Architect or Practical House Carpenter:* Reprint 1988 Dover Publications, NY

Blumenberg, Ben (1990) *The Backing Out Plane: Plane Talk XIV p.236*

Bopp, Carl (1978) *Scratches, Prickers or Gauges:* Plane Talk III #1 p.4

Bopp, Carl (1978) *A Plane for Wedge Finials:* Plane Talk III #3 p.7

Burchard, Seth & Walker, Philip (1985) *The Earliest Planemaking Industry?:* Tools & Trades Vol.3 pp.96-111

Burchard, Seth (1984); Letter to Editor, Fine Tool Journal Vol.27 #4 p. 62

Chippendale, Thomas (1762) *The Gentleman & Cabinet-Makers Director:* Reprint 1966 Dover Publications, NY

Coaldrake, Wm.H.(1990) *The Way of the Carpenter:* Weatherhill, Inc., NY

Comstock, William T. (1881) *Victorian Domestic Architectural Plans and Details:* Reprint 1987 Dover Publications, NY

Constantine Jr., Albert (1975) *Know Your Woods:* Charles Scribner's Sons, NY

D.L.H. (1702) *L'Art de Charpenterie de Mathurin Jousse:* Thomas Moette

Davidson, Marshall B. (1975) *Early American Tools:* Olivetti, Italy

Diderot, D. & D'Alembert, J le R (1751-1772) *Encyclopédie:* Reprint, Inter-Livres Paris

Dunbar, Michael (1977) *Antique Woodworking Tools:* Hastings House, NY

Dunbar, Michael (1989) *Restoring, Tuning and Using Classical Woodworking Tools: Sterling Publishing Co., NY*

Farnham, Alexander (1984) *Early Tools of New Jersey and the Men Who Made Them: Kingwood Studio Publications, Stockton NJ*

Feirer, John L. (1970) *Cabinetmaking and Millwork:* Chas. A. Bennet Co., Peoria IL

Félibien, A. (1676) *Principes de Architecture:*.Paris

Feller, Paul & Tourret, Fernand (1989) *L'Outil, Dialogue de l'Homme avec la Matiere:* Albert de Visscher, Bruxelles

Ferguson, Alan (1984) *Collectors Cornered:* TATHS newsletter #6, pp.15-23

Frid, Tage (1979) *Tage Frid Teaches Woodworking Vol I:* Taunton Press, Newtown CT

Gabriel & Sons, *Stock Inventories:* Reprinted in Goodman (1978); see below.

Garvin, James & Donna-Belle (1985) *Instruments of Change:* New Hampshire Historical Soc., Cconcord NH

Gilbert, Katherine Stoddert, Ed. (1976) *Treasures of Tutankhamun:* Ballantine Books, NY

Goff, David (1973) *Wooden Scoop Shovel Making:* Faulkner Printing, Sherburne NY

Goodman, W.L. (1964) *The History of Woodworking Tools:* David McKay Co., NY

Goodman, W.L. (1972) *Industrial Archaeology,* Vol.9 No.4

Goodman, W.L. (1978) *British Planemakers from 1700, 2nd Ed.:* Arnold & Walker, Needham Market, Suffolk, England

Goodman, W.L. (1983) *Gabriel & Sons Stock Inventories:* Chronicle 36#3 pp.53-61

Gooch, Bob (1984) TATHS Newsletter #4 p.45

Gorlin, Jack (1978) Plane Talk Vol III #2 p.15 and #3 p.4

Graham, Robert (1978) *More Notes on the Yankee Plow:* Plane Talk III-1 p.7

Graham, Robert (1982) *The Yankee Plow Revisited:* Plane Talk VII-2 p.16

Graham, Robert (1983) *A Chat with a Plow:* Plane Talk VIII-1 pp.11-13

Gray, George (1991) *Unique Piggy Back Sash Plane:* Plane Talk XV pp.324-325

Greber, Josef M. (1956) *Die Geschichte des Hobels:* Reprint 1987, Th.Schäfer, Hannover Germany

Harris, Cyril M. Ed.(1977) *Illustrated Dictionary of Historic Architecture:* Reprint 1983, Dover Publications, NY

Hasluck, Paul N. (1903) *The Handyman's Book:* Reprint 1987, Ten Speed Press, Berkeley CA

Hayward, Charles H. (1970) *Antique or Fake?:* Evans Bros., London

Hayward, Charles H. (1975) *Woodwork Joints:* Sterling Publishing Co., NY

Hayward, Charles H. (1975) *Practical Woodwork:* Emerson Books, NY

Heicher, Ted (1991), Plane Talk, Vol.XIV p.316

Heine, Günther (1990) *Das Werkzeug des Schreiners und Drechslers:* Verlag Th.Schäfer, Hannover, Germany. (see also Schadwinkel)

Hennel, Thomas (1947) *The Countryman at Work:* Architectural Press, London

Heseltine, Alastair (1982) *Baskets and Basketmaking :* Shire Publications, Aylesbury, Bucks, U.K.

Hoadley, R. Bruce (1980) *Understanding Wood:* Taunton Press, Newtown CT

Holtzapffel, Charles (1875) *Turning & Mechanical Manipulation Vol II:* Reprint 1982, EAIA

Hommel, Rudolf P. (1937) *China at Work:* Cornwall Press, Cornwall NY

Hopfel, Kenneth (1992) The Toolshed, CRAFTS of NJ, June p.7

Hummel, Charles F. (1968) *With Hammer in Hand:* University Press of Virginia

Hummel, Charles F.(1965) *English Tools in America: The Evidence of the Dominys:* Winterthur Portfolio Vol II., Reprinted by EAIA

Industrial School Ass'n of Boston (1882) *How to Use Woodworking Tools:* Reprint 1977, Roger Smith, Athol MA

Ingraham, Edward, *WPINCA II* pp.29-50, Ken Roberts Publishing Co., Fitzwilliam NH

Isham, Norman M. & Brown, Albert F. (1900) *Early Connecticut Houses:* Reprint 1965, Dover Publications, NY

Joyce, Ernest (1979) *Encyclopedia of Furniture Making:* Sterling Publishing Co., NY

Katz, Laslo (1970) *The Art of Woodworking:* PFC Publishing, NY

Kean, Herbert & Pollak, Emil (1990) *Collecting Antique Tools:* Astragal Press, Mendham NJ

Kean, Herbert (1988) *Spring Marked Planes:* Plane Talk XII-2 pp.88-89

Kean, Herbert (1989) :*Spring-Marked Planes — An Addendum:* Plane Talk XIII-4 p.216

Kebabian, Paul & Witney, Dudley (1978) *American Woodworking Tools:* New York Graphic Society, Boston

Kebabian, Paul B. (1982) *An American Bridle Plane:* Plane Talk VII-3 pp.15-16

Kebabian, Paul B. (1987) *A Rarity: The Shoe Peg Plane:* Plane Talk XI #4 pp.52-53

Kilby, Kenneth (1971) *The Cooper and his Trade:* John Baker Ltd, London

Kilby, Kenneth (1977) *The Village Cooper:* Shire Publications, Aylesbury, Bucks, U.K.

Klatt, Erich (1961) *Die Konstruktion alter Mobel:* Julius Hoffman Verlag, Stuttgart, Germany

Knight, Richard (1983) *Two Early English Screw-stem Ploughs:* Tools & Trades Vol.1 pp.39-42

Knight, Richard (1984) Reeding Planes: Tool and Trades Newsletter 5, pp. 20-24

Krenov, James (1976) *A Cabinetmaker's Notebook:* Van Nostrand Reinhold Co., NY

Krenov, James (1977) *The Fine Art of Cabinetmaking:* Van Nostrand Reinhold Co., NY

Krenov, James (1979) *The Impractical Cabinetmaker:* Van Nostrand Reinhold Co., NY

Krenov, James (1981) James Krenov, *Worker in Wood:* Van Nostrand Reinhold Co.,NY

Lanz, Henry (1985) *Japanese Woodworking Tools:* Sterling Publishing, NY

Layton, Dudley (1977) *Let's Collect Old Woodworking Tools:* Jarrold & Sons Ltd., Norwich, England

Mannoni, Edith *Outils des Métiers du Bois:* Ch. Massin, Paris

Marshes and Shepherd catalog ca.1940, reprinted in Roberts' *Some 19th Century English Woodworking Tools* (1980), p.257

Martin, Richard A. (1977) *The Wooden Plane:* EAIA

Martin, Thomas (1813) *Circle of the Mechanical Arts:* London 1813

McGrail (Ed.) (1982) *Woodworking Techniques before AD 1500:* National Maritime Museum, Greenwich, England.

Mercer, Henry C. (1929) *Ancient Carpenter's Tools (5th Ed., 1975):* Bucks County Historical Soc.iety

Mesirow, Kip & Herman, Ron (1978) The Care and Use of Japanese Woodworking Tools (Rev. Ed.): Woodcraft Supply Corp., Parkersburg WV

Moody, John A. (1981) *The American Cabinetmaker's Plow Plane:* The Tool Box, Evansville IN

Mowat, W. & A. (1985) *A Treatise on Stairbuilding & Handrailing:* Linden Publishing Co., Fresno CA

Moxon, Joseph (1703) *Mechanick Exercises:* Reprint The Astragal Press, Mendham NJ 07945

Nicholson, Peter (1823) *The New Practical Builder and Workman's Companion:* London

Nicholson, Peter (1825) *New Carpenter's Guide:* Jones & Co., London

Nicholson, Peter (1837) *Carpenter's new Guide:* Grigg & Elliot, Philadelphia PA

Nicholson, Peter (1849) *The Mechanic's Companion:* John Locken, Philadelphia PA

Nicholson, Peter (1851) *Practical Carpentry:* Thomas Kelly, London

Norman, G.A.(1954) *Hovelens Historie:* Lillehammer

Odate, Toshio (1984) *Japanese Woodworking Tools:* Taunton Press, Newtown CT

Palladio, Andrea (1738) *The Four Books of Architecture:* Reprint 1965, Dover Publications, NY

Parke Jr., David L. (1981) *Wooden Planes at the Farmers' Museum:* Farmers' Museum, Cooperstown NY

Perch, David G. & Lee, Leonard G. (1981) *How to Make Wooden Planes:* Lee Valley Tools Ltd., Ottawa

Philipson, John (1897) *Coachbuilding:* Reprint 1986, Sheridan Press, Hanover PA

Pollak, Emil & Martyl (1987) *A Guide to American Wooden Planes 2nd Ed.:* Astragal Press, Mendham NJ

Pollak, Emil & Martyl (1989) *Supplement to American Wooden Planes:* Astragal Press, Mendham NJ

Proudfoot, Christopher & Walker, Philip (1984) *Woodworking Tools:* Charles E. Tuttle Co., Rutland VT

Radford, William A.(1911) *Radford's Portfolio of Details of Building Construction:* Reprint 1983, Dover Publications, NY

Reagan, Don (1989) *Reuben Fretz, Clay City IN, 1837-1920:* Grist Mill #56 pp.16-17

Rees, Mark (1987) *Airtight Casemaking-The Planes and Their Uses:* Tools & Trades Vol.4 pp.73-83

Reichman, Charles (1986) Chronicle Vol.39 #3, p.45

Robert, J.-F. (1985) *Les Rabots (Cahier No 1 Musée du Bois):* Musée du Bois, Lausanne, Switzerland

Robert, J.-F. (ca 1985) *Clé pour la Determination des Rabots:* Musée du Bois, Lausanne, Switzerland

Roberts, Kenneth & Jane (1971) *Planemakers and Other Edge Tool Enterprises in New York State (2nd Ed.):* Ken Roberts Publishing Co., Fitzwilliam NH

Roberts, Kenneth D. (1978) *Wooden Planes in 19th Century America* (Abbr. WPINCA): Ken Roberts Publishing Co., Fitzwilliam NH

Roberts, Kenneth D. (1980) *Some Nineteenth Century English Woodworking Tools* (Abbr. NCEWT): Ken Roberts Publishing Co., Fitzwilliam NH

Roberts, Kenneth D. (1983) *Wooden Planes in 19th Century America Vol II* (Abbr. WPINCA II): Ken Roberts Publishing Co., Fitzwilliam NH

Roubo, J.A. (1769-75) *L'Art du Menuisier:* Paris

Roubo, J.A. (1772) *Le Menuisier en Meubles:* Reprint, Inter-Livres Paris

Rumayor, Edwardo A. (1976) *Wooden Plane Making in the 20th Century:* Plane Talk Vol.1 #3 pp.1-3

Sainsbury, John (1984) *Planecraft:* Sterling Publishing Co., NY

Sahlman, Frank (1974) Chronicle Vol.27 #3 P.44

Salaman, R.A.(1975) *Dictionary of Woodworking Tools:* Charles Scribner & Sons, NY

Salaman, R.A.(1989) *Dictionary of Woodworking Tools (Rev.Ed.):* Taunton Press, Newtown CT

Sayward, Elliot (1985) *:Tools & Trades:* Newsletter #7, p.36

Schadwinkel, Hans-Tewes & Heine, Günther (1986) *Das Werkzeug des Zimmermanns:* Th.Schäfer, Hannover, Germany

Schaffer, Erv (1988) *A Pre-production Self-adjusting Plow:* Plane Talk XII-3 p.114

Schuler, Stanley (1973) *Illustrated Encyclopedia of Carpentry & Woodworking:* Random House, NY

Sellens, Alvin (1978) *Woodworking Planes:* Sellens, Augusta KS

Sellens, Alvin (1990) *Dictionary of American Hand Tools:* Sellens, Augusta KS

Sheraton, Thomas (1802) *The Cabinet-Maker and Upholsterer's Drawing Book:* Reprint 1972, Dover Publications, NY

Sloane, Eric (1964) *A Museum of Early American Tools:* Ballantine Books, NY

Sloane, Eric (1965) *A Reverence for Wood:* Ballantine Books, NY

Small, Tunstall & Woodbridge, Christopher (1930) *Molding and Turned Woodwork of the 16th, 17th and 18th Centuries:* Reprint 1987, Stobart & Son Ltd., London

Smith, James (1816) *Panorama of Science and Art I:* Caxton Press, Liverpool

Smith, Joseph (1816) *Explanation or Key to the Various Manufactories of Sheffield:* Reprint 1975 EAIA

Smith, Roger K. (1981) *Patented Transitional and Metallic Planes in America* (abbr.PTAMPIA)*:* Roger Smith, Athol MA

Smith, Roger K. (1992) *Patented Transitional & Metallic Planes in America-Vol.II* (PTAMPIA II): Roger Smith, Athol MA.

Spon, E. & F.N. (1889) *Mechanic's Own Book:* London & NY

Stanley, Philip (1981) *A Unique Chamfer Plane:* Plane Talk VI-3 p.6

Sturt, George (1923) *The Wheelwright's Shop:* Cambridge University Press

Townsend, Raymond R.(1991) Fine Tool Journal Vol.41 p.22

Vandal, Norman (1982) *How to Make a Molding Plane:* Fine Woodworking Vol.37 pp.72-77

Walker, Philip (1980) *Woodworking Tools:* Shire Publications, Aylesbury, Bucks, U.K.

Walker, Philip (1983) TATHS Newsletter 2, p.26

Walker, Philip : see also Proudfoot & Walker, Burchard & Walker

Warne, E. J. (1923) *Furniture Moldings:* Reissued by Roy Arnold, Needham Market, England

Warren, William L.(1978) *Isaac Fitch of Lebanon:* Antiquarian & Landmarks Soc., Hartford CT

Wattermaker, Firch, & Joyaux (1981) *European Tools From the 17th to the 19th Century:* Flint Institute of Arts

Wertheim, Fr.von (1869) *Werkzeugkunde:* Vienna

West Jr., Karl (1987) *Paired Cornice Planes:* Fine Tool Journal, Vol.34 #3 pp.40-41

Wildung, Frank H. (1957) *Woodworking Tools at Shelburne Museum:* Shelburne Museum, Shelburne VT

Witsen, Nicholaes (1700) *Scheeps-Bouw En Bestier,* as quoted in Plane Talk III-2 pp.8, 19

MANUFACTURERS' AND RETAILERS' CATALOGS

Abbreviations for Sources:

[AP] Astragal Press, Mendham, NJ (Reprint)

[APT] Association for Preservation Technology (Reprint)

[D] Dover Publications, NY (Reprint)

[E] Early American Industries Assn. (Reprint)

[ETC] Early Trades & Crafts, Long Island (Reprint)

[KR] Ken Roberts Publishing Co. (Reprint)

[M] Midwest Tool Collector's Association (Reprint)

[NCEWT] *Some Nineteenth Century English Woodworking Tools*, Kenneth D. Roberts

[RA] Roy Arnold, Needham Market, England (Reprint)

[RS] Roger Smith, Lancaster, MA (Reprint)

[WPINCA I] *Wooden Planes in Nineteenth Century America Vol. I,* Kenneth D. Roberts

[WPINCA II] *Wooden Planes in Nineteenth Century America, Vol. II,* Kenneth D. Roberts

Arrowmammett Works: Middletown, CT (1858) [AP]

Auburn Tool Co.: Auburn, NY (1869) [AP]

Bartlett A.C.: Chicago, IL (1899) *WPINCA I,* p.233

Barton D.R. & Co.: Rochester, NY (1873) [AP]

Brombacher, A.F. & Co. Tools for Coopers, New York (1922)

Chapin, Hermon: Pine Meadow, CT (1853) *WPINCA II,* pp.102-105

Chapin, Hermon: Pine Meadow, CT (1858) *WPINCA II,* p.119

Chapin, Hermon: Pine Meadow, CT (1859) *WPINCA II,* pp.129-134

Chapin & Sons: Pine Meadow, CT (1865) *WPINCA II,* pp.193-200

Chapin's Son : Pine Meadow, CT (1874) *WPINCA II,* pp.256-296

Chapin's Son: Pine Meadow, CT (1882) *WPINCA II,* pp.297-301

Chapin's Son: Pine Meadow, CT (1890) [M]

ChapinStephens Co.: Pine Meadow, CT (1914) [AP]

ChapinStephens Co.: Pine Meadow, CT (1925) *WPINCA II,* pp.400-405

Chapin, Philip: Baltimore, MD (ca.1850) *WPINCA I,* p.31

Charbonnel Fils, Dordogne, France (1910)

Colwell Cooperage (1929), Cited in *Fine Tool Journal* 25, p.55

Dalpe, Sem.: Roxton Pond, Quebec (1889)

Denison, John: Winthrop, CT (ca.1850) *Chronicle* 26 p.58

Emond, V.A.& Co.: Quebec (1889)

Feron & Cie.: Paris (ca.1940) Burchard Translation [E,M]

Gabriel Inventory Lists: see Goodman in Bibliography

Gleave & Son, Joseph: Manchester, England (ca.1915)

Greenfield Tool Co. Illust.Cat.: Greenfield, MA (1872) [AP]

Greenfield Tool Co. Price List: Greenfield, MA (1854) [AP]

Hammacher, Schlemmer & Co.: Bowery, NY (1896) [E,M]

Howarth, James & Sons: Sheffield, England (1884) [RA]

Kellog planes sold by Burditt & Williams: Boston (ca.1880) *WPINCA I*,
    p.218

Lachappelle Fils: Strasbourg, Alsace, France (1945)

Lang & Jacobs: Boston, MA (1884) [ETC]

Marples, Wm.Hibernia Works: Sheffield, England (1909)

Marshes & Shepherd: Sheffield, England (ca.1840) NCEWT p.257

Mathieson & Sons: Scotland (1899) [KR]

Nooitgedagt, J.: Ijlst, Netherlands (ca.1890), Reprint H.K.Rode,
    Netherlands : [AP]

Ohio Tool Co.: Columbus, OH & Auburn, NY (ca.1910) [M]

Preston, Edward & Sons Ltd.: Birmingham, England (1901) [AP]

Roberts, E.L.& Co.: Chicago, IL (1903) [D]

Russell & Erwin Mfg.Co.: New Britain, CT (1835) [APT]

Sandusky Tool Co.: Sandusky, OH (1877) [AP]

Sandusky Tool Corp.: Sandusky, OH (1925) *WPINCA I*, pp.238-243

Sears, Roebuck & Co.: Chicago, IL (1908) [DBI Books Reprint]

Shannon, J.B.: Philadelphia, PA (1873) [M]

Sheffield List: Sheffield, England (1870) *NCEWT* pp.258-261

Sheffield List (1889): Reprint 1974 Arnold & Walker

Stolp, D.: Zutphen, NL (1915) Burchard Translation [E,M]

Summers-Varvill Ebor Work: York, England (ca.1850)
    Tools & Trades #3 pp.7879

United Hardware & Tool Corp: New York (1925) [M]

Walters, (Wm.P.) Sons: Philadelphia, PA (1888) [RS]

Weiss, Joh.& Sohn: Vienna (1870), *ATLAS osterreichscher Werkzeuge
    fur Holzarbeiter*

Weiss, Joh.& Sohn: Vienna (1909) Burchard Translation [E,M]

Wilks J.,Ironmonger: Sheffield, England (1829) *NCEWT* p.254

Woodline, the Japan Woodworker, Alameda, CA (current)

TOOL DEALERS' CATALOGS

Arnold & Walker: Needham Market, England
Birchland Antiques: Wm. Neyer, Landisville, PA
Blumenberg, Bennett: Lincoln, MA
Catalog of American Wooden Planes: Michael Humphrey, Sherborn, MA
Clouser, Jack: Ye Olde Tool Shed, Cornwall, NY
Comerford, Dan & Kathy, Stony Brook, NY
Finch, Bob: Two Chiselers, Lakewood, CO
Gustafson, William: Austerlitz, NY
Habicht, Peter & Annette, Sheffield, MA
Heritage House Antiques: Jos.Dziadul, Enfield, CT
Hida Tool and Hardware Co., Berkeley, CA
Iron Horse Antiques (continued as Fine Tool Journal)
Japan Woodworker, Alameda CA
Mechanick's Workbench: Don & Anne Wing, Marion, MA
Moody, John A.: The Tool Box, Rockville, MD
Old Tool Store: Ashley Iles, Lincolnshire, England
Steere, Bud: Antique Tools, N.Kingston, RI
Tashiro's, Seattle, WA
Whitney House Antiques: Linda Mariconda, Pompton Lakes, NJ
Witte, Tom: Mattawan, MI
Yaun, Cliff: West Hurley, NY

AUCTIONS and AUCTION CATALOGS

Bates & Brown: Hockessen, DE
Bittner, J.P.: Putney, VT
Brown Auction Services: Reading, PA
Crane, Richard: Hillsboro, NH
Gustafson, William: Austerlitz, NY
Hurchalla, Barry: Pottstown, PA
Roberts, Tyrone: Norfolk, England
Stanley, David: Leicestershire, England
Witte, Tom: Mattawan, MI

Index

- Numbers with colons are figure numbers; text adjoins.
- Complex molding planes are not indexed; they are presented alphabetically in Chapter 11.